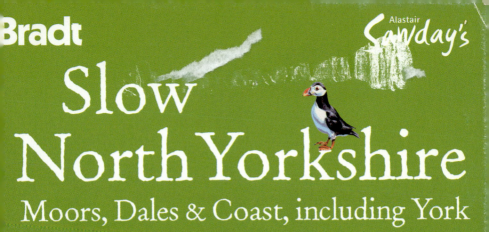

Bradt

Alastair
Sawday's

Slow
North Yorkshire
Moors, Dales & Coast, including York

Local, characterful guides to Britain's special places

Mike Bagshaw

Contributing author Caroline Mills

Edition 1

...el Guides Ltd, UK

...lishing Co Ltd, UK

...ot Press Inc, USA

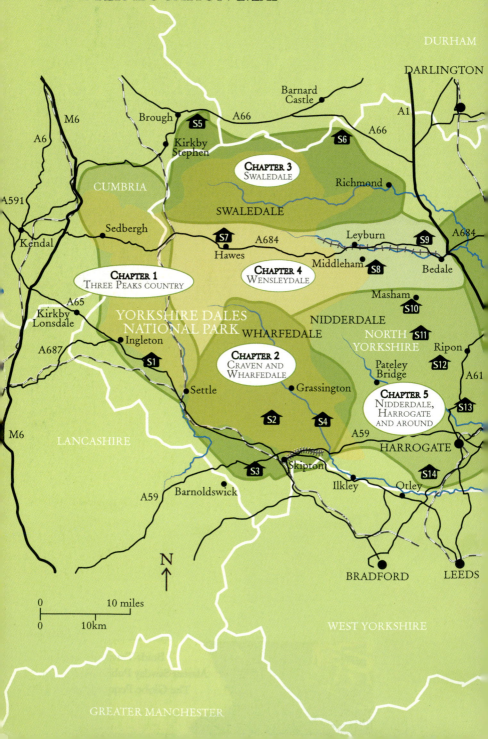

CHAPTER LOCATION MAP

DURHAM

DARLINGTON

Barnard
Castle

A66

M6

Brough

S5

A66

A1

Kirkby
Stephen

CUMBRIA

CHAPTER 3
SWALEDALE

Richmond

A6

A591

SWALEDALE

Sedbergh

Leyburn

S9

A684

Kendal

S7

A684

Hawes

Middleham

S8

Bedale

CHAPTER 1
THREE PEAKS COUNTRY

CHAPTER 4
WENSLEYDALE

Kirkby
Lonsdale

A65

YORKSHIRE DALES
NATIONAL PARK

Masham

S10

NIDDERDALE

A687

Ingleton

WHARFEDALE

NORTH
YORKSHIRE

S11

Ripon

CHAPTER 2
CRAVEN AND
WHARFEDALE

S12

A61

S1

Settle

Pateley
Bridge

CHAPTER 5
NIDDERDALE,
HARROGATE
AND AROUND

Grassington

S13

M6

S2

S4

LANCASHIRE

A59

HARROGATE

S3

Skipton

S14

Barnoldswick

Ilkley

Otley

A59

N

10 miles

0

10km

BRADFORD

LEEDS

WEST YORKSHIRE

GREATER MANCHESTER

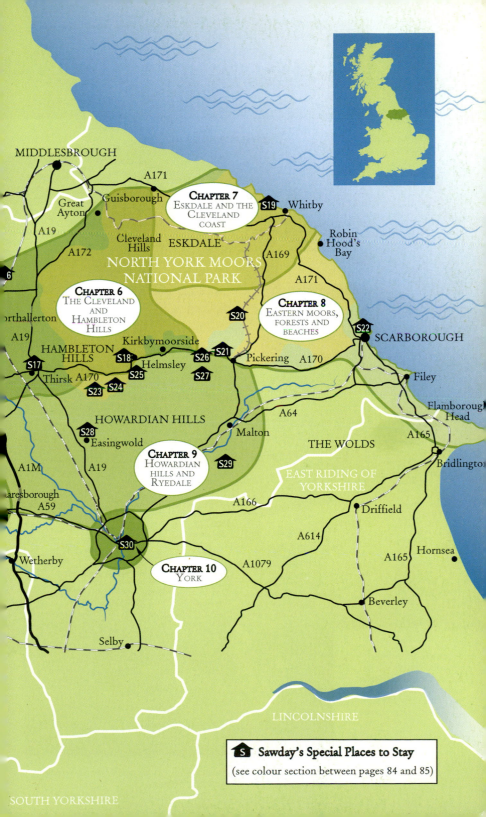

MIDDLESBROUGH

A171

Guisborough

Great
Ayton

A19

A172

Cleveland
Hills

CHAPTER 7
ESKDALE AND THE
CLEVELAND
COAST

S19 Whitby

Robin
Hood's
Bay

ESKDALE

NORTH YORK MOORS
NATIONAL PARK

A169

A171

CHAPTER 8
EASTERN MOORS,
FORESTS AND
BEACHES

S22

SCARBOROUGH

6

rthallerton

CHAPTER 6
THE CLEVELAND
AND
HAMBLETON
HILLS

A19

Kirkbymoorside

S20

S21 Pickering A170

S26

Filey

HAMBLETON
HILLS

S17

Thirsk A170

Helmsley

S18

S25

S23 S24

S27

A64

Flamboroug
Head

A165

HOWARDIAN HILLS

Malton

THE WOLDS

Bridlington

S28 Easingwold

CHAPTER 9
HOWARDIAN
HILLS AND
RYEDALE

S29

EAST RIDING OF
YORKSHIRE

A1M

A19

aresborough

A59

Wetherby

S30

CHAPTER 10
YORK

A166

Driffield

A614

A165 Hornsea

A1079

Beverley

Selby

LINCOLNSHIRE

S Sawday's Special Places to Stay

(see colour section between pages 84 and 85)

SOUTH YORKSHIRE

A North Yorkshire Gallery

A young member of the grey seal colony at Ravenscar, dozing in the sunshine above the high water mark. (TL)

A couple of serene wooded meanders on the River Wharfe near Grassington, one of the country's finest wild swimming spots. (WTY)

A living skin of yellow water lilies on Semer Water, a Yorkshire Wildlife Trust Nature Reserve. (TM/PCL)

Pony trekking is an exhilarating way of dashing through the North Yorkshire countryside without using your own legs, as here near Pickering. (WTY)

Wildlife and wild places

The wild is never far away in this part of the world and the natural profusion is home to many interesting rarities.

Robert Fuller, the Wolds artist and barn owl conservationist, with one of his own-design nest boxes and occupant. (YP)

The limestone of the Yorkshire Dales nurtures many rare flowers and plants. One of its star species, the purple saxifrage, displays its colourful blooms on the gritstone of Pen-y-ghent's summit. (MB)

Visible from the tower of York Minster, Kilburn's white horse, though a Victorian fake, has become an emblem for the Hambleton Hills. (WTY)

Living landscapes

From rocky crags to river floodplains, windswept moors to wooded dales, there's more variety here than almost anywhere else in England.

Dry stone walls and field barns are characteristic features of Upper Swaledale. (CM)

The heather-covered hills above Rosedale are part of the largest expanse of moorland in England, with a rich and ancient archaeology. (WTY)

A pavement of water-eroded limestone has formed at the very edge of Malham Cove, with pastoral Airedale beyond. (DN/PL)

The scenically spectacular Three Peaks Challenge can be faced running, walking, biking … or a combination of all three! (WTY)

A lone walker on a quiet corner of the summit plateau of Ingleborough, probably the best known of the Three Peaks. (AS/PL)

Handmade cakes and tarts are the specialities of Bettys Café Tearooms in both Harrogate and York. (WTY)

Wensleydale's lush valley pastures produce the milk for its famous cheese, made here in Hawes. (WTY)

The Tan Hill Inn above Swaledale is the highest, and surely most isolated, pub in England. (CZ/FL)

Stonegate, one of York's oldest streets, boasts the ancient Olde Starre Inn and its unusual, road-spanning sign. (WTY)

Gastronomic delights

There are more breweries here than in any other county, plus top quality food and even the odd vineyard. You won't go hungry here.

Two coopers at work at the Theakston Brewery, Masham, one of the few breweries still to produce its own wooden barrels. (WTY)

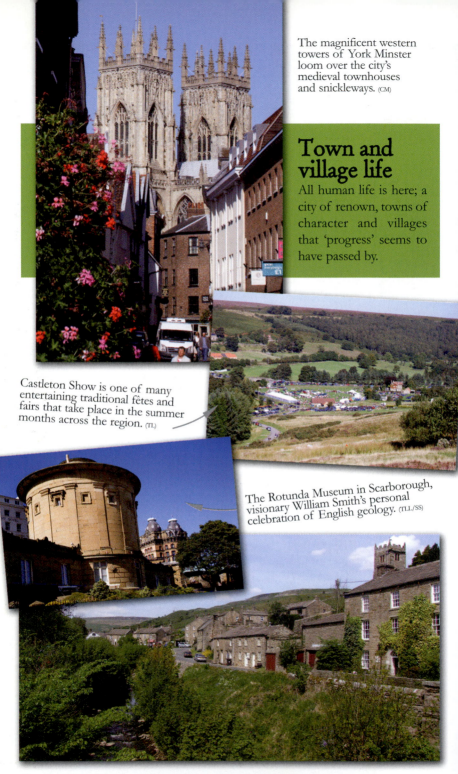

The magnificent western towers of York Minster loom over the city's medieval townhouses and snickleways. (CM)

Town and village life

All human life is here; a city of renown, towns of character and villages that 'progress' seems to have passed by.

Castleton Show is one of many entertaining traditional fêtes and fairs that take place in the summer months across the region. (TL)

The Rotunda Museum in Scarborough, visionary William Smith's personal celebration of English geology. (TLL/SS)

Sleepy and solid, Muker in Swaledale epitomises the Dales village. (CM)

Rowing your own boat along the River Nidd is surely the slowest and most relaxing way to view Knaresborough. (CM)

A tour along the length of Wensleydale on a vintage 1960s single-decker bus makes a fine nostalgic experience. (TS/FL)

Moored cobles sheltering up Staithes Beck – a view beloved of artists over the centuries. (WTY)

Mini longships in design, these traditional 'double-ender' boats are still used by the inshore fishermen of Runswick Bay. (JC/PL)

The Wolds meet the sea at Flamborough Head, home to hundreds of thousands of seabirds. (JC/PL)

Pantile-roofed cottages cluster on Whitby's east side lifeboat piers. (TG/FL)

Lythe Bank is an ideal place from which to view a northerly swell arriving in Sandsend Bay, with Whitby visible three miles in the distance. (TLL/SS)

Where North Yorkshire meets the sea

Spend a day on the coast and you will see why most of North Yorkshire's cliffs and beaches have justly earned themselves Heritage Coast status.

Scarborough Castle towers over the town's harbour and South Bay. Yorkshire's surf is excellent, but you need a good, thick wetsuit for the North Sea. (WTY)

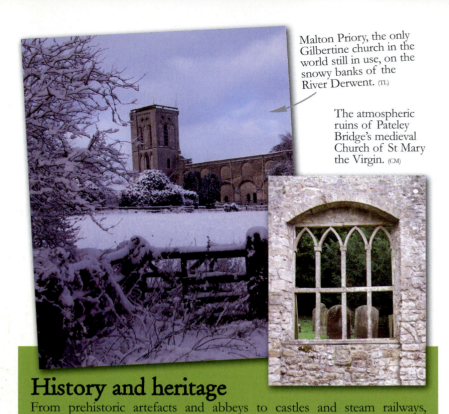

Malton Priory, the only Gilbertine church in the world still in use, on the snowy banks of the River Derwent. (TL)

The atmospheric ruins of Pateley Bridge's medieval Church of St Mary the Virgin. (CM)

History and heritage

From prehistoric artefacts and abbeys to castles and steam railways, thousands of years' worth of human history can be seen here.

Whitby Abbey was founded by St Hilda. Here it is reflected in one of its own monastic fishponds. (JC/PL)

Pickering Station, restored to its 1930s glory, is once again a stopping point for period locomotives on the North Yorkshire Moors Railway. (WTY)

Harrogate's Valley Gardens are the place to soak up the genteel side of North Yorkshire. (WTY)

April daffodils provide a splash of colour in front of the grandiose façade of Castle Howard, near Malton. (WTY)

The intimidating entrance to the Forbidden Corner near Middleton hides a folly garden that is deliberately designed to get you lost. (SD)

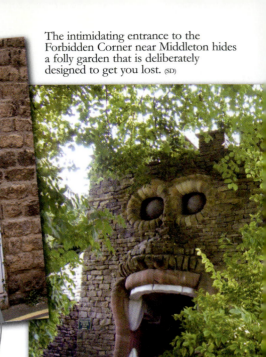

The house that appeared overnight in Knaresborough is in fact a trompe l'œil mural, painted on the side wall of a building society as part of an arts festival. (CM)

Yorkshire Quirks

'There's nowt so queer as folk,' as they say in Yorkshire, and the evidence isn't hard to find.

York celebrates its Viking roots with the ceremonial burning of a longship during the Jorvik Festival. (BOV/PL)

Slingsby's famous 41ft maypole in full swing. (RW/PL)

Author

Mike Bagshaw is a Lancastrian by birth and a zoologist by training. After four years as a student in Sheffield he qualified as a biology teacher and has taught full-time ever since. Initially this took place indoors in school classrooms, but for the last 22 years he has worked in outdoor education centres, introducing children and adults to the delights of water-sports, mountaineering, forest education and how to understand and appreciate the natural world.

In his spare time he has travelled the wild places of the world as a naturalist and explorer, often in a canoe or kayak, and written about his experiences for outdoor magazines. He contributes monthly nature columns to local newspapers and has had a book of poetry published.

Author's story

On the face of it, a Lancastrian 'townie' writing about rural Yorkshire is an unusual phenomenon, but the truth is that I have spent more of my life in this adopted county than in the one of my birth.

My first experience of Yorkshire, a seaside holiday in the late 1960s, was a shocking one; for a ten-year-old boy used to the Gulf Stream waters of north Wales, swimming in the North Sea came as a very rude awakening.

Fast forward three or four years and I am back over the border again, this time on the other side of the county in Dentdale, where we teenagers enjoyed many residential stays in the school's country cottage. With hindsight, those first exposures to real country life – windswept hills, clean rivers and undisturbed wildlife – were life-changing experiences, for which I am eternally grateful.

That initial love affair with the Yorkshire Dales has been consummated every Easter since, for 30 years, accompanied by a handful of like-minded school friends, and during that time we reckon to have visited just about every hill-top and decent pub available. That, coupled with my 21 years living and working in the North York Moors, led me to believe that I knew pretty much all there was to know about North Yorkshire. How wrong I was.

The very welcome opportunity to write this guide has allowed me to see familiar places in a new light, and discover corners that for years I had unwittingly missed. It also gave me the incentive to go and do some of those things that I'd always promised myself, like watch an early-morning black grouse lek, or brave the descent of Gaping Gill cavern. Best of all, it's re-kindled my desire to go out exploring again, and see what else I might have missed in this wonderfully varied county.

First published May 2010
Bradt Travel Guides Ltd
23 High Street, Chalfont St Peter, Bucks SL9 9QE, England
www.bradtguides.com
Alastair Sawday Publishing Co Ltd
The Old Farmyard, Yanley Lane, Long Ashton, Bristol BS41 9LR
www.sawdays.co.uk
Published in the USA by The Globe Pequot Press Inc, 246 Goose Lane,
PO Box 480, Guilford, Connecticut 06437-0480

ISBN-13: 978 1 84162 323 8

Photographs, illustrations and maps
Photographs Mike Bagshaw (MB); Sally Dixon (SD); Flickr: craigzz2006 (CZ/FL), Tall Guy
(TG/FL), Timothy Saunders (TS/FL); Tim Locke (TL); Caroline Mills (CM); Photolibrary:
Britain on View (BOV/PL), Joe Cornish (JC/PL), David Noton (DN/PL), Andy Stothert
(AS/PL), Richard Watson (RW/PL); Pictures Colour Library: Tom Mackie Images Ltd
(TM/PCL); SuperStock: Travel Library Limited (TLL/SS); Welcome to Yorkshire (WTY);
Yorkshire Post (YP)
Maps and illustrations Chris Lane and Chris Nairne-Clark (Artinfusion Ltd)
Cover artwork Neil Gower (www.neilgower.com)

Typeset from the author's disc by Artinfusion Ltd
Production managed by Jellyfish Print Solutions and manufactured in the UK

Foreword

Slow travel is a philosophy that is so natural to Yorkshire that we should have, if it were allowed, copyrighted it. North Yorkshire especially doesn't lend itself to rushing. Why rush when there is so much to take in, to absorb, slowly, and to appreciate? As a sheep farmer in Leyburn in my spare time, I know what a wonderful place it is to be, in liquid sunshine or on a bright and brilliant summer's day. You feel like if you blink you'll miss something, so perish the thought of rushing through. This is why we were so delighted to be involved in the *Slow North Yorkshire* guidebook. Yorkshire is attracting more visitors than ever and we want them to spend more time exploring our wonderful county and to keep coming back (with their friends and family!) to discover new – or rediscover old – favourites. Yorkshire has inspired award-winning writers, artists, photographers and film makers from across the world and the landscape covered in this guide has been widely captured on canvas, celluloid and in thousands of pages of print. Yet nothing can ever re-create the sense of actually being there. For me, the view from Sutton Bank is one of the finest in England – I never tire of seeing it – and you need to have visited it yourself to realise that photos can only do it so much justice. I hope that this guide will take you to many places you have seen on screen or heard about but not actually visited before, and that the experience of seeing them will be something that will stay with you and keep you coming back for years to come. Anyway, enough of my words. You will only fully appreciate how special the people, the landscape and the places of North Yorkshire are by immersing yourself in all they have to offer and by adopting the slower pace of life for which this guide is suited. Savour everything you see, don't rush, for I am sure I will be welcoming you back to Yorkshire soon enough.

Gary Verity,
Chief Executive of
Welcome to Yorkshire

Contributing author

Caroline Mills, author of the Nidderdale and York chapters, is a freelance writer of travel guides and contributes to various national magazines on travel, food and gardens. Though not officially of Yorkshire stock, she has many family connections with the county she classes as her second 'home'. Having lived in York, she returns to North Yorkshire regularly. Caroline writes, 'It has been great to return "home" for this guide. When you live in an area, it's easy to take your surroundings for granted and stop exploring. Returning to Yorkshire, I've visited with a fresh pair of eyes and have been able to talk with residents about places they didn't know were on their doorstep.'

Acknowledgements

A big thank you goes to all those people that have helped me with this, my first book. All those Yorkshire contributors who shared a little of their lives and passions and allowed me to quote them; Caroline Mills for contributing two chapters of writing; and everyone in the Bradt team, especially Tim Locke for being so professional and patient, and Hilary Bradt and Janice Booth for sound advice and words of real encouragement.

Dedication

To my partner Lois who has been unofficial researcher, typist, editor, proofreader and general life coach for the past year; without her this book would not have been possible.
Mike Bagshaw

CONTENTS

The Slow mindset

From Alastair Sawday, founder of Alastair Sawday Publishing
One of my early literary 'heroes' was John Stewart Collis, a poet who wrote about his work as a farm labourer during World War II. "Now, as far as I can see in any direction, a plantation free (of entanglements) meets my eye, accomplished by the labour of my hands alone. Nothing that I have ever done has given me more satisfaction than this, nor shall I hope to find again so great a happiness." If you are a gardener, have an allotment, make things or simply revel in the slow creative labours of others, you will know what Collis meant.

Going Slow is a way of thinking, living, eating and being. It is also a sophisticated response to unsophisticated, vacuous commercialism – the Slow movement offering something that is life-affirming, rooted in a deep understanding of human needs.

Slow is serious, yet it is fun too. The ideas go deep, but so do the pleasures – for Slow can be seen as a 'bridge from panic to pleasure'. These Slow books are awash with stimulating examples of people who have turned their backs on hectic and empty lives to find deep pleasure in living in a different gear.

Sawday's *Go Slow England* book has enabled thousands of people to enjoy themselves innocently, slowly and greatly. This collaboration with Bradt Guides, a delightful company with whom we have much in common, will lure readers more deeply into the crannies and nooks of England in pursuit of deeper and even slower pleasures.

From Hilary Bradt, founder of Bradt Travel Guides
At a Bradt editorial meeting some years ago we started to explore ideas for guides to our favourite country – Great Britain. We pretty much knew what we wanted: to recruit our best authors to write about their home areas. They had shown that they could write wittily and perceptively about distant lands, so why not ask them to explore closer to home? We wanted a series of books that went beyond the usual tourist attractions and found something different, something extraordinary in familiar villages and landscapes. To quote T S Eliot: 'We shall not cease from exploration, and the end of all our exploring will be to arrive where we started and know the place for the first time'. Exactly.

We have long been impressed with Alastair Sawday's approach to life and travel, and he prepared the way for this series. The Slow philosophy matched our concept perfectly: the ideal partnership. So take time to explore. Don't rush it, get to know an area – and the people who live there – and you'll be as delighted as the authors by what you find.

GOING SLOW IN NORTH YORKSHIRE

Pre-1974 Yorkshire was enormous, bigger than some small countries, and by far the largest county in England. By definition, a Slow appraisal of a place shouldn't skim, but needs to look at the detail, so the whole of the historic county is beyond the scope of one volume. Even the Vikings realised that its size was unwieldy, so split Yorkshire into thirds or 'ridings', with the North Riding being the most rural. The new county of North Yorkshire pretty much corresponds to the old North Riding, and this book takes a long, slow look at its places, landscapes and people.

Even pared down, North Yorkshire is still England's largest county, and an incredibly diverse place. Over 100 miles separate the lofty peaks of the Pennine west from the sea-cliffs and sandy strands of the east, with pastoral limestone dales, rich farmland and rolling heather moors nestled in between.

I have been a little flighty with borders, choosing to include the whole of both national parks, and consequently allowing chunks of Cumbria and Cleveland to stow away on board; I have omitted the extreme south of the county around Selby. East Yorkshire's Flamborough Head also sneaks in, quite simply because it is very visible from North Yorkshire – and I like it. As for York, I could hardly leave out the county town, especially as it is also one of the most fascinating, historic and slow cities in the country.

Where I do have feelings of guilt and regret are towards the places not mentioned, old East and West Riding, new South Yorkshire and even pockets of North Yorkshire; there will be corners that I've had to leave out, and many characters that I haven't met yet, but they are pleasures for the future.

My old neighbour Frank, God rest his soul, led an extraordinary life, that many of us in this day and age could not imagine, not because of what he did, but for what he didn't do. During all of his 70-odd years, Frank never left Yorkshire, not a single step over the border for one minute. He was born on a farm in Goldsborough, near Whitby, worked there all his life and brought his family up in the house next door. In his spare time he played football and cricket for the village, and occasionally took exotic holidays – to a caravan on another farm in the Yorkshire Dales. When I asked Frank why he hadn't travelled more, his reply was that he had no need to, that Yorkshire was as good as anywhere else, and gave him all he wanted for a happy and contented life.

Frank and his beloved Goldsborough are not unique, and that's what makes North Yorkshire so special in the Slow stakes. Whilst many places are re-discovering the value of the traditional, real and genuine, and renewing connections with their history and landscape, many corners of rural North Yorkshire never lost them in the first place. This old-fashionedness has attracted some good-natured humour, and not a little malicious ridicule, in its time, but, as far as I'm concerned (all the more so the older I get), it's an attribute rather than a fault.

So-called progress has brought us cheap, mass-produced goods sold in supermarkets the size of villages and even bigger shopping malls. Thankfully, a backlash is taking place, and rural North Yorkshire is at the forefront of the push to preserve those things that make places different, interesting and... well, real. Folk are fighting hard to keep their village shops open, promote locally produced, high-quality food and drink, and encourage their own artists and artisans. These are the special people – the brewers, potters, shop-keepers, cheese-makers, farmers, wood-carvers, butchers, bakers and candlestick makers – that have managed to capture a little of the essence of their corner of this singular county, and enable you to feel it, smell it, taste it or even take a little of it away with you.

I hope this book inspires you, not just to read about North Yorkshire, but to live it – to come and meet these people, spend some slow-time where they live and get to know it as they do.

Climb a few hills, stroll through the woods and meditate in a ruined abbey, eat a pork pie from the village butchers by the river-side and finish the day in an old stone pub, with a glass of your favourite tipple and a crackling fire to toast your feet on – I can think of worse ways of passing time. Maybe Frank had it right – why go anywhere else?

The National Parks

The first five chapters of this book cover that area of the Pennines traditionally known as the Yorkshire Dales, with all but one sitting predominantly in the National Park of the same name. Nidderdale was left out in the cold on the park's inception, but has since been rightly granted its own status as an Area of Outstanding Natural Beauty (AONB).

North Yorkshire is blessed with two national parks. Chapters 6, 7 and 8 cover the other one, the North York Moors, plus some towns with slow credentials and great character that gather around its perimeter, and the full length of the county's Heritage Coast.

The Yorkshire Dales

Time is a continuum, with change going on constantly, but for the Yorkshire Dales there have been four milestone events. The first of these moments was a long one, the Carboniferous period lasting 140 million years in fact. During this time, the overwhelmingly dominant rock of the Dales, its limestone, was laid down, as multi-layered coral reef in a shallow tropical sea.

Ten thousand years ago, the next big event was drawing to a close, as the Devensian ice finally retreated, to reveal the shapes it had carved into the underlying land surface; classic 'U'-shaped valleys, ice-plucked crags with cascading waterfalls and bare, soil-less hilltops.

Man's first real impact came in the Bronze Age, when a vast, blanketing wildwood was cleared for agriculture, and finally, all the newly revealed features were named by the Vikings just over a thousand years ago. Fell, dale, foss, ghyll and beck are all pure lingua-Scandinavia, as are most of Yorkshire's town and village names.

Obviously, a lot has happened since the Danes arrived –castle-building in Norman times, lead-mining and the Industrial Revolution for instance – but 1954 will always be a particularly important year with the formation of the Yorkshire Dales National Park. As in all 13 other national parks, the authority is charged with maintaining and enhancing the landscape, nature, culture and history of the Park, for us visitors, and the people that live in it, to enjoy. In striving towards these ideals, it has made itself a champion of all things traditional and sustainable, and a tremendous source of information and expertise for those of us that wish to go Slow in the Dales.

What they do particularly well is enable travel and discovery without a car, even having a separate web-site devoted to **green travel** (www.traveldales.org.uk). **Cycling** is strongly encouraged, both on roads (www.cyclethedales.org.uk) and off-road on mountain bikes (www.mtbthedales.org.uk). For many other outdoor activities, the website, or friendly staff in the visitor centres, will direct you to clubs and national governing bodies, but for one fairly new and enjoyable outdoor pastime, they are being a lot more pro-active. **Geocaching** is a sort of computerised treasure hunting, using GPS (global positioning system) receivers, and is a great activity for families, especially those with children who need to be given a reason for setting out on a good walk. You can download information onto your own GPS in one of the visitor centres, or hire one for £5 a day (£50 deposit).

One final activity that the National Park does not mention at all, possibly because these days it seems a little radical and alternative, is **wild swimming**. All the main rivers in the Dales have hidden corners where the water is clean, clear, the right depth and safe enough to swim in, and one or two, the Wharfe and Swale in particular, boast some of the best wild bathing in the country. If you want advice on where to swim, then try www.wildswimming.co.uk or www.river-swimming.co.uk, but I prefer a less formal approach. If I happen to be walking along a river bank on a warm, sunny day and find a likely and private place, I'll slip off my clothes and plunge in. If you've not done it, have a try – it's one of the most refreshing and life-affirming experiences you can have.

For **information** about the Yorkshire Dales National Park before you visit, go online to their website, www.yorkshiredales.org.uk, or get hold of a copy of their annual guide/newspaper, *The Visitor*.

The North York Moors

When William Smith produced the first geological map of England, he was particularly fascinated by outcroppings of Jurassic rocks that run in a broad band from the Dorset coast, diagonally up the country to meet the sea again in North Yorkshire. Just before they disappear beneath the cold, grey waves of the North Sea, these rocks bulge up in a range of rolling, flat-topped hills.

The sandstone that capped these uplands produced a thin, acid soil that could only support sparse forest, which Bronze Age people found relatively easy to clear. This natural woodland has never returned, but hundreds of square miles of alien coniferous forest were planted in the 1930s. Although not popular with many naturalists and landscape purists, these woods are now maturing into a certain Scandinavian-style beauty, which I feel adds more to than it detracts from the character of the region. Certainly the Forestry Commission now comes across as a much more enlightened, visitor-friendly and Slow organisation than it has done in the past.

Across the rest of the hill tops, acid-tolerant **heather** has taken over, resulting in the largest uninterrupted expanse of heather moorland in England, with an abundance of Bronze Age settlement remains. The North York Moors (as in, moors north of the city of York, not moors in North Yorkshire) were designated as a National Park in 1952, primarily to preserve this internationally important habitat (Britain has 70% of the world's heather moorland), its wildlife, and rich archaeology, both ancient and industrial, and the dramatic Heritage Coast, where the hills abruptly meet the sea.

The **National Park Authority** has a delicate balancing act to perform, working with the big grouse-shooting estates that actually own and maintain most of the moors, whilst opening up these glorious acres for visitors to enjoy. On the whole they do a magnificent job, especially in educating visitors about what you can see and do here, and giving practical help to get you out experiencing it.

They produce leaflets detailing a variety of **cycle** routes around the park, and similar help for **horseriding**, with a *Horse Riders' Guide to the North York Moors* and *Newtondale Horse Trail*, a guidebook to a 35-mile circular route specifically for horses.

If **walking** is your thing, then you will be very well looked after; the Park provides free, down-loadable walk leaflets, details of 15 routes accessible to wheelchair users and invaluable information regarding access to wild country. The right of access to open land, which became law in 2005, has been a welcome arrival for those of us that enjoy exploring our country's uplands; for lovers of the North York Moors it has been a revelation. This right means that you can walk just about wherever you wish, across swathes of spectacular moorland, once jealously guarded by the shooting estates and out of bounds to the public. The National Park gives detailed advice for responsible use of this new privilege, online and at 26 moorland access points which are marked on the OS map.

For more **information** about what the North York Moors National Park has to offer to Slow visitors, log on to their website (www.northyorkmoors.org.uk) or get hold of a copy of their annual guide/newspaper, *Out and About*.

Maps

I love maps and can get almost as much pleasure from reading one as I would from a novel. By far the most complete and useful maps for walking, cycling, horse-riding and general sightseeing are the OS 1:25,000 Explorer series. Those covering the region described in this book are as follows:

OL2 Yorkshire Dales – Southern & Western Areas

OL19 Howgill Fells and Upper Eden Valley

OL 30 Yorkshire Dales – Northern & Central Areas

298 Nidderdale

OL26 North York Moors – Western area

OL27 North York Moors – Eastern area

301 Scarborough, Bridlington & Flamborough Head

300 Howardian Hills & Malton

290 York

Request for feedback

North Yorkshire is stuffed with people who have specialist knowledge on their part of the county, and although we've done our best to check our facts there are bound to be errors as well as the inevitable omissions of really special places. You can post your comments and recommendations, and read the latest feedback from other readers online at http://updates.bradtguides.com/northyorkshire.

How to use this book

The **colour map** at the front of this book shows which area falls within which chapter. Each chapter begins with a more detailed **chapter map** highlighting places mentioned in the text.

(1) (2) (3) To guide you round, each featured place is given a **circled number** corresponding to the same circled number on the map. Points are numbered consecutively as they occur in the text, making it easy to locate them on the map.

SP This symbol denotes a **pub** recommended in Alastair Sawday's *Pubs & Inns of England & Wales*.

S1 S2 These symbols appear on the chapter maps at the start of each chapter, as well as on the colour map at the start of the book. These refer to the 30 **Sawday's Special Places to Stay**, which are described fully in the second colour section.

To give clarity to some descriptions of localities – particularly walks – simple **sketch maps** are included. They are intended merely to set the scene rather than to provide detailed information.

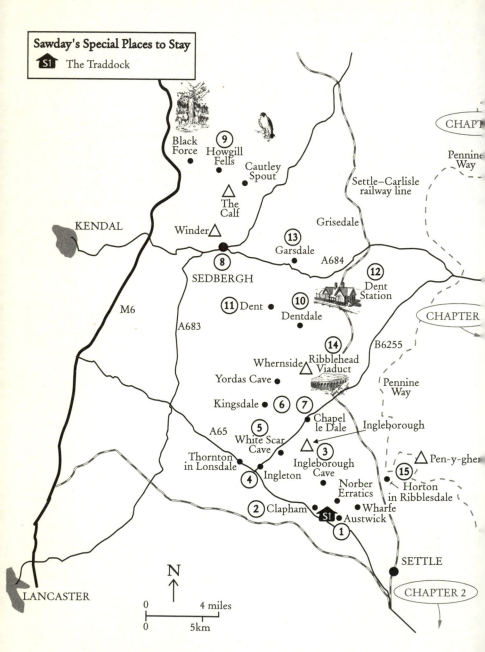

Sawday's Special Places to Stay
S1 The Traddock

Black Force
9 Howgill Fells
Cautley Spout
The Calf
Winder
KENDAL
Settle–Carlisle railway line
Griesdale
CHAPT
Pennine Way
13 Garsdale
A684
SEDBERGH
8
12 Dent Station
M6
11 Dent
Dentdale
10
A683
CHAPTER
B6255
14
Whernside Ribblehead Viaduct
Yordas Cave
Pennine Way
Kingsdale 6 7
Chapel le Dale
Ingleborough
A65
5
White Scar Cave
3
Pen-y-ghe
Thornton in Lonsdale
Ingleborough Cave
15
4 Ingleton
Norber Erratics
Horton in Ribblesdale
2 Clapham
Wharfe
S1 Austwick
1
SETTLE
N
CHAPTER 2
0   4 miles
0   5km
LANCASTER

THREE PEAKS COUNTRY

1. THREE PEAKS COUNTRY

Some of the highest land in Yorkshire lies on the western side of the Yorkshire Dales (which actually stray into Cumbria), where the rivers Dee, Skirfare, Greta and Ribble bubble into life. It is an area dominated by three great, brooding hills, Whernside, Ingleborough and Pen-y-ghent, that collectively give this area its unofficial name. Ironically, none of these flat-topped heights could remotely be called a peak but a much-tramped long-distance challenge walk linking the three coined the name and it has stuck.

The legendary walking-book author Alfred Wainwright, in his 1970 *Guide to Walks in Limestone Country*, said of the area, 'This is a region unique, without a counterpart, but its charms are shyly hidden. Those who seek and find them are often enslaved, yet few visitors come looking.' He would probably be astonished and appalled at the numbers of visitors that do come now, but his observation that a little bit of searching can reveal enchanting hidden places still holds true. Some of my first real exploring as a schoolboy was done here, and the hidden places that I discovered then have left indelible marks, and remain very special to me.

This is not as uniform a region as the eastern Dales, but an area of borders, watersheds and transformations. Even before the 1974 county boundary changes bit off a huge chunk of the North Riding and called it Cumbria, Lancashire was never far away, and the local Yorkshire accent has a distinct 'lanky' twang to it. Most of the rivers flow west, to join the Lune, and eventually Morecambe Bay; and where the limestone runs out, the hills develop a distinctly Lake District feel to them.

Getting there and around

Trains

This is the only part of the dales reasonably served by rail. There are two lines, both part of the national rail system, not private (08457 484950; www.northernrail.org). The **Settle–Carlisle** line has seven trains a day in both directions on most days, serving the east of the locale and stopping at **Horton** (from where you can walk up Pen-y-ghent), **Ribblehead, Dent** and **Garsdale**. The **Day Ranger ticket** (hop-on, hop-off, unlimited travel) is a good deal. **Clapham** is the only other place accessible by train, five times a day on the **Skipton–Lancaster** line.

Buses

All the towns and villages have some sort of bus service, but for some it is very sparse indeed.

Ingleton can be visited from Settle, Austwick, Clapham and Kirkby Lonsdale

(581, nine buses a day). **Sedbergh** can be reached from Kendal (564; eight buses a day, three Saturday, none Sunday); Kirkby Stephen (564, via Cautley; four buses a day, none Sunday); and Dent (564A/B, one a day on Wednesday and one on Saturday). **Garsdale Head** is linked to Hawes (113; four times a day); and Ripon (127, via Wensleydale; one a day, summer Friday to Sunday). **Horton** has just one bus service, to Settle (B1; four times a day, none Sunday).

Dales Rover tickets are good value and discounts are offered in some businesses if you show a bus or train ticket; look for the 'Dalesbus' logo or contact 0113 245 7676; www.dalesbus.org.

Walking

The scope for exploring on foot here is very extensive, from the three official long-distance paths that pass through the region, the **Ribble Way**, **Pennine Way** and **Dales Way**, to the scores of shorter rambles and ambles you'll find described in leaflets which you can pick up at national park and tourist information centres.

The best known is the **Three Peaks walk** itself; an unofficial 24-mile challenge of Whernside, Ingleborough and Pen-y-ghent. Horton in Ribblesdale is the traditional start point, especially if you wish to be registered in the 'club' by finishing within the allotted 12 hours, but you could start and finish anywhere along the route. If, like me, your preferred walks avoid other people then this is not the route for you as the Three Peaks, both individually and collectively, are extremely popular. The footpaths along the route hold the dubious distinction of suffering the worst erosion of any in the country.

One solution to the crowd problem could be to reach the summits individually and by different routes to the 'challenge', because these are three magnificent eminences that each deserve a visit. **Whernside**, to my mind, is best tackled from Whernside Manor in Dentdale, up the bridleway to 'Boot of the Wold' then over open fell-side to the summit via the tarns. This is the highest and quietest of the peaks – relish the solitude. A direct descent west takes you into Deepdale where you can hitch down the road or follow beck-side footpaths to your start. **Pen-y-ghent** is the peakiest of the three, neat and well defined. My choice would always be to ascend its precipitous southern nose, from

Horton if I've arrived by train, but preferably from Silverdale Road if I have my own transport. This latter option allows a horseshoe walk taking in Plover Hill and returning to the road via Lockley Beck. **Ingleborough** is a hill that's packed with interest from top to bottom. Limestone pavements, disappearing rivers, pot-holes, an Iron Age fort on the top – and you don't even have to make a round walk of it. Just start at Ingleton, walk the direct path to the summit, then down via Gaping Gill and Ingleborough Cave to descend into the oasis of Clapham village, where a surprisingly regular bus service gets you back to Ingleton.

For those that like someone else to do their navigating for them, **guided walks** are available free from the Friends of the Settle–Carlisle line (01729 825454; www.settle-carlisle.org) and Dalesbus (see above), or, for a fee, from the National Park Ranger Service (0300 456 0030; www.yorkshiredales.org). The National Park also suggests some linear walks incorporating a bus or train to return you to your start point. There is only one wheelchair-accessible route, a 600-yard length of path at Killington New Bridge Nature Reserve near Sedbergh.

Finally, three of my favourites: **Flinter Gill and Dentdale** (a five-mile, not too strenuous circuit – see page 21); **Carlingill and Blackforce** (a deceptively testing scramble in the Howgills – see page 18); and **Crummack Dale** (a gentle historical potter from Austwick – see page 5).

Cycling

Two long-distance road routes find themselves skirting the Three Peaks. The **Yorkshire Dales Cycleway** and **Pennine Cycleway** join forces to creep up Kingsdale and plummet down Deepdale. When they reach the bottom of Dentdale they part company, the former heading down the dale to Sedbergh and the latter uphill to Hawes.

It is no surprise that official routes are well represented in **Dentdale**, because its network of relatively flat and quiet lanes just beg to be biked around. The National Park's Cycle the Dales people have recognised this with a 'family ride' circuit of 13 or 19 miles up one side of this picturesque dale and back down the other. You can start anywhere en route but Dent village or Sedbergh would make sense, or of course Dent station if you arrived by train. If you want more of a workout, then their 25-mile route linking Sedbergh, Kirkby Lonsdale and Dentdale takes in an uphill leg traversing the hidden Valley of Barbondale – hard work, but worth it for the dramatic scenery.

Off-road options are not as extensive here as in other parts of the Dales: no big forests or networks of old mine tracks and sadly, many of the green lanes that should be ideal for biking have been irreparably damaged by 4x4 vehicles and trail bikes. However some rewarding rides of varying difficulty are described in a whole library of guidebooks as well as on the **MTB the Dales** website (www.mtbthedales.org.uk). The latter features a good, testing 19-mile circumnavigation of Pen-y-ghent and a severe expedition over the Howgills, but the one they call Tunnels and Bridges suits me best. It is a fairly forgiving 12-mile tour of the bridleways around Clapham and Austwick. For those with a competitive edge, and a touch of lunacy, the 38-mile **Three Peaks Cyclocross race** takes place every September.

Finally, the **upper reaches of Garsdale and Dentdale** have some quiet and really enjoyable rides that are a mixture of track and tarmac, with the advantage that they are accessible by rail. You could arrive by train at either Garsdale or Dent station and finish your ride at the other, saving a slog over the Coal Road at the end of the day.

Tourist information

Horton Pen-y-ghent café ☏ 01729 860333.
Ingleton Main car park ☏ 015242 41049.
Sedbergh Main St ☏ 015396 20125.

The southern fringe

Ingleborough's flanks mark the southwestern boundary of the Yorkshire Dales National Park and it is here that the villages of **Austwick** and **Clapham** nestle beneath limestone crags by the centuries-old coach route from Skipton to Kendal, now the A65.

A few miles further west, this road crosses the River Greta where the small town of **Ingleton** clings to the valley side. Once a busy quarrying and mining community, Ingleton is now the caving capital of Britain and largest 'town' in the locality.

① Austwick

Like many place names in North Yorkshire, this one is Viking in origin, but unusually it was not given by the Danes colonising from the east. The Lancashire coast Vikings were Norwegian, and the furthest they settled up this valley was here, hence Austwick, or 'East Farmstead'. With their pervading sense of solid antiquity, the buildings in and around the village green look as if they've been standing in the Pennine drizzle for centuries. Many structures date from the 1600s, including the fine restored medieval cross on the green.

For me though, Austwick's best feature is the glorious walking country just to the north, in the tiny valley of Crummack Dale and the gentle hills that encircle it. **Norber** barely qualifies to be a hill in its own right; it is really just an extended spur from the Ingleborough massif, but geologists get particularly excited about it because of a group of scattered boulders on its eastern slope. The **Norber Erratics**, as they are known because they don't really belong here, are blocks of a hard, dark rock called greywacke, some the size of small buildings, that were carried up the hill by a wayward glacier 10,000 years ago, and marooned when the ice melted.

The summit plateau of Norber is dotted with cairns, probably placed here by shepherds in years past as landmarks. They did not, however, do their job for one 18th-century farmer, Robin Proctor, whose horse was trained to take him home after a skinful in the Gamecock. At the end of one particularly heavy night he mounted the wrong horse which didn't know the route and promptly walked him off the top of the crag, which bears his name in memorial. Robin Proctor's Scar marks the precipitous southern end of the Norber.

If Farmer Proctor's fate does not entice you up to the tops, then the valley bottom is the place for you. This is excellent, short-distance rambling territory with an intricate network of paths and bridleways, a relict from the pre-Tudor monastic sheep estates. Sunken walled lanes weave their way between tiny meadows, and cross Austwick Beck repeatedly on ancient single-stoned 'clapper' bridges. The beck itself is remarkable, as it emerges fully formed from a cave at the dale head, provides a couple of inviting swimming holes and a waterfall or two lower down, before dwindling to a trickle just before the serene and snoozy hamlet of Wharfe.

Before you make your way back to Austwick, it is well worth detouring south to Oxenber and Wharfe woods. These are a double rarity, woodlands on limestone pavement, and very old, a combination which makes them floristically very rich. A large proportion of the woodland is hazel coppice, and local people still have ancient commoners' rights of not just sheep grazing, but also nut gathering. Although privately owned, these woods are open access land and walkers are allowed anywhere within them.

Austwick Traddock Graystonber Lane ☎ 01524 251224 🖰 www.traddock.co.uk. A hotel that serves really high-quality lunches and evening meals. They also do teas, coffees and snacks at other times of day.
Feizor Refreshments Home Barn, Feizor, LA2 8DF ☎ 01729 824114. A legendary little farm tea room. Cyclists divert here to call for a cuppa and locals walk over from Austwick for snacks.
The Game Cock The Green ☎ 01524 251226 🖰 www.gamecockinn.co.uk. A fine archetypal village pub right on The Green, serving traditional, good-value food and real ale from Thwaites. The bar is just like a bar should be, unfussy and uncluttered.

② Clapham

Walk a longish mile west of Austwick, and you will find yourself amongst the buildings of its more popular sister, Clapham, stretched out along the sides of a chuckling beck. Although about the same size as Austwick it has far more facilities for visitors; its shops, cafés, car park, pub and information point all contribute to making Clapham a very busy little village at times. This tourist drawing-power was boosted significantly by the opening of the Victorian railway station, the trains delivering carriage loads of visitors to the newly discovered Ingleborough Cave a mile up the valley of Clapham Beck.

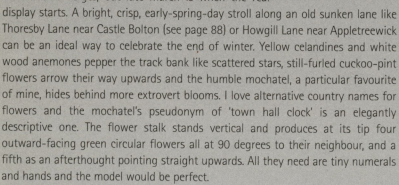

Flowers of the Dales

Lime-rich soil, a history of traditional non-intensive agriculture and lots of rain: these are the three blessings bestowed on the Yorkshire Dales that allow a fabulously rich flora to bloom in the spring and summer months.

Down in the valleys, away from the biting wind and chance of a late blizzard, early March can see odd pioneers like butterbur and coltsfoot appearing on roadside verges, but late March is when the real display starts. A bright, crisp, early-spring-day stroll along an old sunken lane like Thoresby Lane near Castle Bolton (see page 88) or Howgill Lane near Appletreewick can be an ideal way to celebrate the end of winter. Yellow celandines and white wood anemones pepper the track bank like scattered stars, still-furled cuckoo-pint flowers arrow their way upwards and the humble mochatel, a particular favourite of mine, hides behind more extrovert blooms. I love alternative country names for flowers and the mochatel's pseudonym of 'town hall clock' is an elegantly descriptive one. The flower stalk stands vertical and produces at its tip four outward-facing green circular flowers all at 90 degrees to their neighbour, and a fifth as an afterthought pointing straight upwards. All they need are tiny numerals and hands and the model would be perfect.

May is the time for the woodlands of the region, when the great floral carpets are unrolled; wild garlic or ramsons and the incomparable bluebell. There cannot be many better displays anywhere in the country than Skipton Woods (see page 34) or Hag Wood near Richmond. Out in the fields, hawthorn hedges paint lines of white may blossom up hillsides and wet roadsides dance with bobbing heads of water avens.

If you can only visit the Dales once in the year to experience its flowers, then June has to be the time. This is when the display is at its peak: daylight hours are at their

The cave lies on the land belonging to the Ingleborough Estate which, in the 18th century, belonged to the Farrer family. They had constructed what is still by far the biggest building in the village, **Ingleborough Hall** (now an outdoor education centre; see below), but it was a great-grandson, Reginald Farrer, who had the most lasting influence. He was a botanist and plant collector in the early years of the 20th century, who brought back many exotic species from the Himalayas and planted them in the estate grounds. He could be very imaginative in his planting techniques, having once fired alpine rock plant seeds at a cliff face from a shotgun to give a 'natural' spread of flowers later.

The estate charges a nominal fee to follow the **Reginald Farrer Nature Trail** along the main Ingleborough track, although it is more of a landscaped garden stroll, and a free bridleway alternative runs parallel, to the cave and beyond.

maximum and plant growth is so fast you can almost hear it. This is when the iconic limestone flowers appear, trademark verge and hedge blues like meadow cranesbill and nettle-leaved bellflower, traditional hayfield species including yellow rattle and betony, and the real stars of the show, the orchids. Many of the family are lime loving (calcicoles) so it is no surprise that more than ten species of orchid grow within the National Park. All are beautiful, none is very common and some are extremely rare.

The lady's slipper orchid is arguably the best looking and without doubt the rarest flower of all: only one native wild lady's slipper orchid plant exists in Britain and it grows in a secret ash-wood location somewhere in the Craven and Wharfedale locale. In pre-Victorian times this orchid was also found in Derbyshire, Durham and Cumbria but was never common. Wholesale picking for markets and uprooting for collections was its downfall, the attraction, of course, being its stunning appearance. The maroon perianth crowns the golden-yellow shoe-shaped lip which gives the plant all of its names; *Cyripedium calceolus* literally means 'little shoe of Venus', and 'Mary's shoe' is a vernacular Yorkshire name.

Now other lady's slippers grow in one or two dales and Cumbrian woods but these are all artificially propagated from seeds collected since 1987 from the one 'wild' plant. Natural England is coordinating this Species Recovery Programme, which is now starting to blossom – literally. It takes 11 years for a lady's slipper plant to flower once established, and in 2000 the first of the new scheme's offspring did just that near Ingleton. Let us hope that the efforts of the scientists are successful – that these magnificent flowers return to their old haunts, no longer secret and guarded, and we can all marvel at the plant that so nearly disappeared.

Every summer the National Park organises a 'Flowers of the Dales Festival' with nearly a hundred events: walks, meetings, talks and such like, across the whole park. The festival runs from the beginning of May until the end of September and is an excellent way to learn about and celebrate the flora of the Dales. For details contact the Yorkshire Dales Millennium Trust (01524 251002; www.ydmt.org).

Estate connections apart, a good deal else to see in Clapham can easily fill half a day. An excellent guide for pottering around the village is the free map/leaflet produced by the village development association (www.claphamyorkshire.co.uk) and found in all the shops and cafés. It shows where little St James church is hidden away in the trees; how to find Witherspoons Craft Emporium, the village hall that often has displays of local artists; and exactly where the five bridges over the beck are. Interestingly, two buildings in the village not featured on the map as they are not open to visitors, but which locals are very proud of hosting, are **The Dalesman** magazine, bastion of Slow principles, which has offices in a small cottage near the village hall, and the headquarters of the **Cave Rescue Organisation**, the building next to the pub.

The underground emergency service

An unassuming, plain, grey building, next door to the New Inn in Clapham, is something of a shrine in caving circles. It was once a pub, then stables for the inn next door, but now is known simply as the C R O Depot, which stands for Cave Rescue Organisation. It possesses such a generic title because, like the F A Cup, it was the first of its kind in the world, and didn't need a name to distinguish it from other cave rescue teams – there weren't any. Since its formation in 1935, the C R O has rescued nearly 3,000 unfortunate folk, many from underground, but also walkers and climbers on the surface, as the organisation doubles as a mountain rescue team.

The modern C R O is a large and very professional organisation, but amazingly, all 80 team members are volunteers and the whole operation is funded by donations.

Food and drink

Brook House Guest House and Café Station Rd ☎ 01524 251580 ⌂ www.brookhouse-clapham.co.uk. Home-cooked rustic dishes.

Croft Café Church Ave (no phone). In a delightful setting overlooking the river. Afternoon teas are a speciality.

Growing with Grace Station Rd ☎ 01524 251723 ⌂ www.growingwithgrace.co.uk. A Quaker co-operative organic farm shop selling a wide variety of vegetables, fruit and whole foods. Closed Sun and Mon.

New Inn Hotel ☎ 01524 251203 ⌂ www.newinn-clapham.co.uk. A large 18th-century coaching inn opposite the market cross. Two bars with open fires serving Yorkshire real ales. Main bar has a collection of caving cartoons by Jim Eyre, one of the local early cave explorers.

Shopping and activities

Beckside Gallery Church Ave ☎ 01524 251122 ⌂ www.becksideyarns.co.uk. A shop that celebrates the local tradition of wool knitting. A wide variety of yarns for sale and a sit'n'knit self-help group you can join in with.

Ingleborough Hall ☎ 01524 251265 ⌂ www.ingleboro.co.uk. Run by Bradford Metropolitan District Council as an outdoor education centre, primarily for Bradford schoolchildren, but they do offer day and half-day activities for non-residents in expert-led climbing, caving and gorge scrambling.

The Old Manor Bunkhouse Church Ave ☎ 01524 251144 ⌂ www.claphambunk.com. Home to Witherspoon's Craft Emporium shop selling local produce. Also a licensed bar with food at weekends and cheap and cheerful accommodation.

③ Ingleborough Cave

The entrance to the cave is a very obvious large hole in the side of the Clapham Beck valley, just over a mile upstream from Clapham village, so to say the cavern was discovered in 1837 would be stretching the truth. The cave's existence had been known to locals for hundreds of years, but the 19th century's upsurge in both scientific exploration and commercial development prompted the estate to blast away a rubble barrier a short way into the chamber. What they found beyond turned out to be a link to one of the most extensive cave systems in Britain, and a goldmine for their fledgling tourist industry.

Thousands of visitors have enjoyed the guided tour in the subsequent 170 years. Visitor numbers to Ingleborough cave reached their peak in the 1960s when the health and safety culture was not quite as obsessive as today. The cave is now fully lit throughout and hard hats are compulsory, but 40 or so years ago visitors were advised to 'mind their heads' and were given individual candles to light their way. Alan, one of the cave guides, was telling me of an entertaining recent visit from a deceptively harmless-seeming elderly couple. 'We've actually been here once before,' the old gentleman said, 'Back in 1961 or 62 when we were both teenagers. I'm afraid we didn't behave particularly well. I wrote my initials on the cave ceiling in candle soot, and my wife set fire to the person in front of her with her candle. It was an accident I think.' Alan pointed out the offending graffiti, which were still there after nearly 50 years.

For a reasonable fee, the guides, mostly serious ex-cavers themselves, provide a friendly and informative tour, taking about 50 minutes to travel a third of a mile in and returning the same way. The cave is dry, the paths level-ish and the only discomfort a bit of stooping here and there… not at all the claustrophobic experience you might expect.

If you do want a truly adrenalin-charged underground experience, you need not look much further. A mile uphill from Ingleborough Cave, following the dry valley of Trow Gill, you come to an area of 'pot holes' and 'shake holes', one of which warrants a safety fence around it. This is **Gaping Gill**, a slightly ominous name for something genuinely awe-inspiring. Fell Beck, tumbling down the eastern side of Ingleborough thousands of years ago, found itself a crack in the soluble limestone to disappear down. Over the millennia this crack has widened into the largest cave chamber in Britain and Fell Beck's freefall descent into it forms the highest waterfall in the country, albeit not seen by many people. Sadly more than a few careless people eager for a closer look have also made the quick and fatal descent, 365 feet to the floor of Gaping Gill, so take care near the edge.

The great news is that a much slower descent of Gaping Gill is possible, but only on two weeks of the year, the week of Whitsun bank holiday and the week leading up to August bank holiday. Local caving clubs set up a winch to lower willing members of the public down to the bottom of the cave and back for a nominal fee. Bradford Potholing Club run it in May (01484 683260; www.bpc-cave.org.uk) and Craven Pothole Club in August (no phone; www.cravenpotholeclub.org). There must be a catch, I hear you say, and there is. So popular is this service that the wait for your turn at the top can be five hours at busy times. What you can do is put your name down then walk up nearby Ingleborough until it's time for your turn.

My descent into Gaping Gill

The karabiner clicked. 'Sit right back and keep your feet in,' my minder instructed, then he looked me in the eye, 'Okay, you ready? Away you go.' With that, a trap door opened and my chair disappeared down into absolute blackness with me in it, clutching to my midriff the items on Chester's list.

I'd been talking to Chester the night before in the bar of the New Inn in Clapham about my morning descent into Gaping Gill. 'You'll love it, it's a great experience but take something warm and waterproof,' he said, 'Too many people turn up at the winch in shorts, and bikinis even, not realising just where they are going. They treat it as a funfair ride – but it's a bit more than that. A head torch will be useful and a bit of food if you're planning on staying down a while. A roll-up keeps me warm enough but some folk like to have a small flask of coffee.' About ten seconds into the descent was the first of the several times that I was glad of Chester's advice. The potholing club members above had temporarily diverted the beck that created the main shaft, away from it, but there was still a fair amount of water around and I got well sprayed. Gaping Gill is a little like an inverted funnel in shape, so after the initial narrow entrance, although I couldn't see it, I could feel I was in a huge space – large enough to contain York Minster it turns out. It was a vulnerable feeling to be suspended in the middle of that with just tiny lights visible on the floor below and the roar of the waterfall echoing around the chamber. Almost before I knew it the chair came to a halt at the cave floor and I was helped out and moved to somewhere slightly drier to watch Kevin, the next descender, join us. 'God, did I just do that?' I thought as the chair hurtled out of the dark spray and into the dim light where we were.

The two of us had a brief tour from another club member and were then let loose to explore with head torches (cheers, Chester). Twenty minutes later, with more and more people arriving, and queueing for the chair out becoming a possibility, I went back up. Chester had said that the ascent would be different and it was. 'You'll see more 'cos your eyes are acclimatised to the dark; look out for Colley's ledge.' This is as far as Colley, the first caver to brave the descent, reached. He looked down into the black, couldn't see the floor and declared Gaping Gill bottomless. What Chester didn't tell me was that for some reason it's a lot wetter going back up.

I stepped out of the chair at the top, completely drenched and in a daze, handed in my numbered wristband (it's handy for them to know how many are still down there) and went to the checking-in tent to thank the team. I had, and still have, a real feeling of gratitude towards everyone in the Craven Pothole Club for enabling me to have such a privileged experience. It took the direct involvement of eight people to get me down and back: two doing the checking in, a winch man, a top chair man, two bottom chair men, a guide and an overseer. All were volunteers here on holiday and what did I pay? £10 – a bargain. Long may it continue.

④ Ingleton

Ingleton is most definitely a town, albeit a small and friendly one, and it is a town that has very successfully re-invented itself after the collapse of a busy industrial past. The last of the coal mines closed in the 1930s, limestone quarrying stopped ten years later and the town lost its rail link courtesy of Dr Beeching in 1967. Most folk would agree that Ingleton has benefited from the first two changes, but not the last one: a locomotive in full steam, crossing the town viaduct on its way to Kirkby Lonsdale, would be an inspiring sight today.

Ingleton is thriving now because of tourism, with most visitors using it as a service base to explore the scenic delights of its hinterland. The nearest sample of this beautiful countryside is right on the doorstep, the **Ingleton Waterfalls Trail**. This is one of two walks (the Reginald Farrer Nature Trail near Clapham being the other), where a fee is charged by the landowner for the privilege. I'm not madly keen on the principle of paying to walk, but I'll bite the bullet, since it's such a spectacular path.

If you have found yourself here on a lousy weather day, or you're just feeling lazy, indoor diversions in Ingleton – a smattering of arts and craft shops, the pottery being the best, a few tea-shops and four pubs, could be your option. Two of the cafés, Bernies and Inglesport, have an interesting history; next door to each other, Bernies was a café and Inglesport a caving equipment shop. When Inglesport started selling food and drink, the café next door replied by selling caving gear and they now exist in a state of healthy rivalry.

Inglesport also operates Ingleton's **indoor climbing wall** which is available for experienced climbers. If you aren't, but would like to have a go anyway, then ask in the shop about freelance instructors who can coach on the wall, or even take you down a cave. If all that sounds a little too adventurous but you would like some exercise then maybe the swimming pool is for you. Ingleton is one of the few places hereabouts to boast a heated **outdoor pool**, which you can find down by the riverside behind the church. The pool was built by striking coal miners in the 1930s, at the height of the lido boom.

Too cold for a swim? Then maybe a country-lane stroll half a mile past the pool to the tiny village of **Thornton in Lonsdale**. Sir Arthur Conan Doyle was married in St Oswald's church here and celebrated afterwards in the Marton Arms opposite. You would do well to emulate him as it is a great old pub, but mind your behaviour, as the old village stocks are still fully functional nearby.

Food and drink

Bernies Café Main St ☎ 01524 241802 🖰 www.bernriescafe.co.uk. Basic hearty nosh surrounded by cavers and bikers. Also sells outdoor gear.

Ingleborough Limestone Beef Whaitber Farm, Westhouse, LA6 3PQ ☎ 01524 241442. Meat reared on the high fell, available from the farm.

Marton Arms Thornton in Lonsdale ☎ 01524 241281 ⌨ www.martonarms.co.uk. The building dates from the 13th century and retains a lot of its old charm. Food is standard pub fare but for drinkers this is an exceptional place with up to 15 cask ales, beers and ciders available at any one time, and over 200 malt whiskies to choose from.

The Wheatsheaf High St ☎ 01524 241275 ⌨ www.thewheatsheaf-ingleton.co.uk. All the pubs in town have real ale and the Masons Arms has the best-value food, but overall this is the best of the bunch for food and beer quality, and general ambience.

Shopping and activities

Ingleton Pottery Under the viaduct ☎ 01524 241363 ⌨ www.ingletonpottery.co.uk. An old Unsworth family business. You can watch stoneware pottery being hand thrown and buy the results.

Activities

Inglesport/Ingleton Climbing Wall Main St ☎ 01524 241146 ⌨ www.inglesport.co.uk. Probably the biggest caving shop in the country, with a café upstairs, and operators of the climbing wall.

Ingleton Swimming Pool ☎ 01524 241147 ⌨ www.ingletonpool.co.uk. Open in summer months.

Ingleton Waterfalls Trail

This 4½-mile walk is a little classic. The walkers' oracle Alfred Wainwright himself declared 'Surely, of its kind, this is the most delightful walk in the country. And not only delightful; it is interesting, exciting, captivating and, in places, awesome.' The trail is well signposted in Ingleton and starts down in the valley bottom where the Thornton road crosses two small rivers, just above their confluence to form the embryonic River Greta. If you are in a car it is worth parking down here by the café rather than up in town, as your walk entrance fee includes parking.

Traditionally the route is clockwise ascending the valley of the River Twiss first; do not be tempted to go maverick, starting with the River Doe and travelling anti-clockwise. You may think that you are avoiding the crowds (and the fee) but in reality you will meet everybody else travelling in the opposite direction at some point, probably on all the steep and narrow staircase sections! For solitude, and that would always be my choice on a walk as beautiful as this, the advice is go early. Last time I visited, the nice man in the ticket office said, 'We officially open at nine o'clock and I couldn't possibly condone anyone setting off before then as they would not be covered by the owner's insurance (said with a twinkle in his eye). In any case, it never gets busy until about 11 in the morning… lazy lot these trippers.' Another alternative recommended by Wainwright, who was a confirmed sociopath, is to do the walk in winter when there are no crowds and the falls are either roaring with flood water or festooned with ice sculptures.

As soon as you enter the limestone gorge of Swilla Glen near the start of the walk, it becomes obvious why this area is deemed so special, Natural England designating it as a Site of Special Scientific Interest (SSSI) for its geology alone. The fenced path clings to the valley side as it passes through a tunnel of overhanging ash and hazel boughs on its way to Manor Bridge and the first of the cascades, **Pecca Falls**, as it leaps over a hard band of greywacke rock. In the next 500 yards the river tumbles over seven rock steps at **Pecca Twin Falls, Hollybush Spout**, other nameless rapids and finally, **Thornton Force**, at 46 feet the highest of them all. This time the hard ledge is limestone and the soft rock beneath is vertically folded slate.

For the laid-back and sedate, this is the ideal spot for a laze and/or picnic, whilst the bold and restless members of the party brave the slippery walk behind the falls or swim in the plunge pool itself. Not far above Thornton Force, the route leaves the Twiss valley to contour around the hill on the very old Twisleton Lane track and reaches a high point of 934 feet above sea level before joining the valley of the **River Doe** for the descent.

Beezley Falls marks the start of the most dramatic section of the whole walk, and is closely followed by **Rival Falls** and the dark depths of **Baxengill Gorge**. The inaccessible nature of this place has left the woods relatively undisturbed to form one of the best remnants of ancient semi-natural forest in the area. The giant mature oaks, rare mosses and liverworts, and nesting pied flycatchers and redstarts are in the care of the Woodland Trust, who own and manage this part of the valley.

Snow Falls is one of the last spectacular diversions on view, before the path passes through an old limestone quarry and back into Ingleton.

⑤ White Scar Cave

North of Ingleton, Twisleton Dale carries the main road to Hawes, past White Scar Cave and through the little hamlet of Chapel le Dale. The White Scar experience is very different to that of Ingleborough Cave in many ways. It is the longest show cave in Britain so at 80 minutes the tour lasts longer. The beck that created Ingleborough Cave has moved to a lower system leaving the show cave dry, whereas White Scar is an active cave with the noise and moisture of its creative beck still very much in evidence, giving a real risk of the cave closing in very wet weather. There is car parking at the cave entrance, a shop and a well appointed café; you can even have a virtual tour of the cave on the new website without leaving home. It is convenient, modern and slick, which I suppose is good, but I have to admit I prefer the 'slower' experience of Ingleborough.

White Scar Cave ☎ 01524 241244; www.whitescarcave.co.uk. Open daily Feb–Oct plus weekends in winter (weather permitting).

⑥ Kingsdale

By car, the way to Kingsdale is a narrow, poorly signposted minor road that sets off from Ingleton in the wrong direction entirely, then doubles back at Thornton in Lonsdale if you follow the sign for 'Dent'. Up a steep hill, down another one, round a bend and suddenly there it is; a hidden valley, tiny and tucked away. This is one of Wainwright's 'shyly hidden places' where 'life here is as it should be; two farmsteads the only habitation, animals graze undisturbed and birds enjoy sanctuary.'

Kingsdale is just a great place to be, an almost guaranteed deserted oasis for those that need solitude to wander, which was why I was surprised on my most recent visit, in May 2009, to see what looked like an impromptu campsite near the head of the valley. I assumed that it was a meet of the caving fraternity but on closer investigation found myself in the middle of an archaeological excavation. The group conducting the dig were from the local Ingleborough Archaeology Group and one of their number, Dave Johnson, kindly showed me around the site.

'In 2006 we were excavating a known medieval building when we found remains of a fire pit which was dated to between 6960 and 6660BC, putting it within the Mesolithic (or Middle Stone Age) period,' he explained. 'What we're doing now is concentrating on features to the side of the fire pit that may be remains of post-holes for a temporary shelter used maybe by hunters, foragers or chert knappers.' (Chert is the limestone equivalent of flints in chalk, I learnt from Dave.) The group offers the opportunity for volunteers to join their number, be trained up in a variety of techniques and assist on digs. If you are interested in future projects contact them (01524 271072; www.ingleborougharchaeologygroup.org.uk).

When I chanced upon the archaeologists, I was on my way to a place in Kingsdale that, in Victorian times, was quite a tourist draw. **Yordas Cave** was once a show cave with an admission fee but is now a little-visited hole in the hillside. An inscribed date of 1653 on one of the internal walls testifies to how long this place has been known about, indeed the name indicates an even older heritage. Yordas was a legendary Norse giant who would lure boys into the depths and devour them. Putting aside the dangers of being eaten by Vikings, Yordas is considered one of the safer caves to enter without a guide or specialist equipment, although in today's paranoid health-and-safety culture the British Caving Association would probably never put that in writing. Although not signposted it is marked on the OS map and is relatively easy to find. Just before the last building in the dale where the road is gated is a wooded dry valley. Beyond the low entrance a torch is all that is needed, and the bigger the better, to see your footing and the details of the roof formations 60 feet above. At the back of the cave, 30 yards from the entrance, Yordas Gill flows across the floor from right to left, having fallen in through the roof as an elegant waterfall. This is a great place for sensible freelance exploration but not after very wet weather when the cave floor can flood and be very muddy afterwards.

On the fell-side above Yordas Wood, just below the summit of Gragareth, lies an area referred to on the map as Turbary Pasture. Turbary is the ancient commoners' right to collect turf or peat, and the fuel was transported via the Turbary Road which is present as a track and makes an excellent terrace walk or cycle along the side of Kingsdale.

⑦ Chapel le Dale

A church, a pub and some caves; that is just about it for Chapel le Dale, but the church is delightful, the pub magnificent and the caves have some of the weirdest names you have ever heard.

This hamlet is named after 'the church in the valley', **St Leonard's**, a tiny 17th-century building with a history intrinsically linked to the railway that crosses the head of the dale. The church is made of local limestone. On the west wall of the nave is a black Dent marble memorial which reads: 'To the memory of those who through accidents, lost their lives, in constructing the railway works, between Settle and Dent Head. This tablet was erected at the joint expense, of their fellow workmen and the Midland Railway Company 1869 to 1876.' The railway company obviously felt some small responsibility for these accidental deaths as it paid for an extension to the graveyard (hardly a gesture that would have earned them an 'Investors in People' logo today) – but not for the many more that perished from smallpox or fights; some of those victims lie in unmarked graves here.

By far the most visited building in Chapel le Dale is the **Old Hill Inn**. Although it started its long life as a farm in 1650, this building has been a pub of repute, and sometimes ill repute, for a long time. Sheep drovers were their main customers in the 17th and 18th centuries but in the late 1800s, railway building time, the pub was more like a wild-west saloon with 6,000 navvies needing to be watered and entertained. Last century quieter times returned, with hill-walkers and cavers the main clientele… and the occasional celebrity visitor; Winston Churchill was a regular when visiting the Dales.

The 1970s and 80s saw a brief return to the wild old days when the Old Hill became a very basic boozer but an extremely popular one. I have many very fond memories of a misspent youth here: some wild and long Saturday nights in a bar packed with cavers and walkers. Things were very informal; one of the bar games was cavers attempting to squeeze through the spokes of an old cartwheel, the bar staff wore wellies to cope with the quantity of beer on the floor and most of the customers staggered out to their tents in the garden in the early hours of the morning. Those days are long gone and the Old Hill is much more sedate now; some would say it has lost a lot of its character but one thing is for certain, the quality of the beer and food is higher than it has ever been.

The recommended slow route linking Chapel le Dale with Ingleton is not the busy main road but the old Roman road on the other side of Twisleton Dale. It is a pleasant drive and an even better cycle, quiet and relatively flat until Meal Bank at Ingleton. This route can be extended into a circular easy walk, or a more testing bike ride, on the bridleway over Twisleton Fell. Big plusses are that you get to pass the wonderfully named Hurtle Pot and Jingle Pot caves near the church, and cross the fantastic limestone pavement on the fell top. The only minus, except for pushing your bike up or down the steep bits, are the unrestricted views of the still-operating Ingleton quarry – a real eyesore.

Old Hill Inn Chapel le Dale ☎ 01524 241256 www.oldhillinn.co.uk. An historic tavern serving excellent local brews from Theakston, Black Sheep and Dent, and delicious food in an intimate dining room. The chef is a master confectioner so the puddings are especially good.

The Cumbrian corner

The minor road that heads up Kingsdale from Ingleton sneaks right over the shoulder of the biggest of the Three Peaks, Whernside. At its highest point it does something very strange; as it starts to drop down steeply into Deepdale, and towards **Dentdale**, it stays within the Yorkshire Dales National Park, but leaves the county of North Yorkshire. Since 1974 this valley down to **Sedbergh** and the parallel valley of **Garsdale** to the north have been part of Cumbria, but you try telling the local farmers that they are not Yorkshiremen if you dare!

Half of the range of hills beyond Sedbergh is also part of the National Park and I have therefore included them. The Howgills are hills apart; distinctly neither the Pennines nor the Cumbrian Fells but rubbing shoulders with both.

⑧ Sedbergh

The little-known River Rawthey squeezes its way between the Pennine hills of the Yorkshire Dales and the Howgill Fells just to their west. On its northern bank, just before it spills into the grand River Lune, sits Sedbergh, a market town with a castle mound and venerable bowed buildings lining a cobbled main street. Sedbergh is a very self-contained little place, comfortable in its own skin, which until recently was really only known to walkers or mountain bikers with designs on the southern Howgills, or those with connections to the prestigious private school whose buildings dominate the land between the main street and the river. **Sedbergh School**, founded in 1525, has by necessity moved with the times and now has modern facilities, day pupils and a significant proportion of girl students. Thirty-five years ago, when I was a schoolboy myself and visiting Sedbergh on a school trip, things were far more traditional. The male-only boarders were ripe for our astonished ridicule as we leant over the school wall and saw the 'posh kids' all in shorts… right up to 18-year-old sixth-formers!

These days mention the name Sedbergh and many people will think of books, because this is officially England's **book town** and partner to Hay-on-Wye in Wales (where it all started) and Wigtown in Scotland. The town's re-branding has been brilliantly orchestrated by a group of local residents who realised after the 2001 foot-and-mouth disease outbreak how vulnerable rural communities dependent on farming were. 'This has been so good for the town,' said Carol Nelson, manager of the project, It's brought more people in, which supports and safeguards the future of the shops that really matter – the butcher, grocer, hardware shop, post office and the like – but it also allows us to celebrate the glory of books. The sort of books people buy in a book town aren't your throwaway airport novellas, but important ones that you are prepared to keep, read to your children and which eventually become old friends.'

Less well known is Sedbergh's importance in the beginnings of the Quaker movement. In 1652, George Fox, the founder of the Society of Friends, preached in and around the town to hundreds of local folk. His sermon from a rock on Firbank Fell, now known as Fox's Pulpit, is widely held to be the founding moment of the Society. Twenty two years after these events local 'Friends' built a meeting house at **Briggflats** by the river half a mile west of Sedbergh. It has survived the intervening 400 years as the oldest meeting house in the north of England, its plain, wood-bench-simplicity, testimony to the 'slow' and minimalist Friends' philosophy. Briggflats is only a mile's stroll away from Sedbergh town centre along the riverside Dales Way path, with a seat in the peaceful burial ground the ideal spot for a moment of meditation before the return path across the fields.

><><><

Food and drink

The Dalesman Main St ✆ 01539 620089 🖳 www.thedalesman.co.uk. A popular old coaching inn and the best of the town's three pubs. Food is sourced locally and seasonally and the menu is imaginative and continental if a little pricey.

Green Door Sweet Shop Main St ✆ 01539 620089 🖳 www.thegreendoorshop.com. Do you ever yearn for the nostalgic taste of pear drops, Pontefract cakes, and sherbet lemons? Then enter the Green Door because they are all here, with hundreds more besides.

The Sedbergh Café Main St ✆ 01539 621389 🖳 www.thesedberghcafe.com. An Edwardian-style gem, serving a wide range of tea and filter coffees from Taylors of Harrogate, and top-quality snacks. Gift and food shop attached.

Bookshops

Sedbergh's five book-town shops are:

Bertram's 16 Back Lane ☎ 01539 620408. General second-hand books, fair-trade percussion instruments and gifts.

The Bookseller 77 Main St ☎ 01539 620991. Local topography, mountaineering and children's books.

Dales and Lakes Book Centre 72 Main St ☎ 01539 620125 🖰 www.sedbergh.org.uk/booktown/dlbc.html. Quality secondhand books on most subjects.

Sleepy Elephant 41 Main St ☎ 01539 621770 🖰 www.sleepyelephant.net. A wide range of books including scarce books on art design etc.

Westwood Books Leisure House, Long Lane ☎ 01539 621233 🖰 www.westwoodbooks.co.uk. A very large stock of new, secondhand and antiquarian books on all subjects.

⑨ The Howgill Fells

The Howgills are a very discreet range of hills, separated from the Yorkshire Dales by the valley of the River Rawthey, with the River Lune, and more obviously the M6 motorway, providing the boundary with the Lake District mountains.

Such is the gentle rounded aspect of these hills from a distance that a friend of mine once likened them to a giant plate of dumplings. Alfred Wainwright,

the great walker and writer, was less obsessed with food, and in his *Walks on the Howgill Fells* preferred the metaphor 'a huddle of squatting elephants'. This is very different country, and what makes it so is an absence of things rather than a list of attributes; no roads or buildings, virtually no trees except in the deepest creases and, most striking of all, no walls – not a single one. This makes for a particularly liberating place to walk in, as you can genuinely just wander where you fancy, terrain permitting – and make no mistake, despite the distant gentle impressions, some serious gradients lie hidden away.

The most accessible Howgill is most definitely **Winder**, a mere morning stroll from Sedbergh, albeit a very steep one, but longer treks allow you to lose yourself in this special place. For a nice, easy stroll into the heart of the Howgills without too much climbing, the walk along the beck from near the Cross Keys to **Cautley Spout waterfall** is highly recommended. The ascent of the Howgills' highest point, **The Calf** (2,220 feet), via Cautley Spout waterfall and then down to Sedbergh makes a fine day's walk, but the plum route for me is **Black Force** via **Carlingill Beck**.

Unfortunately it starts with a six-mile drive/taxi ride/hitched lift on the minor road from Sedbergh, through the hamlet of Howgill to Carlingill. But within minutes of starting, the M6 is out of sight and your only company is grazing dales ponies, wheatears protesting loudly from boulder-tops, and dippers feeding by (and in) the water. You are forced to crisscross the beck as the valley walls close in (it may be impassable after heavy rain) and finally reach the spot of the day, where Black Force Beck tumbles down its ravine to join you. Scan the skyline for ravens and peregrine falcons. Both routes to the tops involve some serious scrambling, up the side of either Black Force or Carlingill Beck and then you are back on gentle grassy slopes again. The route from there is your choice; back to the car or over some elephants' backs to Sedbergh.

The Cross Keys Temperance Inn Cautley, LA10 5NE ☎ 01539 620284
www.cautleyspout.co.uk. A 400-year-old building that looks its age. Delicious rustic meals (rabbit pie with black pudding and bacon is the best seller). Alcohol is not for sale but you can bring your own for free (the pub has been unlicensed since 1902 and has the status of a temperance inn; the present tenant is a Quaker). Usefully placed for walks to Cautley Spout waterfall.

⑩ Dentdale

Whenever I arrive in Dentdale, and the sturdy little village that gives the valley its name, I always feel as if I'm coming home. This is no fanciful imagining brought on by the homely feel of the place, but because I did spend a fair proportion of my formative years here. Some inspired soul in my secondary school, in industrial Lancashire, decided that we 12-year-old 'townies' should experience country life, so the school bought a cottage in **Dent** for us to stay in. My weekend visits to White Hart House in the 1970s were a revelation; I discovered proper hills (Great Coum was my first summit), swam in clean rivers and saw the Milky Way in a clear, black, non-street-lit sky for the first time.

Times have changed, Dent is much busier now than it ever was in my youth, and sadly White Hart House was sold, but the village still retains its character and the dale remains many people's favourite.

The fact that it is a mere ten miles from Dent Head – where the Settle–Carlisle line calls in at **Dent Station** as it crosses the top of the valley – to Sedbergh where it meets the Rawthey valley makes this quite a small dale, but one packed with fascinating detail. The River Dee is at the heart of much of it, especially in the upper dale, tumbling over limestone ledges, squeezing through narrow 'strids', and on numerous occasions playing hide and seek by disappearing underground, only to reappear hundreds of yards further downstream. The Dales Way footpath hugs the riverbank most of the way down, allowing views of the caves, which unusually abound down at valley-bottom level, and the rich and enchanting wildlife. You will probably see more dippers per mile of river here than anywhere else in Yorkshire.

The return of the peregrine falcon

Back in the late 1970s, when I was still in my teens, I read a book called *The Peregrine* by J A Baker, a man obsessed by these most magnificent of birds, and who wrote about them wonderfully. For this passionate and poetic naturalist, peregrines didn't just fly, they sliced a parabola in a smooth outpouring, like water gliding over stone, or fell as a black bill-hook does into splinters of white wood. What's more, his meticulously observed winter's diary wasn't only inspirational prose, but damned good science too.

Some of his passion rubbed off on me and I dreamt of seeing peregrine falcons flying in the wild. Those were dark days for birds of prey generally; organo-chlorine pesticides added to crop seeds had found their way into the food chain via seed-eating birds and had ended up in such concentrations in the bodies of top predators that the poisoning proved fatal. Where it did not actually kill the birds, it weakened eggshells to the point where they smashed easily in the nest and breeding failed. By the 1970s the peregrine was on the brink of extinction in England. Those few pairs that did nest on isolated crags in the north and west of the country were guarded 24 hours a day by dedicated volunteers to prevent the theft of their rare eggs or chicks. Thirty years ago egg-collecting was far more widely practised than today, and the hatched young birds could be sold to unscrupulous falconers for thousands of pounds.

I was introduced to my first pair of wild peregrines by an inspirational schoolteacher, Alan Stoddart, who, when on holiday from teaching me and my peers in industrial Lancashire, lived in a caravan in Dentdale. The nest, or eyrie, was on a crag called Combe Scar near the village of Dent, and one Easter I and a few other equally excited schoolboys were sworn to secrecy and taken up to meet the 'guard' in a derelict barn below the crag.

For the following hour or two we watched entranced through binoculars as the male (tiercel) screamed into view at a speed scarcely believable, to deliver food to the female (falcon) who sat incubating eggs on the nest, their staccato calls echoing around the combe. I have seen peregrines many times since; better views, closer and for longer, but nothing has ever matched that first electric experience.

Thankfully, those poisonous pesticides have long since been banned, and wildlife crime is now very well policed. Consequently peregrine falcons have made a remarkable recovery all over the country, recolonising all their old haunts and even spreading on to the artificial cliffs (tall buildings) in some towns and cities. Even Manchester, Brighton and Birmingham have their own resident breeding peregrines. The Yorkshire Dales now boast about twenty pairs nesting on crags dotted across the national park, including, I am happy to note, the descendants of 'my' pair, still on Combe Scar.

You could come across them anywhere in the dales, usually given away by their distinctive anchor shape in flight, like a squat kestrel, or their phenomenal hunting speed of over 100mph, if you are fortunate enough to see it. For an almost guaranteed viewing though, go to Malham Cove where the RSPB has a viewing telescope set up between Easter and August on the resident peregrine nest.

⑪ *Dent*

The fact that many locals still refer to this place as Dent Town gives us an inkling as to its importance in the past. In its heyday 200 years ago Dent had a market (where the George and Dragon now stands), a race-course and managed to support twelve pubs and inns – venues of 'drunken riots, blasphemy, gambling quarrels and other bygone vices and follies' by all accounts. The industry that fuelled its economy was hand knitting, which was practised by just about everyone in the village; man woman and child (see box on page 22).

Dent's most famous son is undoubtedly Adam Sedgwick, who put his education in Dent Grammar School to good use by becoming professor of geology at Cambridge University, and was a personal friend of Queen Victoria and Prince Albert. His radical thinking in his field led him to being dubbed the father of English geology and prompted a water fountain enclosed in a block of Shap granite to be erected in his honour opposite the George and Dragon. It is probably the most photographed object in the village.

Behind Adam Sedgwick's fountain and down a short alley you will find the old, squat, grey stone church of St Andrew, surrounded by clipped yews and gravestones. As a boy I remember being morbidly fascinated by stories of a vampire's tomb here. In reality George Hodgson was a farmer who regularly drank sheep's blood as a tonic – it can't have done him much harm as he lived to 94 and his 'vampire' grave is in the church porch.

Most of Dent's visitors don't stray far from the main street, which isn't surprising as the cobbled surface and whitewashed cottage frontage give it a very attractive, almost Cornish fishing port, look. Also, this is where its two pubs, both cafés and most of the shops are. I do, however, strongly recommend wandering further afield, namely up the hillside at the back of the village to follow the footpath up the Tolkienesque ravine of Flinter Gill. You may choose just to explore this enchanting place, or you can extend the walk in a variety of directions, and range of distances, on the maze of paths and bridleways on the valley side. My choice would be to continue up to join Green Lane, turn left and skirt the slopes of Great Coum for a mile then descend Nun House Outrake. Back in the valley bottom, Deepdale Beck and the River Dee banks are the most entertaining routes back to Dent.

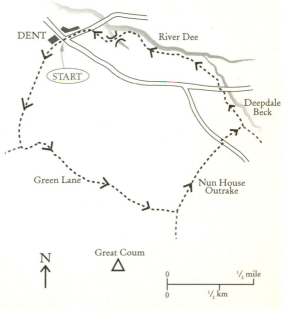

The terrible knitters of Dent

Peering through a Dent cottage window on an 18th-century winter's evening could reveal an eerie and disturbing sight. Ten or twelve adults, men and women, sit around the outside of the room, swaying their bodies in a circular motion in unison, and singing a rhythmic chant. In the flickering candlelight, the shadows of their rapidly moving hands dance on the walls. Is this the meeting of a sinister religious cult? No, it's the Terrible Knitters of Dent.

'Terrible' referred not to the quality of their work but to the incredible speed with which they moved the wool and needles. They were paid on completed garments and a good knitter could start and finish a whole smock in a day. Every week, a cart would arrive from Dover's Mill in Sedbergh loaded with wool and would return full of completed garments – miner's jerseys, army stockings and caps, bump-caps for the slave colonies and high-quality woollens bound for the stores of London; they were all made in the parlours of Dentdale.

⑫ *Dent Station*

Dentdale, like neighbouring Garsdale, displays a typically Viking pattern of settlement – a scattering of farmsteads, with few if any villages. A cluster of buildings, near the top end of the dale, that don't quite manage to form a hamlet, are sometimes lumped together as Cowgill, but more often than not nowadays this corner is named after its most illustrious building.

Dent's railway station sets some kind of record for being further away from the place after which it is named than anywhere else in Britain – the village is a whopping four miles away. Many people have been caught out, stepped off the train and then been faced with a yomp into town, but it's much worse the other way around. Walking from the village to the station is up a killer hill, as Dent station holds another record: at 1,150 feet above sea level, it is the highest mainline station in England.

Most of the other buildings at this end of the dale are lower down, snuggled along the banks of the Dee, which is at its photogenic and playful best here. The whitewashed Sportsman's Inn sits in an enviable spot, with the chapel not far away, and a short mile upstream, a favourite spot of mine, is the old YHA building. Unfortunately, it's closed as a hostel now, but you can still stay there by hiring it as a private self-catering house. Not far from the old youth hostel, at Stonehouse, the highly sought-after **Dent black marble** was quarried and polished. You can see it used decoratively in St Andrew's Church, Dent, and the Railway Memorial in St Leonard's in Chapel le Dale.

Two walks here that I always enjoy are a stroll down the river to Ibberth Peril waterfall and back, and an ascent of Great Knoutberry Hill (possibly the best view in the Dales from the top) via Arten Gill.

Food and drink

Stone Close Café Main St, Dent ☎ 01539 625231. Housed in a 17th-century listed building this well-established café prides itself on the fresh, local, seasonal, organic, and fair-trade credentials of its food and drink.

⑤ Sun Inn Main St, Dent ☎ 01539 625208. The best of the three pubs in the dale, housed in a fabulous whitewashed stone 16th-century building. Traditional and basic pub grub and cask beer from Dent Brewery.

Shopping

Dent Craft Centre Helmside, LA10 5SY ☎ 01539 625400 ⌂ www.dentcraftcentre.co.uk. An outlet for local crafts and a tea-room in an old hay barn, two miles from Dent.

Hill Studio Main St, Dent ☎ 01539 625354 ⌂ www.johncooke.org. The studio of the nationally renowned artist John Cooke upstairs and the Best Cellars craft shop below.

Sophie's Wild Woollens The Shop on the Green, Dent ☎ 01539 625323. Sophie carries on the Terrible Knitters tradition. Lots of colourful modern designs all knitted locally.

⑬ Garsdale

This most northwesterly of the Yorkshire Dales holds the odd double distinction of being one of the most visited of the dales but the least known. The main road west out of busy Wensleydale snakes along the whole length of Garsdale, from top to bottom, but hundreds, sometimes thousands, of people a day pass through, on their way to scenic Wensleydale, or the wild and peaceful Howgills, unwittingly bypassing a landscape with all the same attributes in humble Garsdale. Key to this phenomenon is that there is no village in Garsdale to tempt visitors to stop, and few side roads to draw them off the A684, and slow them down.

It takes a conscious effort to pause and explore here, but try it, because the rewards are rich. The two best opportunities are where minor roads leave the A684, one at Tom Croft Hill, only two miles from Sedbergh, which gives access to Rise Hill and footpaths following the gorgeous River Clough, and the other higher up the dale, the old road to Grisedale.

Grisedale is often labelled the 'Dale that Died' after a 1970s television programme of the same name which documented the last days of the farming families of the dale. It is a deserted place now but great walking country, especially since recent 'open access' legislation has made the surrounding hills available for walkers. Both Wild Boar Fell here, and Rise Hill on the other side of the dale, are strangely devoid of public rights of way, so until open access they were no-go areas.

Red squirrels

Garsdale is isolated enough to be one of the harassed red squirrel's few islands of refuge from its aggressive and disease-carrying cousin, the grey. This is one of 17 woodland areas in northern England where active management is taking place to help the beleaguered reds. Mature cone-bearing Scots pines and larches are encouraged instead of the oaks and hazels preferred by the greys, and any unwanted aliens that get in are trapped and killed – controversial but necessary. Let's hope it works.

Look out for ginger 'tufties' in Grisedale, Dodderham Moss above Dent station and Coat Weggs Woods near Garsdale church.

The Moorcock Inn Garsdale Head, LA10 5PU ☎ 01969 667488
🖰 www.moorcockinn.com. A welcoming sight at a lonely moor-top crossroads. The inside environs may be rustic and the beer traditionally Yorkshire (Black Sheep and Copper Dragon), but the menu is extensive and imaginative with a continental twist.

Ribblesdale

The River Ribble does not spend much time in Yorkshire before it defects to Lancashire. A good way to see every inch of the valley is to follow the Ribble Way footpath which starts at the official source of the river, four miles northeast of the railway. Consequently, the place **Ribblehead**, where the much-photographed viaduct straddles Batty Moss, isn't actually the head of the valley, but let's not split hairs. The gloriously lazy way to see most of Upper Ribblesdale is to board the train at Ribblehead and rattle away south, with Ingleborough filling the window on the starboard side and Pen-y-ghent likewise to port. They both come closest to the train and each other at **Horton in Ribblesdale**, the official start and finish of the Three Peaks Challenge. Six miles down the line at Settle, the railway and river both leave the National Park and go their separate ways.

⑭ Ribblehead Viaduct

To Network Rail this is the site of 'Bridge 66 and station'; to everyone else it is one of the most iconic railway landmarks in the world – the Ribblehead Viaduct. Over 400 yards long, 104 feet high and with 24 arches, it took 6,000 men to build, with 200 losing their lives in the process. To learn about the drama of the viaduct construction and its subsequent history you can visit the Ribblehead visitor centre in the station or get hold of a copy of *Thunder in the Mountains: The Men Who Built Ribblehead* by W R Mitchell. Now in his 80s, Bill, a former editor of the *Dalesman* magazine and self-confessed sufferer of the incurable disease of 'Settle and Carlisle-itis', has produced a riveting account of the soap opera goings-on at Ribblehead. Life in the shanty towns of Jerusalem and the Jerico, rat infestations in Belgravia, the doings of Welsh Jack and Nobby Scandalous, earthquakes, floods and murders – it's all covered here.

The only other building at Ribblehead is its pub, the **Station Inn**, but scattered farmsteads appear as the Chapel le Dale and Horton roads drop down to less exposed climes. A short way down this latter route, and accessible on foot from the station, is **Ribblehead Quarry**, disused since 1999 and now being recolonised by wildlife. The quarry is part of **Ingleborough National Nature Reserve** and a 1½-mile walking trail leads you around its waterfalls, ponds and rock gardens (pick up a leaflet from the station or download one from www.naturalengland.org.uk). Look out for ravens, oystercatchers and ringed plover that breed here, but especially a small plant with five-pointed-star flowers; Yorkshire sandwort is one of the rarest plants in Britain and grows only here on Ingleborough, with its nearest relatives in Sweden.

Just beyond the quarry nature trail, **Colt Park Wood** is one tiny but exceptional part of the NNR. It has been described as the best example of an aboriginal scar limestone ash wood in the country, and the variety of exotic and scarce plants is astonishing. Visit in early summer and you could see globe flower, baneberry, alpine cinquefoil, yellow Star of Bethlehem and the eccentrically named angular Solomon's seal.

The Station Inn Ribblehead ☎ 01524 241274 ✇ www.thestationinn.net. This has always been a lifesaver for Three Peakers, especially on bad days when the fire is roaring. The best of the food is the traditional English dishes; pies, mash, sausages, and the range of Yorkshire beers is impressive. This is an atmospheric boozer but don't expect too much comfort.

⑮ Horton in Ribblesdale

The system of adding an address to a place name, like Skipton on Swale or Thornton in Craven, makes sense when there is another place nearby to confuse it with. Horton's 'in Ribblesdale' makes no sense, as it is the only one for miles, and the nearest is deep in Lancashire – and also in Ribblesdale!

Strange names apart, Horton has much in common with many Dales villages; two pubs, an old arched bridge over the river, a Norman church dedicated to the ubiquitous St Oswald, monastic rule in medieval times and later, a bad dose of the plague.

What singles Horton out today is the influence of outdoor pursuits: caving (at nearby Alum, Hall and Hunt pots and the Long Churn system), cycling and, overwhelmingly, long-distance walking. The Pennine Way and Ribble Way converge here, but the Three Peaks Challenge is by far the most popular. This route was never really invented, it just sort of evolved and then was popularised by Alfred Wainwright's description of it in *Walks in Limestone Country*, and by the Pen-y-ghent café's 'Three Peaks of Yorkshire club'.

The fell-running race over much the same route has a more definite history. It was first run in 1954 with six runners starting, all from Lancashire, and only three finishing. In April 2009, the 55th race had a staggering line-up of 900 starters, with the fastest time an equally impressive 2 hours 55 minutes, and this time a Yorkshireman won it.

Fell running

One question that has always intrigued me about fell runners is not where they do it, how they go so fast, or even what the best technique is – but *why* they do it?

Peter Pozman, a 57-year-old teacher from near Wetherby, put me right. 'You know', he said, 'That's a question I ask myself every race, not long after the start, on the first uphill bit when me lungs are starting to scream. I'd always enjoyed walking up the fells, but the older I got the more I realised that I was running out of time to do them all, so I thought I'd better speed up a bit. By jogging, I found I was doing a whole afternoon's walks in less than an hour and seeing loads of countryside in the process. I was doing this once from Nidderdale, up a fell called Great Whernside, when I met someone near the top who looked at me and my tracksuit and trainers and said, "You must be a fell runner". Jokingly I said, "In my dreams I am", but then I thought, "Yeah, I like the sound of that, I am actually fell running her", and I started to take myself a bit more seriously, eventually actually entering some races.

One of my finest moments was finishing first in the Male 55 and Over class, in a race in the North York Moors, run by a bloke called Dave Parry from Commondale. I love Dave's races - they're really informal. There'd be 80 to 100 of us stood at the start and Dave would shout, "Right, well, it's been snowin' out there and it's startin' to melt, so it'll be real slippy. Last year someone in too much of a hurry took a bit of a tumble, so you might want to go bit easy – Go!" And off we went. It was really horrible but I think the conditions suited me; my hill craft as a walker, and understanding of rough ground kept me out of the freezing water, and my feet stayed relatively dry, whilst the elite athletes couldn't get going. Later in the Eskdale Inn at Castleton, I was watching other people get prizes, when Dave said, "M 55, winner Pete Pozman", and I thought, "Wey hey! Fantastic! Three bottles of wine and my name in print!"

I had my feet plonked firmly on the ground last week though, as I was struggling up a really steep slope, and a fella was keeping up with me walking. "So this is fell running", he said, "Is it hard?", "Yes", I gasped, "especially when I have to talk to people like you at the same time." '

Pen-y-ghent Café Horton ☏ 01729 860333. This place unashamedly caters for outdoor types in need of carbohydrate and rehydration, so food is hearty and simple (excellent, huge vegetarian breakfasts) and tea comes in pints. Can be very busy, especially at weekends.

The Moughton plateau

I wouldn't like visitors to go away with the impression that all the fell-sides around Horton are crowded with bikers, runners and walkers dashing hither and yon. There are undisturbed acres nearby, and one of the easiest to lose yourself in is Moughton (pronounced 'Mooton'), a vast limestone plateau west of Horton. To reach it, follow the Three Peaks path towards Ingleborough, past the offensive eyesore of Horton Quarry, then divert south across one of the most extensive and wildest limestone pavements in the Dales. You could spend hours here striding across the raised ridges of dazzling white rock or sunbathing in the sheltered, flower-filled hollows in between. This other-worldly environment has been created by rainwater dissolving the limestone over thousands of years; in Yorkshire-speak the ridges are clints and the hollows grykes.

To complete a fine five-mile circuit, descend back to the valley bottom at Foredale and follow the riverside Ribble Way back to Horton. That way you will get to see a feature revered by geologists – the **Foredale Unconformity**. This crag at the back of a disused quarry displays Carboniferous rocks lying directly over much older Silurian deposits, with all the intervening layers in between missing – thus not confirming to the usual order of things and earning itself such an odd label.

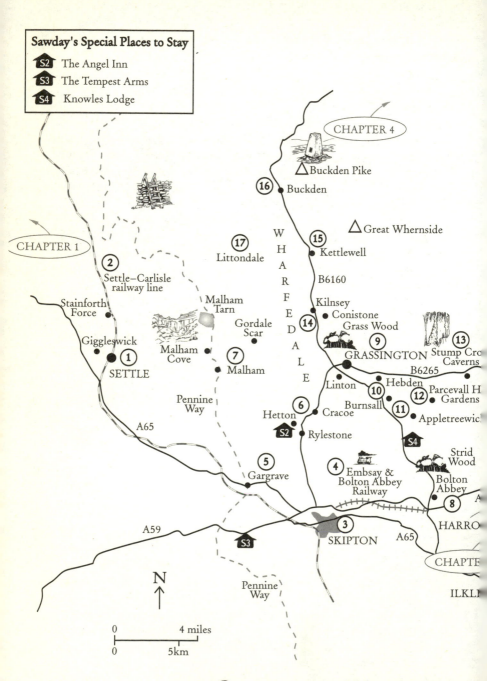

Sawday's Special Places to Stay
S2 The Angel Inn
S3 The Tempest Arms
S4 Knowles Lodge

CHAPTER 4

△ Buckden Pike

16 Buckden

CHAPTER 1

2

Settle–Carlisle
railway line

Stainforth
Force

Giggleswick

1

SETTLE

17 Littondale

Malham
Tarn

Gordale
Scar

Malham
Cove

7 Malham

W
H
A
R
F
E
D
A
L
E

15 Kettlewell

B6160

Kilnsey
Conistone
Grass Wood

14

△ Great Whernside

9 GRASSINGTON

13 Stump Cro
Caverns

B6265

Linton
Hebden
10
Burnsall

6 Cracoe

Hetton

12 Parcevall H
Gardens

11 Appletreewic

Pennine
Way

A65

S2 Rylestone

5 Gargrave

4 Embsay &
Bolton Abbey
Railway

Strid
Wood

S4

Bolton
Abbey

8 A

A59

S3

N
↑

Pennine
Way

0   4 miles
0   5km

3 SKIPTON

A65

HARRO

CHAPTE

ILKLI

CRAVEN AND WHARFEDALE

2. CRAVEN AND WHARFEDALE

This southernmost part of the Yorkshire Dales only just makes it into North Yorkshire, and its closeness to the big cities of Leeds and Bradford makes it probably the most visited region in the national park. Three rivers drain south here: the Ribble, which then escapes westwards into Lancashire, the Aire, and the longest of the Dales watercourses, the Wharfe.

Wharfedale's corridor-like nature sets it apart from the other Yorkshire Dales, that and the river that created it. If forced into a choice, I would have to plump for the Wharfe as my favourite Yorkshire river. Its deep, clear pools, strids, riffles and cascades provide unsurpassed variety of watery landscape, and arguably the richest wildlife in all of the National Park.

Craven, the wild acres of high land to the west of Wharfedale, is a geological wonderland of all things limestone; potholes, 'clint and grike' pavements, disappearing rivers, collapsed caverns and amphitheatres – it's all here, and at its most spectacular around Malham.

Getting there and around

Trains

Unlike in the Three Peaks area, no rail lines travel through the heart of Craven or Wharfedale but Skipton, on the edge, is very well served. Trains from Leeds arrive on average every 20 minutes through the day and from Lancaster every hour. Links to **Carlisle via Settle** on one of Britain's most scenic lines go on average every two hours.

A private steam railway runs between Embsay and Bolton Abbey. Unfortunately trains do not continue the extra two miles from Embsay to Skipton on the national rail line although there are plans for them to do so in the future.

Buses

Skipton is very well served by buses all year from Keighley (65, 66, 66A, 66C; every half-hour weekdays, every hour Sunday), Burnley (215; every hour), Preston and Clitheroe (280, X80; every hour), Leeds and Ilkley (X84; hourly).

Buses out from Skipton to the rest of the region are as follows: **Malham** (210, 211; four buses a day via Gargrave, Coniston Cold, Newfield, Airton and Kirkby Malham); **Grassington** (72; hourly, 11 buses in all via Cracoe, with 7 continuing on to Hebden and 6 to Kettlewell and Bucken in Upper Wharfedale); **Settle** (580; hourly); **Embsay** (214; hourly on average).

In **summer** extra services are put on from Skipton, especially on Sundays as part of the Dales Bus scheme, to **Malham**, **Bolton Abbey** and **Upper Wharfedale**. The pick of the routes to my mind is the 890 **Malham Tarn**

Shuttle, operated by the National Trust, which takes you on a scenic one-hour round trip from Settle, over Craven plateau to Malham Tarn and Malham. Best of all, this is a hail-and-ride service which can take a limited number of bikes and will stop just about anywhere you wave at it en route. Five buses run hourly through the middle of the day. For Sunday and bank holiday travel I strongly recommend a **Southern Dales Rover ticket** which gives you unlimited travel in the whole of Craven and Wharfedale (and beyond) for a day; Dales Rover tickets cover the whole of the Dales.

Boat trips

The Leeds and Liverpool canal at Skipton is the one and only boating venue but offers a variety of options. You can join half-hour or one-hour trips in and around town, or hire a boat for a day, weekend or entire week. West is the more rural and unspoilt direction to sail from Skipton, but even this choice turns away from the Dales and into the lowlands, on its journey towards Lancashire; a tour of farm country, nice, and certainly Slow, if tame.

Pennine Boat Trips Coach St, Skipton ☎ 01756 790829 🖱 www.canaltrips.co.uk. One-hour public cruises on a 58-foot narrowboat. Catered private charters available. Also has self-drive five-seater motorboats.

Pennine Cruisers Coach St, Skipton ☎ 01756 795478 🖱 www.penninecruisers.com. Half-hour public cruises around the back of the castle. Daily self-drive hire of 30-foot narrowboat for up to ten people, also evenings. Half-week holidays from £360 (four berth), £525 (eight-berth) and full weeks from £540 (four-berth), £790 (eight-berth).

Snaygill Boats Bradley ☎ 01756 795150 🖱 www.snaygillboats.co.uk. A similar day and holiday hire service to Pennine Cruisers but from a village two miles away.

Cycling

Road biking is biased towards the fit and experienced rider here purely because the only roads small and quiet enough to be pleasant on a bike tend to have really steep hills on them at some point. The Yorkshire Dales National Park's **Cycle the Dales scheme** (see page ix) has searched out some gentler routes termed as family rides, five of which fall into this region. They start at Settle, Skipton, Gargrave, Bolton Abbey and Grassington. My favourite of these, because it is a circuit that manages to keep off the main Wharfedale Road almost entirely, goes for 14 miles between Grassington, Conistone, Kettlewell, Hawkswick, Arncliffe and Kilnsey; join the route wherever.

For a longer day's ride with some testing hills but nothing gargantuan, try 29 miles of **Into Wharfedale**, a circuit taking in Skipton, Bolton Abbey and

Grassington. For dedicated tourers, part of the Pennine Cycleway passes through here, and a fair chunk of the 130-mile Yorkshire Dales Cycleway, starting as it does in Skipton.

Off-road cycling is even less forgiving to the more leisurely rider than the local roads. No big forests with gentle tracks, or those nice, flat disused railway lines here. It's mainly fell-side tracks with serious inclines more suited to two-wheeled athletes. On the plus side, because this is well-drained limestone country, mud isn't generally a problem and many of the bridleways double as green lanes, so are fairly substantial. Again, the National Park has a scheme that helps; **MTB the Dales** (www.mtbthedales.org.uk) describes seven routes in Craven and Wharfedale, with a ten-mile Settle Loop being the least testing, and therefore the one for me. It crosses Langcliffe Scar and Ewe Moor, taking in the impressive Scaleber Force waterfall, and with only two short difficult sections punctuating a moderate ride.

Hopefully there will be one gentle alternative available soon. Off-road biking doesn't get any flatter than canal towpaths, and there are plans to extend the very popular Aire Valley Towpath Route on the Leeds and Liverpool canal, from where it finishes now at Bingley, to Skipton. Watch this space.

Off the Rails Station Yard, Settle ☏01729 824419 🖱 www.offtherails.org.uk. Daily adult bike hire, including tagalong, trailer and child seat.

Horse-riding

If availability of trekking centres is a good measure, then this is the epicentre of horse-riding in the whole of the Dales. Of the five centres in total, three are here:

Draughton Height Riding School Draughton, Skipton ☏01756 710242.
Kilnsey Trekking and Riding Centre Conistone ☏01756 752861 🖱 www.kilnseyriding.com.
Yorkshire Dales Trekking Centre Holme Farm, Malham ☏01729 830352 🖱 www.ydtc.net.

If you bring your own horse then you, along with the mountain bikers, have access to the area's enormous mileage of bridleways, plus a new national trail primarily aimed at horse-riders, the **Pennine Bridleway**, is under construction. Part of it, the Settle Loop (*see Cycling*), is already open and well used. Accommodation for horses can be had at **Craven Country Ride** Pot Haw Farm, Coniston Cold (01729 850277; www.cravencountryride.co.uk).

Backpacking and walking

Two long-distance trails cross this region on a north/south line: the **Pennine Way** following the River Aire, and the **Dales Way** likewise but along the River

Wharfe. Unless you are actually following either of these classic routes they are best avoided. More than enough alternative **day and half-day routes** exist with fewer people to share them with. My preferred strategy is to spread out the OS map (Explorer OL2 *Yorkshire Dales Southern and Western Areas*) and plan my own, but there are heaps of walking guides to do it for you if you prefer. The Harvey's *8 Walks Centred On* series has three maps for this area, all excellent; Settle, Skipton and Grassington. Two walks that don't make it on to any of these maps but are definitely in my hall of fame are Great Whernside from Kettlewell (see page 51) and a five-mile/three-pub crawl from Buckden, taking in Cray, Yockenthwaite, and the verdant hillside meadows above Hubberholme.

Tourist information

Grassington National Park Centre ☎ 01756 751690.
Malham National Park Centre ☎ 01966 652380.
Settle Market Place ☎ 01729 825192.
Skipton High St ☎ 01756 792809.

Craven

While for the most part the individual dales of the Yorkshire Dales fit into easily identifiable chunks of scenery, the Craven district is a strangely nebulous idea with no neatly defined edges. I am taking it as stretching from the River Ribble in the west, handy as 'Ribble' means boundary in Anglo-Saxon, to the catchment of the Wharfe in the east. The small town of **Settle** sits along the east bank of the Ribble with the frivolously named **Giggleswick** on the opposite side. Behind Settle the land rises steeply at the start of well over 100 square miles of wild upland dominated by carboniferous limestone. Geographers name this sort of landscape after the Karst region of old Yugoslavia, and Craven is absolutely classic Karst scenery. The hills are not so rugged as to be inaccessible to four wheels, and small roads crisscross the area, calling in on **Malham** from where it's a stroll to the huge cliff of **Malham Cove**, an extraordinary limestone pavement, and the gorge and waterfall in **Gordale Scar**. **Malham Tarn** is the source of the River Aire which, after a spell underground, winds southwards to **Gargrave** where it picks up the Leeds and Liverpool canal as a travelling partner for the remaining five miles to **Skipton**. A market town of fair size, Skipton is unquestionably the capital of the Craven district and one that, although not in the national park, proudly labels itself 'Gateway to the Dales'.

① Settle

Settle grew as a small market town at the crossing of two important trade routes. It still has its market but passing trade is much less now since the A65 bypassed the town. Settle really would have been a sleepy backwater if its other transport link had deserted it, as it very nearly did in the 1980s, but the **Settle–Carlisle line** remains open, and attracts many of the town's visitors. Settle itself is unassuming with nothing really exceptional to crow about but I like it for all that, especially the maze of old streets creeping up the hillside towards Upper Settle and Castlebergh, the wooded crag that peers over everything.

A short stroll over the river via a small footbridge will bring you to the photogenic village of **Giggleswick** with two notable places of worship, a private boarding-school chapel with a striking copper dome and the parish church with a very unusual name. Only two St Alkelda's churches are to be found in the country, this one and one at Middleham in Wensleydale where she lived, died and was sainted. If her name is obscure, what about the manner of her death; not many nuns meet their end by being strangled to death by two Viking women using a napkin!

Settle's biggest attribute is the river and fell scenery around it and one six-mile loop walk gives a taste of both. The outward leg, upstream on the Giggleswick bank, is actually on the route of the Ribble Way which takes in the hamlet of Stackhouse on the way to **Stainforth**. Here is an old pack-horse bridge to cross and the impressive waterfall of **Stainforth Force** to admire; keep an eye open for leaping salmon in late autumn. For half-way refreshment, try the pub in Stainforth. On leaving the Craven Heifer, the footpath back first scales Stainforth Scar before contouring the hillside along to Settle via Langcliffe, giving a bird's-eye view of your outward journey all the way.

Market day in Settle is Tuesday with a farmers' market on the second Sunday of every month.

For such a small town Settle is rich in good restaurants. All worth visiting are **The Little House** Duke St ☎ 01729 823963; **Ravenous** Market Place ☎ 01729 822277; **Ruchee** Commercial Courtyard; ☎ 01729 823393; and **Thirteen** Duke St ☎ 01729 824356. For a brew and a snack, the best two cafés are **Ye Olde Naked Man** Market Place ☎ 01729 823230; and **Poppies** Bishopdale Court (no phone).

Falcon Manor Hotel Skipton Rd ☎ 01729 823814 ⌂ www.thefalconmanor.com. This place is worth visiting just for the building – a former rectory that looks like the Addams Family house. Food is well priced, especially Wednesday and Friday steak nights and Sunday lunch. The Falconers bar has a hexagonal pool table and beer from Copper Dragon and Tetleys.

Harts Head Inn Belle Hill, Giggleswick ☎ 01729 82086 ⌂ www.hartsheadhotel.co.uk. Not the most attractive building, but the best beer drinker's pub in the vicinity by a country mile. An ever-changing range of real ales; always a choice of at least four including local brews. Food is reasonably priced, and there's a fair range.

② The Settle–Carlisle line

Some people who have heard of this famous line assume that it is one of those privately run steam railways reopened and kept going by volunteers at weekends. In fact it is part of the National Rail network with a regular scheduled service. The line never did quite close but it came within a hair's breadth of it in the 1980s and its present fame owes more than a little to the vociferous and successful campaign to save it. The Settle–Carlisle line was, and is, so well loved because of its spectacularly scenic and, it has to be said from an engineering point of view, daft, route. In the 1860s, the Midland Railway Company relied on goodwill from the owners of the two existing lines to Scotland, the London and North Eastern Railway and the London and North Western Railway, to transport its freight and passengers north. When the companies fell out, the Midland had no alternative but to build its own line along the only route left available; not the flat land to the east or west of the Pennines, but straight up the middle and over them. This resulted in an incredible 72 miles of line possessing 14 tunnels and 20 viaducts; arguably the most stunning route in the country, providing an ever-changing catalogue of panoramas. Scarcely a moment passes when you are not crossing a towering viaduct over a hillside beck or emerging from the darkness of a tunnel to be presented with another valley and another vista. Marvellous!

Although the line is busier now than ever in its history, those 1980s campaigners and their 21st-century counterparts are not complacent. Various interested charities and trusts have teamed up to form the Settle–Carlisle partnership and their joint website www.settle-carlisle.co.uk is the definitive reference point for anything to do with this iconic railway line. For the most spectacular section, ride from Settle as far as Appleby-in-Westmorland.

③ Skipton

In Yorkshire Dales terms, this is a large town which owes its origins to those white, woolly, grass-eaters in the surrounding fields – hence the 'sheep-town' label. Its commercial and industrial prominence owes more to its rail and canal links with the bigger towns of West Yorkshire.

All the wool and cotton mills are closed now, but the railways are always busy, taking commuters out to Keighley, Bradford and Leeds, and bringing tourists in. Many of these visitors do use Skipton as a gateway to the rest of the Dales, but lots don't get any further, as there are a wealth of diversions to occupy them in and around the town. The **Leeds and Liverpool Canal** is a big draw, whether you're chugging along it on a narrowboat, strolling beside it on the towpath or just sitting in a waterside café or pub watching other people chug or stroll. I think that the most attractive bit of the canal is a small dead-end offshoot called the Spring Branch that curls around the back of Skipton Castle giving walking access to Skipton Woods – well worth a potter, especially in May when the carpets of wild garlic and bluebells beneath the trees are at their peak.

If you fancy more than a short potter along the canal towpath the walks up the main canal in either direction are pleasant enough. The western route, ten miles there and back to **Gargrave**, has an alternative return on footpaths following the railway line. Eastwards takes you to Low Bradley, which together with neighbouring High Bradley has the quaint joint name of **Bradleys Both**. A return riverside footpath completes a six-mile circuit, which can be extended slightly to visit the village of Cononley, if only for half-way refreshment in its cracking little pub.

Skipton Castle

I'm a bit fussy about castles. All too often I find them, and abbeys for that matter, a little samey; a set of ruins given the standard English Heritage treatment, but Skipton Castle (01756 792442; www.skiptoncastle.co.uk) is definitely not in that category. What makes it different is its completeness; it is a fully roofed and incredibly well preserved medieval building, a fact for which we have one woman to thank – Lady Anne Clifford. She was the incumbent owner at the time of the Civil War when Skipton Castle, a Royalist stronghold, held out under siege for three years before finally falling to Parliamentarian forces in 1645. On Oliver Cromwell's personal instructions the castle was 'Puld downe and demolisht allmost to the foundacon', and that could have been it – another ruin. However, in 1658, with the monarchy restored, and that bounder Cromwell gone, Lady Anne set to rebuilding the castle, finally, personally planting a yew tree in the central courtyard to celebrate the completion in 1659. Ironically, Lady Anne was the last Clifford to live in Skipton Castle as she died without heir and the estate was sold.

I am a little embarrassed at how many visits to Skipton it took me to finally visit the castle. I suspect many visitors like me admire the magnificent gatehouse but, because the main building is only two storeys high and all hidden behind trees, assume that there's not much else to see, but there is, with over twenty rooms to visit (and children's activities too). Check for special events because these can really make your visit memorable; I was lucky enough to be there in May during the War of the Roses re-enactment, which the children watching got really excited about, and so did I, if I'm honest. The boy next to me said, 'I liked the sword fight best when they were really going at it and clanging their swords. It's a good job they were wearing armour 'cos they could easily have chopped each other's arms off. I wish I could have had a go with my brother.'

Aeolous Greek Restaurant Cavendish St ☎ 01756 791996 🖰 www.aeolous.co.uk. Locals rate this the best restaurant in town. The staff are really welcoming and the authentic delicious Greek dishes arrive in such large portions it's also great value.
The Narrowboat Victoria St ☎ 01756 797992 🖰 www.markettowntaverns.co.uk. A refreshing change this, a wine bar that has reverted to a pub, and a good one at that.

A wide range of North Country and European beers always includes Black Sheep and Timothy Taylors, the wine list is reasonable and the food all fresh and home-cooked. Despite its size, the building has an intimate feel, particularly the upstairs gallery area which sports a unique canal mural.

J Stanforth – Celebrated Pork Pie Establishment Mill Bridge ☎ 01756 793477. Pork pies so delicious that customers write poetry about them: 'When in Skipton, call and get one/ Stanforth's are the best/ If you walk by and get no pie/ You'll curse the day you left'. They also sell other locally sourced meat products.

S **The Tempest Arms** Elslack, BD23 3AY ☎ 01282 842450 ⌂ www.tempestarms.co.uk. A 16th-century inn regarded equally highly by connoisseurs of food, beer, wine and comfort. The atmosphere is friendly and relaxed and the food traditional English, all sourced locally. House beer is Moorhouses and guests include Dark Horse's Hetton Pale Ale.

Verdes Swadford St ☎ 01756 700822 ⌂ www.verdes.biz. A multi-purpose establishment. Delicatessen and coffee shop open every day and a restaurant (Fri and Sat eves) with a very good local reputation.

④ Embsay and Bolton Abbey Steam Railway

Oh Dr Beeching, what have you done? Only five miles of the original Skipton–Ilkley railway remain and three of those are managed by the volunteers of the Yorkshire Dales Railway Museum Trust. They operate trains, mainly steam, between Embsay and Bolton Abbey, every Sunday of the year and every day in August (01756 710614; www.embsayboltonabbeyrailway.org.uk). While this is a fun 15-minute nostalgic experience it is not a particularly useful mode of transport from A to B. Now, if the steam railway succeed in their negotiations with Network Rail to access the remaining two miles of line and Skipton station, that would be a different matter. I would be tempted to take myself and my bike (free) from Skipton to Bolton Abbey and start my cycling there. Both stations have a shop and café, and you may be tempted by occasional special events like Thomas the Tank Engine day for the little ones, or Strawberry and Cream evening specials and first-class Stately Specials for the big ones.

⑤ Gargrave, ⑥ Hetton, Rylstone and Cracoe

The name **Gargrave** is old English for triangular wood but the trees that led to this label are long gone, cleared to make way for the host of transport links that squeeze through this narrow section of Airedale. The Leeds and Liverpool Canal and Skipton–Lancaster railway have both had their golden age, but the A65 trunk road through the village has never been busier. Pennine Way walkers have to dodge the traffic as they cross on their way north and the villagers are understandably campaigning for a bypass.

Gargrave has one or two points of interest to occupy visitors, notably the site of a Roman Villa, a neat arched stone bridge over the river and canalside walks, but to be honest most travellers pass through.

Some head on a minor road north, a welcome respite from the A65, and find themselves in **Hetton**, a sleepy hamlet with an exceptional pub, the **Angel Inn**, and a farm-based brewer. The Dark Horse Brewery is one of the newest and smallest breweries in the Dales but is fast earning itself a formidable reputation for quality. 'We're just concentrating on keeping the beer consistent and growing the business slowly,' said brewer Richard Eyton-Jones, 'so the fact that our Hetton Pale Ale managed to win a "Yorkshire's perfect pint" trophy last year was a bonus.'

Nearby, **Rylstone** is a humble hamlet that no one would have heard of had it not been for the exploits of its Women's Institute. It was they that famously took their clothes off for a calendar photo shoot to raise money for leukaemia research, a story told in the film *Calendar Girls*. Many of the photos were taken down the road in the Devonshire Arms, the village pub of **Cracoe**. Look out for the village postman – he was one of the few people to appear in the film as himself.

A choice of two enchanting walks links these three villages, a two-mile low-level potter along Chapel Lane or a five-mile circuit including the war memorial on the summit of Cracoe Fell.

⑤ The Angel Inn Hetton, BD23 6LT ☎ 01756 730263 🖱 www.angelhetton.co.uk. An old drover's inn with a good balance – staunchly traditional with well-kept local ales, including the village's own brew, but also a stylish and fashionable eatery. The menu is seasonal and has a European slant with an excellent selection of wines to accompany. Very popular, booking advised.

The Dalesman Café High St, Gargrave ☎ 01756 749250. Particularly popular amongst cyclists. Wear lycra if you don't want to feel out of place. No-nonsense and good-value food and drink in a tea shop doubling as a traditional sweet shop.

The Devonshire Arms Cracoe ☎ 01756 730237 🖱 www.devonshirecracoe.co.uk. A very popular roadside tavern, with decent pub food. Real ale from Marstons.

Jacksons of Cracoe Cracoe ☎ 01756 730269 🖱 www.jacksonsofcracoe.co.uk. This is basically a butchers with a twist. Not only can you buy top-quality local meat, including limestone beef, but also they have some of the best sausages in Yorkshire, home-made cakes and preserves and Brymoor Farm ice cream (see page 96). The in-house tea-shop allows you to sit in and sample the local produce.

⑦ Malham

The first time that I visited Malham I was astonished at how small it was. How could such an insignificant hamlet be so well known? The truth is that it's not the buildings of Malham itself that are famous but the surrounding countryside; **Malham Cove**, **Gordale Scar** and **Malham Tarn** primarily. Hundreds of thousands of people come to see these natural wonders and they need somewhere to stay, park, eat and drink, so a service machine has developed including two pubs, three cafés, eleven places to stay and the National Park Centre to tell you about it all. Ironically, some visitors don't make it any further than the village; they see a picture of Gordale Scar in the visitor centre, buy a postcard of the cove, have a cup of tea and drive to the next place without seeing anything real – which is such a shame because the real things here are magnificent. Malham has two big events during the year, an animal-themed activity week called the **Malham Safari** during Whit week and the much more traditional **Malham Show** on August Bank Holiday Saturday.

Upper Airedale has two other villages, **Kirkby Malham** a mile downstream from Malham, and **Aireton** the same distance again. Both are peaceful modest places with unusual buildings used as hostels. Kirkby Malham's is the Parish Hall (01729 830277) and Aireton's the Friends' Meeting House (01729 830263). Kirkby also has the parish church for the whole dale, a 15th-century building on a much older site, and the best pub in the dale, the Victoria Hotel. Aireton boasts a farm shop selling all sorts of local produce, and cups of tea, at Town End Farm (01729 830902).

Malham Cove

I am not sure which experience of Malham Cove has left the biggest impression on me. The first time I stood below it gazing at the breathtaking scale of the curved wall in front maybe, or later that same day lying at the top with just my face over the overhang lip and 260 feet of dizzying space below. Wherever it is viewed from this is an awe-inspiring place that well deserves its place in a recent list of Seven Natural Wonders of Britain.

The geology of the place seems simple; a beck flows out of Malham Tarn just over a mile north of the cove, but very quickly disappears underground as limestone rivers often do. The dry valley continues southwards, finishing as a notch at the top of the cove, and a river appears from the foot of the cliff. The obvious assumption is that it is the same water top and bottom and the river used to flow over the top of the cliff, creating the cove by erosion – but not so. The reality is a lot more deceptive: the cliff was formed millions of years ago by an upthrust of the mid-Craven fault. Much later, at the end of the last ice age, meltwater from a glacier formed a monstrous waterfall that eroded the cove four miles back into the hillside and sculpted it into its present curving shape. When the ice melted, the waterfall disappeared. Just to make it even more confusing, water-dye experiments have shown that the water from Malham Tarn does not reappear at the cove but travels at a lower level, reaching the surface south of the village at Aire Head Spring. The beck that bubbles out at the base of the cove is a different river entirely.

You really need to get close up to Malham Cove to experience the full effect; fortunately it is easily accessible for everyone, wheelchair users included. An easy mile from the main car park/bus stop brings you to the bottom of the cove from where you can marvel at the scenery, admire climbers scaling the crag or visit the RSPB base and watch the nesting peregrine falcons. Other birds to look out for here are little owls, green woodpeckers and one of the few natural-site nesting colonies of house-martins. The steep slog up the Penine Way to the top of the cove is worth the effort, particularly for plant lovers, because the **limestone pavement** behind the cliff edge is a lush arctic/alpine rock garden in summer. Rarities like alpine bartsia, mountain pansy, bird's-eye primrose and mountain avens all thrive here in the sheltered crevices, or grykes.

Gordale Scar

When the 19th-century romantic artists and writers went in search of wild nature in Britain some of them discovered Gordale Scar and were suitably impressed. Wordsworth attempted to persuade others to visit: 'Let thy feet repair to Gordale-chasm, terrific as the lair where the young lions crouch.' Not modern-day brochure-speak, but he obviously liked it here. Thomas Gray the poet was a little more delicate; he declared that he could only bear to stay for quarter of an hour, and even then 'not without shuddering'. All agreed that no painting could do justice to the scale of the ravine, except James Ward who solved the problem by producing one of the largest canvases ever attempted. His 14-foot by 12-foot painting is regarded as one of the most important 'sublime landscapes' of its time, and hangs in Tate Britain.

So, does it merit all the hype? Yes, is the answer. Gordale Scar is impressive enough as a deep and fairly dry canyon now, but it must have been a terrifying place when the glacial meltwater river that excavated it was still raging. Despite its drama, Gordale is remarkably accessible along its flat lower section, about a third of a mile of wheelchair-negotiable track to the foot of the dual waterfall. It's even more convenient for those staying at Gordale Campsite (01729 830333) as this will save you the walk from Malham (there is no parking at Gordale). If you do arrive on foot, a convenient alternative return route to Malham is to follow Gordale Beck downstream as it leaps over Janet's Foss, and babbles through Wedber Wood en route to join the newly emerged River Aire. It is possible to escape out of the top end of Gordale Scar, but it does require a serious scramble alongside the waterfalls. It is worth doing, just for the fun of it, but it will also lead you towards Malham Tarn and make a fantastic full-day, eight-mile walk possible, linking all of Malham's celebrity venues – the cove, the foss, the scar and the tarn.

Malham Tarn

The Malham Tarn estate is now under the stewardship of the National Trust but a clue to one of its earliest owners lies in the name of the highest fell in the region. At 2,169 feet high, Fountains Fell rises over nearly 12 square miles of prime limestone sheep country, and reminds us of the huge power and influence the monks of Fountains Abbey had, from a good 25 miles away near Ripon. After the dissolution of the monasteries the estate passed through many hands and finished up in the possession of the Morrison family. In the 1850s James

Morrison converted what was a Georgian hunting lodge into Tarn House, then promptly died, leaving the estate and an awful lot of money to his son Walter. As a very rich socialite, Walter invited all and sundry up to Malham with celebrity guests including influential thinkers John Ruskin, Charles Darwin and John Stuart Mill. Writer Charles Kingsley was a regular visitor and much of his *Water Babies* was inspired by Malham Tarn.

In 1946 the last private owner of the estate bequeathed it to the National Trust and with them it remains, although they do lease Tarn House itself to the **Field Studies Council** (01729 830331; www.field-studies-council.org/malham tarn) as a residential centre for the study of environmental sciences. The FSC run over 30 different courses a year on subjects as diverse as earthworms and other invertebrates, painting the flora of Malham Tarn, and the geology of the Dales. Their choice of venue is a good one because the tarn itself is a **National Nature Reserve**, ecologically important through being one of only eight upland alkaline lakes in Europe. The lake has breeding great crested and little grebes with winter bringing more waterfowl like pochard, wigeon, teal and goosanders. Alongside the open water are rich floral fen and bog areas. Access to all of the Nature Reserve is free of charge except for a wheelchair- accessible boardwalk across the bog which has a token £1 fee. The National Trust also produce very informative leaflets for four **waymarked walks** around the estate, from an easy 4½ miles around the tarn **to** an eight-mile yomp up Fountains Fell. Another excellent leaflet is for a 4½ mile family **bike ride**. All can be obtained from their visitor centre in Malham village or are downloadable from their website (01729 830416; www.nationaltrust.org.uk).

Lister Arms Malham ☎ 01729 830330 🖑 www.listerarms.co.uk. A big, traditional 17th-century coaching inn selling Thwaites cask beer and food sourced from local farmers.
Old Barn Café Malham ☎ 01729 830486. A nice, small unfussy café (muddy boots welcome) in the village centre. All-day breakfast recommended.
Town End Farm Tea Room Scosthrop, Aireton ☎01729 830902. Part of a farm shop on a working farm, and selling snacks and drinks. Closed Mon.
Victoria Hotel Kirkby Malham ☎ 01729 830499. A quiet and peaceful village pub and, because of that, easily my favourite in the dale. Changing list of mainly Yorkshire cask ales.

Mid Wharfedale

Most of the River Wharfe's length is downstream of the Yorkshire Dales, and into the county of West Yorkshire, but our interest lies upstream in its mid-section. **Bolton Abbey** sits at the border, just in North Yorkshire and the National Park, and mid Wharfedale continues nearly 10 miles northwards from here to the small town of **Grassington**, with much to please in between.

⑧ Bolton Abbey

The ecclesiastical remains at the tiny village of Bolton so dominate, that the whole place is now called Bolton Abbey. Ironically, for a building that was never completed, it is one of the most intact priories in the country with the original nave still used as the Priory Church of St Mary and St Cuthbert.

Location, location, location – that must have been the watchword for 12th-century monks. This riverside site ranks with Rievaulx and Fountains as one of the most awe-inspiring positions for an abbey anywhere. No wonder the Augustinians moved here from their original Priory in Embsay. At the Dissolution, all the Abbey lands were given to the Duke of Devonshire and the Cavendish family still own and operate the estate (www.boltonabbey.com).

Their lands extend upstream to include **Strid Woods** and **Barden Tower** and on the other side of the river, the wide tracts of **Barden Moor**. These are the places to head for if you are seeking solitude because most visitors stay around the Priory or on the river banks between Bolton Bridge and a charismatic Victorian building. The Cavendish Pavilion is still doing what it was designed for in 1898, serving tea and cakes to thousands of visitors from the industrial cities of West Yorkshire, although the menu and catchment area are both a lot more extensive now. Children won't be interested in that though; once they have had their ice cream they will be drawn like magnets to the river to paddle, fish for minnows and swim in the deeper pools, and it is safe to do so here unless the river is running high and fast. The estate doesn't actively encourage swimming but they don't discourage it either, which is good. Rod fishing is also possible in the river; trout or grayling day tickets can be purchased, and it's obviously best where the swimmers and paddlers aren't. Tuition is also available.

If you have children who are not interested in the river, or it is too cold or flooded, there are other things to keep them interested; a green man trail or nature bingo in Strid Woods or a simple treasure hunt on the welcome leaflet. For really enquiring youngsters or mature learners, the estate produce two teacher's packs with worksheets that are just as interesting for adults and families. The *Valley of Desolation* pack improved my walk up Barden Moor no end – I learnt loads about the geology, natural history and the past flood damage that gave the place its name.

Sample local **arts and crafts** at Strid Wood Exhibition Centre where ceramics, paintings and furniture are on display. You may even see Richard Law, the bodger, at work if you are in Strid Woods as he has his outdoor workshop there (www.flyingshavings.co.uk). If you fancy actually doing the art yourself then drawing and painting classes are available from professional artist Nigel Overton, at the Tea Cottage, most summer Saturdays (01943 608447; www.overtonfinearts.co.uk).

The estate also runs almost monthly **Country Fairs** throughout the year in the main car park, a great mixture of farmers' market and art-and-craft display.

Other **events** worth finding out about if they float your boat are kite workshops (Fridays in the summer holidays), giant puppet shows, autumn fungus walks and Christmas carol singing.

Strid Wood

This area of woodland, though not very big or containing any especially rare or spectacular species, is a delight. The trees, mainly oak, cling to the deep sides of Strid Gorge and support a rich population of birds in the spring and fungi in the autumn. The dawn chorus here in June features all the signature woodland birds of Yorkshire: redstarts, pied and spotted flycatchers and wood warblers. Dead wood is drummed on and excavated into by green and great spotted woodpeckers, and nuthatches and treecreepers scuttle around on the wrinkled trunks. The woods are special, but it is the River Wharfe that makes this place exceptional, and gives it the name.

Strid is local dialect for stride and refers to one place where the river narrows to a step's width across. In reality it is more like a leap, and a brave one at that, because the whole river thunders through the gap below. The Strid is even more dangerous than it seems because both banks are actually suspended ledges of limestone covering deep undercuts on both sides. Numerous swimmers over the years have been taken under them by wayward currents and drowned. On less vigorous stretches of the river dippers bob on the rocks, grey wagtails leap for flies in sunny spots and, if you're lucky, a common sandpiper will trill its alarm as it disappears upstream.

Six waymarked trails can be found in Strid Woods, some very short and wheelchair accessible and all less than two miles long. They can get very crowded on summer weekends, especially on the car-park side of the river.

A walk from Bolton Abbey

My favourite walk from Bolton Abbey is a longer one that includes Strid Woods but continues up river to Barden Bridge, ascends the fell-side to the summit of Simon's seat and travels back via Barden Moor and the spectacular Valley of Desolation. At the end of this 8^1/$_2$-mile walk, if your legs are up to it, detour a couple of hundred yards up the road to Laund House to pay your respects to a venerable old-timer. The Laund Oak, by the roadside, is one of the oldest oak trees in the country, a peer of the Sherwood Forest Major Oak, and over 800 years old.

Barden Tower

This imposing building has lots going for it, not least the fact that wandering around it is completely free of charge. Despite its name, it is more than just a tower, but not quite a castle, and has had a few changes of role in its long life. Originally a Norman hunting lodge, it was later extended into a fortified house by Sir Henry Clifford, who fancied living in the country rather than Skipton Castle. That accomplished renovator, Lady Anne Clifford, got her two-penny-worth in during the 1650s but on her death the tower passed to the Earls of Cork and fell into decline. After a spell as a farmhouse in the late 18th century it was abandoned.

The building next door to the tower was never abandoned: the Priest's House was built by Sir Henry Clifford for his personal chaplain and is now what must be one of the most atmospheric restaurants in the country. The old stables of the tower next door have been converted into a very convenient self-catering bunkhouse for large parties of evening diners in the restaurant – or anyone else wanting accommodation in this desirable spot. If you fill it with 24 people it costs less than £8 per person per night.

The Cavendish Pavilion ✆ 01756 710245 🖰 www.cavendishpavilion.co.uk. There are five cafés in Bolton Abbey: the pick of them on location alone is this, and you can sit outside. Food is good but a bit pricey, although the afternoon tea special is good value.

S🎵 The Fleece Addingham, LS29 0LY ✆ 01943 830491 🖰 www.thefleece addingham.co.uk. The only real pub anywhere near Bolton Abbey but it's a belter and worth the three-mile journey downstream. Its bags of character come from big open fires, solid tables, flagged floors and low beamed ceiling. Food is good quality and value; local, seasonal and rustic. Beer is a choice of four Yorkshire cask ales. Open all day every day.

The Priest's House Restaurant Barden, BD23 6AS ✆ 01756 720616 🖰 www.thepriests house.co.uk. A unique Grade 1 listed building and really good-quality food. Not a huge menu but all done well. Sunday lunch is particularly good value and in good weather when the tea terrace operates as a café, there can't be many more pleasant places to be. Very popular, book early. Open Thu–Sat lunch and evenings, Sun lunch only.

⑨ Grassington

'Now that's a good question and I wish you had asked someone else,' said the welcoming lady at the Devonshire Institute reception. 'I could flannel on for ten minutes trying to answer it but, to be honest, I don't know. If you do find out come back and tell me.'

My question was a simple one, or so I thought. 'Is Grassington a town or a village?' I had been given a variety of conflicting answers by other locals up to this point. 'Village of course… too small for a town,' (barmaid). 'Town I think. Isn't that what the "ton" means?' (Local artist). 'No, this is a village, Skipton's the town,' (farmer). My definitive answer eventually came in the introductory paragraph of an excellent little £1 guide, *One hundred things to see on a walk through Grassington* by Ian Goldthorpe. It is a town; the official reason being it was granted a charter for a market and fair in 1282. Grassington has played a few roles in its time, originally as the name suggests as a place for grazing cattle, then a market for selling them. The town was very involved with both the long-gone lead mining and textile booms, and the railway made a fleeting visit then left again. Now this is the administrative centre for Upper Wharfedale in the background but its public face, especially from Easter to October, is tourism. Grassington is one of the best loved and most visited places in the Dales. It has a National Park Centre, small folk museum, three pubs, five cafés and numerous art and craft shops, mostly clustered around the Market Square.

The creative theme reaches its peak during two weeks in late June every year when the town is completely taken over by a **music and arts festival** (01756 752691; www.grassington-festival.org) – a wonderful mix of everything from big-name comedians to school brass bands, magician or dry-stone walling workshops, jazz, opera, folk, rock and world music, readings, plays, and visual arts displays in houses and fields… you name it and it's here. It doesn't all stop in winter either; three Saturdays in December, in the run-up to Christmas, the town goes all Victorian with a Dickensian festival.

If the crowds in town get too much, two nearby rural diversions are within easy walking distance, **Grass Wood** upstream and **Linton Falls** in the opposite direction. If you continue downstream on the Dales Way footpath, or back roads, there are a series of very photogenic and individual villages to visit: **Burnsall** right on the river and **Hebden** and **Appletreewick** just above it.

Grass Wood

As I'm a naturalist, this is one of my favourite places in the Dales – no, not just in the Dales, anywhere. A circular walk from Grassington of not much more than three miles takes in one of the most beautiful stretches of the River Wharfe, a Woodland Trust reserve, a Yorkshire Wildlife Trust Nature reserve and one of the most important archaeological sites in Yorkshire. Doing the route clockwise the river comes first and, if it is warm enough, you may be tempted to have a swim in one of the deep pools. The Wharfe is probably the best river in Yorkshire for wild swimming (see page ix) and this mile section is one of its best but take care near Ghaistrill's Strid; it is another powerful 'narrows' with dangerous undercuts like its Bolton Abbey namesake.

If you are lucky enough to be here in early summer, the floral display once you enter the wood will blow you away if you are that way inclined. This is an ancient woodland designated as a Site of Special Scientific Interest (SSSI) and especially rich in flower species; carpets of bluebells in May give way to betony, St John's wort, basil, marjoram, lily of the valley and herb paris to name but a few. Keep an eye out for orchids as some rare ones have a foothold here.

Higher up on the hillside as the trees thin to meadow on the limestone pavement butterflies are everywhere; fritillaries, peacocks, blues and heaths, and the rare northern brown argus if you are lucky. Another scarce insect lives here – the yellow ant; you may well not see them but the distinctive grassy humps of their anthills testify to the antiquity of the meadows.

The return route to Grassington is on the Dales Way footpath passing extensive archaeological remains of old settlements. For 2,000 years the inhabitants of the dales have been gradually moving their homes down towards the river, leaving faint footprints behind – Bronze Age at the top, Iron Age and medieval in sequence lower down.

Linton and Linton Falls

The dramatic natural cataract of Linton Falls on the River Wharfe is nearer to Grassington than the village of Linton, so the choice of name is a little odd. It possibly has something to do with the church on the riverbank a quarter of a mile downstream. This is Linton's parish church of St Michael and All Angels, a long name for a tiny medieval building but  in a magical setting. The church is even further from the village than the falls, probably because it re-uses the site of an earlier pagan shrine, so it is perhaps apt that the Green Man, a pagan symbol, should be carved into the church roof timbers. Despite there being no footpath from the river to Linton village it is still worth strolling up the road for half a mile to see the pretty village green and packhorse bridge and have a meal or drink in the Fountaine Inn. If water levels are low enough you can re-cross the river via stepping stones to return to Grassington.

Grassington has lots of cafés close together, a sign of healthy competition and good quality all round.

Forester's Arms Main St ☎ 01756 752349. My favourite pub in Grassington, this is a friendly and welcoming place with well-kept cask Yorkshire beers and good food. I enjoyed the tenderest lamb shank that I have ever had here.

S♥ Fountaine Inn Linton, BD23 5HJ ☎ 01756 752210 ⌨ www.fountaineinnat linton.co.uk. A welcoming pub in a great setting, tucked into a corner of the village green on the beck-side. Named after a local man who made his fortune in London at the time of the Black Death – burying bodies! Cask Tetleys and John Smith's beer.

Retreat Café and Tearooms Main St ☎ 01756 751887. One of several cafés in Grassington.

⑩ Hebden and Burnsall

Hebden is a solid little village with a decent café and pub and a very obvious lead-mining past. Lots of small miners' cottages line Mill and Back lanes as they creep down the hill to the river. Stepping stones and a footbridge here allow the Dales Way path to cross the Wharfe on its way to Burnsall. This is a dramatic half mile of water course as the river eats into high limestone banks to form the precipitous crags of Loup Scar and Wilfred Scar, popular 'leaping' rocks into the deep river pools. St Wilfred also gives his name to the very old church close by, but undoubtedly the village's most iconic landmark is its graceful five-arched stone bridge spanning the river.

Burnsall's most famous event is its annual fell race which was first run in the 1870s making it the oldest of its kind in the world, a fact that the villagers are fiercely proud of. Evidence that sporting events have been part of the Feast of St Wilfred since before Elizabethan times gives it an even more impressive claim of antiquity. St Wilfred's day is the first Sunday after August 12th, and the Burnsall feast takes place the following week with the races on the Saturday.

The 'Classic' fell race, as it is called, starts from the bridge with competitors aiming for a flagged cairn on Burnsall Fell about a mile and a half away and 1,000 feet above the village. The best runners make the flag in just over ten minutes, which is quick, but nowhere near their suicidal descent speed, as some of them manage the return in less than three minutes.

The Fitton family flag

Burnsall Feast Sports are rife with tradition, none more closely followed than the fixing of the flag on race day. This job has fallen to the Fitton family since the 1930s, as Chris Fitton recalls.

'I don't know how old I was when I first climbed the Fell on Sports Day, possibly four or five. My father had been doing it for many years prior to the war and established it as a family ritual. The object of the exercise was to carry the flag up and put it securely into the cairn which still stands proud at the top of Burnsall Fell. Then, as now, it represented blessed relief to aching legs as the halfway point round which all competitors in the Classic Fell Race must pass prior to the heart-stopping descent.

Since that first time around 1948, I and assorted family members have climbed the Fell faithfully every year. The group of between five and ten has included pregnant mothers, newly born toddlers, grandchildren, children, adults up to their late 70s together with boyfriends, girlfriends and occasionally somewhat reluctant strangers who, full of ale in the Red Lion the night before, having heard of the annual pilgrimage swear they would join us and more often than not, did.

This motley group would always assemble around 7am outside the car park hopefully with the flag. The flag is, and always was, the great problem. No one can ever find it.

Committee members provide storage space for the various accoutrements of the Sports Day, and the night before it is all brought down to the Green. As often as not the flag is missing. Over the years it has taken the shape of an old cream bed sheet, a St George's flag, and once, bizarrely, a National Benzole flag.

Sometimes there is a pole but no flag, and sometimes a flag but no pole.

The route taken never varies, and we have a breather at the top of the field before reaching the summit around 7.30, to drain a celebratory flask of whisky once the flag is securely installed. Finally, the view is admired and we stick out our chests and say to each other that we should do this more regularly. We never do.

On our return home, a vast and well-earned breakfast is consumed and I offer up a prayer that whoever brings down that flag gives it to someone who can remember, 12 months later, what he did with it.'

The Red Lion Burnsall ☏ 01756 720204 🖰 www.redlion.co.uk. An ancient building with 900-year-old cellars that have a resident ghost who likes to turn the beer pumps off. Food features game in season and locally sourced meats and cheeses. A range of cask beers are served, most from Yorkshire.

Wharfe View Tearooms The Green, Burnsall ☏ 01756 720237. A basic but welcoming café, very popular with walkers and bikers.

⑪ Appletreewick

If ever a name conjures up pastoral loveliness it's this one, but over the years locals have tired of the full tongue-twisting mouthful and shortened it to 'Aptrick'. Sunday name or not this is a very agreeable place, especially down in the valley bottom where the river bounces and swirls its way through a series of rapids, beloved of slalom kayakers. Not many villages of this size manage to support a pub these days, but Appletreewick keeps two going comfortably. One of them, the Craven Arms, incorporates the village's most remarkable building, not the pub itself but a cruck barn behind it. This is a new building made to a very old design and with a heather-thatched roof, the first of its kind built for 400 years in the Dales.

I'm sure Aptrick has also produced many remarkable people over the centuries, but for the one that made the biggest impact on the world stage we have to go back to the early 1600s. William Craven, a humble village lad, was sent off to London to apprentice as a draper and, to cut a long story short, did quite well for himself. By the time he returned he had made his fortune, earned himself a knighthood, spent a term as Mayor of London and married the King's sister. I can imagine his reception on returning to the snug of the Craven Arms, 'Na then Billy. Tha's not done badly... tha' round, methinks'.

You can take a stroll downstream to the stepping stones near Howgill. This is another inviting, swimmable section of river and quiet enough to offer a really good chance of seeing the local wildlife. I know that there are otters and crayfish here, even though I haven't seen either of them alive. On my last swimming visit here I landed on a mid-river rock that held the chewed-up remains of a native white-clawed crayfish, its one remaining claw bearing its furry killer's teeth marks.

⑤ Craven Arms Inn Appletreewick, BD23 6DA ☏ 01756 720270 🖰 www.craven-cruckbarn.co.uk. A wonderfully atmospheric building restored to the original oak beams, flag floor, gas lights and open fires state. Traditional pub games, good food and a range of Yorkshire and Lancashire beers. Open every day.

New Inn West End, Appletreewick ☏ 01756 720252. Unspoiled village local, for many years ahead of its time as the only non-smoking pub in the country. Serves a wide range of Yorkshire real ales and good food. Open every day.

⑫ Parcevall Hall Gardens

'Serene' was the word that sprang to mind when I first set foot over the threshold here, which is no surprise, as that is the feeling its creator was trying to achieve. I say 'creator' although Sir William Milner did not build the hall from scratch, but renovated a derelict Elizabethan building in the late 1920s. He definitely did create the garden though, skilfully laying out borders, terraces and woodland – transforming what was previously open agricultural fell-side. Sir William came from a wealthy socialite family, a world that he did not fit into easily. He was quiet and retiring, writing once of his delight in 'sitting with a friend in front of a roaring log fire, in companionable quiet over coffee'. He was a deeply religious man so it is apt that his legacy, the hall, is now leased to the church to be used as a retreat, and the rest of us can use the tea room and gardens for the same purpose. Slightly at odds with this genteel ambience but testimony to the huge changes Sir William managed here, the hillside above Parcevall Hall is so wild and intimidating, the Anglo-Saxons named one ravine the Troll's Arse, now Trollers Ghyll, and there are still tales of the ghostly dog with giant shining eyes called the Barquest, whose appearance foretold a death.

Parcevall Hall Gardens BD23 6DE ☏ 01756 720311 ⌨ www.parcevallhallgardens.co.uk. Tea shop ☏ 01756 720630.

⑬ Stump Cross Caverns

The name suggests that there was once an old way-cross near here, on the Grassington to Pateley Bridge packhorse route, but no evidence of it can be

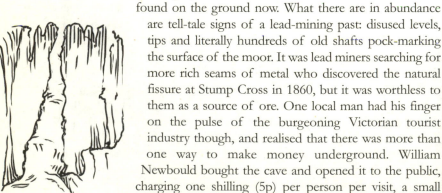

found on the ground now. What there are in abundance are tell-tale signs of a lead-mining past: disused levels, tips and literally hundreds of old shafts pock-marking the surface of the moor. It was lead miners searching for more rich seams of metal who discovered the natural fissure at Stump Cross in 1860, but it was worthless to them as a source of ore. One local man had his finger on the pulse of the burgeoning Victorian tourist industry though, and realised that there was more than one way to make money underground. William Newbould bought the cave and opened it to the public, charging one shilling (5p) per person per visit, a small fortune in those days.

In the subsequent 150 years, the Stump Cross cavern system has been extensively explored and found to extend over four miles. Most cavers visit just for the thrills, but some important scientific discoveries have also been made along the way. We know, for instance, that the cave was open to the outside about 90,000 years ago, because animal bones dating from this time have been found inside. The Yorkshire Dales must have been a very cold place then, as these remains are from animals that all live in today's Arctic regions. Fragments of skeletons from bison and reindeer have turned up, but the prize find was the well-preserved skull of a wolverine, one of the few ever to be found in Britain.

Entry into the cave (with a 20-minute film show) is reasonable value, but if going underground doesn't appeal, then the modern information centre, gift shop and café at ground level are all free of charge to visit.

Stump Cross Caverns HG3 5JL ☏ 01756 752780 🖱 www.stumpcrosscaverns.co.uk.

Upper Wharfedale

Further upstream, Wharfedale heads between the high fells beyond the twin villages of **Kilnsey** and **Conistone**, splitting into the two arms of **Littondale** and **Langstrothdale** which then wrap around the top of Craven in a cosy embrace. Usually, as you head up a hill-country valley, settlements become sparser and smaller; Wharfedale does not deviate from this norm, and beyond Grassington there is nothing even remotely resembling a town.

Kettlewell justly claims to be the largest of the Upper Wharfedale villages, and will be familiar if you have seen the film *Calendar Girls*, as this was the location used for much of the action. The valley's only road winds its way through **Starbotton**, and reaches another parting of the ways at **Buckden**. If you are using wheeled transport you have a choice here; right takes you to **Cray** and then over to Bishopdale and Aysgarth and, at 1,400 feet, it is the highest bus route in the Dales – a spectacular run on the number 800 but only once a week in summer (Sunday, noon from Kettlewell returning 16.00 from Hawes). A left turn at Buckden follows the Wharfe through **Hubberholme** and then a much higher pass over the flank of Dodd Fell direct to Hawes – much too high and steep for a bus unfortunately, but an enjoyable drive in a car. If you manage it on a bike, you deserve a medal.

⑭ Kilnsey and Conistone

These two villages, though they have half a mile of clear valley and a river separating them, have been tied since the 14th century when they were known as Conyston cum Kylnesey. They still have a joint church and village hall (and one of the biggest agricultural shows in the Dales in early September) but Kilnsey has the lion's share of the visitors. This must be partly down to the attention-grabbing cliff that looms over the village.

Kilnsey's other big draw is **Kilnsey Park and Trout Farm** (01756 752150; www.kilnseypark.co.uk), a business unashamedly aimed at families with fun fishing, an adventure playground and trails, and cuddly animals to pet. For adults this is a working trout farm where you can learn to fly fish, hire rods, buy smoked, frozen or fresh fish, or just eat it in the restaurant. This is the only place I have ever heard of that does battered trout, chips and peas.

Kilnsey Park is also serious about its environmental impact, generating its own hydro-electric power, and running a red-squirrel breeding programme and demonstration beehives in conjunction with Wharfedale Beekeepers Association.

Extreme climbing in Wharfedale

At 170 feet high, Kilnsey Crag is not huge, but the glacier that scraped away its bottom section thousands of years ago has left a bizarrely suspended lump of rock that doesn't look as if it should stay up. The 40-foot overhang is a magnet for extreme climbers and there are numerous described routes on Kilnsey Crag. The first person to complete a new route has the honour of naming it; 'Sticky Wicket' I can see the logic of but 'Let them eat Jellybeans'...? The most difficult climb, Northern Lights, was climbed in the year 2000 by S McClure and graded 9a – that's 'virtually impossible' to you and me.

S♥ The Tennant Arms Kilnsey, BD23 5PS ☎01756 752301 ᛘ www.tennantarms.co.uk. A big place with a large central stone-floored bar and smaller opulently decorated rooms. Slightly unnerving stuffed animals everywhere, but cask Taylors and Black Sheep beer and very good-value food, especially the Sunday carvery. Open all day weekends.

⑮ Kettlewell

Transport on foot, whether two or four, has long been a theme here. Kettlewell grew up at the meeting place of packhorse and drovers' routes and is now quite a centre for walkers, using many of those old bridleways of course. I'm sure our ancestors would find our walking for leisure odd though, especially the habit of heading for the highest hilltops. Their walks were everyday practical means of journeying from village to village and valley to valley via the lowest and easiest route. They wouldn't dream of aiming for the summit of **Great Whernside**, which is my favourite destination from Kettlewell.

Other facilities for modern-day walkers are the Over and Under outdoor equipment shop (01756 760871; www.overandunder.co.uk) and a village store.

Zarina's Tea Room Beckside, Kettlewell ☎ 01756 761188. If you have a thing about drinking tea from a china cup, you're in luck. The home-made cakes are raved about.

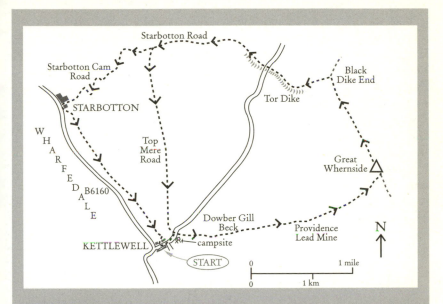

The ascent of Great Whernside

The outward route tours the full length of the village to Fold Farm campsite then follows Dowber Gill Beck up the hillside, with birds your only company; meadow pipits and wheatears mainly, but ring ouzels breed in the quiet corners. The public footpath stops after a mile or so, at the remains of Providence Lead Mine, but, as this is all open-access land, you can head straight up the slope to the summit. You will have earned the next flat mile of ridge walk north, with glorious views of Nidderdale to your right and Wharfedale to the left (weather permitting). After a steep descent to Tor Dike the return route is an historic one along ancient bridleways with an optional mile-and-a-bit extension to Starbotton. Back in Kettlewell you can re-hydrate in one of two cafés or three pubs, a fairly good choice but not a patch on the 13 hostelries that existed at the height of the village market's importance a couple of hundred years ago.

⑯ Buckden

A Bronze Age stone circle at Yockenthwaite provides archaeological evidence of people living in this valley for thousands of years, but Buckden is a relative latecomer. The name gives a clue as to why; Buck-dene, the valley of deer, refers to the Norman hunting forest of Langstrothdale and the village was created as their forest keeper's headquarters. Only later when the forests were cleared and the last deer had been killed did Buckden become a market town dealing in sheep and wool. The market is long gone but there is a village store open every day, a local artists' gallery that doubles as a National Park information point and a farm shop stocked with local Heber Farm lamb and beef. Like Kettlewell it is now a tourist centre with a high proportion of visiting walkers.

Most stick to the gentle pastoral strolls in the valley bottom, but some are tempted up the hill behind the village and **Buckden Pike** can be a tremendous little excursion. This is not a long walk, less than two miles from pub to summit, but it is steep and exciting. Normally, a circular route is just as good done in either direction, but this is one walk I would always start by following the direct route up alongside Buckden Beck. This way the scenic delights are more visible, a tricky, slippery descent is avoided and my dodgy knees don't get such a hammering. If you can manage to be there on a sunny day after a spell of wet weather then you are in for a treat because Buckden Beck's descent is precipitous to say the least. The OS map mentions three waterfalls, but there are at least four times that number, of various sizes. High up the hill the beck emerges from the remains of Buckden lead mine, a peaceful place away from the roar of water to rest and contemplate. A direct line uphill across open access land will bring you to the summit ridge; turn left and it's a short stroll to the trig point at 2,303 feet. Turn right on a short detour and you will arrive at a cross marked on the map as 'Memorial Cross', the site of dramatic and tragic wartime events (see box).

There's also a terrific lower-level four-mile circular walk that's potentially a pub crawl – linking up Bucken, Cray and Hubberholme (each of which has a pub). Follow the track rising north from Buckden – you can later drop to Cray and find a path that goes along a glorious natural terrace with exquisite views right down Wharfedale. When you reach **Hubberholme**, pop into the church – a beauty, with a rare rood-loft dating back to 1558; from there you can follow the Dales Way back, along the lane and then along the river to Buckden.

West Winds Yorkshire Tearooms by Buck Inn, Buckden ☎01756 760883. 100-year-old family cake recipes. Tea garden or by log fire depending on the weather.

🅢 **The White Lion** Cray, BD23 5JB ☎ 01756 760262 🌐 www.whitelioncray.com. An isolated pub with farm attached, on an old drovers' route. Wholesome English food and cask Taylors and Copper Dragon beer. Equally good on a hot summer's day on benches outside or in front of a crackling fire mid-winter. Open all day every day.

⑰ Littondale

This tributary valley of the Wharfe shares with Wensleydale the unusual feature of taking its name from a small village in the dale and not the river. The River Skirfare begins its life at the head of the valley where Foxup Beck and Cosh Beck meet, after which it flows serenely down the middle of a typical small Yorkshire Dale past the hamlets of Halton Gill, Litton, Arncliffe and Hawkswick. Remnants of the ancient hunting forest cling to the steep valley sides and support rich mixtures of limestone flowers. Herb paris is one of them and is known as a primary woodland indicator species, one that only grows in very old and undisturbed woodland, so its presence in Hawkswick and Scoska Woods in particular testify to their age.

Arncliffe is the largest of the dale's hamlets and takes its name from the days when eagles were found in Yorkshire, 'erne' being the old English name for the white-tailed eagle. Two minor roads link Littondale with neighbouring valleys, Halton Gill to Stainforth in Ribblesdale and Arncliffe to Malham in Airedale. Both routes are spectacular and only suitable for healthy cars or very fit and healthy cyclists. It's a shame that they're too steep for buses as they would make superb scenic routes.

The Falcon Inn Arncliffe, BD23 5QE ☎ 01756 770205 🖰 www.thefalconinn.com. A time-warp gem courtesy of generations of Miller family landlords. No frills or false hospitality here, just beer straight from the cask in a jug and lunchtime snacks including pie and peas. A classic. Closed afternoons and some winter days, phone to check.

Queen's Arms Litton, BD23 5QJ ☎ 01756 770208. Friendly rustic pub with generous portions of bar food and Litton Ale brewed on the premises.

The sole survivor

'That plane is too low', thought 12-year-old Norman Parrington, as he stared up into the snowy sky, from his school playground in Kettlewell on 31 January 1942.

The all-Polish, six-man crew of the Wellington bomber that Norman had seen were oblivious to the danger that they were in because of the blizzard, so did not see the summit ridge of Buckden Pike looming up until it was too late. The plane clipped a stone wall at 200mph and hit the mountain, slithering several hundred feet before stopping. The rear gunner's turret, with Joe Fusniak in it, was completely knocked off the aircraft on the initial impact, a fact which probably saved his life.

Concussed, and with a broken ankle, he crawled to the remains of the rest of the plane to find only one companion still alive, and him seriously injured. With the blizzard still raging, Joe realised that he needed to get off the mountain to save both their lives. He crawled nearly a mile through the snow, hopelessly lost, until he chanced upon a set of fox tracks which eventually led him down to the White Lion Inn at Cray, and safety.

Sadly, the Parker family living in the pub couldn't understand Joe's broken English as he tried to explain the plight of his crewmate. By the time he managed to convince them that he wasn't a German pilot, and that a rescue was needed, the weather was too bad to send out a search party. The following day the plane was found, but too late; Joe's friend Jan Sadowski had died in the night.

In 1942 in recognition of his bravery, Sergeant Joseph Fusniak was awarded the British Empire medal by George VI, but was haunted for years afterwards by memories of his lost companions. In 1973 he personally erected a stone cross near the site of the crash, with fragments of the aircraft embedded in its base, and a small sculpture of a fox attached, in thanks to the animal that saved his life.

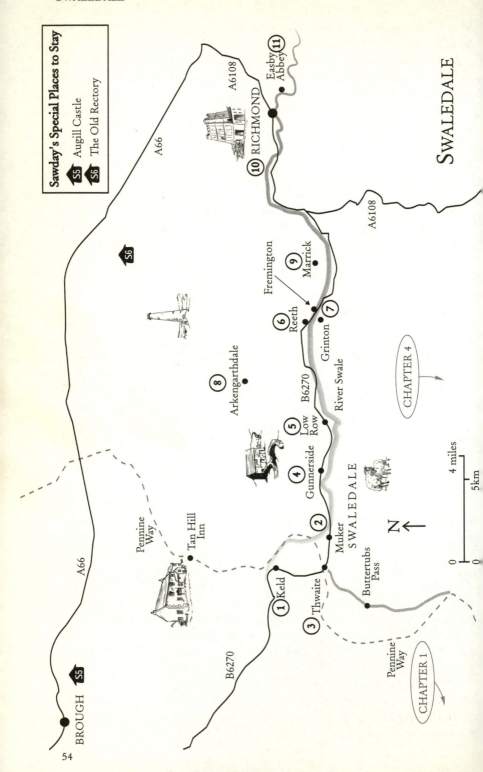

SWALEDALE

Sawday's Special Places to Stay

S5 Augill Castle
S6 The Old Rectory

CHAPTER 4

CHAPTER 1

54

3. Swaledale

The Yorkshire Dales vary in character, with each valley possessing its own unique quirks, but Swaledale always seems to me more different than the others. It is a dale apart, with much more of a northern feel to it; place names are almost all unadulterated Norse, woods are few and far between, and people almost as thin on the ground. Swaledale is the least populated of the Dales, with no towns at all above Richmond, and no main roads. It is quiet and wild and for those reasons alone is many people's favourite.

For the past thousand years Swaledale's economy and landscape has been shaped by two things, sheep and lead. The lack of trees is down to historical forest clearance for grazing but doesn't come close to the devastation wrought by the huge **lead-mining industry** of the 18th and 19th centuries. Most of the Yorkshire Dales still bear the scars of this former activity, but Swaledale more than most.

The dale takes its name from the River Swale which bubbles into life high on the flanks of High Pike Hill, but only earns its name down in the valley, just above the village of **Keld**. It careers downhill, leaping over waterfalls at every opportunity, past the villages of **Muker** and **Gunnerside** and catching its breath a little at **Reeth**. This is the largest village and unofficial capital of Upper Swaledale and **Arkengarthdale**, sitting as it does at the point where the two valleys meet.

During the next nine miles, the river gets its second wind, speeding up and racing on through the rapids at **Marrick Priory** to arrive in style at Town Falls in **Richmond** below the walls of the castle.

Getting there and around

As befits the most isolated of the Yorkshire Dales, public transport is very limited.

Public transport

Richmond's **rail** link to Darlington closed in 1969, leaving no railways anywhere in the region. Nearest main line stations are Darlington and Northallerton, both about 14 miles to the east of Richmond on the East Coast main line, and Kirkby Stephen ten miles over the fells to the west of Keld. Leyburn has a station on the Wensleydale Railway and is only 11½ miles from Richmond.

To get anywhere by **bus** in Swaledale you have first to get to Richmond, which is fine if you are travelling from Darlington. A very good service runs every 15 minutes during the day, every hour in the evenings and half hourly on Sundays

(X26, X27, 28). Northallerton is quite accessible too, with buses eight times a day (54, 55) but nothing evenings or Sundays. Buses run from Leyburn (159) every hour and Ripon (159) and Barnard Castle (79) every two. From Richmond, one solitary service goes up the dale (30) with seven buses a day to Reeth, five of them continuing on to Gunnerside and three to Muker, Thwaite and Keld. None in the evenings or on Sundays, I'm afraid.

Cycling

I have two measuring scales for the bike-friendliness of an area. Swaledale scores highly on one, absence of traffic, but not on the other, absence of nasty gradients. However, anyone hale and hearty enough to consider riding the Yorkshire Dales Cycleway will laugh in the face of hills and this route visits Swaledale. It arrives at Gunnerside via the Oxnop Beck road from Askrigg and returns to Wensleydale from Grinton on the Greets Moss road.

For **road cycling**, Cycle the Dales (www.cyclethedales.org.uk), the cycling arm of the Yorkshire Dales National Park, has turned this section of the big tour into a stand-alone 33-mile day circuit, the Two Valleys Route, along with two others, the 27-mile Swaledale Circular and 52 miles of Tan Hill Toughie. Thankfully for me, and most people I suspect, Cycle the Dales also suggests a gentler family ride in Swaledale. The 15-mile Exploring Swaledale route is actually two loops linked, which could easily be done separately. One loop goes from Gunnerside to Isles Bridge down the main valley road, over the river and back to Gunnerside via Crackpot – five miles and one short steep hill. The other loop links Healaugh, Reeth and Grinton returning on the Harkerside road – seven miles and one not-so-steep hill. I have another favourite road circuit, not official because of one short section off tarmac, but an exhilarating eight miles starting and finishing at one of the best pubs in the dale. From the Punchbowl at Low Row, go over Isles Bridge to Crackpot (get off and push by the waterfalls). Continue uphill to Summer Lodge where the road gives way to a well surfaced track. When you reach tarmac again turn left and enjoy four miles of gentle downhill freewheeling to the main road, then back to the Punchbowl for a well-earned pint.

For **off-road biking**, I reckon that this is the best to be had in the whole of the Dales, because of the huge choice of bridleways and green lanes. Most are remnants from the lead-mining days so are substantial tracks rather than those irritating spectral bridleways – bold green lines on the map that turn out to be imaginary trails in real life, buried under waist-deep heather. Mountain-biking guidebooks abound, with suggested routes; and of course the National Park's *MTB the Dales* web page (www.mtbthedales.org.uk) gives details, including very useful difficulty grades for each section, of two short loops – Booze (10 miles) and Crackpot (15 miles) and one long loop 'The Edge' (24 miles) which can be broken down into short circuits.

If you are a **social biker**, the event for you is on the Spring Bank Holiday weekend every year. The Richmond Meet is a traditional fair, but with a wide variety of cycling events included. Your local contact for all things two-wheeled is the Dales Bike Centre near Reeth (see page 65).

Horse-riding

Only one small family-run trekking centre operates in Swaledale but they are very good: **Arkle Moor Riding Centre**, Arkengarthdale Road, Reeth (01748884731; www.arklemoor.co.uk). They offer rides for all ages and abilities, from half an hour to full days, or you can sign up for a 2–3-day trekking holiday.

Walking

The **Pennine Way** is the only National Trail to enter Swaledale, and it only just dips its feet in, up at the western end, calling on Thwaite, Keld and Tan Hill.

A much more popular route these days is the **Coast-to-Coast Walk**, not an official trail but an invention in the 1960s by the inspirational walker and writer Alfred Wainwright. AW, as he is often affectionately known, claimed modestly that he laid a ruler on the map from St Bees in Cumbria to Robin Hood's Bay in the east, and the route almost chose itself. Don't believe a word of it; it could easily have followed Teesdale just to the north or Wensleydale to the south but he deliberately picked Swaledale as the most rewarding walking hereabouts, and I agree. Unless you are on the full sea-to-sea challenge you're unlikely to want to complete the 30-mile traverse of the dale from Nine Standards Rigg to Richmond, although I do like the idea of following a river from its source. A more practical challenge is perhaps to catch the number 30 bus up the dale and walk back along a section or sections of AW's route. There are a variety of choices: **Keld to Reeth** (11 miles across the lead-spoil desert of Melbecks Moor), **Keld to Gunnerside** (6 miles of some of the best riverside walking in the country), **Gunnerside to Reeth** (another lovely 6 miles, this time along the hillside and through one of Swaledale's few forested areas, Rowleth Wood: an early summer sylvan paradise, with rare lime-loving plants in bloom and warbler song in the air), and **Reeth to Richmond** (10–11 miles; AW gives a choice of riverside or hillside walking, but both routes take in the ruins of Marrick Priory).

Tourist information
Reeth Hudson House, The Green ℂ 01748 884059.
Richmond Friary Gardens, Victoria Rd ℂ 01748 828742.

Upper Swaledale

Keld, **Muker** and **Thwaite** form a triumvirate of tiny grey-stone hamlets at the three corners of a triangle, with the isolated hill of Kisdon in the centre. Kisdon is almost an island in fact, being practically surrounded by water; Straw Beck to the south flowing through Muker and the embryonic River Swale hugging its north and east flanks from Keld downstream. Finally, on the western side, a small stream, with the odd name of Skeb Skeugh, wriggles its way through tiny fields and under dry-stone walls to Thwaite. Because of its splendid isolation Kisdon is good walking country, and, weather permitting, you'll always have a panoramic view in one direction or another. Strange then, for such an obvious vantage point, not to have a path to its 1,637-foot summit; last time I was up here, with a walking partner, we both bemoaned the slog through deep heather to reach the cairn (with particularly colourful language on her part). Once there though we revelled in its inaccessibility, sharing a big sky of scudding clouds with no one but soaring buzzards and passing ravens.

① Keld

For such a small place, the number of buildings barely making double figures, Keld boasts unexpected fame. Its strategic position at the crossing point of the Pennine Way and Coast to Coast Walk helps, but these trails were both deliberately routed here for good reason – the scenic delights of Keld Gorge (if you want to make a round walk of it, use the bridleway that rises over Kisdon Hill for the return leg).The River Swale tumbles over a series of waterfalls, Wain Wath, Catrake and Kisdon Force amongst others, beloved of adrenaline kayakers when in spate and wild swimmers at gentler times. Many of these swimmers and paddlers stay in Keld, on the lovely riverside campsite or in the bunkhouse run by the Rukin family at Park House Farm.

From the 1950s Keld was known as a 'dry' village, with the old Cat Hole Inn bought by the Temperance Society and closed – spoilsports! Further bad news in 2006 was the closure of the youth hostel, but this was tempered by its reopening as a pub/hotel, Keld Lodge: the village is no longer dry.

One building just outside Keld, in a stupendous position gazing down Kisdon Gorge, is Crackpot Hall. Originally a shooting lodge, then game keeper's house and finally farm, it ended its occupied life in the 1950s and is now a forlorn but atmospheric ruin.

><><><

Keld Lodge ✆ 01748 886259 🖰 www.keldlodge.com. On the top road just out of the village, the old youth hostel is now a hotel with restaurant and bar – effectively the new village pub.

Rukin's Park Lodge Farm, DL11 6LJ ✆ 01748886274 🖰 www.rukins-keld.co.uk. A village-centre farm providing a-bit-of-everything service, campsite (gloriously cheap and simple by the river), basic groceries and tea shop.

② Muker

Muker is the largest of the three villages, with one of my favourite Dales pubs, the Farmers Arms, and a couple of shops. The old vicarage, built in 1680, is a characterful building housing the general store, which also doubles as the village tea shop and tourist information centre. Muker's church, dedicated to St Mary the Virgin, was a welcome arrival, relatively late in the day; until 1580, locals had to carry their dead ten miles along the 'Corpse Road' to Grinton, the nearest consecrated graveyard.

Brass-band music has often been a traditional leisure activity in mining communities, and the lead-miners of Swaledale were no exception. The miners are long gone but two bands remain in the dale, one in Reeth and the other based here in tiny Muker. All the players in Muker Silver band, aged between 10 and 70, live in the vicinity of the village, and the community is fiercely proud of its musical ensemble. Look out for them at shows and fêtes in the summer, and Christmas carol events as far away as Richmond. They are always high on the bill at Muker show, on the first Wednesday of September, where you will also be entertained by local produce and craft judging, sheepdog trials and fell races.

Food and drink

Farmers Arms ☏ 01748 886297. A really welcoming village local selling Theakstons and a guest beer, and traditional bar snacks – pies, bakes and such like.
Muker Village Stores and Tea shop ☏ 01748 886409 🖥 www.mukervillage.co.uk. Sells a bit of everything, including a range of teas, filter coffee and snacks.

Shopping

Swaledale Woollens ☏ 01748 886251 🖥 www.swaledalewoollens.co.uk. Swaledale and Wensleydale sheep provide the wool to keep the hand-knitting tradition alive, and the garments and rugs created by 30 local knitters are sold here.

③ Thwaite

The tiny hamlet's fame lies in its situation rather than its buildings, and in two celebrity old boys. John Kearton, a 19th-century sheep farmer, had two sons – Richard, and the unusually named Cherry – whose phenomenal natural-history knowledge from an early age was their passport out of their humble-born lives. While 'beating' on a grouse shoot, the young Richard called in a grouse to one of the shooters, and so impressed was the gentleman with the farmer's lad's abilities that he offered him a job where he worked, at Cassell's publishing house in London.

Cherry later joined his brother, and the two of them went on to have illustrious careers as writers, broadcasters and nature photographers, befriending royalty and American presidents, and inspiring a youthful David Attenborough. Richard was a noted lecturer, so in demand that he could flout normal after-dinner dress codes; I think I would have liked a man who refused to wear any suit he would not feel comfortable climbing a tree in. The brothers are remembered in various local plaques and inscriptions, on their old school in Muker and cottage in Thwaite, and in the name of the Kearton Country Hotel in the village.

The patchwork of fields around Thwaite encompasses some of the most unspoilt, traditional hay meadows in the whole of the dales. The National Park rightly prizes them, and the field barns, or 'laithes', that dot the pastoral landscape. They encourage farmers to keep the old ways going, like late hay-cutting (rather than the modern practice of silageing), which encourages a wonderful floral display in June and July, and is a joy to walk around for all but hay-fever sufferers.

Thwaite is on one of Swaledale's few links to the outside world, along the road to **Buttertubs Pass**. This strange name refers to caves near the highest point, that either resemble traditional butter containers, or really were used to keep it cool in transit, depending on which old story you choose to believe.

Kearton Country Hotel ☎ 01748 886277 🖰 www.keartoncountryhotel.co.uk. A hotel with a tea shop and restaurant attached, open to non-residents.

④ Gunnerside

I had one of those it's-hard-to-imagine moments whilst basking in the sun, sipping a cup of tea on a bench outside the tea room in Gunnerside. The only sounds were the tinkling of water from the nearby beck, and the odd distant clang of a blacksmith's hammer. Enveloped in this rural comfort blanket, it was indeed astonishing to consider the frantic industrial past of 150 years ago, when Gunnerside was nicknamed Klondike. Some insight into the lead-mining boom can be had in the old smithy, which has operated since 1795, and now doubles as a museum. The present blacksmith, Stephen Calvert, is this generation's representative in an unbroken line of six Calvert blacksmiths. Other survivors from the great lead rush are the methodist chapel and the village pub, the Kings Head.

If you follow Gunnerside Beck for a mile or two upstream from the village, you not only are rewarded with a delightful wooded walk, but will get first-hand experience of the impact of past lead-mining in this little valley.

Food and drink

Kings Head ☎ 01748 886261 🖰 www.kingsheadgunnerside.co.uk. A basic, no-nonsense local, recently rescued from closure by the villagers.

Ghyllfoot Tea Rooms and Penny Farthing Restaurant ✆ 01748 886239. A day-time café and evening restaurant, tucked into a corner and selling lead-miners' recipe cheese cake. A real penny-farthing bike over the door illustrates the name.

Shopping

Old Working Smithy and Museum ✆ 01748 886577. Open in the summer for a small fee and displaying a fascinating mix of artefacts all originating from the smithy. Also a working blacksmith's workshop.

⑤ Low Row

Even smaller and quieter than Gunnerside, Low Row is really just a string of buildings punctuating the main Swaledale Road for mile or so, three of which are worthy of mention. On the fell-side above the hamlet, by the side of the Corpse Road route, sits a little-visited barn with the uninviting name of the Dead House. In medieval times coffin carriers, on their way to the church at Grinton, would temporarily leave their cadaver and nip downhill to the local ale house for refreshment, before continuing their solemn journey. We don't know where Low Row's pub was, or what it was called, before the 1600s, but from that time it has been the Punchbowl Inn, next to the church in an area called Feetham.

The third building of note here, especially if you have children with you who need entertaining, is **Hazel Brow Farm** – a working organic farm where the young (and young at heart) can get up-close to the animals and follow the nature trail whilst the grown-ups relax in the café.

Hazel Brow Farm DL11 6NE ✆ 01748 886224 🖰 www.hazelbrow.co.uk. Visitor centre, café, shop, organic farm produce, walks and children's play area including animal feeding and donkey rides. Free entry to café, shop and walks, fee for the rest and open Tue, Thu, Sun and bank holidays.

⑤ Punch Bowl Inn Low Row ✆ 01748 886233 🖰 www.pbinn.co.uk. The beers here are well-kept local brews – Theakstons, Black Sheep and Timothy Taylors – but the emphasis is on food. Meat and game from the dale and fish from Hartlepool are served in the restaurant that sports a 'Mouseman of Kilburn' carved bar.

Mid Swaledale: around Reeth

⑥ Reeth

Reeth is a Saxon name meaning 'by the stream' which is odd, because it isn't. Two watercourses are not far away though, the River Swale to the south and Arkle Beck to the north draining the valley of Arkengarthdale. Reeth sits strategically between the two valleys, raised safely out of flood range of both boisterous rivers. I like Reeth but it doesn't have the cosy atmosphere of some villages: the village green is disproportionately large, giving the place a spread-out feel.

Reeth was, and still is, the capital of Swaledale, and site of the only market above Richmond, hence the size of the Green. The days when the market would fill this space are long gone but one is still held every Friday. All of Reeth's pubs face on to the Green and it does well to support three today, but this is nothing compared with the early 1800s at the height of Swaledale's lead-mining boom. Reeth was the centre of the industry and had a staggering ten pubs at the time. The spiritual needs of the miners were met by three chapels, two of which are still open for worship. Reeth has never had its own church, being part of the parish of Grinton with the church a mile away.

Tourism is by far the biggest employer here now. Virtually every visitor to Swaledale calls in on Reeth and they are well served here by a National Park Visitor Centre, three gift shops, a bookshop, three general stores, and a post office. You won't go hungry or thirsty here either; besides the three pubs there are six places to get a cup of tea, and a source of freshly baked bread and cakes at **Reeth Bakery** on Silver Street (01748 884735; www.reethbakery.co.uk). If

There's lead in them there hills

Yorkshire lead can be found in the paint on the frescoes of Pompeii, in the plumbing of classical Rome and on the medieval roofs of Antwerp and Bordeaux. The fascinating story of how it found its way to all of these places starts millions of years ago. Geological movements caused thousands of small cracks to form in the limestone surface of the north Pennines, which filled with mineral-rich hot water from deep below the earth's crust. When it cooled it deposited crystals of various minerals, including galena or lead sulphide, and this is the ore that has been extracted on a small scale for thousands of years. We know that the Romans delved here because a block or 'pig' of lead was found stamped with the Emperor Trajan's name. Later, the rich monasteries at Fountains, Rievaulx and Jervaulx kept records of their 15th-century trade with Belgium and France.

Lead-mining went large-scale between 1650 and 1900 and its impact on the landscape and rural society was devastating. Valleys that had previously only known woodland crafts and sheep farming now became brutal and polluted industrial centres. Forests were felled and hillsides shaved of peat to fuel the furnaces, and miles of tunnel were blasted out underground. One particularly destructive practice was called 'hushing', where a beck was dammed to form a reservoir above a hillside with a known lead vein. The dam was deliberately breached to cause a flash flood which would scour off all the surface soil and rock thus exposing the valuable seam beneath.

As for the social impact, thousands of outsiders moved into the dales, living in squalor for the most part, sometimes ten or twelve to a two-roomed cottage with shared beds slept in on a rota. A whole sub-culture developed, almost with its own language. A young miner would for instance, strike a 'bar-gain', or join a 'gang' who would work underground on a 'stope'. 'Bouse' would be taken out by 'kibble' or you appreciate arts and crafts then carry on up Silver Street from the Green and find the **Dales Centre**, a modern set of industrial units which is home to a painter, a clock restorer, two furniture makers, two sculptors, a jeweller and a worker in stained glass. They produce wonderful work, it's just a shame that the modern centre they are in is so uninspiring. For a little educational entertainment there is a **Swaledale Museum** (01748 884118; www.swaledalemuseum.org) in the old Methodist schoolroom on the corner of the Green, a quaint and very traditional local history archive with small shop and café attached.

If you don't need educating or entertaining, just a bench in a quiet corner to sit and muse or read in the sun, then the **Community Orchard Garden** is the place. It's easily found, at the side of the tourist information office, free and accessible to wheelchairs.

Reeth's busiest week of the year is undoubtedly over Whitsun, in late May to early June, when the Swaledale Festival (www.swaledale-festival.org.uk) takes place – a celebration of music and the arts.

'whim' to fill a 'bouseteam'. This was emptied on to the 'dressing floor', the 'deads' were rejected and the remainder was 'spalled' and 'bukkered' to make it small enough to be sieved in a 'hotching tub' and then the 'slime' collected in a 'running buddle'. The ore was then 'smelted' and cast into a 'pig'. Got that? Good. Working life started at ten years old and ended on average (life that is) at 45. Life expectancy was so short because of long working hours, bad air in the mines, poisonous fumes from the smelters, TB from cramped living and general poverty. Some miners were so poor they knitted clothes as they walked to work to sell for a few extra pennies.

Faced with this human cost, I can't help feeling that the collapse of lead-mining in the early 20th century was a blessing. Virtually no veterans with a first-hand memory of the industry survive, and the economy of the dales has returned to sheep and, latterly, tourism. Socially, outside of museums and archives, it's as if nothing had ever happened, but up on the fell-sides, scars will take longer to heal. The problem is that the lead that still remains in the 'hushed' areas and vast spoil heaps, being poisonous, stopped the vegetation regenerating. The moors around Greenhow in Nidderdale and above Grassington in Wharfedale are grim, bare and uninviting places, but nothing compared with the north side of Swaledale. The walking-guide guru, Alfred Wainwright, deliberately routed his Coast-to-Coast Walk through the worst of the damaged landscape because he felt people needed to see the consequences of irresponsible land use.

Every cloud does have a silver lining though, and in this case it is *Minuartia verna*, the spring sandwort, a beautiful and rare plant; rare, that is, virtually everywhere except on lead-mine spoil heaps. This is one of the few British plants tolerant to high levels of lead and its neat cushions are sometimes the only life in a heavy metal desert.

A waterside wander

Reeth has a wealth of appealing walks, but if you only have time or energy for one it has to be a circular tour of both rivers. First go south from the Green to Back Lane, then over the River via the footbridge. Watch sand martins flit in and out of their river bank burrows in summer as you follow the bridleway downstream to Grinton. Here you can resist the temptation to enter the fine Bridge Inn, or not as the case may be. Return to Reeth across the field footpath, diverting up Arkle Beck for a short explore before re-entering the Green at its northern end. A delightful 2½-mile easy stroll.

Food and drink

Black Bull Hotel ℓ 01748 884213 🖰 www.theblackbullreeth.co.uk. None of Reeth's pubs can compete with the excellent hostelries in the surrounding villages but they do all have cask beer and the Black Bull is worth a look for its upside-down sign, a gesture of rebellion from a previous landlord to the National Park over a planning dispute.

Ice Cream Parlour The Green ℓ 01748 884929 🖰 www.reethicecreamparlour.co.uk. Sixteen flavours of Brymoor ice cream from Jervaulx, or hot drinks for those chilly days.

The Kings Arms ℓ 01748 884259 🖰 www.thekingsarms.com. Deserves a visit on a cold evening for the fireplace alone, as it must be one of the biggest in the country. When the fire is well banked up the bar feels like a sauna.

Overton House Café High Row ℓ 01748 884332 🖰 www.overtonhousecafe.co.uk. A café in the daytime and restaurant in the evening, very popular, booking required.

Shopping

Dales Centre Studios Silver St. Within these are (among others) **Peter Cummings Furniture** (🖰 www.petercummings.co.uk), **Philip Bastow Cabinet Maker** (🖰 www.philipbastow-cabinetmaker.com), **Clockworks** (🖰 www.clockmakers.co.uk), **Stef's Models** (🖰 www.stefottevanger.co.uk), **Michael Kusz – Sculpture** (🖰 www.graculus.co.uk) and **Pendangles Jewellery** (🖰 www.pendangles.biz).

⑦ Grinton and Fremington

Neither of these neighbouring hamlets has enough to warrant village status today, but an amateur historian will enjoy piecing together jigsaw pieces of a busy and influential past. The bridge linking Grinton and Fremington is at the first point on the River Swale above Richmond where the river could be forded, hence its importance. The oldest evidence is from the Iron Age, with the remains of a fort just east of Grinton by the river, a settlement a mile and a half upstream at Maiden Castle, and boundary earthworks between the two hamlets, blocking the valley bottom completely at one time.

For 400 years St Andrew's Church in **Grinton** was the only one in upper Swaledale, and had the biggest parish in Yorkshire. This accounts for the size of

the building which led to its nickname, 'Cathedral of the Dale'. Although most of the church fabric is now fairly recent, there are fragments of the original Norman church, built by the monks of Bridlington Priory, a long way from home. Bats inhabit the church, both real pipistrelles in the roof space, and striking copper sculptures hanging from the walls, courtesy of Michael Kusz from the Dales Centre Studios in Reeth.

More recent, but still old and interesting, buildings are **Fremington corn mill**, with a rare wooden waterwheel, **Grinton Lodge**, once a shooting lodge but now a youth hostel, and the village pub.

A maze of footpaths and bridleways links all these places, in a choice of pleasant valley-bottom strolls, but two obvious higher-level walks also warrant a try: **Fremington Edge** on the north side of the valley, and **High Harker Hill** on the Grinton side. Another alternative is to hire bikes from the Dales Bike Centre and go for a pedal.

Bridge Inn Grinton ☎ 01748 884224 🖥 www.bridgeinn-grinton.co.uk. A 13th-century coaching inn, well-loved by locals and visitors. Food is a balance of traditional English and continental, but high quality across the board. Unusually, the beer is Jennings from Cumbria, but a local guest ale often accompanies it. Day fishing licences and rods for hire behind the bar.

Dales Bike Centre Fremington ☎ 01748 884908 🖥 www.dalesbikecentre.co.uk. An old barn converted to everything two-wheeled. Road and mountain bikes for hire, bike shop, service and repair, skills training courses, bike wash and showers (not just for riders, sweaty walkers as well). Snacks and drinks are on the menu in an attached café and accommodation is also available. All in all a very handy facility, and not just for bikers.

⑧ Arkengarthdale

If the name of the valley itself isn't eccentric enough, then what about some of the places in it? Booze, Whaw and Faggergill could easily have been words picked at random for their comedy value. Arkle Town sounds as if it should be the largest settlement here, but there is virtually nothing of it; that title goes to the compact village of Langthwaite, straddling Arkle Beck with a graceful, stone, arched bridge that featured in the TV series *All Creatures Great and Small*.

The lower dale is surprisingly lush and wooded for Swaledale, but if you travel up the valley on the road towards Brough, the landscape turns much less cultivated and more open. Just beyond the head of the dale, and right on top of the moor, where the words wild and bleak usually apply, a most unexpected sight materialises out of the cloud, mist or snow – an inn, the Tan Hill Inn to be precise, at 1,732 feet above sea-level the highest pub in Britain (and one of the most remote from other habitation, too).

The not-so-famous grouse

It's 5.45 on a cold April morning and I'm not tucked up in bed but huddled in a wall corner of an old sheep shelter in Arkengarthdale. I'm wearing most of the clothes I possess, a woolly hat down over the ears and sporting a drip on the end of my nose. Why? I hear you ask. Well, following a tip-off from a bird-watching friend, I'm in the right place to wait for dawn to break and witness a unique stage show. Two of the players are already here. I can see them through a convenient hole in the wall, on a stage of short cropped grass surrounded by tussocky rushes and heather. As the morning brightens, colour washes into the landscape and I can make out detail in the birds. They are the size and shape of small chickens, very dark in colour with intense red eyebrows – they are male black grouse or moorcocks (*Tetrao tetrix*).

The two birds are suddenly joined by a third which struts into the arena and spreads its tail to reveal a white pom-pom of feathers beneath. He opens his mouth and, in a bubble of warm misty breath, produces a bizarre series of indignant burbles and hisses aimed at the other two males, who reply in a similar fashion. What I was witnessing was a communal courtship display called a 'lek' which is performed by black grouse and only two other species of bird in Britain. By the time I'd seen enough and slunk away downhill out of sight, six males were giving it what for, and an audience of female grey hens was watching from the periphery, selecting their preferred mate – presumably the most impressive strutter and burbler.

What makes this seem doubly special is its increasing rarity. The black grouse is in serious decline nationally: Swaledale's is the most southerly population in England and the only one in Yorkshire. Since 1996 a consortium of interested parties, including the RSPB, Natural England and shooting organisations, have initiated the Black Grouse Recovery Project for the north Pennines. Their main push is on habitat improvement, reducing sheep grazing on moor edges and encouraging traditional hay meadows, and it seems to be working.

In an inspired move they have also managed to recruit the help of Famous Grouse whisky who have produced a new blend, which incorporates the aromatic peatiness of Islay malt. It's already got rave reviews and is selling well, with 50p from every bottle going to the recovery project. So, if you want to help, go and search out this new whisky and buy a bottle, or ask for it by name at the pub. What's it called? The Black Grouse, of course.

The Tan Hill Inn

I'll ask the obvious question. Why would anyone in their right mind build a pub up here? Coal, is the short answer. The black stuff has been dug out of the ground on Tan Hill since the 12th century, and remnants of the pits, shafts and quarries still dot the moorland around the inn. The current 17th-century building replaced an earlier one which catered to the miners' needs in this lonely spot, and has been here ever since.

The last mine closed in 1929, but the pub managed to keep going because of its high-altitude fame, and more passing trade began in 1965 on the opening of the Pennine Way footpath, which goes right past the front door. Television adverts for double glazing, an annual sheep show in May, and regular live folk and rock music have kept people making the pilgrimage up the hill. Is it worth it? Absolutely: this is a place full of character, almost a world apart.

More often than not, a roaring fire warms the bar, which is a comfort if you can get close to it – access is often blocked by the resident cats and dogs, and sometimes even sheep, toasting themselves by the hearth. If you come in winter, be prepared for a long stay, as the pub can be cut off for weeks on end after heavy snow, and consequently has its own caterpillar-tracked snowmobile.

><><><><

SD Charles Bathurst Inn Langthwaite DL11 6EN ☎ 01748884567 www.cbinn.co.uk. A large roadside inn named after the local lord of the manor and lead-mine owner. CB Inn, as it's known, is friendly and popular, valued for its cask beer from Black Sheep, Theakstons and Timothy Taylors, extensive wine cellar and very good food. Meat and game are all sourced from Swaledale.

SD Red Lion Inn Langthwaite DL11 6RE ☎ 01748 884218 www.langthwaite.free-online.co.uk. A marvellous, atmospheric little village local, almost as different to the CB Inn as you could get. Black Sheep beer, hot drinks, local honey and preserves and bar snacks, but nowhere near the emphasis on food of its near neighbour.

Tan Hill Inn Tan Hill DL11 6ED ☎ 01833 628246 www.tanhillinn.co.uk. See description above.

⑨ Marrick

What is now a favoured haunt for white-water canoeists and kayakers was obviously once likewise for builders of monasteries, because two are here, one on either side of the river. The remains of Ellerton Priory, constructed in the late 12th century for Cistercian nuns, were incorporated into a Victorian shooting lodge which is now a private house on the south bank of the river. Nearby, but on the opposite side of the river, were the Benedictine nuns at **Marrick Priory**. I like to imagine those medieval ladies dressed in different coloured habits, waving to each other across the rapids. Not surprisingly, considering its position, Marrick Priory is now an outdoor education centre (but still owned by the Church of England). Whilst it caters mainly for groups of school children, the centre's instructors and equipment can be hired for a day or half day. **Marrick village** lies about half a mile up the hillside, at the top end of a very pleasant walk through Steps Wood.

Lower Swaledale: around Richmond

The scenery is still exquisite here; Richmond itself is handily placed for walks into the dale, with paths along the valley and high up along the level-topped cliff of Whitcliffe Scar.

⑩ Richmond

This isn't just Richmond, this is *the* Richmond – the one that all 56 others worldwide are named after, including its more well-known Surrey counterpart and far bigger sister in Virginia, USA. The name is pure French, Riche Mont meaning Strong Hill, and refers to the defensive site the Norman **castle** is built upon, high above a loop in the river and still massively imposing.

The Swale has made no concessions to civilisation; it is still wild and frisky, plunging over the spectacular cascade of **Town Falls**, directly below the castle. Riverside Road follows its northern bank and is a lovely place to walk, cycle, picnic or paddle, but take note of the signs warning of dangerous, fast-rising water levels at times.

In the town centre, all roads seem to lead to the cobbled **marketplace**, and it does take your breath away when you emerge into it as it is enormous – one of the largest in the country. Prince Charles was certainly taken with it, likening it to the grand Tuscan piazza of Siena in Italy. On most days this exotic ambience is not obvious as the marketplace doubles as a large free car park, but empty it is impressive, and at its very best on Saturdays when the big market takes place. The third Saturday of the month is particularly good as it also incorporates a farmers' market.

North of the marketplace modern Richmond begins to intrude, but there are three places to seek out, the **Georgian Theatre Royal**, the **Richmondshire Museum**, and the **Friary Gardens**. Where the green space of the last of these is now was once the site of an old Franciscan Friary: it still retains the statuesque ruins of an old bell tower, and a monastic sense of peace and serenity. There's also a good deal of conspicuously handsome **Georgian streetscape**, in Newbiggin Broad and elsewhere, and some alluring back alleys, or **wynds**, such as Cornforth Hill, leading steeply down through two of the surviving town gateways.

For some strange reason Richmond town does not venture south of the river at all, the only building of note on this side being the **old railway station**. The rest remains as park or farmland, ideal country for walking, with grandstand views of the castle in old town. An upstream stroll takes you on to the roundhouse nature trails, a series of scenic woodland loops, linked to make one four-mile walk, or individual shorter circular walks. If you head in the other direction from town, one mile downstream you will find the riverside ruins of **Easby Abbey**, and a return path on the other side of the river following the old railway line. This route is called the Drummer Boy Walk (see box, page 70). For exploring the town itself on foot, three very good town trails are available free online (www.richmond.org) or from the Tourist Information Centre.

It's no surprise that Richmond is the cultural centre of Richmondshire (an old un-official fiefdom and now a district council area), and it hosts a wealth of regular events throughout the year. If you want peace and quiet you had best avoid them, but if you want lively entertainment then time your visit for two in particular. **The Richmond Meet** is an annual fair, with floats, parades, cycle events and general carnival atmosphere, held over the Spring Bank Holiday weekend, and during the last week in September the **Richmond Walking and Book Festival** (www.richmondbooksandboots.org.uk) features guided walks for all abilities during the days and evening events to celebrate the written word.

Richmond Castle

Few towns are more dominated by their castle than Richmond, partly because the town is relatively small but also because this is a genuinely impressive building. The 100-foot-high keep towers over everything and, in my opinion, provides a viewpoint from the top to equal any in Yorkshire. Swaledale snakes away westwards while to the east lies the flat Cleveland plain laid out like a green patchwork quilt, with industrial Teeside hinted at in the distance.

Back in 1066 William the Conqueror had a dilemma. He was now boss of a lot of foreigners in their own country who didn't like him. His strategy was to delegate – allocate big chunks of land to his trusted earls and barons and let them control the resident Anglo-Saxons. His cousin Alan Rufus was given this corner of North Yorkshire and he must have had a healthy respect for the locals as he immediately set to building a castle on a 'strong hill' to defend himself. Most of the other Norman lords started with a temporary wooden fort, but Alan went for stones straightaway, making Richmond castle the equal-oldest stone Norman castle in England with those in Durham and Colchester. Big as it is, the castle was once even more extensive as it included what is now the market place within its walls. During the 14th-century worries about Scottish invasion, the town populace was allowed behind the protective outer bailey which stood where the crescent of market-side Georgian buildings is now. When the Scots danger passed, the bailey was gradually dismantled leaving the marketplace as part of the town and not the castle. This explains the odd position of the castle chapel, Trinity Church, outside the walls; it now houses the **Green Howards Museum**.

English Heritage charge a reasonable entry fee into the castle and it is money well spent; you can access walkways around the walls, a small museum and a shop, but the keep alone is worth the fee. Don't neglect the outside of the building either. If anything I think this is even more interesting than inside.

The Richmond drummer boy

I can remember being told this story as a child and hoping that it wasn't true, the horror of a solitary underground death filling my young mind with nightmares. It's said that soldiers in Richmond Castle chanced upon a small hole in a cellar wall which seemed to continue as a passage. It was too narrow for an adult to enter so they sent in a young drummer boy, complete with drum, to explore. He was instructed to bang his drum as he walked so the soldiers could track his progress by listening above ground. They followed the faint drumbeats across the marketplace and Frenchgate towards Easby Abbey for half a mile when the sound suddenly stopped. The unfortunate boy was never heard or seen again but a stone was laid at the point where the drumming was last heard, and it can still be seen in a field at the end of Easby Wood. Ghostly subterranean drumming can also be heard on still evenings... in my nightmares at least.

Richmondshire Museum

This small local history museum tucked away in Ryder's Wynd near the tourist information office covers life as it was in Richmond and Swaledale in a gentle, traditional style. No touch-screen virtual experiences here or even audio-visual presentations, just artefacts, models and reconstructions. Subjects covered include lead-mining, a village post office, a town chemist's shop, toys through the ages and, of course, a set from the ever popular *All Creatures Great and Small*. Admission is very reasonable and the museum is open daily, April to October.

Green Howards Museum

The Green Howards Regiment has been in existence since 1688, but has only been based in Richmond since 1873. The unusual name originates from an early Regimental Colonel, Charles Howard of Castle Howard fame, but as another Howards Regiment existed at the time, they had to distinguish between the two. Based on colour of uniforms the Green Howards and the Buff Howards were born.

Many of the Green Howards were killed in World War I, after which a number of their private memorabilia collections were sent to the Regiment. The collections of mainly medals and uniforms were housed in barrack rooms, huts and sheds from 1922 until the empty Holy Trinity Church came up for sale in 1970.

If you have a military background or Green Howard connections then you will love this place but for others like me who have neither, it risks being very stuffy. The Museum Trust realised this and have worked hard on much-needed modernisation recently. Popular new additions are the Kidzone where children can dress up (always a winner) and the Family History Research Centre. Open all year, closed Sundays. Children free.

The Georgian Theatre Royal

My choice of production was *A Midsummer Night's Dream* by Bill the Bard or *Bouncers and Shakers*, an 1980s-style comedy with a warning about strong language. I suppose I should have gone traditional when visiting the country's oldest surviving Georgian Theatre building (01748 823710; www.georgiantheatre.com) but I never could resist a John Godber play (and he is from Yorkshire). The show was brilliant, well directed and acted, with the character of the venue adding to the experience. This is a wonderful place, part Grade I listed building, part museum, but also a very busy working theatre.

It was built in 1788 at the height of Richmond's heyday by actor/manager Samuel Butler, but, faced with dwindling performances, closed in 1848. Miraculously the buildings were still intact in the 1960s when a group of local campaigners formed a non-profit trust and the theatre reopened. Although the facilities were extended in 2003 the auditorium remains unchanged and still only has a capacity of 214 in a sunken pit, boxes on three sides and a gallery. It is quaint, intimate, authentic and as far removed from a modern concert arena as you could get, and I loved it. So did Cathy and Graham, the couple sitting next to us. 'We come here at least once a month, sometimes twice in the same week. There's all sorts on – comedy club last week, that was good, rock music tribute bands, Shakespeare, lots of jazz evenings next month. We don't really mind what we see; it's the place we love. The "Poetry and Pints" evenings in the bar we always come to because they are free and next week is Museum Week where they convert everything back to its 1788 state, candlelight, wooden benches, hand painted scenery, Georgian costumes, the lot – it's great.' There are hourly **tours** of the theatre, six days a week, during day time for much of the year.

Food and drink: in Richmond

Richmond is a little disappointing on the gastronomic front. From a selection of ten pubs there is one worth visiting for food, one for beer.

Black Lion Finkle St ☎ 01748 826217 ✆ www.blacklionhotelrichmond.co.uk. A characterful Georgian coaching inn. The food is not cheap but portions are generous. Beer is Black Sheep with one other guest cask ale.

Cross View Tea Rooms Market Place ☎ 01748 825897. This place is always busy, which has to be a good sign. Prices are very reasonable and although the coffee is nothing special, the fresh cakes are.

Delhi-cious Cutpurse Lane ☎ 01748 824916. A double winner: the best Indian food in town and the best takeaway of any variety. Worth the journey out to the northern outskirts. Open every evening.

The Frenchgate Restaurant Frenchgate ☎ 01748 822087 🖰 www.thefrenchgate.co.uk. This is the place in Richmond to get dressed up and treat yourself if you are into fashionable European cuisine. The food is excellent, but expect your wallet to be a lot lighter when you leave. Open every lunchtime and evening.

Ralph Fitz Randal Queens Rd ☎ 01748 828080 🖰 www.jdwetherspoon.co.uk. A former post office given the Wetherspoon treatment and turned into a rather cavernous pub. That said, this is unquestionably the best place for beer in Richmond with a minimum of six cask ales on tap at any given time.

Food and drink: out of town

Holly Hill Inn Holly Hill, DL10 4RJ ☎ 01748 822192 🖰 www.hollyhillinn.co.uk. A country pub but within walking distance from Richmond town, half a mile away. The food is excellent value and with a good reputation locally, especially the grills and pies, and the Ivy restaurant is a lot cosier than many pub eating rooms. Black Sheep supply the ales. No food Mon.

The White Swan Inn Gilling West, DL10 5JG ☎ 01748 821123. A very lively, welcoming village local in a 17th-century building with a resident ghost called Jack. There are always two guest micro-brewery beers on sale plus Black Sheep; this is one of their select 'flagsheep' pubs. Food is basic, traditional and good value.

Richmond's Old Railway Station

Richmond's old railway terminus, or 'The Station' (www.thestation.co.uk) as it is now known, is probably busier now than it ever was when trains arrived daily from Darlington and beyond.

This building has a very special place in the Richmond community's heart; the local people fought tooth and nail to keep the railway open in the 1960s but lost out in the end. Their successors, and maybe some of the original activists, formed the Richmondshire Building Preservation Trust in 2003 and have steered the project that has produced this cultural centre. I like the fact that they have not forgotten the building's roots; the railway theme is everywhere, with evocative black-and-white images of steam locomotives, and a heritage centre devoted to rail memorabilia.

Hundreds of people a day pass through the doors to visit the cinema, café-restaurant, art gallery or heritage centre and many, myself included, leave with bags laden with goodies produced on-site by four artisan food makers (below).

The Angel's Share Bakery (no phone). Heavenly breads, quiches, terrines, tarts and cakes baked daily.

Archers Jersey Dairy Ice Cream ☎ 01748 850123

🖰 www.archersjerseyicecream.com. John and Susan Archer made a bold move when they lost their Friesian dairy herd to foot-and-mouth disease. They replaced it with a herd of Jersey cattle and decided to make ice cream. The rich creamy milk is brought straight from the farm to the parlour in the station and made into a bewildering array of flavours... you think of it, they've probably got it. Open every day.

Lacey's Cheese ☎ 01748 828264 🖰 www.laceyscheese.co.uk. They say cheese makes you dream. Simon Lacey learned the craft of cheese making at the Swaledale Cheese Company but dreamt of running his own cheese-making business, and here it is. The cheeses are all hand made using traditional methods and locally sourced products (the Swaledale beer in the ale cheese couldn't be more local), both natural rind and hand-waxed varieties, smoked, matured or flavoured.

Richmond Brewing Company ☎ 01748 828266 🖰 www.richmondbrewing.co.uk. Between them Andy Hamilton and Richard Bowerman have 44 years' beer-making experience with seven different breweries, and it shows. They brew three different ales as I write: Richmond Station Ale (light and golden), Stump Cross Ale (rich and dark) and Swale (smooth session beer). Look out for them as guest beers in pubs or bottles over the counter at the brewery. Closed Mon.

⑪ Easby Abbey

Historians always suspected that Easby had been a Christian site long before the abbey was built, and this was confirmed in 1931 when pieces of ancient stone carvings were found built into the walls of the church. When pieced back together they re-formed a magnificent 8th-century English cross, now in the Victoria and Albert Museum. The dedication of the church to St Agatha was also a clue as her cult was a very early one, at its peak when Christianity first came to Britain. Poor old St Agatha, by the way, was tortured in life by having her breasts cut off and presented to her on a platter. A superficial similarity in shape led to the ignominy of her becoming the patron saint of bakers and bell makers. Recently, and I think a touch more respectfully, she has been venerated as patron saint of breast cancer patients.

The present church was rebuilt in 1152 at the same time as the abbey by the 'White Canons' of the Premonstratensian order, who decorated it with colourful frescoes. Like the parish church in Pickering (see page 186), some of these survived the Reformation by being whitewashed and are now re-exposed in these more liberal times.

The history of the abbey has run along the same lines as many other Yorkshire abbeys; 12th-century founding on land donated by the local Norman lord, 300 years of power and influence followed by an abrupt end with Henry VIII's dissolution of the monasteries. A common practice at this time was for valuable relics in the abbey to be re-used by the, now new, Anglican churches. Easby Abbey's bell and choir stalls found their way into St Mary's Church in Richmond and are still there. The abbey is now owned by English Heritage.

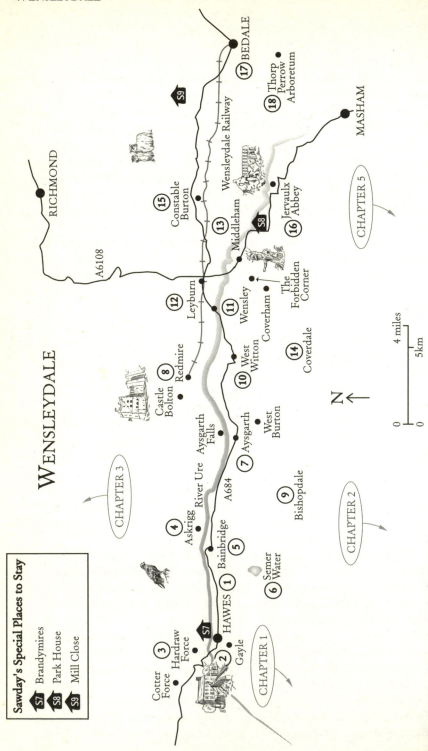

WENSLEYDALE

Sawday's Special Places to Stay

S7 Brandymires
S8 Park House
S9 Mill Close

RICHMOND

A6108

Wensleydale Railway

BEDALE

17 BEDALE

18 Thorp Perrow Arboretum

MASHAM

15 Constable Burton

13 Middleham

16 Jervaulx Abbey

S8

CHAPTER 5

12 Leyburn

11 Wensley

The Forbidden Corner

Coverham

8 Castle Bolton

Redmire

River Ure

Aysgarth Falls

10 West Witton

14 Coverdale

CHAPTER 3

Askrigg

4

A684

7 Aysgarth

West Burton

9 Bishopdale

CHAPTER 2

Bainbridge

5

1 HAWES

Gayle

6 Semer Water

Cotter Force

3 Hardraw Force

S7

2

CHAPTER 1

N

0   4 miles

0   5km

4. WENSLEYDALE

'This is in most places waste, solitary, unpleasant, unsightly, mute and still.' Poor old William Camden didn't much enjoy his visit to Wensleydale in 1590. We tend to place more value on wilderness today, so much so that this valley is one of the most popular tourist destinations in Yorkshire, and in peak holiday season at least you would have to work hard to find the 'solitary, mute and still' elements.

The main valley is the longest of the Yorkshire Dales, and, oddly, named after one of its smaller villages rather than its river, the Ure. A busy 'A' road runs most of its length, linking the busy towns of **Hawes, Leyburn, Middleham** and **Bedale,** and honeypot villages of **Bainbridge** and **Aysgarth**. Wensleydale has a fascinating history and bags of charm; a visit to the museum at Hawes can give you an excellent insight into the area's past, and traditions from quieter times. To escape the crowds try heading away from the valley-bottom roads, up the fell-sides or into one of the tributary side valleys like **Coverdale, Bishopdale** or **Raydale**. Alternatively, visit the main valley at off-peak times, especially after heavy rain when its many spectacular waterfalls are at their best.

Getting there and around

Car drivers beware: the A684 can at times be unpleasantly busy and slow going, and sometimes it seems that every caravan in the county is heading along it. The other side of the valley has an alternative route for part of the way, on a minor road which runs through Redmire, Carperby and Askrigg; a route bypassing Hawes, which can be a real bottleneck at busy times. Because the hills flanking Wensleydale are not too high, quite a number of other minor roads lead in and out of the valley, to Swaledale in the north, Wharfedale in the south and towards the Three Peaks in the west. On clear days these are fabulous scenic drives.

Public transport

The nearest mainline **railway** stations to Wensleydale are Northallerton in the east and Garsdale in the west, with buses from both of these stations. If you catch the half-hourly number 73 from Northallerton to Leeming Bar you can continue your rail journey on the private Wensleydale Railway (0845 450 5474; www.wensleydalerailway.com). A nostalgic 15-minute journey on a vintage train will deliver you to Redmire in the heart of Wensleydale via Bedale and Leyburn. Seasonal timetables operate with usually three trains a day, but not every day; check before you go. The service is diesel most of the time with steam trains in July and August.

Wensleydale may have lost most of its old railway but it is very well served by **buses,** to Leyburn and Hawes at least. From Bedale ten buses a day (nine on Saturday, five on Sunday) serve Leyburn, Hawes and most villages in between

(156, 157 and postbus) via Masham and Middleham. Richmond is linked to Leyburn nine times a day (159) but again, not on Sundays. Hawes is also accessible from the west with four buses a day from Garsdale railway station (113). There is no Sunday service, but in summer the 832 fills this gap, unfortunately only once a day and to Ribblehead station.

In summer, there are three brilliant **vintage tour buses**. The Wensleydale bus (127) runs once a day (Tuesday, Friday, Saturday, Sunday mornings) from Ripon, right up the dale to Hawes, with a second bus just from Redmire (afternoon) continuing to Garsdale Station. On Tuesdays only, the 569 Cumbria Classic Coach runs from Hawes to Kirkby Stephen and the 570 from Hawes to Ribblehead. What is frustratingly difficult is trying to link public transport into a day's circular tour either within Wensleydale or visiting with neighbouring valleys.

Cycling

One long-distance road route, the **Yorkshire Dales Cycleway**, nips into Wensleydale at Hawes and then out again from Askrigg over into Swaledale, returning lower down and running the full length of Coverdale.

The National Park's **Cycle the Dales** website (www.cyclethedales.org.uk) features three day rides that traverse a section of Wensleydale then cross the hills to either Swaledale (33 miles), Wharfedale (45 miles) or the Eden Valley via Tan Hill (52 miles). These are long and hilly routes for fit and experienced bikers only. The website does not list any **easier rides** for families or less masochistic folk, and I would take issue with this as I think some perfectly suitable rides exist. The trick is to avoid the main A684 of course, and this can be done almost completely in a nine-mile circuit taking in Askrigg, Thornton Rust, Aysgarth, Carperby and Woodhall. One or two short, steep sections keep you warm and the roads are relatively quiet. Other very short but highly scenic circular ambles include Lower Coverdale – where you could join up Coverham, West Scrafton, Carlton (six miles) – and Raydale from Bainbridge via Marsett and Stalling Busk (seven miles).

In lower Wensleydale where the hills settle down into hummocks, a triangle of land between Leyburn, Bedale and Masham contains a network of very quiet minor roads – excellent gentle biking country. Those lovely people at the Wensleydale Railway allow bikes on the train for free so you could take a one-way rail journey from Bedale to Redmire, then make up your own route back on little roads for 20 miles... or as far as you fancy, and hop on the train further down the line.

For **mountain bikes**, Wensleydale is as good as anywhere in the Dales. The National Parks **MTB the Dales** website (www.mtbthedales.org.uk) recommends two long and difficult routes; a circuit of Dodd Fell (18 miles) and a tour of mid-Wensleydale from Aysgarth (21 miles). Way too far for my delicate rear on rocky tracks; my favourite **shorter routes** are from West Burton (go east on Morpeth Gate green lane to Witton Steeps, down the road to West Witton and return via Green Gate green lane; six miles) and from Bainbridge (up to Stake Allotments via High Lane and Busk Lane tracks; ten miles, half on tarmac and half on gravel).

Horse-riding

There are three venues in or around the dale where someone else's horse can do your walking for you:

Carthorpe Riding Centre Hall Garth Farm, Carthorpe, Bedale ☎ 01845 567204 ⊕ www.carthorpe.com.
The Highland Pony Riding Centre Swinton, Masham ☎ 01765 689636/689241 ⊕ www.mashamridingcentre.com. Tracks of various length, and lessons for all ages.
Wensleydale Equestrian Gill Edge, Bainbridge ☎ 01969 650367.
⊕ www.wensleydaletrekking.co.uk. Trekking for all sizes and abilities, as well as riding lessons.

Walking

One official long-distance National Trail flirts with Wensleydale. In its upper reaches it is crossed at Hawes by the **Pennine Way** on its way from Fountains Fell to Great Shunner Fell. Hawes is also on the route of an unofficial circular trail of 55 miles, a traverse of both Wensleydale and Swaledale, called the **Herriot Way**. Elsewhere, the 24 miles of dale, daleside, and side dales offer a plethora of full and part-day walks to suit almost everyone. I say 'almost' because those of you searching for the high peaks won't find them here. Wensleydale's hills aren't as extrovertly obvious as the Three Peaks or Wharfedale Fells so consequently don't draw the crowds. These are my sort of hills – empty ones.

The best highish-level walks I think, are Pennhill Beacon above West Witton, Wether Fell from Hawes and a short, sharp pull to the summit of Addlebrough near Bainbridge. Upstream of West Burton is the hidden, unnamed valley of Walden with two short roads that lead in and suddenly stop. During all my time in this secluded corner I have never seen another visiting walker, just farmers going about their business. Cotterdale near Hawes and Hardraw is a similar quiet idyll.

Tourist information

Aysgarth National Park Visitor Centre, Aysgarth Falls ☎ 01969 662910.
Bedale Bedale Hall, Market Place ☎ 01677 424604.
Hawes Dales Countryside Museum, Station Yard; tel:01969 666210.
Leyburn Market Place ☎ 01748 828747.

Upper Wensleydale: Hawes, Gayle and Hardraw

① Hawes

Sitting at the meeting point of at least four ancient packhorse routes, Hawes is undoubtedly the capital of upper Wharfedale and its position far up the dale makes it the highest-altitude market town in Yorkshire. Its popularity has waxed and waned over the years: booms with the building of the Lancaster–Richmond turnpike road and the coming of the railway in the 1870s, slumps when the mills went quiet, and on the railways closure in the 1960s. Hawes is now busier than it ever has been but ironically, the tourists that the town almost completely depends on now are visiting to celebrate many of its old industries: cheese production, textile weaving and rope making.

The Wensleydale Creamery is probably Hawes's busiest attraction but visitors also flock to the old railway station where the National Park has a **visitor centre** with the hugely absorbing **Dales Countryside Museum** attached (01969 666239; www.yorkshiredales.org.uk/dales_countryside_museum). You can spend an entertaining and informative couple of hours here, without noticing the passing of time. It's more a celebration of family life in the country than a set of this-is-what-happened-here displays. Cheese and butter making, sheep farming, lead mining and hand knitting are all brought to life by an outstanding collection of local bygones and domestic objects gathered from all over the Dales. It amply justifies the entrance fee, especially for children,who get in free, and will really enjoy the hands-on displays and dressing-up opportunities.

The shops and businesses of Hawes are a nice mix, with butchers, electrical stores, grocers and hardware shops catering for the locals but also the expected wealth of outdoor gear, gift and craft shops, and numerous cafés of course. One place that manages to hit both markets is **The Ropemakers** at the east end of town, and talking of markets, if you want to see Hawes at its vibrant best then go on a Tuesday outside of school holidays. This is the day of the street stall-market and the livestock auction mart, always an entertaining, multisensory experience.

Wensleydale Creamery

Lovers of real Wensleydale cheese have some unlikely benefactors to thank; the French, a local farmer called Kit Calvert and two Plasticine heroes in the form of Wallace and Gromit.

The recipe for this mild, white cow's-milk cheese almost certainly came over from France with the Cistercian monks and was passed down via farmers' wives, to the dairy at Hawes. Twice in the last 80 years this sole producer of genuine from-the-dale Wensleydale cheese almost closed. The first time, in the 1930s depression, local farmers rallied around one of their own, Kit Calvert, who called the meeting in the town hall and bullied enough support to keep the dairy running. On the next occasion in 1992 the then owners, Dairy Crest, actually closed the dairy and had the effrontery to move production to Lancashire. A team of ex-managers bought the building and opened it under the name of Wensleydale Creamery, but making it a going concern wasn't easy. The breakthrough came when, in *A Close Shave*, one of Nick Park's inimitable Wallace and Gromit animations, Wallace uttered the immortal words 'Not even Wensleydale!' when he finds his lady friend doesn't like cheese and the creamery's steady business exploded. The visitor centre (01969 667664; www.wensleydale.co.uk) now entertains 200,000 people a year who enjoy the 'cheese experience' tour, explore the museum, eat in the restaurant or just select gifts from the now huge selection of branded cheeses and Wallace and Gromit memorabilia in the shop.

The Ropemakers

The Outhwaite family have been making ropes in Hawes since 1905 and on the present Town Foot site from the 1920s. In the early days ropes made from hemp, flax, jute and cotton were taken around the Dales by Mr Outhwaite's personal horse and cart. Most of the Swaledale, Wharfedale and Wensleydale farmers in particular relied on Outhwaite's ropes for sale at weekly markets; such was the well-earned reputation the family developed that their nearest serious competitor was 35 miles away in Lancaster. The business passed from father to son through the 20th century, moving with the times by installing electric power for the twisting machine in the 1950s and using man-made fibres for the first time in the 1960s. In the 1970s Tom Outhwaite was ready to retire but, with no family successor to take over, the business was bought by Peter and Ruth Annison. To this day they carry on the Outhwaite traditions, under the old family name. This is a working ropery that still supplies ropes to farms and industry, but the Annisons were astute enough to realise that people will pay to be hypnotised by the fascinating rope-making process. Hour-long guided tours for groups are available but I was happy enough just to wander around and have a nosy, which is free of charge. There is a lot to entertain and inform, including knot boards where visitors are invited to try their hand at fancy knot tying.

Not counting pubs, there are ten places in Hawes where a brew and a snack can be had.

The Baytree Market Place ☎ 01969 667111; cosy with particularly nice cakes.
The Chippy Market Place ☎ 01969 667663; friendly and good value to eat in or out.

Fountain Hotel Market Place ☎ 01969 627206; 🖰 www.fountainhawes.co.uk. My pick of the Hawes pubs for its good range of Black Sheep and other Yorkshire ales; bar food. It's a shame that it's had 'the knock-through into one big room' treatment though.

Penny Garth Café Market Place ☎ 01969 667066; mainly because of its full English breakfast from 09.00 onwards.

Sheep of the Dales

'Look Mum, a Rastafarian goat!' The **Wensleydale** sheep, so insulted by the teenager leaning over a wall near Hawes, tried not to look offended, but in truth it was one of the oddest looking farm animals that I've ever seen. Wensleydales are the tallest British breed of sheep, but they still manage to grow a full-body set of dreadlocks, so long that they trail on the ground, and make the most valuable sheep's wool in the world. Sometimes called 'poor man's mohair', it is prized by local knitters; the breed almost became extinct in the 1970s, but was saved by the Rare Breeds Survival Trust.

For sheer numbers though, no breed of sheep can match the **Swaledale**, not just in Yorkshire but all of upland northern England. The high fells and moors are dominated by these hardy black-faced and horned ewes to such an extent that a Swaledale sheep's head was chosen as the emblem of the Yorkshire Dales National Park. These days they are crossed with Texel rams to produce good meat lambs, but back in the 1940s they were usually pure-bred.

Transport was more traditional then as well, as Stanley Thackray, the last living drover in Wharfedale, remembers. 'We would walk the sheep and cattle down the dale roads to market in Skipton, yes – our animals and some neighbours', for fourpence an animal. My father had a very good dog in the 40s so we were often called on, especially after another drover, Old Jossy, died. Joe Ibbotson had a cattle wagon, but there was no petrol, it being the war years, so walking the beasts was the only way. It all stopped about 1950 when folk got hold of petrol again, and the roads became too busy – yes.'

The price of lamb today is too low for farmers to make a decent living, so many of them didn't replace their flocks after the 2001 foot-and-mouth outbreak. Both National Park Authorities support those that remain, as sheep are the architects of these upland landscapes – the Yorkshire Dales and Moors wouldn't be the same without them.

② Gayle

This hamlet owes its existence to one building, not a church or castle for a change, but a mill. **Gayle Mill** (01969 667320; www.gaylemill.org.uk) is the oldest virtually unaltered cotton mill in the world. It was built here in 1784 by the Routh brothers, two canny entrepreneurs who saw the business opportunities the new turnpike road would bring to Hawes. They did not really see beyond cotton spinning, but in its long life since, the mill has harnessed water power for a bewildering range of functions, flax spinning, wool spinning, woodworking machinery and electricity generation for the village. 1988 saw the mill finally close its doors as a commercial operation, and the building fell into disrepair.

That could have been it had it not been for local volunteers who joined the Gayle Mill Trust and worked tirelessly to return the mill to its former glory. One of the team, Tony Routh, was its last apprentice back in the 1960s. 'It was like coming home,' he said. 'When we started the project, the building was just as it was the day that I walked out and into a new job – a few more cobwebs perhaps, and a bit more lime off the walls. We've come a long way since then though, and it's great to see it now, completely brought back to life.'

Coming third in the national final of the BBC's *Restoration* series in 2004 proved crucial in securing funds and now the turbines are turning again to produce electricity and work timber once more. The mill is open for tours, and a shop sells hand-crafted wood products made on site. If you want to get involved, sign up for one of their two-day working courses.

Gayle has two other aquatic attractions. **Blackburn Farm** (01969 676524) has a small lake stocked with rainbow trout available for angling, and a footpath to stroll alongside Gayle Beck upstream. A lovely walk in itself, but it has the added bonus of **Aysgill Force** waterfall, about a mile away and especially impressive at high water levels.

③ Hardraw

This sleepy little hamlet follows a typical dales formula; an old pub, a new church on an old site, a stone bridge over a small beck and a scattering of other buildings, some farms and some cottages, with one tea room cum craft shop. What does make Hardraw different is that on land just upstream of the Green Dragon Inn, in fact belonging to it as part of its back garden (so you have to pass through the pub and pay an entrance fee), the beck leaps off an overhanging 100-foot limestone cliff. This is **Hardraw Force**, the highest clear fall waterfall above ground in England (see page 9). The whole place has a steady, timeless air about it – a feeling of permanence but appearances can be deceptive.

Hardraw very nearly didn't exist at all beyond 1899. Hardraw Beck is only a small stream, in fact in mid-summer it is not usually much more than a trickle, and on the morning of 12 July that is just how things were. By the afternoon though, things were very different and at the end of the day known ever since as the Great Flood, Hardraw was all but wiped off the map. Around noon livid black clouds over Shunner Fell burst into ferocious rain with the deafening crack of thunder. Thousands of tons of water roared down the hillside and funnelled into Hardraw Beck. By the time it reached the village terrified residents watched a wall of water yards high tear around the corner and slam into buildings; all were flooded and some demolished. The graveyard was torn up and coffins and gravestones washed two miles downstream. A huge tree smashed a hole in the wall of the Green Dragon Inn and all the bridges disappeared completely. John Sharples was an eyewitness, ' I was only a young man at the time,' he said, ' I worked at a quarry in Garsdale but I'd lamed myself and was at home off work. I was living at Scar End at the time so I'd a wonderful chance of seeing the storm. I'd never seen so much water come down as on that particular day, and the Green Dragon was flooded out. There was water nearly halfway up the walls in the lower room and half a foot of mud on the floors. There was a horse standing belly deep in a stable opposite the Inn, and some pigs next door swam out of the building over the bottom half of the door. They escaped down the fields. It was July and the storm came after dinner. There was thundering and lightning every minute and hailstones as big as marbles. Fish were swept from the river on to the banks, and the low side of Hardraw meadows were covered with mud. Hardraw bridge was swept away and iron railings were bent like tallow by the force of the water.'

Dales folk are resilient and Hardraw was repaired and rebuilt, but one reconstruction not many people are aware of is the waterfall itself. Such was the power of the surge that the lip of the falls was scoured away and Hardraw Force became a cascade down rock and loose boulders, losing its title of highest clear fall in the process. The landowner at the time, Lord Wharncliffe, wasn't having that. On inspecting the damage, he turned to his estate manager and commanded, 'Put it all back.' The very best stonemasons were hired and the lip was rebuilt to its previous shape. Few of today's thousands of visitors to Hardraw Force realise that they are looking at a man-made top to the cliff, still cunningly secured with metal pins.

Not all people visit Hardraw Scar to view the waterfall; the acoustics of the gorge here are perfect for outdoor music apparently, so once a year in early September it is the venue for a prestigious brass band competition.

If Hardraw Force has whetted your appetite for waterfalls, then you will really enjoy Fossdale's neighbouring valley. Cotterdale wraps around the western flank of Great Shunner Fell and is drained by two beautiful becks, East and West Gill, which between them boast nine waterfalls. They join forces to form Cotterdale Beck and produce three more cascades, the final one, **Cotter Force**, being the most impressive. It is also the most accessible, on foot or by wheelchair, 300 yards from the A684 at Holme Heads Bridge.

The Cart House Hardraw ☎ 01969 667691. A bridge-side café offering homemade, and mostly organic, food, and with a craft shop attached.

Green Dragon Inn Hardraw ☎ 01969 667392 🖰 www.greendragonhardraw.com. Worth a recommendation for the 13th-century building and well-kept selection of beers alone. This must be the only pub in the country with its own waterfall; access to Hardraw Force is via here for a fee.

Mid Wensleydale: Askrigg to West Witton

④ Askrigg

It is a sad indictment of our society's priorities, I think, that Askrigg should be most famous as a film set for a television series rather than as a village of great character and rich history. But, it's **James Herriot** country we are in, and this is the fictional village of Darrowby from *All Creatures Great and Small*, the series about a Yorkshire vet.

Askrigg is very old, with evidence of Iron Age settlement, but the name is younger and pure Norse, describing its position admirably on a ridge of high ground (rigg) where ash trees (ask) grow. The village's heyday was in the 1700s when it had the only market in upper Wensleydale, a booming textile industry (hand knitting mainly) and a reputation for clock-making. The local lords of the manor were the Metcalfes who ruled the roost from nearby Nappa Hall, once an impressive 15th-century fortified manor house but now a working farm and a little decrepit. One of many fine short walks from Askrigg takes in the hall and Nappa Mill before returning to the village via the banks of the River Ure.

Askrigg's market ceased trading long ago when Hawes took over as the local commercial centre, but the **market cross** is still here, as is a reminder of a cruel past. An iron ring is still set into the market-place cobbles, where bulls would be tied, to be baited with dogs. The bull-ring was also used for another purpose, a sort of heavy gauntlet-throwing challenge, where a man wanting a fight would turn the ring over and another fancying his chances would turn it back. Presumably they would then set to knocking lumps off one another.

Most of Askrigg's interesting old buildings are clustered around or near the marketplace. St Oswald's Church is here, as is the Kings Arms (TV's very own Drovers Arms in the Herriot series) with Skeldale House Vet's Surgery in nearby

Cringley Lane – its real name is Cringley House. None of the village textile mills is still in operation but one, Low Mill, is very active in another way, as an outdoor activities centre.

A handy waterside walk from the village traces the upstream course of the beck that used to power Low Mill's wheel. Your rewards for following Mill Gill are views of a series of pretty waterfalls wrapped in folds of oak woodland, culminating after a mile or so in the highest, **Whitfield Gill Force**. At this point you can return to Askrigg via an old green lane or carry on uphill to explore the scars, shake holes and swallow holes of Whitfield Fell.

Food and drink

The Crown Inn Main St ☎ 01969 650298. Locals refer to this as the 'Top Pub', the Kings Arms being the 'Bottom Pub', and this is their preferred drinking place. Beer is Black Sheep and Theakstons; traditional pub grub.

Kings Arms Main St ☎ 01969 650817. This is the Drovers Arms of *All Creatures Great and Small* fame as celebrity photos on the walls testify. It was chosen because it looked so traditional-old-Yorkshire and it still does. What's more, the welcome is genuinely friendly; Theakstons, Black Sheep and house beer brewed by Askrigg's own brewery.

White Rose Hotel Main St ☎ 01969 650515 🖰 www.thewhiterosehotelaskrigg.co.uk. Not strictly a pub but with a restaurant and bar open to non-residents. Good, well priced food, and beer from the Yorkshire Dales Brewing Co behind the hotel – couldn't be any fresher.

Outdoor activities

Low Mill Station Rd ☎ 01969 650432 🖰 www.lowmill.com. A residential outdoor centre with a wide range of activities: canoeing, climbing, caving and the like, for groups. At the moment you can hire an instructor for up to ten of you for a day's activity of your choice, but during 2010 it is planned to be available for individuals too.

⑤ Bainbridge

Bainbridge is a mere mile from Askrigg as the curlew flies, but a meandering two via the road over Yore Bridge. It is a similar size to its neighbour and probably at least as old; a Bronze Age earthwork sits just to the south, and on top of Brough Hill a Roman fort. The Latin invaders named this place Virosidum. Modern-day Bainbridge is a strangely sprawling village which suffers more than a little from having a busy A road cut across the village green. It does have one famous old tradition which, after a sad lapse, has recently started again: that of the blowing of the Forest Horn. Back in the 14th century when much of upper Wensleydale was hunting forest, a horn was sounded every winter night at 10 o'clock to guide benighted travellers in the forest safely back to Bainbridge. This custom was continued for hundreds of years but was only documented in the

Alastair Sawday's
Special Places to Stay

We have been building our collection of Special Places to Stay since 1994 and are delighted to dish up a small selection for you here.

How do we choose our Special Places?

It's simple. There are no rules, no boxes to tick. We choose places that we like and are fiercely subjective in our choices. We also recognise that one person's idea of special is not necessarily someone else's so there is a huge variety of places and prices on our website and in our books. Those who are familiar with our Special Places series know that we look for comfort, originality and authenticity and reject the insincere, the anonymous and the banal.

Inspections

We visit every place to get a feel for how it ticks. We don't take a clipboard and we don't have a list of what is acceptable and what is not. Instead, we chat with the owner or manager and then look carefully and sensitively round the house. It's all very informal, but it gives us an excellent idea of who would enjoy staying there. Once chosen, properties are re-inspected every few years to keep things fresh and accurate. In between inspections we rely on feedback from our army of readers, as well as from staff members who are encouraged to visit properties across the series. This feedback is invaluable to us and we always follow up on comments, so do let us know how you get on in these places. You can do this and find out more about each of those Special Places at **www.sawdays.co.uk**.

Disclaimer

We make no claims to pure objectivity in choosing our Special Places. They are here because we like them. Our opinions and tastes are ours alone; we hope you will share them. We have done our utmost to get our facts right but apologise unreservedly for any mistakes that may have crept in.

You should know that we don't check such things as fire alarms, swimming pool security or any other regulations with which owners of properties receiving paying guests should comply. This is the responsibility of the owners.

We hope you enjoy your stay with our owners, all of whom can deepen your understanding and experience of Yorkshire.

ⓢ¹ The Traddock

This family-run hotel is decidedly pretty and sits on southern fringes of the Dales. You enter through a wonderful drawing room – crackling fire, pretty art, the daily papers, cavernous sofas. Elsewhere, a white-washed sitting room opens onto the garden and fabulous local food appears in the restaurant. Bedrooms are just the ticket, some seriously swanky, others deliciously traditional with family antiques, quilted beds, a claw-foot bath. Those on the second floor have a cosy attic feel, all have fresh fruit, flat-screen TVs, homemade shortbread and Dales views. Those looking for a friendly base will find it here.

Bruce Reynolds
Austwick, Lancaster LA2 8BY
- £95-£175. Singles from £85.
  Half-board from £85 p.p.
- 12: 8 doubles, 1 twin/double,
  2 family rooms, 1 single.
- Lunch from £9.50.
  Dinner, 3 courses, about £30.
- 01524 251224
- www.thetraddock.co.uk

ⓢ² The Angel Inn

The Angel has all the ancient trimmings – mullioned windows, beams, stone walls, a working Yorkshire range – yet the feel is bright and breezy, especially in the dining rooms, of which there are several to satisfy the fans who come for the Whitby crab ravioli or the Bolton Abbey mutton. Above, you find exquisite bedrooms. All are different, you may get a French armoire, a brass bed, or a claw-foot bath. One is partly muralled, another has an icon in an alcove. Expect the best fabrics, pretty colours, flat-screen TVs. A super spot – in the middle of a tiny hamlet with Rylstone Fell rising behind.

Pascal Watkins
Hetton, Skipton BD23 6LT
- £130-£155. Suites £155-£180.
  Singles from £115.
- 5: 2 doubles, 3 suites.
- Bar meals from £9.50.
  Sunday lunch £25.
  À la carte dinner £30-£35.
- 01756 730263
- www.angelhetton.co.uk

⌂ S3 The Tempest Arms

A 16th-century ale house with great prices, friendly staff and an easy style. Inside are stone walls and old beams, settles and Yorkshire ales on tap. Dig into raised pork pie with homemade piccalilli, treacle tart with grapefruit sorbet. Bedrooms are just as good. Those in the main house are simpler, but most are ten paces beyond in two newly built stone houses: rather swish with hand-crafted furniture and lovely toiletries, slate bathrooms and flat-screen TVs. They have terraces or balconies overlooking a babbling stream and those at the back have views of the fells. Walkers pile in: the Dales are on the doorstep.

Martin & Veronica Clarkson
Elslack, Skipton BD23 3AY
- £80. Suites £100-£140.
  Singles from £60.
- 21: 9 twins/doubles, 12 suites.
- Lunch & dinner £5-£25.
- 01282 842450
- www.tempestarms.co.uk

⌂ S4 Knowles Lodge

Chris's father built this timber-framed house in 1938 on 18 acres of glorious hillside. It's a comfortable, comforting place to stay. Honey walls and polished floors give the sitting room a light, airy feel, cheerful throws on deep sofas make it cosy, a fine collection of modern art adds interest and there are views from large windows. Bedrooms are attractive with sprightly fabrics and fresh flowers; draw back the curtains and have your morning cuppa in peace. You're superbly well looked after, and you can get married here. Great walking and trout fishing, and the solitude a balm.

Pam & Chris Knowles–Fitton
Appletreewick, Skipton BD23 6DQ
- From £90. Singles £55-£60.
- 3: 2 doubles, 1 twin.
- Packed lunch £5.
  Pubs/restaurants within 2 miles.
- 01756 720228
- www.knowleslodge.com

S5 Augill Castle

A folly castle built in 1841. Outside, five acres patrolled by a family of hens, whose eggs are served at breakfast. Inside, grand interiors with chesterfield sofas, a grand piano, an honesty bar in the drawing room, open fires, fine arched windows. The house is run informally: just Wendy, Simon and their staff to ply you with delicious food, scented hot-water bottles, big pillows, massive tubs. Rooms in the house have the view, there are sofas, interesting art, one huge dining table. A spectacularly remote moorland road rises south east then drops towards Swaledale and Arkengarthdale.

Simon & Wendy Bennett
South Stainmore, Kirkby Stephen CA17 4DE
- £160. Singles £80.
- 12: 6 doubles, 3 twins/doubles, 3 four-posters.
- Dinner, 4 courses, £40 (Fridays & Saturdays).
  Midweek supper, 2 courses, £20.
  Booking essential.
- 01768 341937
- www.stayinacastle.com

S6 The Old Rectory

The views are over glorious Teesdale, the village – solid in stone and right on the border – is perfect, and the cricket club bowls from one county to another! Close to Reeth and Richmond, too. Across the cobbled yard, up a steep stone stair, is an enchanting bedroom in the coach house: a lofty, cross-beamed ceiling, fresh fabrics at little windows, coir and crisp linen. Angela's watercolours add to the artistic mood and, outside, her green fingers have crafted a lovely walled garden. Inside the rectory, antiques and oils (mostly of horses). James and Angela are great hosts.

James & Angie Delahooke
Barningham,
Richmond DL11 7DW
- £85-£90.
- 1 double: Coach house.
- Supper £18.50.
  Pubs/restaurants 10-minute drive.
- 01833 621122

📷 S7 Brandymires

📷 S8 Park House

The Wensleydale hills lie framed through the windows of the time-warp bedrooms; no TV, no fuss, just calm. In the middle of the National Park, this is a glorious spot for walkers. Gail and Ann bake their own bread and make jams and marmalade, and their delicious, well-priced dinners are prepared with fresh local produce and served at your own table. Two bedrooms, not in their first flush of youth, have four-posters; all have the views. If you're arriving by car, take the 'over-the-top' road from Buckden to Hawes for the most bewitching countryside.

The soundtrack could be *Perfect Day*: a scenic drive, delicious cake on arrival, undisturbed peace in the converted estate cottages – partly built with stone from next door's stunning Cistercian Jervaulx Abbey, owned by your hosts. Antique gems stand out among leather bucket chairs, splashes of colour brighten a neutral palette, guest bedrooms are luxurious. Try Carol's bacon, egg and maple crumpets for breakfast – the menu lists local suppliers. Leave pets and children at home but take boots and binoculars for the glorious scenery of Nidderdale: an AONB and a fitting backdrop to a perfect country stay.

Gail Ainley & Ann Macdonald
Muker Road, Hawes DL8 3PR
- From £52. Singles from £31.
- 3: 1 twin, 2 four-posters, all sharing 2 bath/shower rooms (each floor can be let to same party only, by arrangement.)
- Dinner, 4 courses, £18.50 (not Thursday).
- Pubs/restaurant 5-minute walk.
- 01969 667482

Ian & Carol Burdon
Jervaulx, Masham,
Ripon HG4 4PH
- From £75.
  Singles from £55.
- 3: 2 doubles, 1 twin.
- Packed lunch £3-£5. Pub 1.25 miles.
- 01677 460184
- www.jervaulxabbey.com

S9 Mill Close

Country-house B&B in a tranquil spot among fields and woodland; spacious, luxurious and with your own entrance through a flower-filled conservatory. Beds are large and comfortable, there's a grand four-poster with a spa bath, and scones for flickering candlelight. Be spoiled by handmade chocolates, fluffy robes, even your own 'quiet' fridge. A blue and cream sitting room has an open fire – but you are between the North York Moors and the Dales so walks are a must. Start with one of Patricia's famous breakfasts: bacon and sausages from the farm, smoked haddock or salmon, homemade jams. Bliss.

Patricia Knox
Patrick Brompton, Bedale DL8 1JY
- £80-£95. Singles £45-£65.
- 3: 2 doubles, 1 four-poster.
- Pubs/restaurants 2 miles.
- 01677 450257
- www.millclose.co.uk

S10 Swinton Park

Swinton is glorious, a fabulous old pile that flaunts its beauty with rash abandon. Expect marble pillars, vast arched windows, roaring fires. The drawing room is stupendous – like the salon of 17th-century château, the dining room's magnificent ceiling worth the trip alone. There's a bar in the old chapel, a very popular cookery school in the old stables. Bedrooms come in grand country-house style: plush fabrics, huge beds, marble bathrooms, decanters of gin and whisky. Game is from the estate and vegetables from the garden, while hampers can be left in bothies in the park for walkers wanting a rather good lunch.

Mark & Felicity Cunliffe-Lister
Swinton, Ripon HG4 4JH
- £175-£370. Half-board from £125 p.p.
- 30: 25 twins/doubles, 5 suites.
- Lunch from £19. Dinner £42.50-£47.50. Tasting menu £58.50.
- 01765 680900
- www.swintonpark.com

S11 Ashknott Cottage

In a quintessential Dales village is a beautifully looked-after two-up two-down. Smart paintwork and plants at the front, a suntrap little gravelled yard at the back. Sarah will meet and greet, light the wood-burner and leave you local cake... Step straight into the sitting room with deep red and cream walls, beams and wood-burning stove, books, games and CDs. In the shaker-style kitchen, extras include a bottle of wine and some organic doggie treats. Coir-clad stairs lead to a pretty, cream-painted bed and a super bathroom, soft towels and plump pillows. With Nidderdale unfolding all around you, this is a lovely spot.

Sarah Manby
Main Street,
Kirkby Malzeard HG4 3SE
- £250-£475 per week.
- Cottage for 2.
- Self-catering.
- 01423 545787
- www.ashknottcottage.co.uk

S12 Mallard Grange

Perfect farmhouse B&B. Hens, cats, sheepdogs wander the garden, an ancient apple tree leans against the wall, guests unwind and feel part of the family. Enter the rambling, deep-shuttered 16th-century farmhouse, cosy with well-loved family pieces, and feel at peace with the world. Breakfast is generous – homemade muffins, poached pears with cinnamon and a sizzling full Monty. A winding steep stair leads to big, friendly bedrooms, two cheerful others await in a converted 18th-century smithy and Maggie's enthusiasm for this glorious area is as genuine as her love of doing B&B.

Maggie Johnson
Aldfield, Ripon HG4 3BE
- £75-£105.
  Singles from £70.
- 4: 1 double, 3 twins/doubles.
- Pubs/restaurants 10-minute drive.
- 01765 620242
- www.mallardgrange.co.uk

S13 North Dockenbush

An 1800s farmhouse transformed into a handsome B&B with a modern vibe. Animal skins and displays of flowers gleam in the mirrored light of chandeliers; dark red walls flicker in firelight. Sink into Siberian goose down, wake to waterfall showers and Molton Brown treats. Oliver loves country pursuits, housekeeper Jackie provides the feminine touch (and biscuits!) – both radiate energy. Breakfast bacon and eggs are farmyard fresh while port rounds off hearty British meals. Dogs and horses share the stables and the estate, close to Harrogate, is a walker's paradise: you're on the doorstep of the Dales.

Oliver Whiteley
Brearton, Harrogate HG3 3DF
- £90. Singles £65.
- 5: 3 doubles; 2 doubles sharing bath (let to same party only).
- Dinner, 4 courses & half bottle of wine, £30 (min. 4 people). Pub/restaurant 2 miles.
- 01423 797650
- www.northdockenbush.co.uk

S14 Braythorne Barn

Great independence here with your own entrance; inside are paintings, fine furniture, colourful fabrics and rugs. Floors are light oak, windows and doors hand-crafted and sunlight dances around the rooms. Both bedrooms are understatedly luxurious with beautiful rafters, glorious views and a fresh country feel. Bathrooms have Molton Brown toiletries and plump towels; the guest sitting room is gorgeous. Visit charming Harrogate or walk the Priests Way. Chickens in the field and great breakfasts – perhaps brandy-soaked fruit compote... this is a rural idyll with a contemporary twist.

Petrina Knockton
Stainburn, Otley LS21 2LW
- £80-£90.
  Singles from £55.
- 2: 1 twin;
  1 double with separate shower.
- Pubs/restaurants 2-4 miles.
- 0113 284 3160
- www.braythornebarn.co.uk

S15 Gallon House

A bespoke B&B that clings to the side of an impossibly steep hill with a medieval castle tottering on one side, a Victorian railway bridge passing on the other and the river sparkling below. There's Lloyd Loom wicker in the conservatory, an open fire in the panelled sitting room, and delicious communal breakfasts in the dining room. Bedrooms are not too big, but spoiling nonetheless, with bathrobes and white towels, crisp linen and soft colours. Come down to wonderful salmon fish cakes, rack of lamb, pear and almond tart. Best of all is the terrace for one of Yorkshire's best views, and deckchairs to take the strain.

Sue & Rick Hodgson
47 Kirkgate,
Knaresborough HG5 8BZ
- £110. Singles £85.
- 3: 2 doubles, 1 twin.
- Dinner, 3 courses, £27, by arrangement.
- 01423 862102
- www.gallon-house.co.uk

S16 Lovesome Hill Farm

Who could resist home-reared lamb followed by sticky toffee pudding? This is a working farm and the Pearsons the warmest people imaginable; even in the mayhem of the lambing season they greet you with homemade biscuits and Yorkshire tea. Their farmhouse is as unpretentious as they are: chequered tablecloths, cosy and simple bedrooms (four in the old granary, one in the cottage) with garden and hill views, and a proper Victorian-style sitting room. The A167 traffic hum mingles with the odd sheepdog bark; you are brilliantly placed for the Moors and Dales. Good for walkers, families, business people.

John & Mary Pearson
Lovesome Hill, Northallerton DL6 2PB
- £64–£76. Singles £35-£48. Cottage: £70-£84.
- 5: 1 twin, 1 double, 1 family room, 1 single. Cottage: 1 double.
- Dinner, 2-3 courses, £15-£20. BYO. Packed lunch for walkers. Pub 4 miles.
- 01609 772311
- www.lovesomehillfarm.co.uk

Once the residence of the Bishops of Whitby this elegant rectory has a comfortable lived-in air. Both Turner and Ruskin stayed here and probably enjoyed as much good conversation and comfort as you will. Bedrooms are pretty, traditional and with grand views; the drawing room is classic country house with a fine Venetian window and an enticing window-seat. The graceful, deep pink dining room looks south over a large garden of redwood and walnut trees – some are 300 years old. Caroline will give you a generous breakfast; wander at will to find an orchard, tennis court and croquet lawn.

The welcome tea and homemade cakes set the tone for your stay; this is a happy place. No 54 was once two cottages on the Duncombe estate; now it's a single house and Lizzie has made the most of the space. Buttermilk walls, be-rugged flagged floors, country furniture, open fires and a stylish lack of clutter. A single-storey extension has been fashioned into three extra bedrooms around a secluded courtyard. Thoughtful extras – a Roberts radio, fresh milk, hot water bottles – make you feel looked after, and the breakfasts will fuel the most serious of walks. Make a house party and bring your friends!

Tim & Caroline O'Connor-Fenton
South Kilvington, Thirsk YO7 2NL
- From £68.
  Singles from £40.
- 2: 1 double with separate bath & dressing room; 1 twin/double with separate bath & shower.
- Pub opposite.
- 01845 526153

Lizzie Would
Bondgate, Helmsley YO62 5EZ
- £88. Singles from £40.
- 4: 2 doubles, 1 twin;
  1 single with separate shower.
- Dinner, 2-3 courses, £28-£35.
  Restaurants 10-minute walk.
- 01439 771533
- www.no54.co.uk

S19 Estbek House

A super little find on the Whitby coast. This is a quietly elegant restaurant with rooms ten paces from the beach at Sandsend. There's a terrace at the front for drinks and a small bar on the lower ground; watch Tim at work in his seriously swanky kitchen. Upstairs, two airy dining rooms swim in seaside light and come with stripped floors, painted panelling, old radiators and beautiful food. Bedrooms above are warmly designed with cast-iron beds, crisp linen, colourful throws and shuttered windows. Come back down for a delicious breakfast and, as East Beck river passes directly opposite, watch ducks waddle across the road.

David Cross & Tim Lawrence
Eastrow, Sandsend,
Whitby YO21 3SU
- From £120.
- 4: 3 doubles, 1 twin.
- Dinner, 3 courses, about £30.
- 01947 893424
- www.estbekhouse.co.uk

S20 Cropton Forest Lodge Cottages

Forget any previous notion you might have of remoteness – all you will hear is the wind in the trees and the comforting puff of the Moors train. The cottages are a shop front for Ben's carpentry skills and Sue's designer eye, but nothing is prim. Find quirky bric a brac and fresh flowers, books and copious candles, a zany mix of modern and antique furniture and well-designed kitchens. Bedrooms are carpeted, beds are huge and well-dressed. Ben and Sue are in the farmhouse opposite for basics if you run out: there's no local shop! Wander outside and watch the darkness for twinkling stars – no light pollution here.

Sue & Ben Blackburn
Stape, Pickering YO18 8HY
- £335-£735 per week.
- Meadow Cottage for 4. Willow Cottage for 5. Brock Cottage for 4.
- Self-catering.
- 01751 471540
- www.croptonforestlodge.co.uk

S21 The Barn, Middleton Hall

It must be the swishest barn conversion for miles. Light floods through huge windows – and via a soaring, raftered ceiling – to illuminate the vast open living area. Sitting, dining, cooking take place amid smooth white walls and heated floors of polished walnut and stone: a shiny kitchen runs along one side, outside is an Italian-style courtyard with seating and a barbecue. The master bedroom, tucked under rafters on a mezzanine, is softly lit and subtly hued and there's an equally luxurious mezzanine twin. Don your boots for the Yorkshire Moors, stroll to the village pub and the market town of Pickering. Gorgeous.

Noelle Thornton
Pickering YO18 8NX
- Barn £650-£950 per week.
- Barn for 4-5. Coach House (for 4) and Cottage (for 4-6) also available.
- Self-catering.
- 01751 472283
- www.noellescottages.co.uk

S22 Crown House

Scarborough... bracing walks, salty air, fresh fish and buckets and spades. But the Firths have one of those charming listed houses in respectable South Cliff, moments from the Esplanade. Inside find spacious light rooms with contemporary furniture, stunning art (Barbara's passion) and flowers everywhere. Barbara, thoughtful and fun, serves great breakfasts with juices just-squeezed at a large oval table. Bedrooms are cream and stylish with smart TVs and stereos, bathrooms luxurious and sparkling. Coastline and castles by day, home baking on your return, books and CDs to borrow, cats to admire and a theatre just down the road.

Barbara Firth
6 Crown Terrace,
Scarborough YO11 2BL
- £80-£110.
- 3: 2 doubles, 1 twin/double.
- Restaurants 10-minute walk.
- 01723 375401
- www.crownhousescarborough.co.uk

⌂ S23 The Abbey Inn

Fifty paces from the door, majestic Byland Abbey stands defiant after 900 years. As for the inn, it dates to 1845 and once served as a farmhouse for the Ampleforth monks. Refurbished by English Heritage, it's a perfect mix of tradition, eccentricity and elegance. Bedrooms upstairs sweep you back in time: beamed ceilings, panelled windows, fancy beds. Downstairs dining rooms have big fireplaces and carved oak seats on stone flags. TJ's food is British-based and interesting: scallops with cauliflower purée; venison with red cabbage and sloe gin sauce. Breakfast is cooked to order and brought to your room. A glorious setting.

Melanie Drew
Byland Abbey, Coxwold, York YO61 4BD
- £100–£200.
- 3: 2 doubles, 1 suite.
- Lunch from £9.95. Dinner, 3 courses, £15–£30.
  Not Sunday evening, Monday or Tuesday.
- 01347 868204
- www.theappletree.org

⌂ S24 Shallowdale House

Phillip and Anton have a true affection for their guests so you will be treated like angels. Sumptuous bedrooms dazzle in yellows, blues and limes, acres of curtains frame wide views over the Howardian Hills, bathrooms are gleaming and immaculate. Breakfast on the absolute best; fresh fruit compote, dry-cured bacon, homemade rolls – and walk it off in any direction straight from the house. Return to an elegant drawing room, with a fire in winter, and an enticing library. Dinner is out of this world and coffee and chocolates are all you need before you crawl up to bed. Bliss.

Anton van der Horst & Phillip Gill
West End, Ampleforth YO62 4DY
- £95–£115. Singles £75–£85.
- 3: 2 twins/doubles;
  1 double with separate bath/shower.
- Dinner, 4 courses, £35.
- 01439 788325
- www.shallowdalehouse.co.uk

📷 Cundall Lodge Farm,

Ancient chestnuts, crunchy drive, sheep grazing, hens free-ranging. This four-square Georgian farmhouse could be straight out of Central Casting. Homely rooms of damask sofas and bright wallpapers have views to Sutton Bank's White Horse or the river Swale, spotless bedrooms are inviting – family furnishings, fresh flowers, Roberts radios – and tea and oven-fresh cakes welcome you. This is a working farm and the breakfast table groans with free-range eggs, homemade jams and local bacon. The garden and river walks guarantee peace, and David and Caroline are generous and delightful.

Caroline Barker
Cundall, York YO61 2RN
- £75-£90.
- 3: 2 doubles; 1 twin/double.
- Packed lunch £5.
  Pubs/restaurants 2 miles.
- 01423 360203
- www.cundall-lodgefarm.co.uk

📷 Hunters Hill

The moors lie behind this solid, stone farmhouse, five yards from the North York Moors National Park, in farmland and woodland with fine views... marvellous walking country. The house is full of light and flowers; bedrooms are pretty but not overly grand. The attractive sitting room has deeply comfortable old sofas, armchairs and fine furniture, while rich colours, hunting prints and candles at dinner give a warm and cosy feel. The family has poured a good deal of affection into this tranquil house and the result is a home that's happy, charming and remarkably easy to relax in... Wonderful.

Jane Otter
Sinnington, York YO62 6SF
- £80. Singles from £50.
- 2: 1 twin/double;
  1 twin/double with separate bath.
- Dinner, 3 courses, £30.
  Pub/restaurant 500 yds.
- 01751 431196

S27 Little Garth

In gentle hills, short miles from bustling market towns, is an ancient settlement with Norman church and trout stream. Behind the hedge-fringed village street is a dear little house. Turn the key, drop your bags in the flagged hall and leave the world behind. Pots of fresh flowers glow on old pine tops, cotton-covered armchairs are deep and comfortable. A light-filled kitchen, with all the kit, opens to a rose and honeysuckle back garden. Sweetly sprigged bedroom walls, gleaming white woodwork and generously clad beds are blissful after trudging the moors or battling with Friday night traffic. A lovely hideaway.

Pippa Galloway
Normanby, Sinnington,
York YO62 6RH
- £260-£550 per week.
- Cottage for 5.
- Self-catering.
- 01904 431876
- www.holidaycottage-normanby.co.uk

S28 The Durham Ox

At the top of the Grand Old Duke of York's hill is an L-shaped bar of flagstones and rose walls, worn leather armchairs and settles, panelling and big fires. There's a dapper restaurant with seasonal temptations: duck with parsnip mash, red cabbage and port sauce, and chocolate cake with vanilla yogurt ice cream. No need to drive on: four delightfully quirky rooms in the old farmworkers' cottages have been renovated in smart country style. Expect original quarry-tiles, beams and brass beds, smart fabrics and re-vamped bathrooms. The far-reaching views across the valley are stunning: such peacefulness 20 minutes from York.

Michael & Sasha Ibbotson
Westway, Crayke, York YO61 4TE
- £100-£180. Singles £80.
- 5 doubles.
- Main courses £8.95-£18.95; bar meals from £6.95; Sunday roast from £11.95.
- 01347 821506
- www.thedurhamox.com

S29 Low Penhowe

With the Turners at the helm, you are on a safe ship. They see to everything so perfectly – the crispness of the breakfast bacon, the freshness of the eggs from their hens, the homemade bread, the bowls of flowers, the fire in the guest drawing room. Traditional, comfortable bedrooms face south and overlook the garden – lap up the views in summer while birds soar and twitter, Christopher's Highland cattle peer over the fence and the chickens strut and scratch. Castle Howard and the North York Moors are in front of you and all around are abbeys, castles, rivers, ruins and woods.

Christopher & Philippa Turner
Burythorpe, Malton YO17 9LU
- £72-£90. Singles £60.
- 2: 1 double; 1 twin/double with separate bath.
- Packed lunch £6. Pubs 1.5 miles.
- 01653 658336
- www.bedandbreakfastyorkshire.co.uk

S30 10 George Street

Forget magnolia and minimalism! In a quiet pretty residential street, five minutes from York Minster, is a house (once used to lodge brewery workers) dedicated to high Victoriana. Upstairs: a huge four-poster strewn with silk cushions, candlelit sconces by a deep, deep bath, and Crivelli's *The Annunciation* on the wall. Downstairs: a panelled sitting room with dark leather sofas, and a dining room, splendid with oak refectory table and chandeliers. There are more bedrooms – some gentler, a sleek kitchen and a pretty gravelled yard with teak seating. All this, and a parking permit with the house (gold dust in York).

Heather Robinson
Walmgate, York YO1 9QB
- £1230 per week.
- Townhouse for 6.
- Self-catering.
- 01484 841330
- www.10georgestreet.com

19th century when the role of horn-blower was passed down the Metcalfe family. An old cow horn dating back to 1611 was replaced in 1864 with the present one, a huge African buffalo horn that resides in the Rose and Crown Hotel. Starting on 27 September, which is the feast of the Holy Rood for those that don't know, a long, clear blast of the horn echoes around the dale each evening, and continues to brighten the winter nights until Shrovetide the following February.

Corn Mill Tea Room Bainbridge ☎ 01969 650212. Within earshot of the River Bain. Lunches, afternoon tea and snacks. Open Easter–Oct.
Schoolhouse Farm Stalling Busk ☎ 01969 650233. A small tea shop and mini-museum on a farm that produces its own 'Raydale Preserves'. Have a cuppa and a slice of homemade cake and then take away a jar of jam or chutney for later. Open May–Oct.

⑥ Semer Water

Natural lakes are in short supply in Yorkshire so consequently the few that exist tend to earn undeserved fame. Semer Water, in little Raydale, is trumpeted as the largest lake in North Yorkshire but at less than half a mile long it is not going to excite anyone who has visited the Lake District. It is also supposed to conceal a drowned town under its surface, but with a maximum depth of 30 feet it could scarcely hide a solitary two-storey building. Having said all that, Semer Water is a gorgeous place, a haven for winter wildfowl and summer watersports with a rich enough mix of marshland wildlife to prompt the Yorkshire Wildlife Trust to declare it a nature reserve.

The sinking town

The legend of the flooded town, whilst patently not true, is an entertaining moral homily. The gist of the story is that a wandering saint visited bustling Semer Town disguised as a pauper and begging food and shelter. He was rudely turned away from every house save that of a poor, old couple who treated him like one of the family. The following day he cursed the town with the words:
'Semer Water rise! Semer Town sink!
And bury the place all save the house
Where they gave me meat and drink.'

There is car parking at the north end of the lake, for a small fee in summer, but for peace and quiet head down to the other end. This is where the wetland nature reserve is, a glorious place to explore in early summer with the spongy ground festooned with water-loving plants, nothing very rare, but a wide variety including marsh valerian, bog bean, ragged robin, marsh cinquefoil and marsh and spotted orchids, with yellow water-lilies on the open water. Crooks Beck wriggles its way through the marsh to empty into Semer Water, but when it emerges at the other end of the lake it is now known as the River Bain. Its 1½-mile journey to the River Ure makes it the shortest river in England, but in that brief distance it does manage to boast a population of native crayfish and some of the finest brown-trout fishing in the Dales.

⑦ Aysgarth

This is an odd split-site village with the main settlement, presumably the original 'clearing in the oaks', half a mile away from the most visited buildings clustered around the famous Aysgarth Falls. **St Andrew's Church** is here, on the hillside overlooking **Yore Mill** and the river. The church is the probable

original reason for the separation; it is a restored 16th-century building but almost certainly on an older religious site, maybe even pagan, connected with the Falls. It was at the height of its influence in medieval times when the building was owned by Jervaulx Abbey. It is the River Ure that most people come here to see,

or more specifically, its 200-foot descent in the space of less than half a mile that constitutes the **Aysgarth Falls**. There is no single spectacular drop but a series of limestone terraced steps at High Force, Middle Force, Lower Force and a further unnamed waterfall lower down – let's call it Bottom Force. Come here after a dry spell and you will wonder what all the fuss is about but if the river is full the name 'force' becomes more meaningful and the roar of the combined drops can be heard a long way away.

However big and brown the Ure is, the riverside walking is a delight, and accessible for wheelchairs and pushchairs all the way to Middle Force. The only drawback for me is the crowds; it can get very busy with the adjacent National Park visitor centre attracting its quota of visitors. It's not too difficult to find a little solitude though, as most people stroll to the falls and back on the north bank. If you walk through the churchyard and down to the river on the other side you may well find that you have it to yourself. Alternatively, head away from the river into Freeholders' Wood where the National Park have reinstated a traditional hazel-coppicing system and are currently encouraging the return of the common dormouse to its preferred habitat. Look out for their nest boxes in the shrubbery.

Beyond the woods, a choice of **footpaths** can take you to the villages north of Aysgarth and the river; Carperby with its fine pub, the Wheatsheaf, and old market cross; Redmire, the present terminus of the Wensleydale Railway; and

Castle Bolton. South of the river the main valley is joined by the tributary Bishopdale and, slightly removed downstream, the village of West Witton.

Close to the falls, **Yore Mill** is an imposing four-storey building built in 1784, the same year as Gayle Mill (see page 81). It is not quite so precious to industrial archaeologists as it was substantially rebuilt in 1852 after a fire, but it still merits Grade II listed status. It has changed jobs through its long life, cotton spinning first, then knitting yarn and later corn grinding and flour rolling. For ten years after milling finished in the 1950s Yore Mill was a cattle food depot and until recently a horse-drawn carriage museum. At present it just houses a teashop but the owners have plans to restore the building, wheel and turbines to generate power again. Let's hope they manage it.

A big and once-important church with a four-acre churchyard that is reputedly the largest in the country, **St Andrew's Church** was at its most influential during medieval times when the church was owned by Jervaulx Abbey (see page 95). Its present claims to fame are the old abbey rood screen and vicar's stall that were moved here at the time of the dissolution. This work of art was too valuable to dismantle so was carried the 13 miles in one piece on the shoulders of 20 men.

George and Dragon Inn Aysgarth ☎ 01969 663358 ⌂ www.georgeanddragonaysgarth.co.uk. A Grade II listed 17th-century coaching inn with separate bar and restaurant. Excellent food is a mixture of traditional local and fine cuisine. Beer is all brewed in Wensleydale (Black Sheep and Yorkshire Dales beers) and the wine selection extensive. Can get packed; open all day.

Kitty's Tea Rooms Aysgarth ☎ 01969 663423. Very welcoming and comfortable. Open Wed-Sun.

Mill Race Teashop Aysgarth Falls ☎ 01969 663446 ⌂ www.millraceteashop.co.uk. Great views of Upper Falls. Twenty different teas, outrageous hedonistic hot chocolate, real coffee and homemade cakes and scones. Also selling local produce.

⑧ Castle Bolton and Redmire

'My name is Sir Richard le Scrope and I have a licence to crenellate,' sounds like a line John Cleese could have uttered in *Monty Python and the Holy Grail*, but truth can be stranger than fiction. Sir Richard was the builder in 1379 and like all 14th-century castle-builders, he needed a licence to put turrets on his towers.

Bolton Castle (01969 623981; www.boltoncastle.co.uk) is a particularly rewarding place to visit, partly because it is so complete, but also because it is privately owned so hasn't had the corporate treatment some historic buildings suffer. The owner has considerable emotional investment in the place because, incredibly, the castle has remained in one family throughout its entire 600-year history. Harry Orde-Powlett, the present 8th Lord Bolton, is a direct descendant of Sir Richard the Crenellator. Incidentally, the building is Bolton Castle and the village it's in is Castle Bolton.

There is so little damage to the fabric of the building because the royalist defenders surrendered after six months of passive siege in the Civil War, during another Pythonesque episode in the castle's history. Colonel Chaytor, the commander of the Royalists, apparently cut off his own hand and threw it at his enemies in an extreme gesture of defiance but, not surprisingly, this didn't work and the siege continued, with the defenders finally giving up after eating their last horse. The Scropes regained the castle after Cromwell's demise but moved out to the newly constructed luxury mansion of Bolton Hall near Wensley and the castle became a block of flats of sorts with up to nine families living in it up until the 1940s.

Now uninhabited, the castle has been developed as an excellent visitor attraction (open April to October), with the bulk of it restored and accessible. Much is made of Castle Bolton's most illustrious past resident, Mary, Queen of Scots, who spent an eventful six months here in 1568 after her capture by Queen Elizabeth's forces in Scotland. She was ostensibly imprisoned, but local Catholic sympathisers made her stay very comfortable, supplying cart-loads of tapestries, Turkish carpets, luxury clothes and venison – certainly not the conditions that the wretches in the dungeons had to suffer .

The gardens have been re-laid along medieval lines including a herb garden, maze, bowling green, rose garden and what must be one of the most northerly vineyards in the country. Regular special events are held throughout the year, such as armada or medieval weekends, which involve lots of dressing up and period activities – the kids will probably love them, and you can leave them to it while you visit the gift shop and tea room.

A choice of two roads or two footpaths will take you downhill from Castle Bolton to its near neighbour, **Redmire**. This village's oldest resident is the Wesley Oak, leaning heavily on its props at the village green, and named after the famous preacher who spoke from beneath its spreading branches over 200 years ago. What brings most people to Redmire is the **Wensleydale Railway**, this being the present terminus of the line. If you have arrived by rail, and have time to kill before your train back, a three-mile circular walk taking in the ancient sunken track of Thoresby Lane and Castle Bolton is an excellent way to do it.

The Wensleydale railway

'I have a dream', one famous speech began, and so do the volunteers of the Wensleydale Railway Association (WRA). Their aim is to restore the rail link along the full 40-mile length of their beloved valley, from the East Coast Main Line at Northallerton, to the Settle–Carlisle line at Garsdale. This is not just a nostalgia trip by a group of middle-aged beardy types, or a cynical money-making tourist trap, but a genuine attempt to return the service that the local dales-people felt should never have been taken away. 'We'd love our railway to become the branch line it was in the 1920s and 30s', said David Walker, one of the WRA volunteers, 'A thread linking all the communities of the dale from schoolchildren and commuters to tourists coming to visit this lovely part of the world.'

At present, 17 miles of operating line is marooned in the middle, between Leeming Bar and Redmire. Joining up the eastern end should be the easiest task, as it's only five miles to Northallerton, and the track is still in place and used for freight transport – the MOD bringing tanks to Catterick Garrison in the main. The major long-term project will be the re-laying of 18 miles of track from Redmire, the present terminus, to Garsdale Head. This would mean the reopening of stations in Askrigg and Hawes eventually, but the first goal is the next stop along the line after Redmire–Aysgarth.

'It's definitely a labour of love', said David. 'None of us would put this amount of hard work in for free if we didn't enjoy it. It takes my head away from the day job and I've made a lot of new friends from all sorts of backgrounds – and contrary to popular perception, none of them are oddball eccentrics!'

⑨ Bishopdale

Few people are aware of Bishopdale, and even of those that are, not many stop and enjoy its delights. They are usually on their way from Wensleydale to Wharfedale, or vice-versa, on the 'B' road that runs its length. The upper dale is almost-deserted sheep and walking country with a scattering of farms, but lower down there are three villages, each with a pub. For Newbiggin that's just about it, **Thoralby** also has a chapel, post office and waterfall and **West Burton** is a veritable metropolis with all of the above plus school, village hall, general store, butchers and craft shops. It also boasts one of the largest and most oddly shaped market crosses in the country, a strange stretched pyramid of a thing on the extremely spacious village green. What originally brought me to West Burton though, was the same feature that attracted the landscape painter J M W Turner in the 19th century. Yards from the village centre, but hidden away in its own limestone amphitheatre, is **Cauldron Falls**, a beautiful cascade formed by Walden Beck's leap over a 15-foot rock step. Good swimming can be had in the pool below when it's warm and quiet enough. A short stroll of a mile or so follows Walden Beck upstream from the waterfall to Cote Bridge, then back over fields or road to the village.

Fox and Hounds Inn West Burton ☎ 01969 663111 🖰 www.fhinn.co.uk. A 17th-century building on the village green with quoits pitch adjoining. It is the social centre of the village with something going on most evenings including darts and dominoes teams. Cask beers, John Smith's and Theakstons, with other local guest beers.

⑩ West Witton

If you have seen the film *The Wicker Man* then the goings-on here one Sunday every August will send familiar shivers down your spine. The name 'West Witton' is so innocent-sounding, and the local people are very decent really, but on St Bartholomew's Day every year they all take part in a ritual of barbaric pagan origins. It's called the Burning of Bartle and re-enacts supposed real historical events when a local criminal is chased, caught and burned at the stake in place of a sacrificial lamb. The route of the chase is recounted in a chanted verse:

> *On Penhill crags he tore his rags*
> *At Hunters Thorn he blew his horn*
> *At Capplebank Stee he brak his knee*
> *At Grassgill Beck he brak his neck*
> *At Wadhams End he couldn't fend*
> *At Grassgill End we'll mak his end*
> *SHOUT LADS SHOUT!*

To the accompaniment of a rousing cheer from the crowd, a straw effigy is set alight and everyone marches, singing, to the pub for a pint or two – it's very sinister stuff. This traditional ceremony has been carried out for at least 400 years and the villagers are very proud of it, so much so that the local youth club, with help from Rural Arts, North Yorkshire, produced a series of mosaic tiles telling the story. They are in place up on the hillside making up a trail which you can follow during a pleasant four-mile fell walk.

S▷ Wensleydale Heifer West Witton ☎ 01969 622322
🖰 www.wensleydaleheifer.co.uk. I nearly didn't get past the tacky pub sign, and what a mistake that would have been. This is a fantastic fish restaurant in a pub, miles from the sea, not cheap but top quality. Black Sheep beer.

Lower Wensleydale: Wensley to Bedale

⑪ Wensley

In 1956 schoolchildren made a strange discovery in Holy Trinity churchyard, a seemingly deliberately buried market cross. This odd ritual of laying to rest the symbol of a town's identity encapsulates Wensley's sad history and explains why Wensleydale is named after such a tiny village. In the 14th and 15th centuries this was the market town for the whole of the dale, but in 1563 the plague struck and Wensley was particularly badly hit. Most inhabitants died, others moved to nearby Leyburn and certainly no one had any intention of visiting the market. There was probably nothing to sell anyway, the parish crop register noting grimly, 'This year nothing set down.' Wensley has never fully recovered its former importance and, but for Lord Bolton building his hall nearby, might have faded away completely. Now it is one of the most appealing of the dale's villages, and well worth a visit.

The old church is still there, along with the village pub and a Victorian watermill which now houses a traditional candle maker. **White Rose Candle Workshop** (01969 623544; www.whiterosecandles.co.uk) has been the White family business since 1978, producing traditional beeswax and other candles of all shapes, sizes, designs and scents. It is a fascinating experience, and one that I found strangely relaxing, to watch the candles being made. Admission is free and you can also enjoy the small waterfall by the side of the mill. The workshop is open on various Fridays, Saturdays and Sundays throughout the year – check before you go.

🔟 **The Three Horseshoes** Wensley 📞 01969 622327
🍴 www.3horseshoeswensley.com. This cosy village inn is a beer drinkers' pub with a good changing range of well-kept Yorkshire cask ales. Open every evening and most lunchtimes.

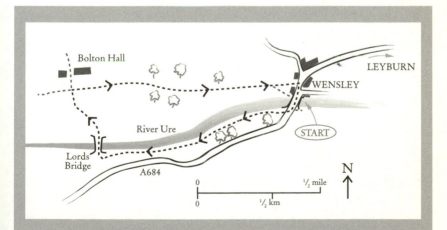

A Ure-side stroll

Very gentle walking starts from Wensley, either up or down the nearby River Ure. If you head upstream (westwards) for a mile along the south bank and over Lords Bridge you can return via Bolton Hall, which isn't open to the public but a public footpath passes right between the hall outbuildings – I'm sure Lord Bolton loves that!

⑫ Leyburn

This pleasant and, seemingly, always busy market town is easily the largest settlement in this part of lower Wensleydale though it has limited attractions of its own. I like Leyburn but I must admit I can't be entertained for very long within the town itself. It desperately tries to borrow a bit of history from Bolton Castle in its Leyburn Shawl story, where Mary, Queen of Scots was said to have escaped from Bolton Castle but dropped her shawl on the cliffs above Leyburn, thus betraying her whereabouts and causing her recapture. Wishful balderdash I'm afraid; Leyburn Shawl Crag's name is much older than the Tudors and has its root in the word 'shielings' or shepherds' huts. Retracing the queen's supposed footsteps back along the Shawl top to the castle makes a splendid walk though, with glorious panoramic views.

No, Leyburn is not an historical centre but it is an effective service centre for the dale with the wide variety of shops, a market every Friday and a farmers' market every fourth Saturday of the month. It also has one of the largest **antiques auction rooms** in the country in the form of Tennants (Harmby Road; 01969 623780; www.tennants.co.uk). The town hosts two big annual events: the Wensleydale Show on August bank holiday Saturday and the Dales Festival of Food and Drink on May Day weekend are both a real treat.

Just downstream of Leyburn and Middleham, the River Ure is joined by the River Cover, the latter having just navigated the length of Coverdale, another little valley on a par with Bishopdale for unspoiled pastoral peace.

Penley's Coffee Shop Market Place ☎01969 623909. Particularly good cappuccino and some very tasty and good-value snacks. Open daily 09.00–17.00 (10.00–16.00 Sun) also evenings Fri and Sat.

Rupali Balti House High St ☎01969 624863/624861; also deserves a mention as one of the best takeaway curry houses I have encountered anywhere in Yorkshire.

S⦿ Sandpiper Inn Railway St ☎01969 622206 ⌂ www.sandpiperinn.co.uk. One of Leyburn's oldest buildings is home to its best food, courtesy of host/chef Jonathan Harrison. Menus are based on local farm produce and game, expertly prepared and reasonably priced. Not especially a drinkers' pub unless your tipple is malt whisky with over 100 to choose from. Closed Mon.

Serendipity Tearooms High St ☎01969 625388. A different sort of place on the first floor over a crafty gift shop. Open daily 10.00–16.45.

⑬ Middleham

Two miles south of Leyburn and perched on high land between the rivers Ure and Cover, sits the village of Middleham. It has three links with royalty: the childhood home of a king, royal treasure and the sport of kings. The impressive remains on the edge of the village are, in fact, Middleham Castle mark two, its predecessor still visible as a mound on William's Hill just south and up the slope. Richard III was brought up here as a lad in the 15th century under the tutelage of the Earl of Warwick. It was then that he met the Earl's daughter Anne, whom he later married, thus inheriting the castle on Warwick's death. He became king on the death of his brother Edward IV in 1483 but

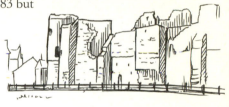

his reign was a short and miserable one. Within the space of two years his only son died in the castle aged 11, his wife went the same way the following year aged 28, and he also uttered those famous words, 'A horse, a horse, my kingdom for a horse,' at the Battle of Bosworth. He didn't get his horse but lost the battle, his kingdom and his life aged 31. We have Shakespeare to thank for the quote and the all-round impression of a vindictive, malicious and selfish character. Modern historians are of the view that the Bard was trying to impress the reigning Tudors with his writing and that Richard was quite a nice chap on the whole. The villagers would certainly agree; their local king is still remembered with much affection and a requiem mass is said in the village church annually on 22 August, the anniversary of his death.

Blue Lion East Witton, DL8 4SN ℂ 01969 624273 ⏏ www.thebluelion.co.uk. Between Middleham and Jervaulx Abbey on the A6108, this old coaching inn is an almost perfect blend of flag-floored, open-fired village pub bar and country house hotel. Whilst the beer is fine, Black Sheep and other local cask ales, the emphasis is on the food which is wholesome traditional fare of fantastic quality. Not cheap but worth it.
White Swan Market Place ℂ 01969 622093 ⏏ www.whiteswanhotel.co.uk. Pleasant old coaching inn right in the centre of Middleham; very decent bar food, plus a range of Yorkshire beers.

The Middleham Jewel

A right royal treasure was found near the castle in 1985 by Ted Seaton, an amateur metal detector. He was about to pack up and go home when his machine picked up a faint signal from just over a foot beneath the soil surface. Ted dug out what he thought was an old compact box and took it home to clean. It was then he discovered what he had; a diamond-shaped gold pendant inlaid with a single sapphire and exquisitely engraved with a scene of the Trinity and a Latin charm against 'falling sickness' (epilepsy). The Middleham Jewel, as it has come to be known, was bought by the Yorkshire Museum in York (see page 261) for the tidy sum of £2.5 million.

An almost perfectly straight two-mile stretch of bridleway leads from Middleham over Low Moor to the west, and on the map it looks like a deserted trackway ideal for a peaceful walk or bike ride. If you do venture up, solitude you won't find but entertainment you will, as on most days, scores of racehorses thunder up and down it on their way to or from the old racecourse on High Moor. There hasn't been an official race here since 1873 but the training tradition, once started, continued. Today no fewer than 15 stables operate in and around Middleham, making it one of the biggest horse-racing centres in the country. If you want to see more than just the horses around the lanes and on the gallops, then pay a small fee and book on a morning stable tour (07775 568374).

⑭ Coverdale

Medieval monks and nuns sought out beautiful and isolated places for their abbeys and priories so it's no surprise that ecclesiastical remains are scattered around Coverham and East Scrafton in this valley. Middleham Church is dedicated to the nun St Alkelda (see page 33); perhaps she was a resident of the abbey in Coverdale. Little documentary evidence has been found concerning the Premonstratensian order (Ordo Praemonstratensis) that lived here – I suspect because few people could either spell or pronounce the name. Coverdale is still relatively isolated and definitely beautiful, a hidden corner some may call it, which is apt because its most popular attraction is the **Forbidden Corner**, a fantasy-based series of mazes and follies in the four-acre garden of an old racing horse stables, Tupgill Park.

The Forbidden Corner

This place in Coverdale, west of Middleham, quite justifiably advertises itself as 'The Strangest Place in the World'. It is brilliantly unique and although it was voted top family day out in a national survey, beating Alton Towers and Legoland, it was never intended as anything more than a private family folly. It was the brainchild of the owner of Tupgill Park, Colin Armstrong, who in the 1980s teamed up with architect Malcolm Tempest to design a series of walled gardens, tunnels, grottoes and towers which linked into a three-dimensional maze for his family and friends to explore. As it developed it was opened to the public and its fame spread by word of mouth, to the point now where it can barely cope with its own popularity.

What makes it so good is that it is a genuine adventure. On arrival you are given a leaflet which is not a map, but a series of cryptic messages. 'All the clues to finding your way around are on the sheet,' a girl at the reception said, 'They're just not in the right order.' The entrance through the gaping mouth of a giant stone monster sets the tone and away you go. I first came here in the early days when my children were small and they absolutely loved it. We spent hours climbing, crawling, getting lost, studying clues, groping along dark corridors, planning routes from battlement viewpoints, getting lost again and finally finding the way to the underground temple. At times I was genuinely unnerved, for example by the revolving room with identical doors, and after two subsequent visits, some secret corners have still managed to evade me.

This is a must-see place, especially if you have children, but I would strongly recommend coming at less busy times to make the most of the sense of exploration.

The Forbidden Corner Tupgill Park Estate, Coverham, DL8 4TJ ☎ 01969 640638 ⌂ www.theforbiddencorner.co.uk. Open daily Apr–Oct and Sun only Nov–Christmas. Under 4s free. Tickets have to be booked in advance online or by phone, or bought on the day from Leyburn Tourist Information Centre if there are any left.

⑮ Constable Burton

You will find this village three miles east of Leyburn on the Bedale road. If you have been looking for it you probably intend to visit the Wyvill Arms pub for some of its very good food, or the Wyvill family home at **Constable Burton Hall** (01677 450428; www.constableburtongardens.co.uk). If you end up near Hull in East Yorkshire, your sat nav has taken you to Burton Constable not Constable Burton – an easy mistake and you're not the first! The hall is a Grade I listed neo-classical Georgian mansion set in a large landscaped park. It is the park and gardens that most people come to visit, partly because they are attractive, and well worth the entrance fee, but mainly because the hall is not usually open to the public.

Constable Burton Hall Gardens ☎ 01677 450428 ⌂ www.constableburtongardens.co.uk. Gardens open daily mid-Mar–Sep; wheelchair access. Hall open for pre-booked groups of 25 or over only.

⑯ Jervaulx Abbey

This abbey suffered more than most under Henry VIII's violent Dissolution and sadly, very little of it remains. It was a very influential daughter house of the Cistercian Byland Abbey (see page 221) with the original French monks probably responsible for starting cheese making in Wensleydale. What remains today are peaceful and atmospheric ruins which the private owners have allowed to become overgrown by 180 species of wild plants – a lovely floral oasis. Entrance is every day of the year by honesty-box payment. The tea rooms and gift shop on the opposite side of the road are open mid-March–October.

Brymor Ice Cream

At High Jervaulx Farm, above the abbey, the Cistercian monks' dairy-produce tradition continues; not cheese nowadays but ice cream. Brymor Ice Cream is available throughout Yorkshire in 30 flavours but what makes it so popular is its rich creaminess – how do they do it? The answer is pedigree Guernsey cows and lush Dales pasture. Brymor is one of the few on-farm producers of ice cream that only uses milk from the farm's own herd so they can guarantee the provenance of the product, and its richness – Guernsey cow milk has one of the highest fat contents of any available. There are three ways you can sample the delights of rum and raisin, experiment with mocha almond crunch or remember nostalgic childhoods with traditional vanilla. You can look out for Brymor Ice Cream served in cafés and restaurants in Yorkshire, you can buy it from good delis and farmers' markets or you can call in to High Jervaulx Farm and get it fresh. Either relax and eat it here in the conservatory or take it away along with some clotted cream and cheese if you wish.

⑰ Bedale

Yet another town that dubs itself 'Gateway to the Dales', Bedale does have a justifiable claim as far as Wensleydale is concerned. If you enter the dale from the east, off the A1, or by train on the Wensleydale Railway, you will pass through this ancient market town.

Bedale is quite small and all the interest is concentrated on the long, thin marketplace, and the beck-side that runs parallel, so you can see just about everything on a half-mile stroll up one and down the other. The best place to start is Bedale Hall at the top of the market, opposite the church, as this is where the town's small, free Bedale Museum is housed (01677 423797, open April to September) – a collection of bygones amassed over half a century and featuring an 18th-century wooden fire engine; from the adjacent tourist office you can pick up a heritage trail leaflet. I couldn't help but notice St Gregory's Church next door, and the disproportionate size of its tower. Apparently this most fortified church in the north of England was refuge for the townsfolk when the Scots came rampaging. Emgate leads from the 14th-century market cross down to the beck, which was part canalised in the 19th-century to link Bedale with the River Swale, but abandoned when the railway arrived. The Harbour, a canal basin, is a reminder of these times gone, but nowhere near as impressive as the small square brick building on the far bank. This Grade II listed structure is unique; Britain's only remaining leech house, a store place for apothecaries' wriggly medical helpers.

Wandering back up the mainly Georgian, cobbled marketplace gives the opportunity for some browsing, especially on Tuesday's market day when the town's five pubs are at their atmospheric bustling best too. Of the four cafés, Aunt Sally's is probably the best.

Aunt Sally's Café Market Place, Bedale ☎ 01677 426634. Probably the best, certainly the busiest, in town.

Big Sheep Little Cow Aiskew Farm, DL8 1AW ☎ 01677 422125
🖰 www.bigsheeplittlecow.com. A bit of a 'fast' children's attraction with an adventure play area and buggy rides, but its slow credentials are earned with farm tours and home-produced ewes' milk for sale. On the eastern edge of Bedale.

⑱ Thorp Perrow Arboretum

What initially brought me to this place south of Bedale was joining a fungus foray event, to learn the useful skill of how not to poison myself eating wild mushrooms. In the process I was captivated by the autumn colours of the trees and shrubs planted by the Arboretum's creator Sir Leonard Roper and also enjoyed a fascinating display of falconry at the bird centre. Other regular events that take place include photography courses, ghost walks, seasonal nature trails and outdoor concerts, and you can call in the Arboretum's tea room and gift shop without paying the entrance fee.

Thorp Perrow Arboretum ☎ 01677 425323 🖰 www.thorpperrow.com. Open all year.
Castle Arms Inn Top of the Green, Snape, DL8 2TB ☎ 01677 470270
🖰 www.castlearmsinn.com. A friendly, low-ceilinged, flagstoned village pub, just south of Thorp Perrow Arboretum. The menu is extensive, good value and top quality. Beer from Jennings and Marstons.

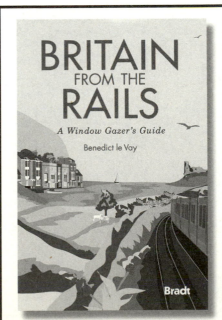

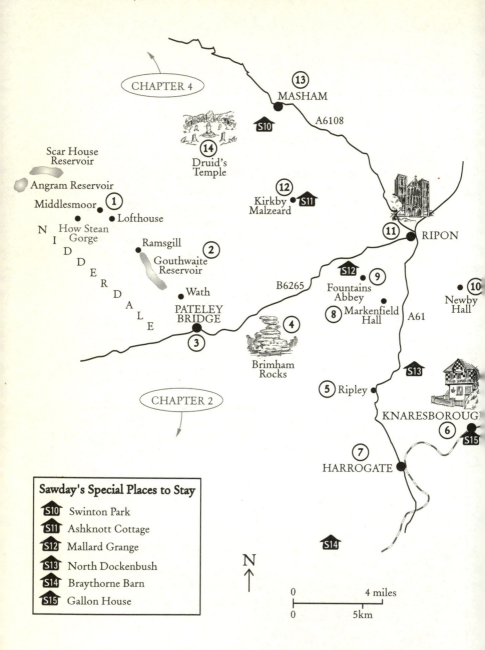

CHAPTER 4

(13) MASHAM

A6108

S10

Scar House
Reservoir

Angram Reservoir

Middlesmoor (1)

• Lofthouse

N
I How Stean
D Gorge
D
E
R
D
A
L
E

• Ramsgill (2)

Gouthwaite
Reservoir

• Wath

PATELEY
BRIDGE

(3)

(14)
Druid's
Temple

(12)
Kirkby
Malzeard S11

RIPON

(11)

B6265

Fountains
Abbey S12 (9)

(8) Markenfield
Hall

A61

Newby (10)
Hall

(4)

Brimham
Rocks

(5) Ripley

S13

KNARESBOROUG

CHAPTER 2

(6)

S15

(7)

HARROGATE

Sawday's Special Places to Stay

S10 Swinton Park
S11 Ashknott Cottage
S12 Mallard Grange
S13 North Dockenbush
S14 Braythorne Barn
S15 Gallon House

S14

N
↑

0   4 miles
|————————————|
0   5km

NIDDERDALE, HARROGATE AND AROUND

5. NIDDERDALE, HARROGATE AND AROUND

Caroline Mills

Swaledale, Wensleydale or Wharfedale would, I'm sure, be the first to be mentioned if someone was asked to name one of the Yorkshire Dales in a pub quiz. But Nidderdale? It tends to play second or even third fiddle to the more well-known Dales. That tends to be because it isn't actually in the area designated as the Yorkshire Dales National Park at all, but sits alongside the national park.

With its lesser status, the main throng of tourists tend to bypass Nidderdale, heading straight for the National Park. That's great for those who enjoy a little extra peace and quiet. In Nidderdale, the lack of people is evident by comparison with other dales in the Park.

Nidderdale is therefore something of an anomaly to the rest of the Yorkshire Dales and yet it is almost impossible to fathom out why it hasn't been included within the park boundary. The countryside around Nidderdale is still spectacularly beautiful, and important enough to be granted the status of an Area of Outstanding Natural Beauty (AONB). The hills that fall across the border between national park and AONB status are the same hills making up the same landscape after all.

Yet Nidderdale is a game of two halves. To the northwest, and closest to the Yorkshire Dales National Park, lies Upper Nidderdale. It's an area that becomes increasingly rugged and remote the further back along the valley you go. It pulls you like a magnet, drawing you further into its midst, tempting you with an ever-changing panorama at every turn, rise and fall. With only one small road that leads to nowhere, the hills of Little Whernside and its giant neighbour Great Whernside creating a wall between Nidderdale and Coverdale, there is no through traffic, unless you happen to be on foot or on the hoof. A string of pearly reservoirs line the route of the River Nidd from the foot of its source, Great Whernside. These watering holes, quenching the thirst of residents in far-flung Bradford, are interspersed with other jewels – tiny hamlets filled with residents going about their daily business. The place is so remote that a good guess would be required as to why anyone should have set up camp here years ago but now they have, it's easy to understand – a quality of life that surpasses many others with peace and fantastic views.

Further east, Nidderdale bottoms out, the hills recede and the land becomes flatter – just. At least, the undulations are less undulating, the distance between villages decreases and the land becomes more cultivated. It's not until you reach **Knaresborough**, a good thirty miles from the river's source (and even longer if you stretched out the Nidd's meandering tendencies into a pencil-straight line), that you get any serious habitation although the elegant town of **Harrogate**, joined at the hip with Knaresborough on its eastern side, is now disastrously sprawling further north and west towards the edge of Nidderdale AONB with a plethora of rather ordinary-looking housing developments.

Past Knaresborough, the Nidd continues for a few more meandering miles east before it disappears for good, its waters mingling with those of the more northerly Swale and Ure to form the mightier Ouse.

The Nidderdale AONB also swallows up the most southeasterly section of Wensleydale. Like its counterpart of Upper Nidderdale, the land furthest west begins harsh and inhospitable on top of Masham Moor before it drops down to greener pastures, great swathes of estate forests and a web of tiny tributaries that gurgle towards the Ure.

For this reason, Masham and Ripon, officially part of Wensleydale, are mentioned within this chapter but, for now, I'll stay with the upper reaches of Nidderdale before moving slowly southeast, just as the River Nidd does, towards Knaresborough and its neighbour, Harrogate.

Tourist information

Harrogate Royal Baths, Crescent Rd ✆ 0845 389 3223 ⌖ www.enjoyharrogate.com.
Knaresborough 9 Castle Courtyard ✆ 0845 389 0177
⌖ www.enjoyknaresborough.com.
Masham Little Market Place ✆ 01765 680200 ⌖ www.visitmasham.com
Nidderdale AONB ⌖ www.visitnidderdaleaonb.com.
Pateley Bridge (for Nidderdale) 8 High St ✆ 01423 711147
⌖ www.enjoyyorkshiredales.com.

Getting there and around

Public transport

The most remote parts of **Upper Nidderdale** and the villages to the east are only accessible by car unless, that is, you take a bus as far as you can and then walk or cycle. For example, the **Scar House** and **Angram** reservoirs, a beautiful spot to walk at the very tip of Upper Nidderdale, are seven miles from Pateley Bridge. The **Dales Explorer** bus will take you as far as **Lofthouse** but from there you need to make the remainder of the two-mile journey to the reservoirs on foot or bicycle.

However the **Dales Explorer** bus (0871 200 22 33; www.dalesbus.org) will get you to most places and will often provide a very scenic journey too. On bank holidays and weekends, the **Nidderdale Rambler** travels to particular attractions such as **Brimham Rocks**, **Gouthwaite Reservoir** and **How Stean Gorge**. Many of these depart from **Harrogate** and **Pateley Bridge**, the latter seen as the gateway to Upper Nidderdale. To really encourage the use of public transport, many cafés, pubs, attractions and bed and breakfasts in the area have signed up to the 'Dales Bus Discount Scheme', offering special deals on drinks, meals and accommodation.

Travelling between the towns of Harrogate, Knaresborough, Pateley Bridge and Ripon is easy with several bus services from which to take your pick. **Transdev** (01423 566061; www.harrogateanddistrict.co.uk) operate several routes between Harrogate, Knaresborough and Ripon, including some of the outlying villages. **Ripley**, famous for its castle and estate-owned village, is accessible on the Transdev 36 route from Ripon to Harrogate. Transdev offer a 'daygold' ticket, providing unlimited travel on all their local bus routes for a day. A train service run by **Northern Rail** (0845 0000125; www.northernrail.org) also connects Harrogate and Knaresborough to York and Leeds.

Walking

Nidderdale has some great walking territory with spectacular views and scenery. There are opportunities for all, with many pre-planned short and medium-length routes across easy-going ground, which make good options for families. Wheelchair users can get out and about too at places like **Scar House**, where approximately two miles of the

four-mile route around the reservoir is totally accessible. For walkers who like to stretch their legs, the **Nidderdale Way** trips its way over 53 miles of ground in a circular route that officially starts in Pateley Bridge. It provides the opportunity to walk around the uplands that nurture the juvenile River Nidd and along the riverbank to the greener pastures of lower-lying land further east. The route quite deliberately wiggles about a bit to take in some worthwhile landmarks such as Brimham Rocks and Ripley Castle but it also links up with many other footpaths and bridleways to provide more localised circular routes for those who don't wish to hike the full distance.

If you'd prefer being part of a group, the **Dalesbus Ramblers** (www.dalesbusramblers.org.uk) organise a number of free, guided walks around the area that are all accessible by bus. Simply catch the bus to the starting point.

Harrogate and **Knaresborough** have some rewarding town walks too, which I will cover later; they can be particularly good for those with mobility issues, taking advantage of tarmac footpaths and pavements.

Cycling

A free **bike-carrying service** is offered on the **Nidderdale Rambler** bus service (see page 100) from Harrogate and Pateley Bridge to Upper Nidderdale and Brimham Rocks although only three bikes per bus can be taken.

With so many lumps and bumps in the landscape, a few gears on the bike are necessary – even along the flatter stretches of the river valley. There's limited opportunity for **off-road cycling** around the cluster of villages and hamlets on the eastern side of the dale, with gentler slopes and quiet country lanes connecting them, makes it easy to join the dots on the map, and there are a few extremely scenic, if arduous, bridleways high above on the moor. And there's always the odd pub or tearooms to experience a bit of convivial communal spirit when you're thirsty.

In **Harrogate** and **Knaresborough**, there are lots of **cycle routes** to get around town. Harrogate Town Council has produced a network map for each town, which can be downloaded from their website (www.harrogate.gov.uk). The **Beryl Burton Cycle Way**, named after the seven-times world champion, connects Harrogate with Knaresborough along a 1½-mile stretch of traffic-free cycle path, thereby avoiding the need to use the busy A59. One suspects the great Beryl might not have been that impressed, though – she was one of the toughest cyclists ever (of either sex) and, based on her 1973 record of 21 minutes 25 seconds for ten miles, it would have taken her less than four minutes to do the distance!

Cycle hire is available from **How Stean Gorge** (☎ 01423 755666 ✆ www.howstean.co.uk) in the heart of Upper Nidderdale. Young families are well catered for too, hiring out child seats and tagalongs.

Secure covered **cycle parking** in Harrogate is available at both the Jubilee and Victoria (next to the bus and railway station) car parks and there are several bicycle shops in Harrogate although **Boneshakers Cycle Shop** (11 Albert St ☎ 01423 709453 ✆ www.boneshakersbikes.co.uk) and **Spa Cycles** (1 Wedderburn Rd ☎ 01423 887003 ✆ www.spacycles.co.uk) come highly recommended for repairs and servicing.

Cycling around the Harrogate area

Formed in appreciation of a good cycle ride, **Wheel Easy!** describe themselves on their website as 'Harrogate's cycling group for people who don't wear lycra (and some who do)!' They cycle every Sunday and Wednesday morning throughout the year and Wednesday evenings during the summer with the aim of appeasing everyone who likes to get on the saddle to enjoy the countryside – distances range from a 'short' ten-mile ride to medium (twenty miles) and long-distance rides.

Encouraging families to take part is crucial for the club but safety is paramount. Therefore cyclists under the age of 18 must be accompanied by an adult and anyone under the age of 15 must be on a tandem cycle, in a child seat or on a trailer bike. There are specific all-age bike rides planned throughout the year that are traffic-free.

The club welcomes visitors to come on their weekly rides – simply turn up at

Upper Nidderdale: Nidd Head to Pateley Bridge

It makes sense to begin at the beginning – where the River Nidd dribbles out from the fells around Great Whernside. Here the land is harsh and inhospitable, where the only sign of civilisation is the odd farmstead over the top of Great Whernside in Coverdale. Much of this land has open access rights so you can walk across the upland freely.

The first sign of human activity in Nidderdale is a couple of miles downstream where the river flows through two reservoirs, first **Angram** followed by **Scar House**. Angram is the older of the two, completed in 1919, while Scar House was the last of the Nidd reservoirs to be built, in 1936. The stone to build the giant dams was quarried from around the valley either side of the reservoirs – it's still possible to see the scars – and just visible poking through the grass like a line drawing, are the scratchy remains of the old village that once housed the 1,200 workers and their families while they built Scar House reservoir.

Owned by Yorkshire Water, the two enormous lakes (Scar House is the larger of the two) supply Bradford via the Nidd Aqueduct. This is one of the most beautiful parts of Nidderdale to spend some time in; I love taking the circular walk around the reservoirs, where the view is constantly changing, as well as the light. Sheep hug the hillsides and stone walls criss-cross the landscape, the rough grasses and heathers providing a shelter for wildlife. Angram tends to be the livelier of the two, the wind whipping across the water that lashes at the dam wall. On the other side, with the river still only a trickle, Scar House is calmer. Its banks are shallower and have beach-like edges. From the top of the dam, you can look out over the wall to see just how high up you are (216 feet) from the valley floor; it does look a long way down especially when you realise that you are looking into the top branches of the deep green pine trees of Scar Plantation below, which hides some of the drowned village.

Hornbeam Park railway station (in Harrogate) at 9.30am on a Sunday (Wednesday morning times vary but usually begin at 9.30 or 10am) or 6.30pm on Wednesday evenings from May to September with a roadworthy bike and a helmet.

Said Malcolm Margolis, one of the organisers of Wheel-Easy!, 'Our name describes exactly what we do; we are all about enjoying a leisurely cycle ride, not about racing so we really welcome anyone who is visiting the area to come on our rides with us and meet any number of our 200 members.' A list of rides is posted on the Wheel Easy! website should you favour a particular route but, whichever one you select, you'll find some great cycling in good company.

Wheel-Easy! Malcolm Margolis ☎ 01423 870333 or Dave Preston ☎ 01423 566541 🖰 www.wheel-easy.org.uk.

Scar House and Angram Reservoirs circular walk

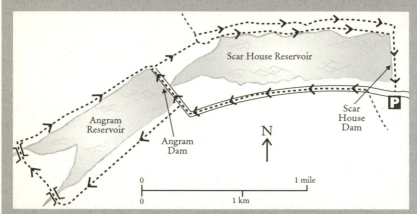

Beginning at the car park and toilets on the southeastern point of **Scar House Reservoir**, follow the tarmac track (owned by Yorkshire Water) that runs along the southern side. This section is popular with families as the walking is flat and easy, and children can zoom up and down on their bikes; it's also accessible for wheelchairs.

Continue past the end of Scar House Reservoir until you come to the Angram Dam; there's a small hut for shelter – but watch out for sheep dung on the seats; woolly beasts shelter in it too! For a longer walk (an additional 2¼ miles) carry on along the shore of **Angram Reservoir** and keep following the route around its edge until you arrive on the other side of Angram Dam. This additional section has some rough and boggy ground and crosses two bridges over rivers.

Sticking to the Scar House circular walk, cross over the Angram Dam walkway, admiring the views across Angram Reservoir to both Great and Little Whernside. At the northern end of the dam, turn right and follow the path, now with grass under your feet rather than tarmac, along the upper reaches of Scar House Reservoir. It's from here that I think you get some of the best views of the reservoir and the valley running downstream, gaining a real impression of the remoteness of the area.

Cross over a stream and continue along the well-trodden path until you come to a ladder stile and a gate. You can either turn right downhill and then left to wander along the shore of the reservoir or you can climb over the stile on your left and turn almost immediately right to follow the bumpy stone track that runs parallel with the reservoir below you. I prefer this route because you get better views along the valley both in front and behind when you turn around for a passing glance from whence you came.

Arriving at the northern tip of the Scar House Dam, cross over the top of the dam to return to the start, not forgetting to look over the top of the dam wall for a glimpse of the valley floor below. The walk is four miles in total (just over six including a trek around Angram) and is a good family walk – my three children, all under ten, managed it convincingly.

① Middlesmoor, How Stean Gorge and Lofthouse

Middlesmoor is the most far-reaching village along the Nidderdale valley; there is no other habitation beyond except the odd lonely farmstead. To reach it by road, you need to climb the 1 in 4 gradient, for the village is perched on top of a hummock, the 15th-century church of St Chad with its castellated square tower acting as a guiding beacon to onlookers. Also a guiding beacon for fell walkers stopping to sup a refreshing pint is the **Crown Hotel** (01423 755204), which, like all the other buildings, is crammed around a tiny square to prevent them sliding off the hill.

The alternative route to Middlesmoor is via the Nidderdale Way. Coming from the north you can pick up the walk at the southeast corner of Scar House Reservoir (close to the car park) and follow the path over In Moor. There's a punishing climb up the very rocky crag to begin but once on top of the moor, the scenery is simply stunning. As the reservoir disappears from view behind, the moor pans out, the purple heather in late summer an electrifying colour against a shiny blue sky. From here, the path cuts straight across the moor above the village giving views along the progressively greener Nidderdale Valley towards Gouthwaite Reservoir.

There are some wonderfully poetic names in this area. Look on a large-scale Ordnance Survey map and you come across places like Foggyshaw Barn, Limley Pastures, Beggar Moat Scar and Goyden Pot. Next on the list of fanciful names is Hard Gap Lane, close to the village of Stean. Actually Stean is no more than a few houses but what makes it famous is **How Stean Gorge**. This vast ravine with umpteen geological features is indeed impressive as a natural attraction, the waters of the How Stean Beck tumbling over giant boulders and smoothing the

limestone into bizarre creations as it flows through the towering gap before wending its way to join the River Nidd. It's impressive enough to warrant SSSI (Site of Special Scientific Interest) status, but frankly I found the entrance fee less than impressive – or rather impressively high (currently £18.50 for a family of four) – when subsequently greeted with some ramshackle metal fencing around the gorge that needed more than a coat of paint to warrant the maintenance costs. Personally, unless you want to visit the accompanying cave, I'd avoid the fee and take a glimpse of the gorge from the various footpaths, including the Nidderdale Way, that run alongside – and across – the beck.

The first village to actually straddle the Nidd is **Lofthouse**. While by no means a picture-book tourist village, it makes a good starting point for a number of walks, including a footpath that runs right alongside the Nidd. A short-cut narrow road across Masham Moor to the village of Masham also begins at Lofthouse. Even if you have no plans to go right across the moor (a nicely rugged and bleak stamping ground) take a moment to climb the steep Trapping

Hill out of Lofthouse and look back along the valley towards Gouthwaite in the southeast and further round towards the hummock of Middlesmoor in the northwest. The views towards the green pastures dotted with trees and the higher fells behind will leave a lasting impression indelibly marked in the mind.

Crown Hotel Middlesmoor is welcoming with autumnal log fires on a frosty day. Lofthouse has its own pub, also confusingly called **The Crown Hotel** (☎ 01423 755206), which is a useful stopping off point when out for a walk. Both serve ales brewed by the Black Sheep Brewery at Masham.

② Ramsgill, Gouthwaite Reservoir and Wath

Of all the villages in Upper Nidderdale, Ramsgill is the jewel. It sits at the northern head of Gouthwaite Reservoir, a grouping of comfortably proportioned stone cottages. The houses are centred around a large open green that's always immaculately kept, and a perfectly harmonious church. At its head is the striking, old shooting lodge that is now **The Yorke Arms**, iced with ivy. Also in the village is the lovely **Ramsgill Studio** (01423 755098; www.ramsgillstudio.co.uk), a small art and craft gallery exhibiting and selling work from various artists including the owner Sarah Garforth, who specialises in painting scenes of Nidderdale. Sarah also runs small and intimate workshops in her studio for painters of all abilities (or none!). It's hard to say whether such beautiful surroundings will prove inspirational or distracting.

This village too, makes a good base for a walk, the Ramsgill Beck playfully splitting the village in two, the halves joined by a tiny bridge. Wander over a second bridge that crosses the Nidd a little north of Ramsgill and follow the road to the hamlet of **Bouthwaite**. From there, on slightly higher ground, you get wonderful views towards Ramsgill with the River Nidd and **Gouthwaite Reservoir** in the foreground. You'll also cross the ghostly tracks of the old railway that once plied the workers building Angram and Scar House Reservoirs with materials.

Gouthwaite Reservoir, also supplying Bradford with water, is not a bit like its more northerly cousins. This one is long, sleek and dark, where the movement of the water is minimal except on the stormiest of days. At its head, close to Ramsgill, the reedy banks provide housing solutions for nesting waterfowl while, two-thirds along the western side, a platform has been set up for birdwatchers to sit and view the mannerisms of the native and migrating wildlife that call the reservoir home, if only for a season.

The Nidderdale Way follows right along both sides of the reservoir while the Dales Explorer bus (see page 100) stops opposite the viewing platform at weekends. There's also a pleasant picnic spot across the road, next to a small and unobtrusive car park.

At the southern end of Gouthwaite Reservoir lies the tiny hamlet of Wath, again just a few houses, this time spread out like beads along a ribbon above the river. The Nidd flows past, the Nidderdale Way following it. Crossing over both on a narrow packhorse bridge, **The Sportsman's Arms Hotel** is one of the finest watering holes to rest one's feet. It has an unusual pub sign outside but, more to the point, it has a spectacular location; the gardens, adjacent to the river, are just the place to enjoy the surrounding scenery.

Sportsman's Arms Hotel Wath ☎ 01423 711306 ⌂ www.sportsmans-arms.co.uk. Fantastic location and a beautiful building both inside and out. While the bar and garden are great for walkers, the elegant restaurant should be reserved for those without a pair of boots on. Accommodation too.

Yorke Arms Ramsgill ☎ 01423 755243 ⌂ www.yorke-arms.co.uk. Winner of several foodie awards, including a Michelin star. Accommodation too.

③ Pateley Bridge

For many visitors to the area, Nidderdale begins and ends at **Pateley Bridge**. It's as if they arrive in the town, 'do' Nidderdale within its confines and leave without going any further up the valley. Oh, what they miss, but Pateley Bridge is a very good start.

The small town is flanked on both sides by the sharply rising, beautifully green, fells on either side, the Nidd adding a very pretty decoration to the town's beauty. It is Nidderdale's gateway – there is no other route to Upper Nidderdale other than through the town – so it remains an important 'capital' to both visitors and local communities alike; Pateley Bridge is home to the annual **Nidderdale Show** (www.nidderdaleshow.co.uk), a major rural event in the area's calendar, held every autumn in Bewerley Park. It is a fantastic day that, perhaps more than anything else, epitomises the beating heart of Nidderdale and what .it means to live and work in the area.

Pateley Bridge expands outwards from its High Street, which rises steeply from the river bridge that gives the town its name. It's understandable why visitors are drawn to the place, with its quaint assemblage of little shops and eateries of every description, the breathtaking scenery and the manicured, floral riverside gardens. Follow the High Street up the hill and turn left along Church Street. If you can handle the queue that's usually filing out of the door, you can purchase a quarter of humbugs in **The Oldest Sweet Shop in England** (www.oldestsweetshop.co.uk), on the corner where the two streets meet. It has one of the largest selections of teeth-rotters and filling-pullers of yesteryear you're likely to find.

At the end of Church Street, opposite St Cuthbert's Church is the **Nidderdale Museum** (01423 711225; www.nidderdalemuseum.com). It is an absolute gem, run by volunteers and a bargain for families – children accompanied by parents enter free of charge, hence our two-hour family visit cost a couple of quid. At first, the museum appears ever so slightly stuffy – a few items from the olden days pinned up on a wall with others displayed in a glass cabinet – but from here, it simply gets better, as visitors become drawn into the fascinating world of Nidderdale life. Each exhibition is split into themed rooms exactly as you would anticipate finding them – the cobbler's shop, the joiner's shop, agriculture room, Victorian parlour, workhouse and general store all bring the area to life, with implements and exhibits donated by local people. Set aside at least an hour, but don't be surprised if you find yourself there for considerably longer.

The **Nidderdale AONB offices** are also located in the same building as the museum. There is lots of information on the walls about the AONB, its geology and environment, and also posted are details of the many countryside events that run throughout the year with relevance to the local area, from pond dipping to dragonfly walks, volunteer fence building to acorn collecting, and guided walks.

Elliots 31 High St ℓ 01423 711851 ⏷ www.elliotsdeli.co.uk. Splendid deli serving all kinds of typically deli things including many local products. Perfect for putting a picnic together.

The Willow Restaurant Park Rd ℓ 01423 711689 ⏷ www.the-willow-pateley.co.uk. Just off the High Street, down a tiny alley. I've been going to this restaurant for years and have always had a good meal.

Yorkshire Country Wines

In the giant, old stone mill at Glasshouses, a building that would seem to look more in keeping with the textile mills of South and West Yorkshire than the Dales, lies a newer industry for Nidderdale, the making of fruit wines. Actually the mill is the legacy of flax spinning, a very important industry that once thrived in Nidderdale. It now houses several small enterprises, one of which is Yorkshire Country Wines set up by Richard and Gillian Brown.

They make wines from fruit grown by local producers or gathered from hedgerows, such as elderflower, blackberry, damson and cherry. Their Visitors' Centre for wine tasting and sales, with its entrance alongside the Nidd, is housed in the old water turbine room, the turbine itself sunken twenty feet below the floor.

In the light and airy Steam Engine Room, which opens out on to a quiet terrace above the Nidd, is the tearoom. It serves delicious lunches and wonderful homemade cakes and in winter time, a good glass of their own warming mulled wassail cup around the fire in The Snug. You can walk from Pateley Bridge direct to the Visitors' Centre alongside the River Nidd (as for the walk mentioned above); it provides the perfect excuse to indulge in a piece of cake.

Yorkshire Country Wines Riverside Cellars, The Mill, Glasshouses, HG3 5QH ℓ 01423 711947 ⏷ www.yorkshirecountrywines.co.uk.

Eastern Nidderdale

East of Pateley Bridge, the land doesn't exactly flatten out but it's not quite so harsh and inhospitable. The hills and valleys begin to look very green, the stone walls that turn the hills into pastures, creating geometric patterns, all the more noticeable. Due east of Pateley Bridge is the extraordinary geological spectacle of **Brimham Rocks**. North and south of these mammoth natural sculptures are two clusters of villages. Some of these villages, in the southern cluster, lie in the Nidd's valley tucked up against the sides of the river; others cling like limpets to the sides of the hills. The northern cluster, centred around **Galphay** and **Kirkby Malzeard**, lie in the Nidderdale AONB but the streams and rivulets that drift through them link up with the River Ure, after its journey through Wensleydale.

④ Brimham Rocks

If there is ever a place to take children for some good old-fashioned life-building skills, **Brimham Rocks** is it. Sure, it may well frighten parents, anxiously watching as their children hurtle from one giant stack of boulders to the next oblivious to the potential pitfalls – literally – but it is a breath of fresh air to find a place where nature prevails and children can pretty much do as they please. They can stand and climb without red tape and risk assessments, and appreciate the magnificence, and significance, of the landscape without 'Don't' signs littering the place; the only warning is that things might be a bit slippery and you need to be aware of sudden drops.

My children love Brimham Rocks. I absolutely love Brimham Rocks. We've had magical times there jumping, climbing, respecting and appreciating. It is nature's playground and if there has to be a theme, it's rocks. These giant stacks of millstone grit, carved by glaciation, erosion and any amount of geological disturbances over more years than one can contemplate, certainly focus the imagination and they make fantastic climbing frames. Perched nearly 1,000 feet up on the heather-cloaked Brimham Moor, they also provide the most incredible views across Nidderdale. The area around the rocks is designated an SSSI (Site of Special Scientific Interest) for its surrounding plant life. Secret paths dart this way and that, the bracken and the rowan trees fighting for space, their late summer show of red berries exploding with colour against the lichen-covered darkness of the rocky giants.

The National Trust owns Brimham Rocks and entrance is free, with just a small car-park charge (free for NT members); there's a small refreshment kiosk on site. You can access the rocks at weekends by using the Dales Explorer bus (see page 100) from Pateley Bridge; the Nidderdale Way passes over Brimham Moor too.

Nidderdale Llamas

I first met Jack and Ike when they were three years old, Ike likened to a stroppy teenager despite his age. Louis was a little younger, just two years old, while Ted was the baby at 15 months, desperately trying to be more grown up like his friends. This is not the result of something in the Nidderdale water, creating a male baby boom at the hands of Suzanne Benson, though these are her babies of a sort. These are her llamas, reared and trained for pack trekking through some of the most inspirational countryside you're ever likely to see in England while with a llama! And if there is ever a perfect way to take things slowly, this has to be it.

Nidderdale Llamas is based at Kiln Farm in Wilsill, a tiny hillside village between Pateley Bridge and Summerbridge. It's run by Suzanne Benson who fell head over hooves in love with llamas when she discovered their intelligent and loving character. I discovered this character too when I took Jack and Ike out for a walk on one of Suzanne's llama treks through Nidderdale.

You don't ride llamas, but you walk with them and they carry your stuff while they amble along at the pace set by you – and sometimes by them should they find an irresistible blade or two of grass to eat on the way! I found it to be one of the most gentle and sociable ways to explore the countryside, strolling at a pace far slower than I would go during a normal hike across the hills. Having first met the llamas in their own environment and been given the opportunity to handle them before setting out on our walk, I felt confident that I knew their personalities a little bit. That tiny speck of knowledge grew into a real bond with Jack and Ike, my llamas for the day, something that is quite common as Suzanne explained during our trek. 'Llamas are very intelligent creatures. They will look you up and down (indeed they

⑤ Ripley

As the Nidd runs its course towards Knaresborough, the dale broadens, turning from bleak moorland to shallow hills dotted with farmsteads and small villages. This is perhaps the kind of landscape that most would associate with the Dales – a gentle river of no great size and a rolling countryside of emerald green that's broken up by stone walls built to a Dales spec.

There is one village that surpasses all others in this area for attracting the tourists – Ripley, three miles north of Harrogate. Upon entering Ripley, signs announce the village lays claim to a famous ice-cream. Actually it's **Ripley Castle** (01423 770152; www.ripleycastle.co.uk) for which the place is famous, the rather beautiful home of the Ingilby family, taking centre place within the small, estate-owned village. While the interior is attractive and the associations with British history are impressive, it's actually the exterior that appeals to me:

did), weigh you up as to whether they can be mischievous while in your care and will work with you as you walk. They are very easy to handle. We have had a very elderly woman who came to trek with the llamas and likewise, a wheelchair-bound visitor who was blind. There was something about the llamas' instinct, they could sense that they needed to be even more gentle and considerate than they usually are and the visitors, despite their immobility, found a true bond with their llamas.'

Kiln Farm is high on a hill and looks straight across the Dale. Other than short walks around the farm, the llamas are trekked along footpaths and bridleways in the area. It's great to be able to learn about the animals as you trek but, because of the slow pace, Suzanne can point out all the beauty of the Dales as you go. Part way through the trek, the llamas are given their break and you get the refreshments that they have been so considerately carrying. One of the longer trekking options is to Brimham Rocks (see page 109).

Suzanne tailors each trek according to the people that are booked. Therefore, it is not possible to simply turn up to the farm unannounced either to look at the llamas (the chances are, they won't be there) or to expect a trek immediately. It's not advisable for children under ten years to trek with a llama because of the pace ('young children tend to get bored with the slow speed,' says Suzanne) but children from the age of twelve will easily be able to lead a llama, so long as they have an accompanying adult with them. Don't be surprised if you find yourself talking to the animals!

Nidderdale Llamas Kiln Farm, Wilsill, Pateley Bridge, HG3 5EF ☎ 01423 711052 🖰 www.nidderdalellamas.org.

the walled gardens with their huge herbaceous borders, the kitchen garden full of rare varieties of fruit trees and the pleasure grounds, with two shapely lakes, silted up from a beck that runs into the nearby Nidd.

The grounds have that archetypal estate feel, planted with specimen trees that defy age. Giant wellingtonia reach for the sky alongside oaks and sweet chestnut trees vying for the biggest and knobbliest girth competition, their trunks showing more warts and pimples than the foulest of imaginary characters.

On your way out, take a peek inside **All Saints' Church**. It has the most beautiful ceiling decorated like a piece of fabric with a repeat pattern in simple reds and greens, embossed with gold. It couldn't be simpler, but it's all the better for it.

The Boar's Head Hotel Ripley ☎ 01423 771888 🖰 www.ripleycastle.co.uk/hotel.html. Housed in a fine building (note the arched windows) in the centre of the village. Refined dining in either the restaurant or the bistro. Sir Thomas Ingilby, owner of Ripley Castle, personally selects the wines for the wine list.

Knaresborough and Harrogate

⑥ Knaresborough

It's hard to tell what is the dominant feature of Knaresborough, a town that perches on a steep bank above the River Nidd. Is it the river itself, the huge viaduct (potentially the most well-known feature as its vista is regularly used to promote the town), the ruined castle that just about stands above the river, or is it actually the town's most famous and oldest tourist attraction, **Mother Shipton's Cave**, tucked away out of sight?

I'm leaving Mother Shipton and her cave out of it for now – they're well known enough and the attraction is only one tiny aspect of a much bigger picture that needs building of Knaresborough. Most of the town sits to one side of the Nidd. On the other are the remains of the Ancient Forest of Knaresborough. The woods, which include hornbeams, oak, ash and beech trees that smell like peaches when you wander through them, cover up Mother Shipton's Cave and the bizarre well that turns everything to stone – including numerous hanging teddy bears. The beech trees are considered to be such fine specimens that every one has a preservation order placed upon it and the Forestry Commission has filed a seed bank for future plantings. You do have to pay to wander through the woods (accessed at the entrance to Mother Shipton's Cave) but, running alongside the river, there's an arresting view of the town and a nice picnic spot too.

On entering Knaresborough, either by train over the viaduct high above the river – what an incredible introduction to the town – or other means, I think the most prominent feature is actually the number of black-and-white chequered buildings. It's a significant trademark of the town and the mysterious reason behind them all makes it all the more intriguing. I've received all kinds of answers when enquiring around the town, including some kind of relationship with the chequered flag used to signal the end of a grand prix! But the most plausible answer is likely to be that the checks used to denote licensed premises (hence pub names like 'The Chequers Inn'); consequently in Knaresborough, it then became fashionable to paint your house black and white, explaining why there are so many. Oddly, these mono houses look right, yet could you imagine if anyone tried to paint their house similarly elsewhere? There could be uproar among neighbours.

Close to the river, and the viaduct, is one of these chequered houses, the Old Manor House. Built in the 12th century, it is where King Charles I and Oliver

Cromwell signed the treaty that ended the English Civil War. The ancient **Knaresborough Castle**, positioned high above a bend in the river, played its part in the War too, with a parliamentary siege on the royalist camp. It is now officially owned by the Queen, although an overnight stay by Her Majesty in this tumbledown residence might not have quite the same appeal that it once had for many of her forbears. It is however the best place to snap a photo of the most traditional of Knaresborough scenes, overlooking the river and the viaduct.

Wandering along **Waterside**, naturally by the river, you begin to get a real feel for the town, a tiered system of beautiful terraced houses each with a miniature garden. You can hire a rowing boat here too, to appreciate the river from another perspective. There are several options to reach the main town area from Waterside but they all involve a good climb, including the steep steps up to the castle, from where you can see the old mill on the opposite side of the river. The fields around Knaresborough used to be filled with the daily flourish of hazy blue flax and the mill was appointed by Queen Victoria to supply linen for all the royal palaces.

The old town is centred around the **Market Place**, still in weekly use for the Wednesday sales, and the **High Street**. I love the centre. It has higgledy-piggledy house roofs and narrow streets that radiate from the centre like spokes on a wheel. Look out for some unusual windows around the town; the 'Town Windows' project is a recent collection of public art that uses the *trompe l'oeil* effect – at first glance you'll believe that someone really is hanging out of a window. That someone is actually one of 12 characters from the town's past and they're used to brighten up some of the blank windows in the town's Georgian buildings, a legacy of the 18th-century window tax.

One of these historical figures is Blind Jack. Born in 1717 Jack Metcalf lost his sight as a child through smallpox yet went on to become a reputed fiddle player and a pioneer in civil engineering, constructing 180 miles of roads throughout Yorkshire. He can be seen playing his fiddle from an upstairs window in the pub that bears his name, in the market square. But you can also sit next to him, again in Market Place, where the bronze figure of Blind Jack rests on a bench, his measuring wheel propped up by his side.

One of Knaresborough's newest places to visit is **Henshaws Arts and Crafts Centre** (01423 541888; www.hsbp.co.uk) on Bond End (the A59 towards Harrogate). This new complex is extraordinary, the circular brick turret-like entrance sandwiched between high stone walls feels as if you're entering through a castle keep. Inside there are shops selling crafts made by visually impaired residents of Yorkshire, a wonderful sensory garden that can be appreciated and enjoyed by all and a gallery café. The Centre also runs a whole range of arts workshops that anyone can join.

I cannot write about Knaresborough without including one final walk. Wander down to the River Nidd and along **Abbey Road**. It follows the river for a mile (actually coming to a dead end) past private riverside gardens; the peace is sublime while the town continues daily life on a cliff top above. This is actually the ancient Pilgrim's Way and tucked back into the rock is one of the sweetest, tiniest chapels that you will come across, the 600-year-old **Chapel of Our Lady of the Crag**. Look for too long at the river and you'll miss it, the powder-blue door is its only clue of existence. Beside it is a beautiful rock garden and it is, I believe, the most restful place to sit in the town.

Knaresborough Bed Race

Knaresborough is also famous for its annual **Bed Race** (www.knaresborough. co.uk/bedrace), a real community-spirited athletic event with the subtle difference of pushing a decorated bed through the streets! It might not make it as an Olympic sport, but at least there is somewhere to snooze after all the strenuous activity. It's usually held every June, and most competitors take a dip in the Nidd during the closing stages of the race.

The Old Dairy Market Place ☎ 01423 865027. Nice deli to pick up some picnic bits.
Rascals Tea Shop Waterside ☎ 01423 863606. Not the finest tea rooms in Yorkshire but undoubtedly has the finest location in Knaresborough.

⑦ Harrogate

Where York has history and Knaresborough has small-world charm, Harrogate has elegance. My father used to say that it was easy to imagine Miss Marple-like elderly spinster ladies daintily sipping tea out of bone china cups and nibbling on cucumber sandwiches while discussing society life. It's an outdated view today, but he does have a point; the centre of Harrogate is about refinement.

Harrogate's elegance is partly owed to the kind of visitor that it has been able to attract over the centuries – wealthy and noble society from across Europe in search of cures for ailments from the town's spa water. They brought money into the area and with it an air of decadence. Today the town regularly comes within the top ten of the best places to live; consequently this shines through when visiting.

Arriving in Harrogate it's hard not to notice the vast open expanse right in the centre of town. It's known as **The Stray** and is an important part of Harrogate community life where joggers breathe a cleaner air, and any number of football matches for all ages take place of a weekend. An act of parliament created the park in the late 18th century, fixing its size at 200 acres, which must be maintained today. There's no doubt that it enhances the look of Harrogate and in winter, when the trees that line its perimeter twinkle with fairy lights, it takes on a magical quality.

Floral Harrogate

Harrogate is renowned for its gardens. The town regularly wins national and regional awards for its floral displays and the volunteer organisation behind it,

Harrogate in Bloom (www.harrogateinbloom.org.uk), has a wealth of community projects to ensure that everyone, of all ages, can take part and be proud of their success. The team has created **Harrogate's Floral Trail** (0905 644 1423; www.moguide.com), a marked route with a sound guide that you can download on to your mobile, ipod or mp3 player. The route takes in 11 public gardens, including the most famous promenading spot of them all, the **Valley Gardens**. The year-round colour here is more than vibrant, a classic spa-town garden with giant specimen trees, lawns and flower borders that show true dedication from their gardeners.

Seasonal displays of autumn crocus and dahlias are replaced with bird-enticing (their presence ever-heard through their birdsong) deep red holly berries, jungle plants hover above streamlets and alpine rockeries make way for formal rose beds, while a giant and ancient wisteria slithers its gnarled trunk up the pillars of a walkway like a serpent. One footpath through the gardens is named the **Elgar Route**. It commemorates Sir Edward Elgar's love of Harrogate; he visited many times from 1912 to 1927 and would walk regularly in the Valley Gardens. The first provincial performance of the composer's Second Symphony was held in the town in 1911.

Harrogate Flower Show

With such a floral tradition, the town is renowned too for having one of the most important events in the gardening calendar, particularly in the north. The Spring (in April) and Autumn (in September) Flower Shows (0870 758 3333; www.flowershow.org.uk), held at the **Great Yorkshire Showground**, draw thousands of gardeners who return home laden with plants and having filled their heads with advice from specialist plant societies and gardening experts.

Unless you're planning on purchasing a lorry-load of plants, you can reach the showground by shuttle bus directly from the town centre, running from **Station Parade**.

There's another garden of significance in Harrogate, the Royal Horticultural Society's northern home at **Harlow Carr**. It's huge and shows all the professionalism that you would expect from the nation's largest gardening organisation. However it is also a trial site, where plants and gardening techniques are assessed for their suitability in a northern climate. It's in danger of becoming an all-singing-all-dancing theme park rather than concentrating on gardening but the stunning new acclimatised Alpine greenhouse and a new Learning Centre (built from sustainable materials and with a zero carbon footprint) should keep Harlow Carr special.

A mile from the centre of town, you can reach RHS Harlow Carr using Bus 106 from **Station Parade**; visitors arriving at the gardens by bus receive half-price entry. Alternatively you can take the very pleasant 1½-mile marked walk through the Valley Gardens and Harrogate's **Pinewoods**, a woodland that's filled with sycamore, birch and rowan as well as pine trees.

A spa town

Tewitt Well, the original iron and sulphur-rich spring that began Harrogate's fortunes as a spa town, is found within The Stray but other locations around the town also have waters bubbling up from the deep. One such place is the **Royal Pump Room**, the refined-looking black and gold building close to the Valley Gardens. It houses a museum exhibiting the history of the town as a spa and you can drink a glass of the water if you feel you must.

Bettys and Taylors of Harrogate

If someone asks me what is the very first thing that comes into my head when you think of Yorkshire, I have to say 'Bettys'. For **Bettys** is a Yorkshire institution. It is a world-renowned family empire of elegant tearooms and a few other things beside. Although now very much a 'Yorkshire thing', the story actually began in Switzerland. Orphaned under tragic circumstances, a young Fritz Bützer, the son of a Swiss miller and master-baker, came to England in 1907 to find work. Getting on to the wrong train in London, he found himself in Bradford without the means to return. After many years of hard work and dedication to learn the art of chocolate making, and a certain amount of moving around Yorkshire, he anglicised his name to Frederick Belmont, moved to Harrogate and opened a café with only the finest-quality furnishings and serving the finest-quality food and drink, with the finest service. All this finery encouraged high society visitors.

Ninety years on, Bettys is owned and run by Frederick Belmont's nephew Jonathan Wild, together with his wife Lesley. There are now four tearooms – in Harrogate, York, Ilkley and Northallerton – all with a very special, individual character and ambience. Having bought out the long-time tea and coffee merchants, **Taylors of Harrogate** (world-famous for 'Yorkshire Tea'), in the 1960s, every aspect of the Bettys business today is maintained with the highest standards. For example, in the craft bakery where all the Bettys products are made, housed in a beautiful 'Swiss chalet' in Harrogate, every process is done by hand, whether it's making speciality breads ready for baking in the traditional brick oven, creating the most divine cakes, tarts and biscuits or making the very finest chocolates.

I paid a visit to **Bettys Cookery School**, based opposite Bettys craft bakery in Harrogate. It was set up by Lesley Wild in 2001 and has the enviable resource of being able to draw on the talents of the craftsmen, bakers, confectioners and cooks that work for Bettys. They still look to their Swiss–Yorkshire heritage for inspiration

I'm not alone in finding it tastes absolutely disgusting. The sulphurous smell that pervades the air around the exterior of the pump room (it's allegedly Europe's most sulphurous spa water) is quite enough to cure many things!

I'd rather head for the town's **Turkish Baths and Health Spa**, *the* place to unwind in the same way that society did in the 19th century, though with a few modern alterations and luxuries. The royal baths are worth visiting simply for the decoration, restored in 2004 and one of the most historically complete of all those that remain in Britain today. With a Moorish design the Islamic arches, decorated pillars, glazed brickwork walls, painted ceilings and terrazzo floors are a work of art and that's before you've dipped a toe into the plunge pool or laid your head on a soft pillow in the rest room. You can simply turn up on spec to use the Turkish baths but it's worth booking one of the many spa treatments for a truly rejuvenating experience.

and it's this that really makes the courses unique and inspiring.

I joined in with the school's pinnacle course, the ten-day 'Bettys Certificate Course', which covers just about everything you need to know for a really firm grounding in cooking, from knife skills and pastry techniques to chocolate making, taught by one of the master chocolatiers from Bettys bakery.

The school kitchen is incredible, a room that is inspiring to cook in before the lovely staff have even said a word. However it is the warmth of the tutors that make the school and the teaching so special. Friendliness abounds but they are helpful and non-judgemental too, turning the most nervous, or newest, of cooks into confident cooks. The most experienced of chefs will gain something from one of their cookery courses too, even if it's simply a fantastic day out and meeting new friends. Of the 'pupils' on the Certificate Course that I attended, some were local to the area while others had made it their holiday in Yorkshire and were full of praise for the School. With breakfast, lunch and dinner thrown in, who could ask for more?

The school is very keen to encourage young cooks too. Said Richard Jones, the cookery school manager who pops around to chat while you're cooking, 'Inspiring children to cook is one of the main reasons that Lesley Wild wanted to set up the school. We offer courses that will ensure that children can cook a proper meal, not simply fairy cakes'.

Personally, I can't wait to return for other practical one-day courses – anything from preparing supper parties, and pasta making (I need to hone the skills that I learnt on the last course!), to cooking with chocolate. But there are two that really grab my eye. One is entitled the 'Flavours of Switzerland', taking students back to Bettys roots. The other is 'Yorkshire Breads', learning to bake traditional loaves and pikelets. I can't think of a better souvenir of Yorkshire.

Bettys Cookery School Hookstone Park ☏ 01423 814016
🖰 www.bettyscookeryschool.co.uk.

Harrogate and art

While its sulphurous waters have brought fame to the town, its connections with the arts are lesser known, although one rather famous crime writer did put Harrogate in the headlines. **The Old Swan Hotel**, close to the Valley Gardens, was the bolthole for Agatha Christie in 1926. A nationwide search for the author was launched following her disappearance but she was found ten days later having checked into the hotel under a pseudonym. It was a plot to match any of her thrillers, involving secret affairs, revenge and the possibility of murder; the mystery remains as to why she chose to disappear, but it was possibly revenge against her husband who had just announced his secret affair with another woman – Agatha's disappearance cast suspicious rumours that he had murdered her.

Between the hotel and the Valley Gardens is the **Mercer Art Gallery** on Swan Road (01423 556188; www.harrogate.gov.uk/mercerartgallery). In a neo-classical building, it's home to Harrogate's fine art collection of 2,000 works although these are not on permanent display. It's only a small gallery, free to enter, and exhibitions change regularly, from works by local artists, photography, national touring exhibitions as well as themed displays of prints, paintings and drawings taken from the permanent collection.

To enjoy art and the company of others, the **Nidd Valley Decorative and Fine Arts Society** (www.niddvalleydfas.org.uk) holds monthly lectures on a wide range of themes and subjects, using experienced and knowledgeable public speakers. Said Sally Wilks, Chairman of the Society, 'We are always delighted to welcome and involve people who are only staying in the vicinity for a short time and who enjoy art. The talks are always informative and are a wonderful way of meeting like-minded people.' Informal lectures are held every third Monday of the month at Christchurch Centre on the Stray; a small donation is requested per visitor.

Bettys Café Tearoom 1–3 Parliament St ☎ 01423 502746
🌐 www.bettysandtaylors.co.uk. The ultimate dining experience in Harrogate, even if it's just for a cup of tea while listening to the resident pianist or people-watching through the plate-glass windows. Visit the Montpellier Bar (closest to the entrance) for a quick, continental-style menu serving open sandwiches and tortes from the bar, or the main tearooms for full-blown at-table service and a more traditional tearoom menu (that includes some Swiss favourites too of course). For a fantastic cup of tea, you can't beat the Tearoom Blend. It's not the cheapest place in town, but you're paying for the whole ambience as well as top-quality food. Freshly made breads, cakes and biscuits as well as Taylors' teas and coffees can be bought in the shop too.
Farrah's Food Hall 31 Montpellier Parade ☎ 01423 525266 🌐 www.farrahs.com. Farrah's are the makers of Harrogate Toffee, a delicious slightly lemony-flavoured toffee that was originally created to take the rather yucky taste of the sulphurous spa water away. Their food hall sells all their toffees, fudges and a whole host of other sweets.

Fodder Great Yorkshire Showground, Harrogate, HG2 8NZ ☎ 01423 546111
🖰 www.fodderweb.co.uk. Opened in the summer of 2009, a fantastic new 'farm shop'
that is owned by the Yorkshire Agricultural Society; 85% of the products on sale are
made, baked or grown in Yorkshire. There's an environmental and sustainable ethos
behind the whole business from the new building to educating children on where
food comes from. There's a great café on-site too.
Harrogate Farmers' Market Cambridge St. Held on the second Thu of the month
from 9am until 3pm. Lots of good, local produce.
Weetons 23/24 West Park ☎ 01423 507100 🖰 www.weetons.com. Weetons describe
themselves as 'the farm shop in the town', opposite The Stray. Owned by local
farmers, it's a fantastic deli, butchers and bakery selling lots of Yorkshire produce
including Ampleforth Cider (see page 223) and a Triple Curd Cheese, made from their
own dairy herd. A good, bustling café is on site too.

North from Harrogate to Masham

While the A1 carves up North Yorkshire, slicing between the Yorkshire Dales
and the North York Moors, the Ure valley to the west is far from dull with a
string of attractive properties, market towns and satellite villages making the
most of their rural location.

⑧ Markenfield Hall

One of the best-preserved – and most beautiful – medieval houses in Britain
today, Markenfield Hall (01765 692303; www.markenfield.com) is most
definitely someone's house, and that is why it works its spell on me. With the
exception of a spot of tinkering over the centuries, it has remained largely
unaltered since it was built in the early 14th century for the de Markenfield
family. Completely surrounded by a fashionable moat (it wouldn't keep out
many marauding armies!) and walled courtyard, this wonderful crenellated
house has seen a remarkable and tragic history, its walls, rooms and tiny chapel
playing a major part in the 1569 Rising of the North, a battle in direct rebellion
to Henry VIII's Dissolution of the Monasteries. This caused the house – and
the family's – downfall.

Today Markenfield Hall, over a mile off the main A61 and three miles south
of Ripon, is once again owned by descendents of the Markenfield family. They
have restored the magnificent Great Hall, winning the Historic Houses
Association Restoration Project of the Year in 2008 (beating Harewood House,
arguably one of Yorkshire's grandest of attractions, in the process). Standing in
the courtyard, listening to the history that befell the property while glancing at
the giant petals bursting opening on the magnolia that climbs the wall by the
entrance way, you can almost hear the whispers and the chatter of disgruntled
Catholics plotting against the forwarding armies.

Markenfield Hall's tiny chapel, restored alongside the Great Hall, is unique too, especially given its past history; it is licensed to hold both Catholic and Protestant services, even if there is only room to fit a dozen or so people in the congregation.

The hall is only open to the public on certain afternoons throughout the year, when you can tour the courtyard and four rooms (including the Great Hall and Chapel). I really urge you to visit but it's advisable to check the website for opening times. Guided group visits can be booked all year round. The Ripon Rowel Walk runs past the moat and gatehouse. Note there are no refreshments at the hall; your best bet nearby is Hob Green (see below).

Hob Green Markington, HG3 3PJ ☏ 01423 770031 ⌂ www.hobgreen.com. Delicious food using fruits and vegetables from their own kitchen garden wherever possible along with local produce; a mile west of Markington itself.

⑨ Fountains Abbey and Studley Royal

Centuries ago, Markenfield Hall had big connections with **Fountains Abbey** (01765 608888; www.nationaltrust.org.uk), now owned by the National Trust.

As the crow flies, this ruined abbey is only a matter of a few fields away; you can easily walk between the two on a slightly protracted route along numerous public footpaths.

The remains of the Cistercian Abbey, four miles southwest of Ripon, are rather romantic. Yes, it would be wonderful to see it as it once stood. But I find a certain charm in willowy grasses and ivy growing out of the roof, wild figs sunning themselves in the abbey courtyard and every crevice and archway stuffed with wild scabious waving in the wind that blows along the valley of the River Skell, and the soothing sound of its waters rushing past the ruins to the adjacent Fountains Mill. The Cistercian monks certainly knew how to pick a good location. We have Henry VIII and his iron will to crush Catholicism to thank (if you can really use the word) for watching the wild scabious grow and the birds flutter in and out under the vaulted arches of the old refectory. There's a steep climb beyond the river valley but take a wander up to the secret lookout named Anne Boleyn's Seat (is that title given in jest with a hint of irony?) and you'll appreciate all the more how magnificent the abbey would once have been.

From Anne Boleyn's Seat you can take any number of paths to visit **Studley Royal**, the formally landscaped 18th century water park that uses the Skell for its feed, and the wider estate that incorporates the Deer Park where you are virtually guaranteed to see some antlered beasts. Last time I visited, the lower branches of the trees around **St Mary's Church**, within the grounds of the estate, were getting a very good pruning! The church is a visual treat inside, with an extraordinarily ornate 1870s interior by William Burges (best known for his adornments to Cardiff Castle), and featuring depictions of angelic musicans and carved parrots against a gorgeous backround of red and gold.

Visitors to Fountains Abbey and Studley Royal arriving on the **Ripon Roweller** bus 139 from Ripon Bus Station, running on Sundays and Bank Holidays from April to October, receive half-price entry. You can also **walk** into Studley Royal via public footpaths, in particular the delightfully secretive Skell valley; Studley Roger is a useful starting point. The licensed restaurant at Fountains serves homemade dishes from locally sourced produce.

⑩ Newby Hall

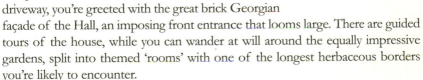

There's no doubt that **Newby Hall and Gardens** (01423 322583; www.newbyhall.com) mid-way between Ripon and the A1M is impressive. Arriving by car, bike or on foot (the Ripon Rowel Walk runs close to the estate) you enter through the majestic parkland, splattered with giant oak trees, under which cattle and sheep fill their bellies. After an eternally long driveway, you're greeted with the great brick Georgian façade of the Hall, an imposing front entrance that looms large. There are guided tours of the house, while you can wander at will around the equally impressive gardens, split into themed 'rooms' with one of the longest herbaceous borders you're likely to encounter.

I first visited the gardens some years ago with a friend who lived nearby but who had never been to Newby Hall. We had a very enjoyable day wafting in the glorious, heady scents from the Rose Garden, getting lost through secret paths and discovering the story behind 'Sylvia's Garden'. So I felt touched that, when my invitation to her wedding arrived twelve months later, I discovered that she had chosen the gardens of Newby Hall as the venue for her reception. You never quite know how visiting somewhere will change a life.

It's the 'extras' that help to keep a place like Newby Hall financially viable, but all too often the added 'attractions' of miniature railways, adventure playgrounds and craft fairs can detract from the beauty of this place. The restaurant here uses locally sourced ingredients.

⑪ Ripon

Ripon, officially, is a city, though it is not a great sprawling metropolis. Very much the opposite, it's a city that is smaller than most towns, with a great history and that characterful atmosphere that provincial market towns seem to acquire. It owes its status to its huge cathedral, one that dominates its surroundings and is vastly out of proportion to the city's size, a sign of the cathedral's importance.

You can see **Ripon Cathedral** as you approach from the surrounding roads

– and the chances are you will approach the city this way, for the railway no longer reaches Ripon. Your only other option is by boat – either on the River Ure or on the Ripon Canal, itself a tiny 2½-mile spur that enters town off the Ure.

Ripon Cathedral

The official title for Ripon's most imposing structure is the Cathedral Church of St Peter and St Wilfrid. The city has recently celebrated 1,300 years of Wilfrid's connections with the cathedral; he became abbot of a Benedictine monastery on the site and built a new church. The crypt of this new church (in 672 anyway!), now the oldest existing Saxon crypt in England, forms the basis of today's cathedral; it became a place of pilgrimage because of the saint. The crypt was built to resemble Christ's tomb as Wilfrid imagined it. It's a tiny, whitewashed room with a ledge for a candle; so very different to the embellishments and adornments that grace the building above. One visitor asked, as he squeezed down the narrow, dimly lit staircase, 'Is this it?' I'm not sure quite what he was expecting to see; indeed, that is all you get, except for a sense of 1,300 years of history.

The cathedral is very much at the centre of Ripon life, just as it has always been. Its history lies within the tombs – the remains of ancient families of significance, such as the Markenfield family from nearby Markenfield Hall (see page 119). But, like so many huge structures of significant age in need of a new identity, it fulfils the differing roles today of art gallery, concert hall and meeting place. Musicians are regularly making the most of the cathedral's acoustics, not least in the free Thursday lunchtime concerts when you may get to hear the organ stretched to its full capabilities or budding concert professionals of the future.

When I was at the cathedral last, there was a community exhibition entitled 'Yorkshire Through the Eyes of Young People' organised by the Cathedral's education department. The artwork, from more than fifty schools in North Yorkshire, was simply stunning, and though by the very youngest of artists, frankly would have hung equally well next to the work of a professional in a modern gallery. Its aim, according to the exhibition coordinator, Eileen Bellett, 'was to encourage young people to reflect and record their own local landscape from direct experience and, above all, a personal response to their Yorkshire.' It was so lovely to see the county through these young eyes, showing a completely different perspective. Thankfully, it is an annual exhibition, held every September. However, at any time of year there is usually some form of community-spirited exhibition displayed within the cathedral.

Ripon Museums

Opposite the cathedral is the **Courthouse Museum** (Minster Road), one of three museums that are linked by their subject matter; the others, five minutes' walk away, are the **Workhouse Museum** (Allhallowgate) and the **Prison and Police Museum** (St Marygate). The titles are a dead giveaway to the buildings and the content, but they have played an important part in the history of the city. Ripon maintained independence from the rest of Yorkshire until 1888, so it had to provide its own law and order. In the courthouse (operational until 1998), you can stand in the dock and listen to a court session where petty thieves were sentenced with deportation to Australia. In the Workhouse, you can try your hand at the same toil that was expected of the Victorian paupers while the prison has some horrific tales of punishment and regime, all the more terrifying when the five-inch thick door is slammed shut! The three museums are something that children will enjoy (collectively they won a Sandford Award for Heritage Education in 2008, the highest honour for educational visits) and there is a special reduced-rate three-in-one ticket to visit all the museums (01765 690799; www.riponmuseums.co.uk).

The Ripon Hornblower

The Ripon Hornblower is the product of 1,000 years of history, when the wakeman was responsible for security, particularly at night. He could impose fines or would have to provide compensation to victims should, for example, a burglary occur during his overnight watch. The job of wakeman effectively became outdated by the 16th century, but even so, the Ripon Hornblower still calls his tune every night at 9pm around the four corners of the obelisk in the Market Square.

Walking round Ripon

Wandering around Ripon is a pleasure. It has an eclectic mix of both stone and brick buildings of every conceivable style and yet, owing to the nature of the materials used, even recently built houses seem to blend in well to the existing structures and streets. If you fancy a quiet stroll, head to the **Ripon Spa Gardens**, a small but verdant oasis. The main entrance (wheelchair accessible) is on Park Street, with other, stepped entrances off Skellbank. A mixture of flower borders, grassy picnic spots and mature trees centred around a traditional bandstand provides somewhere to munch a pork pie from Appletons (see page 124). Regardless of any intention to dip a toe, if you're passing the impressive ornate, brick building that houses the old swimming baths, next door to the Park Street entrance of the spa gardens, poke your head around the door; there's a splendid art-nouveau decorated entrance hall, complete with stained glass, the likes of which you never see in any modern leisure complex. It might be your last chance to see it too. The Council has plans to convert it into luxury maisonettes, a project that's not going down well with some in the town so a Save our Spa campaign (www.saveourspa.co.uk) has been launched to regenerate the old building while maintaining its original purpose, to provide wonderful new spa facilities.

It's the River Laver that runs through the centre of the city, joining up with the River Ure on the outskirts, and the Ripon Canal runs adjacent to the Laver, on the opposite side of the Boroughbridge Road. The canal basin, accessed off Bondgate Green and Canal Road on foot, is hidden away and looks rather lonely despite it being only five minutes' walk from the town centre.

The **Market Place** or the Cathedral is as good a place as any to begin a walk. Indeed a set of waymarked routes begins at the cathedral. The **Sanctuary Way Walk** is based upon the times when Ripon looked after its own law and anyone within the Sanctuary Boundary, marked by a series of posts (one of which still stands today), was granted overnight sanctuary. New markers have been installed, not so much to grant sanctuary to tourists, but to encourage walkers around the town and its outer limits through the countryside. The full circuit is ten miles long but there are shorter walks that visit historically important locations. You can pick up a route map (although the walks are marked) from the **Tourist Information Centre** opposite the entrance to the cathedral.

For a much longer walk, the **Ripon Rowel Walk**, which passes the cathedral, uses 50 miles of existing public rights of way or permissive paths to take a wander through the extended countryside around Ripon. En route, you pass through beautiful villages and some lovely, gentle countryside, river valleys, lakes and one or two impressive buildings such as Markenfield Hall and Fountains Abbey.

Appletons 6 Market Place ☎ 01765 603198. Pork butchers selling the most fantastic pork pies. The best I've ever tasted – dare I say, far better than any Melton Mowbray pie!

The Old Deanery Minster Rd ☎ 01765 600003 ⌂ www.theolddeanery.co.uk. Upmarket restaurant in a beautiful grade-two listed building adjacent to the Cathedral. Award-winning food using local produce and a chef who has worked under Gary Rhodes.

Perk Up Market Place South ☎ 01765 698888 ⌂ www.perkup.co.uk. Delicious dishes while focussing on using seasonal produce. Specialises in fish, although it's not the only thing on the menu.

Ripon Farmers' Market Market Place. Held every third Sun of the month, 09.00–14.30. Seasonal veg and fruit, locally reared meat plus lots of tasty treats.

⑫ Wensleydale in Nidderdale: Kirkby Malzeard and around

Within the Nidderdale AONB a cluster of villages and hamlets here are not directly on the well-known tourist trail, which is partly what makes their character so appealing. This is an area to savour on a bike, along quiet country lanes. I love the quietness of **Laverton**, on the River Laver, and the **Grantley** villages. But my favourite is **Kirkby Malzeard**, one of the larger villages in the area with a long main street and lots of footpaths disappearing off into the fields.

There's a great circular walk just west of Kirkby Malzeard called the **Crackpots Mosaic Trail**. It's 6½ miles long and is based around **Dallowgill**, an area known for its Iron Age forts. The trail is based upon a community project set up in Kirkby Malzeard when a group of residents calling themselves 'The Crackpots' created a series of mosaic pictures depicting important aspects of local life. These 22 mosaics have been placed around the trail and make excellent waypoints as well as bringing in a treasure hunt – great with children. The mosaics include pictures of wildlife and flora that are likely to be encountered along the way. Others depict features along the walk such as a picture of boots and beer, to be found outside the Drovers' Inn, the recommended refreshment stop en route.

The walk extends through woodlands, along tracks, over rivers and streams, along field ditches and up over moorland. It's not suitable for cycling but if you happen to have left a bike in the Drovers' Inn car park, or if your feet will hold out, carry on along the road from the pub, slightly further southwest, up and across **Skelding Moor**. It's a tiny area of moorland that was once used for quarrying and mining – though much of that evidence has gone. Very excitedly, I saw my first ever grouse there, but from the top of the moor there are some wonderful views across Upper Nidderdale in the west and right the way across to the North York Moors. On a clear day you can just make out the White Horse carving on the edge of the **Hambleton Hills** (see page 141).

><><><><

The Drovers' Inn Dallowgill, Kirkby Malzeard, HG4 3RH ℡ 08721 077077. Remote pub that's featured in the Crackpots Mosaic Trail. Makes a useful base to return to for a meal after the Crackpots Mosaic Trail or for a drink en route.
The Grantley Arms High Grantley, HG4 3PJ ℡ 01765 620227
 www.grantleyarms.com. Pleasant pub with a panelled bar and a real log fire.

⑬ Masham

As a tourist, I can't understand why the small market town of **Masham** doesn't make it into the Yorkshire Dales National Park. To me it is the epitome of Dales life, a town with true community spirit that holds its traditions dearly while moving forward. Arrive on any given day and you could be witnessing Yorkshire cricket, judging sheep or supping a pint of the local brew – from not one but two breweries.

I often judge a town by its shops. From them, you can tell the character of the place. In Masham there is no supermarket (except for a tiny Co-op) and the town is all the better for it. Instead, tucked between the old stone houses that line the market square, is a bakery, a butchers and a greengrocers, one after the other. And there are often people queuing out of the door from each shop. I was ecstatic to see this, not so much that I would have to wait a little while to purchase the most delicious looking, locally grown strawberries, but that the residents obviously value their way of life.

To place it on the map, Masham is officially part of Wensleydale, bordering the **River Ure**, though it is many miles from the area that most think of as being Wensleydale around Hawes. The Ure by now is a sizeable river, a rowing boat or a swim required to get from one bank to the other. On entering Masham from Ripon (see page 121), you cross over the Ure before it flows past the recreation ground and cricket ground. Sitting listening to the river gurgling behind you, this is an idyllic place to pause for a while or catch up on a few runs, the cricket club regularly serving afternoon teas at weekends during a match.

There is one thing in particular that has placed Masham on the map – beer. The older of the two breweries is **Theakstons** renowned for its 'Old Peculier' ale. Established in 1827, the brewery is still under the ownership of the Theakston family, although a brief spell with a multinational conglomerate before being bought back by the Theakstons split the family. From the Visitor Centre, named **the Black Bull in Paradise** (you'll find out why when you visit) you can take a guided tour of the old Victorian brewery concluding, naturally, with sampling some of the ales in the visitor centre bar. Though what really interests me is the cooperage, with the brewery having one of the few remaining craft coopers in the country; it's fascinating to see how they make the traditional barrels.

However, there is another side to the story of brewing in Masham. When Theakstons was sold to an international corporation for a while, it caused friction within the Theakston clan and one family member, Paul Theakston, decided to go it alone. He set up a rival brewery in the town using traditional brewing methods. With Masham's long association with sheep (the traditional sheep fair is still held in the town annually), and the background to the brewery's formation, it was named the **Black Sheep Brewery**. It too is now a massive part of Yorkshire life with worldwide fame. Like their rival, you can take a tour of the brewery here and compare notes of the two brewing houses, although there should be no industrial espionage required; the family members have 'kissed and made up'!

Black Bull in Paradise Visitor Centre Theakstons Brewery ℡ 01765 680000
🖰 www.theakstons.co.uk. Selling Theakstons' legendary ales from the brewery on-site.
S⟩ Black Sheep Brewery Visitor Centre Masham ℡ 01765 689227
🖰 www.blacksheepbrewery.co.uk. On the site of the brewery (you can smell the hops as you enter), there's a bistro serving food all day and evening meals. The bar serves the ales; I recommend the 'Golden Sheep' ale – superb!
King's Head Hotel Market Place ℡ 01765 689295 🖰 www.kingsheadmasham.com. Traditional coaching inn in the heart of Masham overlooking the Market Place. They serve both Theakstons and Black Sheep cask ales.
The Mad Hatters' Tea Room 2 Church St ℡ 01765 689129. Traditional tearoom serving morning coffee, lunches and afternoon tea.

Swinton Park Cookery School

A part of the spectacularly imposing Swinton Park hotel, the cookery school here is open to day visitors and hotel residents. Housed in the renovated Georgian stables overlooking the crenellated castle entrance, this is a cookery school with a difference. For a start, the 'celebrity TV chef' Rosemary Shrager has made it her headquarters, whipping students into shape with her inimitable style.

The kitchen has a very informal, homely feel, like a personal farmhouse kitchen complete with a huge Aga as the centrepiece. Students prepare and cook food around a giant central table, topped with a slab of smooth granite just waiting for some pastry and a rolling pin.

After the hard work has been done, you adjourn to the cookery school's fine dining room (not your average school dining room), where the food that you prepared is served to you. If you have a partner who has been keeping well out of the way for the duration of the course, they can join you in the dining room to taste your culinary delights.

Day courses cover all kinds of tastes and techniques: there's a Dinner Party course, with a module focussing on different kinds of game. A Grow and Eat Your Own course takes you into the hotel's walled kitchen garden to collect and pick your produce before cooking it while the Wild About Food course involves a ramble around the estate grounds gathering wild fruits and nuts before preparing a meal. There are children's courses too, including private family tuition for groups of two adults and two children who like to cook together.

Swinton Park Masham, HG4 4JH ☎ 01765 680900 ⏣ www.swintonpark.com. The hotel and cookery school is situated approximately 1½ miles from Masham.

⑭ Druid's Temple

West of Masham, a narrow lane rising from the village of Ilton heads up into forest plantation and abruptly stops. Very soon you may find yourself blinking in disbelief at a bizarre curio that is the folly of all follies: a scaled-down Stonehenge plonked amid the trees. Actually it's Stonehenge with knobs on – more lintels than the real thing, and a stone table, cave and altar to boot. Only it's far from prehistoric, having been created by the local landowner, William Danton, in the 1820s as a job creation scheme. He even engaged someone to play the role of a hermit, though it's said that whoever took on the role didn't stick it out for long before going slightly off the rails.

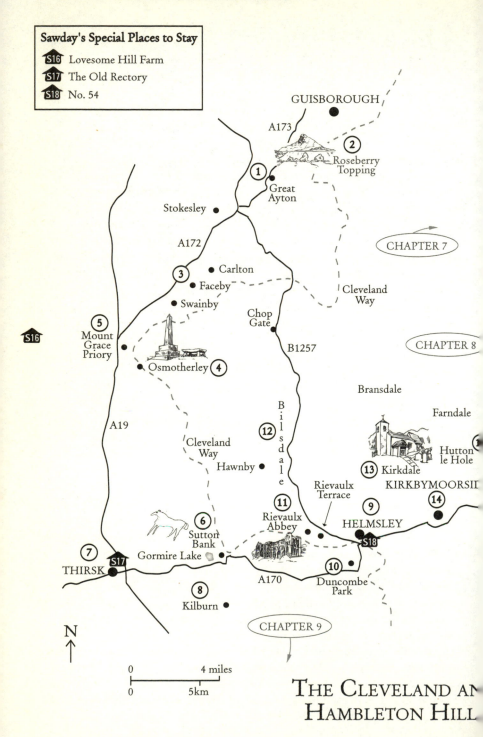

Sawday's Special Places to Stay

S16 Lovesome Hill Farm
S17 The Old Rectory
S18 No. 54

GUISBOROUGH

A173

2 Roseberry Topping

1 Great Ayton

Stokesley

A172

CHAPTER 7

3 Carlton
Faceby
Swainby

Chop Gate

Cleveland Way

5 Mount Grace Priory

Osmotherley 4

B1257

CHAPTER 8

Bransdale

Farndale

A19

Cleveland Way

Hawnby

Bilsdale

12

13 Kirkdale

Hutton le Hole

KIRKBYMOORSI

Rievaulx Terrace

11 Rievaulx Abbey

9 HELMSLEY

14

S16

6 Sutton Bank

7
THIRSK
S17
Gormire Lake

S18

10 Duncombe Park

A170

8 Kilburn

N

0   4 miles
0   5km

CHAPTER 9

THE CLEVELAND AN
HAMBLETON HILL

6. The Cleveland and Hambleton Hills

Travelling up or down the Vale of York you are likely to be moving at speed, whether in a car on the A19 or a train on the East Coast Main line. Either way, to the east of you will be a range of hills stretching in an almost unbroken escarpment from Thirsk in the south up to Teesside in the north. Occasional crags stand proud from the slopes, tree-muffled valleys bend teasingly out of sight and ruined castles and priories poke just their heads into view. You may be sorely tempted to break your speedy journey, turn off the fast route and go-slow in the hills for a while. Succumb to temptation, because this is low-gear territory par excellence, from the limestone country of **Kirkbymoorside**, **Helmsley** and **Hambleton** to the brooding sandstone giants overlooking **Osmotherley**, **Great Ayton** and **Guisborough**.

Getting there and around

Road links to here are very good. Once you have found your way around York from the south, or Teesside from the north, traffic is usually light. Thirsk and Helmsley are the only places that can get snarled up and difficult to park in, but a way of avoiding that, for the latter at least, is to park and ride from Sutton Bank National Park Visitor Centre. The parking fee is refunded when you buy an all-day Moorsbus ticket.

Public transport

The East Coast Main Line skirts the area but with only two stops, at **Thirsk** and **Northallerton**. A word of warning here; in both places the railway station is a fair walk from the centre of town and bus station, over a mile in the case of Thirsk. A variety of different buses call, all heading to the market square, not at regular intervals but on average every 30 minutes. Up in the north the Middlesbrough–Whitby line has three stations in this region: Great Ayton, Battersby and Kildale. Kirkbymoorside is peripheral enough to be most accessible from Malton railway station on buses via Pickering (see page 214).

The extent of the bus network comes as a pleasant surprise: it serves every village of any size except in one blank area between Thirsk and Osmotherley. **Helmsley** is very well linked, with hourly services (bus 128) to Sutton Bank and Scarborough, five daily to Thirsk (M7, M71; April to October), five to Stokesley (199, M2), four to Malton (195, 196), four to Osmotherley (M91), and one direct bus a day serves York via Easingwold (M15). **Thirsk** is a fair-sized town with bus links to Northallerton ten times a day (58, 70), Ripon eight times a day (70, 147) and York four times a day (58). From **Osmotherley**, buses go to

Northallerton and Stokesley hourly (80, 89) and Helmsley and Sutton Bank four times a day (M91). **Great Ayton** benefits from the regular Stokesley–Teesside service (29, 81) that calls in here three times an hour except on Sundays.

Cycling

If you are okay with testing hills then **road biking** here is good, particularly on the National Route No 65 which traverses a good chunk of the region from Hutton Rudby in the north to Kilburn in the south, on two alternative routes. A circuit of the minor roads in Farndale is a favourite of mine, but don't go at daffodil time if you want quiet, safe roads.

Off-road biking is exceptional. Testing routes for fit and experienced riders are easy to find; just spread out a copy of the 1:25,000 OS Explorer map OL26 and link together bridleways and green lanes across the moor tops. Some particularly good, but deserted, routes head out of the heads of Farndale and Bransdale. For flatter and easier riding, **Farndale's** high-level disused ironstone railway is a fabulous five miles from Blakey Ridge, that can be extended to a ten-mile horseshoe using the Westside Road green lane. A steep descent will bring you to the pub at Church Houses, a mile from the start point but unfortunately over 1,000 feet lower. Another flattish high-level route is the Cleveland Way north of **Sutton Bank**. The first half a mile is footpath so you need to detour to Dialstone Farm or walk the bike, but from Whitestone Cliff there are three loops of four, six and eight miles, easy enough for families and returning along the tarmac Hambleton Road. This last route takes you close to the best forest track riding in the region, in **Boltby Forest**.

Unfortunately, no bike hire is available anywhere in the region, but for bike parts, repairs and maintainance you have two choices:

Bike Scene Park Lane, Guisborough ☎ 01642 610735 ⌂ www.bikescene.co.uk. Mountain bikes only.
Bike Traks High St, Great Ayton ☎ 01642 724444 ⌂ www.biketraks.com. Road and mountain bikes.

Horse-riding

You will find lots of scope to ride here, with or without your own horse, on hundreds of miles of bridleway, green lane and permitted forest track. Three riding centres (below) provide trekking or hacking.

Bilsdale Riding Centre Hawnby ☎ 01439 798225 ⌂ www.horseholiday.co.uk.
Boltby Pony Trekking and Trail Riding Centre Boltby ☎ 01845 537392
⌂ www.boltbytrekking.co.uk.
Helmsley Riding School Helmsley ☎ 01439 770355.

If you bring your own horse, places offering horse accommodation can be found in the booklet *Horse Riders' Guide to the North York Moors*, produced by the National Park.

Walking

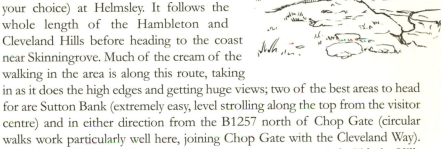

The one official National Trail in the region is the Cleveland Way (110 miles) with one end (whether it's the start or the finish is your choice) at Helmsley. It follows the whole length of the Hambleton and Cleveland Hills before heading to the coast near Skinningrove. Much of the cream of the walking in the area is along this route, taking in as it does the high edges and getting huge views; two of the best areas to head for are Sutton Bank (extremely easy, level strolling along the top from the visitor centre) and in either direction from the B1257 north of Chop Gate (circular walks work particularly well here, joining Chop Gate with the Cleveland Way). Other less official but still very popular long-distance routes are the Tabular Hills Way (48 miles), heading east from Helmsley to join the two loose ends of the Cleveland Way together, the Lyke Wake Walk (40 miles), a very old traditional route from Osmotherley to Robin Hood's Bay and the Hambleton Hillside Mosaic Walk (36 miles), a circular trail from Sutton Bank.

Shorter sections of all these trails make good day or half-day walks, the perennial problem being transport, as they are not circular routes. Some sections that can use public transport one way are **Kildale to Great Ayton via Captain Cook's Monument** (a pleasant, mainly woodland walk of three miles using the Esk Valley Railway as a shuttle); Carlton to **Swainby via Carlton Bank** (an airy five-mile moorland traverse with extensive views of the Vale of Mowbray; buses 89 and M9 get you back); and **Sutton Bank to Rievaulx or Helmsley** (five or seven miles, along the lovely valleys of Nettle Dale and Ryedale – best done this way as it is downhill; use buses 128, M71, M91 for the return leg). In **Farndale** and **Rosedale** some of the best walking takes in the valleys themselves and the high moors just above, though the route-finding through fields can be very intricate; once you're up on the moors, though, it's a different world with easily managed tracks; or in Farndale, the riverside stroll between Church Houses and Low Mill is a perennial delight, especially magical at daffodil time.

Tourist Information

Great Ayton High Green Car Park ☎ 01642 722835.
Helmsley Castlegate ☎ 01439 770173.
Sutton Bank National Park Visitor Centre ☎ 01439 770657.
Thirsk Market Place ☎ 01845 522755.

The Cleveland Hills

The gradually rising land of the North York Moors has its precipitous swan-song in its north-western corner; a final celebration of altitude in a series of buttresses, overlooking the Cleveland plain. Clustered around the ankles of these hills are a string of old villages, the largest being Great Ayton and Osmotherley.

① Great Ayton

Soon after your arrival in Great Ayton you may begin to suspect the existence of a famous old boy, one James Cook, whose former presence is writ large, though he only spent nine years of his youth living here. Born in 1728 in Marton

(now a suburb of Middlesbrough), James Cook was one of the great explorers, and his sea voyages charted much of New Zealand and Australia. The Cooks moved to Great Ayton when he was a child, and his father worked nearby at Aireyholme Farm on the slopes of Roseberry Topping where the family lived; the Cooks also had a cottage in the village, dismantled in 1933 stone by stone and re-erected in Melbourne, Australia. The **Captain Cook Schoolroom Museum** (open afternoons April to October, all day July and August; 01642 724296; www.captaincookschoolroommuseum.co.uk) is in the very school the young James attended for four years, and has displays about his life and the village's past.

The main street running parallel with the river has a village green at either end, Upper and Lower, and is overlooked by a Quaker school, the Great Ayton Friends' School, founded in 1841, but sadly closed in 1997. The railway line here doubles as the boundary of the National Park, with Great Ayton outside, and this spectacular branch of the Cleveland Hills most definitely in. Two summits stand out, **Easby Moor** with its tall memorial pillar and the unmistakable outline of **Roseberry Topping**.

For **shopping** head three miles south to the market town of Stokesley (two excellent pubs and a Friday market), or four miles north to the much bigger town of Guisborough. This former capital of Cleveland also has a market (Tuesday, Thursday, and Saturday), and impressive priory ruins.

Mill Riggs Organic Farm Store Stokesley TS9 5HQ; ☎ 01642 715784. A farm shop on the A174, selling mainly meat and eggs.

Spread Eagle High St, Stokesley ☎ 01642 710278. A small and unspoilt market-town pub with good-value, home-cooked food and a range of real ales including guests from micro-breweries. The beer garden backs on to the River Leven and has duck-feeding potential.

Suggits Café and Shop, High St ☎ 01642 722522. An ice-cream shop since the 1920s, old-fashioned sweet shop and very popular cyclists' café. Very much a local institution.

The White Swan West End, Stokesley ☎ 01642 710263

⌂ www.captaincookbrewery.co.uk. A typical 18th-century, one-room pub with an interesting 'J'-shaped bar, and excellent beer from the Captain Cook Brewery next door. The only food available is cheese, bread and pickles. Come at Easter time and you will be treated to a Beer and Cheese Festival.

② Roseberry Topping

Some high mountains disguise their altitude with a humble show of rounded slopes and flat, grassy tops. Roseberry Topping is the opposite, a hill with delusions of grandeur, sometimes even referred to as the Matterhorn of Yorkshire. Such is its prominence, with an abrupt conical shape and rocky summit, that its height is constantly over-estimated. At 1,057 feet, not only does it fail to make highest mountain in Yorkshire status (a common claim), but it does not even manage the altitude title for the Cleveland Hills, as nearby Round Hill on Urra Moor is over 300 feet higher. That said, this is possibly the most recognised, best-loved and most often climbed peak in Yorkshire, probably deserving the title of 'Little Mountain' after all.

A history of reverence is hinted at in the name, which probably derives from Odin's Berg, the Vikings associating it with their chief god, but later generations treated it with far less respect. One local historian commented that Roseberry Topping is an industrial summary of the North York Moors... almost everything that has been taken from the ground in Cleveland has been pillaged from its slopes – jet, coal, alum, sandstone, fossils, ironstone and basalt. This last surprising mineral product was quarried up until the 1980s from the Whinstone Ridge, a ruler-straight igneous intrusion crossing the moors and breaking the surface here, and also at Egton Bridge, Goathland Moor and Sneaton Forest.

Despite its human ravages, Roseberry Topping provides a fine venue for a walk, inviting from every angle, especially the Cleveland Way extension from the east, and with a panoramic view from the top, hard to beat anywhere else in the country. The most direct route of ascent is from the hamlet of Newton under Roseberry, just north of Great Ayton, and if you happen to be here on the first Sunday of the month, then after your walk call in on the farmers' market at Pinchinthorpe Hall, another mile up the road.

A walk to the Captain Cook Memorial

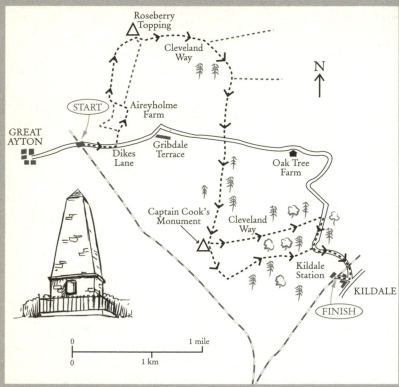

A shortish walk to the south is the massively prominent **Captain Cook Memorial**. Thank goodness common sense prevailed in 1827 when sites for a memorial to Captain Cook were discussed, and Roseberry Topping was rejected in favour of Easby Moor. This flat-topped hill is enhanced by the 51-foot tower whereas the Topping needs no help in catching the eye. Ringed with old sandstone quarries, capped with heather and a healthy population of red grouse, this is good walking country, though rarely quiet, as the Cleveland Way crosses the top. My preference is to link it with Roseberry Topping to create a five-mile walk from Great Ayton to Kildale, returning by train. This strategy has the added advantage of calling in on the excellent café near Kildale Station.

Glebe Cottage Licensed Tea Room and Coffee House Station Rd, Kildale ☎ 01642 724470 ☍ www.glebecottagekildale.co.uk. Closed Thu.
Pinchinthorpe Hall Pinchinthorpe TS14 8HD ☎ 01287 630200
☍ www.pinchinthorpehall.co.uk. A country house hotel with non-residents bar and dining, and the North Yorkshire Brewing Company (organic) on-site. Farmers' market on the first Sun in the month except Jan.

A death foretold

Many local stories have Roseberry Topping as a backdrop but probably the oldest is the tragic tale of the death of Prince Oswy. It had been prophesied that King Osmund's beloved only son would drown before his second year was out. In a desperate attempt to thwart the prediction the King sent his infant son, with his mother, as far from water as he could find in his Kingdom of Northumbria – the summit of Roseberry Topping. On Oswy's second birthday, the queen dozed in the sun on the hillside and the boy wandered off. Her frantic search for him on waking ended with the tragic discovery of his body, lying face down in a shallow pool of spring water. Roseberry Well, now merely a marshy patch of ground, is marked on the OS map.

③ Carlton in Cleveland, Faceby and Swainby

Both these villages, and the smaller Faceby in between, are close enough to the A19 to cater mainly for the commuters of Teesside, but each has attractions for visitors. All three have a pub, **Carlton's** being the pick of the bunch, and old churches with unusual dedications; St Botolph's in Carlton is the most northerly in the country to be named after this Lincolnshire monk, whilst **Faceby**'s St Mary Magdalen's church has a fine collection of 'Mouseman' carvings (see page 142). Carlton has an outdoor activity centre, if you fancy exerting yourself, and one of the most unusual cafés in the country at Lord Stones, near the top of the steep Carlton Bank road.

Swainby is one of those settlements that moved sites after the ravages of the Black Death. All that is left of the old village of Whorlton are ruins of the 11th-century castle, and nearby, probably even older, Church of the Holy Cross. Modern Swainby is an attractive collection of stone buildings lining the banks of Scugdale Beck, including a bustling village shop that had its post office counter taken away recently, so converted the space into a small coffee shop.

Two roads lead uphill out of the moors end of Swainby, one the scenic back lane already mentioned, to Osmotherley, and the other, the winding, dead-ended road up Scugdale. Being a no-through valley, this is a haven of peace and quiet, the only visitors being walkers, and climbers coming to play on its crags.

Food and drink

The Blackwell Ox Carlton in Cleveland ☎ 01642 712287 🖥 www.theblackwellox.co.uk. A typical village local pub with caravan site attached. The extensive menu is predominantly Thai, and the permanent Hambleton beer fronts a range of cask ales.
Lord Stones Café Carlton Bank TS9 7QJ ☎ 01642 778227. Situated near the point where old boundary stones marked the meeting of three estates, and built into the hillside in a megalithic-bunker architectural style, this is a bizarre and unexpected licensed café. Very popular with cyclists and Cleveland Way walkers, especially as the home-cooked food is very good value.

Potto Grange Organics Potto DL6 3HH ☎ 01642 700646
📠 www.pottogrange.co.uk. Organic beef, lamb and pork, direct from the farm or via
Stokesley farmer's market.

Outdoor activities

Carlton Outdoor Education Centre Carlton in Cleveland ☎ 01642 712229
📠 www.carltonoutdoors.org. A wide variety of half-and full-day activities, like
climbing, canoeing, bush-craft, caving and archery, is available at weekends and
school holidays.

④ Osmotherley

The most satisfying mode of arrival into Osmotherley
is by foot, from the south along the Cleveland
Way. This route treats you to tempting
glimpses, from high up on Black Hambleton
Hill, of the village tucked into a fold of the
valley-bottom fields, and descends through the
verdant woods of Oak Dale.

Even using wheeled transport, it is possible
to visit Osmotherley avoiding the nearby A19
dual carriageway, by approaching via the spectacular moor road over from
Bilsdale, or the minor back road from Swainby. This latter route could well have
been the one followed by the Queen of Northumbria and her dead child (see
page 135). According to legend, she buried Oswy at the church in Tivotdale, and
joined him soon afterwards when she died herself, of grief and guilt. Tivotdale's
name changed to commemorate Oswy-by-his-mother-lay – a far-fetched, but
nice story.

However you arrive, you will find yourself at the village green, decorated by
an ornately carved market cross and stone barter table, where goods were
exchanged. The table is more famous now for one of Osmotherley's many
religious connections, as it was used as a preaching pulpit by John Wesley in
1745. He obviously made an impression, as one of the oldest Methodist chapels
in the world is hidden away down a cobbled alley across the road.

Chequers Tea Room DL6 3QB ☎ 07958 610095 📠 www.chequersosmotherley.co.uk.
Ex-drovers' inn (the Slapestone Inn), high on the Hawnby road overlooking
Osmotherley. A very popular refuelling place for cyclists and Cleveland Way walkers.
Coffee Pot North End ☎ 01609 883536. The only café in the village.
⑤ Golden Lion West End ☎ 01609 883526 📠 www.goldenlionosmotherley.co.uk.
A dark-stone inn overlooking the village green. Inside, wood is the theme in the bar,
and beer sourced from Timothy Taylors, Hambleton and the continent. The menu
is refreshingly simple with an excellent range of gluten-free meals, and the wine
list extensive.

Heather, grouse and honey

The existence of the North York Moors as a national park depends almost solely on one plant. It is also responsible for a significant proportion of the economy of this region; it's not a timber tree or a farmer's crop, but a wild, woody perennial called *Calluna vulgaris*, or ling – the humble, common heather. It dominates the moors to a staggering degree, but ironically only because we let it. Without human management, by controlled burning or mowing, and sheep grazing, these upland heaths would soon revert to their natural vegetation of oak forest.

An awful lot of landowners' time, effort and money goes into keeping these vast acres covered in heather, not for us to ooh and aah over their colour in August, or have long, uninterrupted views on our walks, but to encourage the populations of one species of wild bird – the red grouse.

Grouse are very specific in their habitat requirements, needing young heather shoots to eat, and old heather bushes to nest in, so a moorland gamekeeper's job is to maintain a mosaic of different-aged patches of heather on the land. 'Most estates do this by burning old heather, small areas at a time, and then allowing it to regenerate,' explained Simon Bassindale, one of the National Park's rangers. 'We depend on the gamekeepers doing this well, to maintain the National Park landscape, and it's quite a skill of theirs, choosing the right day to do it. If the ground is too dry, or the wind too strong, the fire can burn out of control which can be disastrous.' A good population of grouse means a healthy income from the autumn and winter shoots, with customers paying upwards of £1,000 a day for the privilege of bagging a brace. Love it or hate it, without grouse shooting, the North York Moors would not exist as we know it.

What's good for grouse is fortunately also attractive to lots of other unique wildlife, and this area is a real stronghold for adders, lizards, curlews, golden plover, short-eared owls and, my favourite of all, a dashing little falcon called the merlin.

One other harvest that can be taken from the heather is that of nectar, which bees can transform into what is widely regarded as the best-quality honey available. Rows of hives, moved up on to the edge of the moor, for the mass purple-flowering, are a common sight in August. Sadly, honeybees have been hit hard by disease in recent years, so you may find getting hold of locally produced honey difficult, but your best bet are specialist food shops in the villages, and farmers' markets.

⑤ Mount Grace Priory

Of the bewildering array of orders of monks and nuns to have lived in Yorkshire, the Carthusians, the last to arrive from the continent, are perhaps the least known. There have only ever been ten Carthusian priories, or Charterhouses, in England and Mount Grace is the best preserved of them all. Its position displays the usual monastic good taste for beautiful locations, tucked as it is beneath the steep wooded slope of Swinestye Hill. What struck me on my first visit here was how different Mount Grace was to more traditional sites like Fountains and Rievaulx; no one, big, dominating abbey church here, but smaller, homely buildings. This reflects the Carthusian philosophy of solitary hermitage, with each monk or nun living silently in their own cell, meeting only for chapel services and one long, communal walk, the only time they could speak – I bet that was a noisy affair.

Mount Grace Priory is owned by the National Trust but, oddly, administered by English Heritage. Areas of interest include a reconstructed cell, an exhibition upstairs in the attached manor house, a shop and activities for children. The gardens are full of wildlife, notably a family of famous stoats that have featured in various BBC wildlife documentaries.

Mount Grace Priory ✆ 01609 883494; ⊕ www.english-heritage.org.uk. Open Thu–Mon, Apr–Sep; Thu–Sun, Oct–Mar.

The Hambleton Hills

When the heathery tops of the Cleveland Hills give way to grass, you will know that you have arrived in the limestone country of Hambleton. The most public face of these hills is its steep, scarp slope, often refered to as **Whitestonecliffe**, that stretches ten miles south from Thimbleby, and looks out west over **Sutton-under-Whitestonecliffe**, to **Thirsk** town, and the rest of the Vale of York. At its more hidden, southern end, it tumbles down to **Kilburn**, to then merge imperceptibly with the Howardian Hills.

⑥ Sutton Bank

The village of Sutton-under-Whitestonecliffe has two claims to fame, the longest place name in England, and the cliff itself that provides the label. The busy road that passes through Sutton is one of the main routes into the North York Moors, but as the many warning signs insist, it is not recommended for lorries or towed caravans. Sutton Bank, the hair-pin section up Whitestonecliffe, is blocked by stranded vehicles with monotonous regularity. At the top of Sutton Bank you will find the **National Park visitor centre** of the same name (01845 597426; www.northyorkmoors.org.uk), with a shop, exhibition centre and tea rooms inside. A very entertaining half-hour can be spent with a cup of tea or coffee, gazing out of the window at one of the busiest bird feeding stations that I've ever seen.

From the centre, six waymarked **walking trails** can lead you between two and nine miles astray, the best to my mind being a five-mile circuit taking in Gormire Lake; or just for a blast of air and the sublime views, head across the A170 on the dead-level, dead-easy stretch of the Cleveland Way, which heads along the top of the great cliff that is Sutton Bank for a very easy mile or so towards the **White Horse of Kilburn**. On your walk, don't just gaze down to the lake, woods and Vale of York, but glance upwards every now and again, and you may be treated to the sight of a glider drifting silently overhead. If it seems like an idyllically peaceful way to travel, and you fancy having a go – the good news is that you can! The **Yorkshire Gliding Club**'s base is hidden away in the trees less than a mile from Sutton Bank, and they offer trial lessons where, under the expert guidance of an instructor, you can actually fly the glider with no previous experience.

A map detailing six circular bike routes from the centre, between 11 and 23 miles, is also available.

Gormire Lake

Beneath the Hambleton Hills scarp and one of the few natural lakes in North Yorkshire, this is also one of its most beautiful. With the pale cliff above and surrounding lush forest reflected in its crystal-clear limestone spring waters, the name hardly seems deserving, as it literally means 'filthy swamp'. Gormire is not only a haunting and evocative place, it's a prized haven for wildlife. The rich limestone woodland surrounding it is managed by the Woodland Trust, mainly for its flora, and the lake itself supports important numbers of winter waterfowl, like goosanders, tufted duck, pochard and kingfishers. The whole area is designated as a Site of Special Scientific Interest (SSSI).

Probably because lakes are such a rarity in this part of the world, many legends have grown up around Gormire Lake, some involving it being bottomless, or telling of it swallowing witches or geese and spitting them out in wells miles away (Gormire has no in-or out-flow river). The most common theme though, a white mare leaping off the cliff and into the water, complete with doomed rider, possibly derives from White Mare Crag, the alternative name for Whitestoncliffe. This refers to the shape of a horse that used to be visible in the rock face, not the White Horse at nearby Kilburn.

$ **The Hare** Scawton ☎ 01845 597769 ✆ www.thehareinn.co.uk. An inn once reputedly used as a brewhouse by the monks of Rievaulx Abbey in the 13th century, and now a dining pub with traditional English menus, Yorkshire ales from Timothy Taylors and Black Sheep, and an extensive wine menu.
Yorkshire Gliding Club Low Town Bank Rd, Sutton Bank ☎ 01845 597237 ✆ www.ygc.co.uk. The clubhouse has a restaurant and bar open to the public, an ideal vantage point to watch the gliders come and go. Gliding courses and lessons are available, and the club also operates a campsite.

⑦ Thirsk

This small town has ticked along, minding its own business, for over a thousand years. Nothing momentous has ever happened here, no battles or royal visits to the castle (because there's no castle), just a lower-league manor house and an old, but fairly average, church. For me, it is a celebration of ordinary Yorkshire life through the centuries, centred on trade, in its busy market square and surrounding shops and inns. Market days are still the high points of the week (Mondays and Saturdays), with the cattle market moved to a purpose-built venue on the trading estate (Thursday) and a farmers' market there on the first Saturday of each month.

How apt then, that the town should earn some outside fame from the venue of a favourite local pastime, its racecourse, and the reminiscences of an ordinary working man, who just happened to write about his experiences particularly well.

Alf Wight was the local vet in the 1940s, but the world knows him better under his pen-name of **James Herriot**. His entertaining stories appeared in print in the 'vet' series of books of the 1970s, but it was when they were televised as *All Creatures Great and Small* that a legend was born, and Thirsk became Herriot country.

His original surgery, in Kirkgate, the real-life Skeldale House, has been restored to its 1940s state to tell his story, and opened to the public as the **World of James Herriot** (01845 524234; www.worldofjamesherriot.org). It is open every day, all year except Christmas and early January.

Another museum faces this one in Kirkgate. **Thirsk Museum** (01845 527707; www.thirskmuseum.org) celebrates life in the town from Saxon times to the present day, and famous pre-Herriot old boys, like Thomas Lord (of Lord's cricket ground) whose house this was.

Food and drink

Arabica Market Place ✆ 01845 523869. A small modern coffee shop with a good range of coffees and free wireless internet.

Yorks Tearoom Market Place ✆ 01845 526776. A traditional café serving quality Taylors teas and coffees, and substantial snacks – not cheap but very good.

As you would expect of an active market town, Thirsk's eight pubs rub shoulders with each other around the market place and Kirkgate. Unfortunately, in this case, competition hasn't pushed up standards, but travelling out of town you will find the following:

Crab and Lobster Dishforth Rd, Asenby ☎ 01845 577286
🖰 www.crabandlobster.co.uk. A 17th-century thatched pub with a formidable reputation for gourmet food in its restaurant. Sea-food is the speciality and influences are French and Italian.

The Nags Head Pickhill ☎ 01845 567391 🖰 www.nagsheadpickhill.co.uk. Out of town to the west, this two-hundred-year-old coaching inn has got the balance just right; a cosy pub tap-room, comfy lounge bar and sumptuous restaurant, with good food and drink served in all three rooms.

🆂 Pick-your-own

Spilman and Spilman Church Farm, Sessay YO7 3NB ☎ 01845 501623
🖰 www.spilmanfarming.co.uk. Pick your own soft fruits in June and July; strawberries, raspberries, gooseberries, redcurrants and blackcurrants.

Art

Zillah Bell Gallery Kirkgate ☎ 01845 522479 🖰 www.zillahbellgallery.co.uk. A nationally renowned gallery featuring mainly Yorkshire artists. Regularly changing exhibitions.

⑧ Kilburn

The unofficial emblem of the Hambleton Hills, logo of a local brewery and name of numerous local pubs, is carved into the side of Roulston Hill above this village, and consequently bears the name, the **White Horse of Kilburn**. Impressively large and visible for many miles (from York Minster tower for instance) it was created in 1857 by a local schoolmaster with the aid of his pupils.

The village itself has something of a Cotswoldy charm, with a beck gurgling down the side of the main street (in a deep unfenced trench – so beware), but is very small, and would be relatively unknown but for a famous former resident, Robert 'Mouseman' Thompson, woodcarver. The Mouseman Visitor Centre (01347 869102; www.robertthompsons.co.uk) has outgrown his old workshop and is now in the old blacksmith's buildings over the road.

Kilburn also has a busy pub and village store.

🆂 **Black Swan** Oldstead ☎ 01347 868387 🖰 www.blackswanoldstead.co.uk. It's well worth the mile stroll, or cycle, over from Kilburn to this 400-year-old gem. Low beams, roaring fires and wooden floors make this a comfortable space in which to enjoy superb food and quality tipple. The wine list is classy, the cask beer is from Yorkshire and you can spoil yourself at the end of the meal with a vintage port or malt whisky.

The Mouseman of Kilburn

There's no doubt that Robert Thompson was an extremely talented woodcarver, whose skills alone may well have earned his fortune, but from the moment he came up with the inspired idea of carving a mouse on to every item he produced, his international fame was assured.

He was born in 1876 and, as a young man, took over his father's joinery business in Kilburn. His early work was mouse-less but his reputation grew, and Thompson carvings began to appear in many local churches and Ampleforth Abbey. The idea for the emblem apparently came when his carving companion, whilst working on a church screen, commented that their jobs left them as 'poor as church mice'. Robert had a lightbulb moment and carved his first mouse there and then.

By the time of his death in 1955 'Mousey' Thompson's work was to be found all over the country, including York Minster and Westminster Abbey. Such is his fame, that a letter sent from Australia with just a picture of a mouse and the word 'woodcarver' on the envelope, was delivered safely to his workshop. The Mouseman Visitor Centre is still an operating workshop employing 30 craftsmen, but also a shop and café. Some of the furniture isn't cheap, but they produce smaller items such as napkin rings that make excellent souvenirs.

Robert's other legacy has been an upsurge of interest in quality, hand-carved furniture in the area. Ten workshops are included in the Thirsk Furniture Trail (www.thirskfurnituretrail.co.uk), each of which has its own motif carved on to every item, of course. You will have fun finding the hidden unicorn, fox, wren or beaver, but I suspect none will ever have the impact of that original humble church mouse.

The western dales

Three valleys bite into the southern slopes of the Cleveland Hills, and channel their rivers and becks to the Vale of Pickering. The upper reaches of Farndale, Bransdale, Bilsdale and Ryedale are rural in the extreme, with some of the most inaccessible acres in the whole of the National Park. Where these hills meet the Vale's rich farmland, is where most of the villages, and the area's two small towns, **Helmsley** and **Kirkbymoorside**, nestle.

⑨ Helmsley

Helmsley is an incredibly popular little town, possibly attracting more visitors in relation to its size than anywhere else in the North York Moors. And, it has achieved this pulling-power without resorting to anything 'fast' or tacky. The town has unconsciously carved itself a niche as an upmarket resort and, perhaps incongruously, a destination for touring motorbike clubs, who almost fill the market-square car park some weekends. Families will not find a huge amount here to entertain young and active children, but it has a wealth of historic buildings, serene walled gardens, aristocratic connections and quality, speciality shops.

When Helmsley is at its busiest the crowds spoil the experience for me, so I try to visit on off-peak days. My favourite is on Friday when the street market is held, and the town is bustling and vibrant without being heaving. This is a very small town so almost all the interest is around the market square or, in the case of the outrageously ornate **Feversham monument**, smack bang in the middle of it. Here is where all four of Helmsley's old coaching inns are, along with most of its ten cafés and two exceptional **food shops**: Hunters (01439 771307; www.huntersofhelmsley.com) and Perns (run by the Star at Harome; 01439 770249; www.thestaratharome.co.uk).

Behind the library you will find yourself in Castlegate; carry on around the castle walls to the **tourist office**, which doubles as the entrance to **Helmsley Castle**. Signs here will direct you to **Helmsley Walled Garden**, once part of the **Duncombe Park** estate, supplying the big house with fruit and vegetables, and now hiding away behind the castle.

Two more venues away from the centre are worth seeking out; one for daytime entertainment and the other evenings. **Helmsley Arts Centre** (01439 771700; www.helmsleyarts.co.uk) lies a short walk away up an alley off Bridge Street. This old Quaker meeting-house is the town's very active theatre, putting on a wide variety of plays, films, concerts and readings. The volunteers that run it are never less than really welcoming and the place always seems full. Slightly further afield is a welcome rarity for outdoor swimmers. The River Rye is not quite big enough for wild swimming but **Helmsley open-air swimming pool** (07772 395368; www.helmsleypool.org), in Baxton Road, opens afternoons and early evenings, late June to early September. Check before planning a visit, as refurbishment work planned for 2010 may mean the pool having to close for a period.

Helmsley Castle

This jagged ruin (01439 771580; www.english-heritage.org.uk) merits a brief peep, but does not have the spectacular position of Scarborough, the royal connections of Pickering or the level of preservation of Bolton in Wensleydale. It was however, founded by a character with one of my all-time favourite names from English history – Walter the Woodpecker, or Walter L'Espec as he was known to his Norman compatriots. He was succeeded by Robert de Roos who was responsible for most of the fortifications, and later the Manners family built the Elizabethan mansion which is still partly intact. English Heritage now maintain it and have provided complete wheelchair access at ground level with some good hands-on exhibitions in the mansion range.

Helmsley Walled Garden

My first visit to this place was during a 'Green Day', a festival of sorts to celebrate all things environmental and earthy. The place was cluttered with information desks about recycling and nature reserves, stalls selling local honey, cheese and pickles and everywhere the sounds of folk music, sizzling sausages and happy people. It was great, but it was busy, busy, busy.

The second time I went was an altogether different experience, and what

walled gardens are all about. I sat on a bench in a quiet, sunny corner – it's easy to find solitude in a five-acre space. The only sounds were the buzzing of the bees on the nearby roses and a wren trilling within the wall ivy. In the baking heat I could actually smell the apples on the branch hanging over my head, just before I dozed off. To think this lovely garden nearly disappeared, but for the efforts of a concerned group of mainly volunteers, who in 1994 started the long job of restoring the orchards, vine house and orchid house. The gardens are now back in full production and almost everything is available for you to buy.

Its demise up until recent years is a sad and poignant story. From its construction in 1758 until 1914 it supported 19 full-time gardeners and supplied produce to Duncombe Park House. At the start of World War I, all the gardeners answered the call-up and went to serve their country, but not a single one returned. This peaceful place is a fitting memorial to their sacrifice.

Food and drink

Beadlam Grange Farm Shop and Tearoom Pockley YO62 7TD ☎ 01439 770303
🌐 www.beadlamgrange.co.uk. A resident butcher serves locally produced beef, lamb, pork, poultry and game, with fruit and veg and Yorkshire cheeses on the deli counter. The café is in the upstairs granary.
Feathers Hotel Market Place ☎ 01439 770275 🌐 www.feathershotelhelmsley.co.uk. Although Helmsley has more select hotels, this is by far the most welcoming and comfortable as a pub.
Helmsley Walled Garden Cleveland Way ☎ 01439 771427
🌐 www.helmsleywalledgarden.org.uk. Within the garden, the newly restored Victorian vinery houses an atmospheric café beneath the climbing vegetation. Most of the produce is organic, home produced, vegetarian or Fair Trade.
Tudor Rose Bistro Bridge St ☎ 01439 770131. A traditional café that also does more substantial meals, in a building that looks as if it was a pub at one time.

Shopping

The Stickman Cleveland Way ☎ 01439 771450 🌐 www.thestickman.co.uk. Keith Pickering is a walking-stick maker operating from a workshop just outside the Walled Gardens.

⑩ Duncombe Park

Lord and Lady Feversham probably wouldn't thank me for saying this, but Duncombe Park is, in essence, a second division Castle Howard. I don't mean that as an insult, because I actually prefer the Duncombe experience, but just as a measure of scale. They are both massive, opulent, privately owned and run 18th-century houses with surrounding parklands to match, but the Feversham estate is slightly lower key, the house and gardens smaller and, in terms of visitors, much quieter.

The origins of the house are unusual in that it was built from scratch by a commoner. Sir Charles Duncombe was a London goldsmith who made his fortune with more than a whiff of suspicion of insider dealing. He bought the whole Helmsley estate from the Villiers family after the death of the infamous Charles, Duke of Buckingham. Helmsley Castle he declared 'un-liveable' and built The Great House on a green-field site further up the hill finishing it in 1713, three years after Castle Howard. Since then the two major events in the life of the house were a catastrophic fire in 1879 and a 60-year spell on let as a girls' boarding school. This chapter ended in 1986 when the Feversham family decided to return the house to its former glory and open it to the public.

The house has an astonishing 200 rooms, around ten of which you can visit if you choose to go inside, but you can find more than enough to do here for half a day without going in the house, or gardens for that matter. The parklands cover nearly 3,000 acres, a large chunk of which is a National Nature Reserve, primarily to protect some of the oldest and biggest hardwood trees in the country, and the rare invertebrates and birds which depend on them. Two waymarked walks will take you through the best of the wild areas; the Country Walk and River Walk are both about three miles long but can be easily combined to create a five-miler for those who fancy a decent stride out. The hub of the garden landscape design is a half-mile-long terrace adorned at each end by two classical 'temples' – strikingly similar in conception to Rievaulx Terrace, three miles up the valley above Rievaulx Abbey.

At the end of your walk, or instead of it if you're feeling lazy, refreshments are available at Fountain Tea Room adjoining the ticket office/shop in what was originally the estate's fox-hound kennels (01439 771115). It sells the usual hot and cold snacks and drinks (including beer and wine), fresh and locally sourced or Fair Trade, and not overly priced.

Like Castle Howard, many outdoor special events are held here throughout the year, but mainly in the summer. You may want to time your visit to coincide with point-to-point racing, or a brass band concert, or a steam fair… or avoid them altogether for a quiet day away from the crowds.

Duncombe Park ☎ 01439 770213 ✆ www.duncombepark.com. Open Easter Sun–late Oct (closed Fri and Sat) 11.30–17.30 (park, gardens and tea room). House tours 12.30, 13.30, 14.30, 15.30. Good-value family and season tickets; under 5s free.

⑪ Rievaulx

With a name like that, there has to be a French influence. It was 12th-century Cistercian monks who brought themselves, and the name, over from the continent to settle in this breathtakingly beautiful bend of the valley of the River Rye. They were granted vast areas of land by the then Lord of Helmsley, Walter L'Espec, and quickly became very rich and powerful landowners. The monastery's influence peaked in the early 1400s when the community numbered more than 200, and then went into steady decline, with the Black Death hitting particularly hard. By the time Henry VIII spoilt the party completely, numbers were down to 23. Even though the abbey was significantly dismantled during the Reformation, it remains a stunning building, '… the most beautiful monastic site in Europe,' according to the landscape painter, Turner. English Heritage also obviously rate it highly as it scores 50p more than Helmsley Castle on their strange sliding scale of entrance fees.

Traffic can be unpleasant on the narrow lanes around Rievaulx but a bus does call here regularly in summer, from Helmsley or Sutton Bank. By far the nicest way to get here, though, is to walk or bike the three miles from either Helmsley, Scawton or Old Byland.

Arguably the best views of the abbey are from a landscaped grassy walkway on the hillside above, called **Rievaulx Terrace**, although no access exists from one to the other, except via the road. Ownership here is a confusing issue; both the abbey and the terraces were the possession of Duncombe Park estate, but they sold the former to English Heritage and the latter to the National Trust, along with the two neoclassical temples that grace either end of the walk: a rotunda called the Tuscan Temple and a lavish banqueting hall called the Ionic Temple and resplendent with painted ceiling and wood carving. The Trust keep the main part of the terraces mown as per its original design, but manage the verges as flower meadows. They are a rich riot of spring and summer colour: cowslips, yellow rattle and early purple orchids in May with spotted orchids, betony and cranesbills later in the year. The obvious similarity to the terrace at Duncombe Park is not coincidental; it was once all part of the Duncombe estate and was laid out in 1758 by Thomas Duncombe III, the grandson of the creator of the Duncombe Park version.

Rievaulx Abbey Rievaulx ☎ 01439 798228 ⌂ www.english-heritage.org.uk.
Rievaulx Terrace and Temples Rievaulx ☎ 01439 798340
⌂ www.nationaltrust.org.uk.

⑫ Bilsdale

Too few motorists bother to stop and explore here, which is a shame, because walking on both sides of the valley, and neighbouring upper Ryedale, is as good as anywhere else in the moors. In particular you might revel in exploring the remains of **jet mines** here. In my ignorance I always assumed that the jet industry was confined to the coast around Whitby, so was staggered at the number of jet mine spoil heaps I found lining the side of Tripsdale (Grid ref NZ 5897).

Hawnby is the largest village hereabouts, with a very pleasant pub, a bridge which replaced one lost in the flash floods of 2003, and a horse trekking centre. Woodland walking just to the north of the village, along the banks of the infant Rye, is tremendous.

The highest point on this route, the top of **Chop Gate** pass, is quite a geographical landmark, as it marks the watershed between two major river systems; to the north all waters flow into the River Tees, whilst southwards, it's a much longer journey to the Humber estuary.

A walk around Bilsdale Head

The best of Bilsdale Head can be taken in during a five-mile horseshoe walk, including Urra Moor, the Wainstones climbing crag and Cold Moor. Start at either the hamlet of Chop Gate, or Clay Bank car park (where the B1257 crosses the Cleveland Way).

The views throughout this breezy moorland route are glorious and constantly changing, although its finest section is undoubtedly along the Cleveland Way.

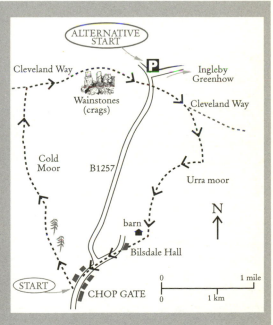

The Inn at Hawnby Hawnby ☎ 01439 798202 🖥 www.innathawnby.co.uk. A light and airy bar, usually serving three Yorkshire ales, which can also be enjoyed in the beautiful beer garden, weather permitting. The menu features local game, often cooked in a continental style.

Post Office Tearoom Hawnby ☎ 01439 798223. This is one of those cornucopia places, post office, general store, source of all knowledge and café, that does particularly good cream teas and breakfasts.

Jet-setters, Whitby-style

A chat-up line that I would love to try out is 'Did you know that your dangly, black ear-rings were once part of a log, floating down a river 180 million years ago?' but I'm not sure how successful that would be.

Jet is fossil wood, but from one particular species of tree only, the *Araucaria* or monkey-puzzle tree. This very particular specification makes it beautifully carveable and polishable but also rare – the only place in Britain where it can be found is under the North York Moors.

A common misconception is that the Victorians invented jet jewellery in Whitby. They were certainly the first to mechanise the process, and Queen Victorian's morbid obsession with all things black popularised it, but jet artefacts have been found in Bronze Age tombs and at almost all Roman excavations. As for its presence at the coast, these are merely the most visible exposures of the seams; more than half the jet that ended up in the Whitby workshops was dug from beneath the western moors.

Wherever river valleys had cut down far enough through the rock strata to expose the jet series, miners would tunnel 'drifts' into the hillsides, leaving a telltale line of spoil heaps today, in Bilsdale, Scugdale, Farndale and along the Cleveland escarpment. A happy geological accident resulted in a thin band of hard limestone being laid down just above the jet, and this Top Jet Dogger made a very convenient strong mine roof, allowing the drifts to penetrate deep underground. Working so far underground by candlelight, miners could not distinguish the black jet from dark-grey shale, so the whole lot was wheeled out in a barrow and sorted in the daylight.

Jet is still collected from the **coastal cliffs** to supply the small-scale workshops in Whitby, mainly by professional fossillers like Mike Marshall (see page 175) and storm-bound fishermen, but on nowhere near the scale of the Victorian boom-time, when 1,500 jet workers were employed in the town.

Over in the **Cleveland Hills**, the only evidence of this 150-year-old industry are those lines of collapsed tunnels on the valley sides and pub names like the Jet Miners Arms in Great Broughton.

If you do find any black pebbles on the beach or hill-side that you suspect may be jet, here's the test; scratch it on to a piece of pale sandstone and examine the colour of the mark. If it's black, bad luck, you have a piece of coal; if it's chocolate brown you have maybe struck it rich!

⑬ Kirkdale

In its infancy, Hodge Beck flows through the very isolated fields of Bransdale, which in its lower reaches does something very unusual for a valley – it changes its name, twice. It becomes Sleightholmedale for a while, but lower down still, between Kirkbymoorside and Helmsley, it takes on its most widely-known label of Kirkdale, and is visited most for its minster and a cave.

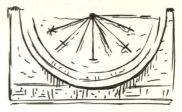

St Gregory's Minster is a tiny church with no village to accompany it, but the fact that it qualifies as a minister, and has a valley named after it, drops the hint of its historical importance. Its south wall carries its most remarkable feature, a **Saxon sundial**, carved into a single block of sandstone seven feet in diameter, and set above an outside doorway. It is the most complete one of its kind in the world and its creator also left us a very informative inscription detailing his name (Hawarth), the owner of the church (Orm) and the priest (Brand).

Fascinating and charming as it is, don't restrict your Kirkdale visit just to the church; a mere 200 yards from St Gregory's you will find a small hole, part-way up a quarry wall. This is the entrance to **Kirkdale Cave**, which, although the longest cave in the North York Moors, is far more famous for what was found in it. In 1821 when quarry workers exposed the entrance, they found it full of the bones of prehistoric, and largely extinct, mammals from around 70,000 years ago. It turns out that this was a cave hyena lair, and the bones were the remains of their many meals, including hippo, lion, elephant and rhino – Yorkshire was obviously a warmer place back then. The cave is not open to the public, and a deep exploration is not recommended, but a short scramble up, to crouch in the entrance and peer into the blackness, is an atmospheric experience.

Kirkdale valley upstream from the cave and minster makes an excellent walking objective. You can follow **Hodge Beck**, one of those disappearing and reappearing limestone watercourses, and enjoy rich woodland, full of flowers in spring-time. A maze of paths on both sides of the beck gives you a range of options for return loops.

⑭ Kirkbymoorside

'Kirby', as it is known to local folk, is a small but busy market town, leaning on the southern slopes of the North York Moors – hence the name. It has many similarities to Helmsley seven miles down the road; it is roughly the same size with a castle, a market square surrounded by old coaching inns, and a nearby stately home and estate. Are the two places friendly, cooperative neighbours then? Not a bit of it. A traditional rivalry exists between the towns that poor old Kirby always seems to lose out on. The castle is a feeble bit of wall built into a younger building, and the pubs, although busy, aren't quite as genteel as those of the 'posh' place. Even the National Park Authority seems to have been deliberately insulting; their headquarters are in Helmsley, whereas the park boundary takes a deliberate detour to completely exclude Kirby. None of this bad press is warranted of course because this is an agreeable little town, especially around the market place, and a start point for some pleasant walks in the hills behind – and a particular favourite bike ride of mine.

Take either of the tiny but cycleable routes of Park Lane or Swineherd Lane from Kirby, and you will find yourself joining Back of Parks Road to Gillamoor (re-hydrate in the Royal Oak), thence to Fadmoor (more refreshment available) and back to Kirby by a choice of minor roads (five or six miles in total).

McConnell Thomas Market Place ☎ 01751 432832 🖥 www.mcconnellthomas.co.uk. Eco and ethical general store.
Newfields Organics The Green, Fadmoor ☎ 01751 431558
🖥 www.newfieldsorganics.com. A wide variety of organically grown vegetables for sale direct from the farm.
S) The Plough Inn Fadmoor ☎ 01751 431515 🖥 www.ploughrestaurant.co.uk. Whilst there are four pubs in Kirby, it's probably worth the trip the couple of miles out to here. Despite the traditional and very cosy bar, serving cask beer, this is first and foremost a restaurant. The meals are simple English affairs but done extremely well, in six separate and intimate rooms.

⑮ Hutton le Hole and Farndale

Hutton or 'Hightown' presumably refers to this village's elevated attitude in relation to nearby Kirkbymoorside and 'le Hole' the pretty hollow it sits in. This is one of the National Park's honey-pot villages, with many visitors drawn here by the excellent Ryedale Folk Museum, but more than a few just to enjoy strolling around the village green, or calling in the pub or café for refreshment.

If pottering around the village isn't enough for you, longer **walks** link the nearby villages of Spaunton, Lastingham and Gillamoor. From the latter, the Shepherds Road bridleway can also take you through the wooded Ravenswick estate to Kirkbymoorside and a bus back to your start.

The delightful river that tumbles over the limestone ledges of Ravenswick is the Dove, fresh from its journey further upstream through Farndale.

As quiet as anywhere in the Moors for eleven months of the year, this valley bursts at the seams with visitors in late March and early April. The reason for this popularity is the best display of **wild daffodils**, or lenten lilies, in the country. Most of the valley has been made a National Nature Reserve to protect the millions of blooms; strangely no-one really knows how they got here and why there are so many of them, although one theory has the monks of Rievaulx introducing them from France. To cope with the 40,000 admirers that arrive during the four-week flowering season, paths have had to be paved, a shuttle-bus service from Hutton le Hole put on and a seasonal Daffy Café opens.

The official **Daffodil Walk** runs from Low Mill to Church Houses but it can be extremely crowded; for almost as many daffs all to yourself walk up the Dove from Lowna Bridge, or catch the bus to Low Mill and walk back.

The Craft Workshops Keld Lane. Five small artisans' studios (wood-worker, chocolate factory, candle-maker, art gallery, stained glass works and garden furniture maker) and a café, next to the folk museum.

The Crown Keld Lane ☎ 01751 417343. Busy and welcoming village pub serving Black Sheep beer and wholesome traditional food.
Feversham Arms Inn Church Houses, YO62 7LF ☎ 01751 433206
⌂ www.fevershamarmsinn.co.uk. An archetypal country pub, with stone flag floors and horse-brasses, serving simple but wholesome pub food and Yorkshire cask beer. Hugely popular at daffodil time.

Ryedale Folk Museum

The small and unassuming frontage to this museum, on the village main street, gives no clue to the delights hidden behind. Over 20 buildings, strung-out down a long, thin, three-acre site, house re-creations of Ryedale country life through the centuries, all the way back to a thatched Iron Age roundhouse. Many of them are genuine historic buildings moved from their original sites, and rebuilt stone-by-stone, to house the artefacts of many rural craftsmen and craftswomen, like blacksmiths, wheelwrights, coopers, saddlers and dairy-maids.

Trails and activities are provided for children, and many hands-on events are put on throughout the year, usually with an old-fashioned theme; the ancient board-game of Merrills, for instance, once had its world championships held here. Recent attractions have included a cottage cooking weekend, archaeology festival, a landgirls' play performance, story-telling weekend, harvest festival and May-pole dancing. The Ryedale Folk weekend is a regular feature in May.

Ryedale Folk Museum ☎ 01751 417367 ⌂ www.ryedalefolkmuseum.co.uk. Open daily except for its winter break during most of Dec and Jan.

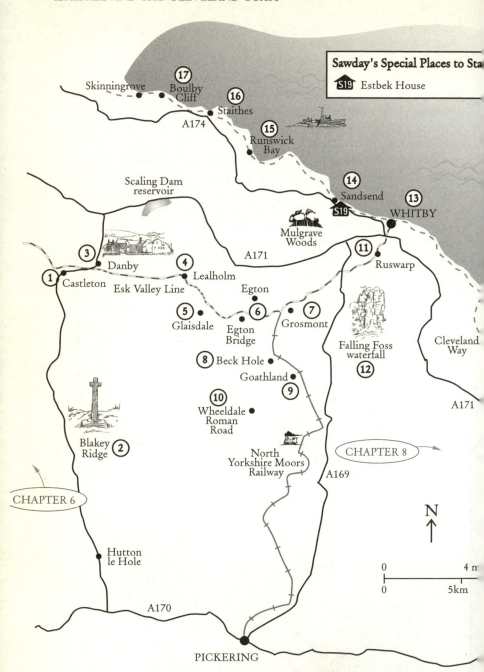

Sawday's Special Places to Sta

S19 Estbek House

Skinningrove

17 Boulby
Cliff

16 Staithes

A174

15 Runswick
Bay

Scaling Dam
reservoir

14 Sandsend

S19

13 WHITBY

Mulgrave
Woods

A171

3 Danby

4 Lealholm

11 Ruswarp

1 Castleton

Esk Valley Line

Egton

5 Glaisdale

6

7 Grosmont

Egton
Bridge

Falling Foss
waterfall

Cleveland
Way

8 Beck Hole

12

Goathland

A171

9

10

Wheeldale
Roman
Road

North
Yorkshire Moors
Railway

CHAPTER 8

Blakey
Ridge 2

CHAPTER 6

A169

N
↑

Hutton
le Hole

0   4 m

0   5km

A170

PICKERING

ESKDALE AND THE
CLEVELAND COAST

7. ESKDALE AND THE CLEVELAND COAST

Eskdale, the 'valley of the winding river', is at the heart of the North York Moors, and the River Esk is the life-blood of the dale. It is only 25 miles long but it punches way above its weight; it has more charm, variety and points of interest than many rivers twice its size. Until recently the Esk was the only salmon-river in Yorkshire, and is the only site in eastern seaboard England with a population of fresh-water pearl mussels.

What I love most about the modern River Esk are its moments of wild inaccessibility. Long stretches where it wanders away from civilisation, often plunging into narrow ravines and crag-shadowed gorges where no tarmac road dare follow, and the only way to explore it is by foot or canoe.

Eskdale ends at the point where the river enters the sea, the entrance to **Whitby** harbour, with this last leg of its journey in a surprising direction. Because of a geographical quirk, this stretch of the Yorkshire seaboard faces due north, so consequently, the coastline to the left, towards Teesside and Scotland, runs away westwards – and what a coastline it is.

The first two miles of it is beach, until the sand ends at a village called simply **Sandsend** – the first of a string of small, former fishing communities, tucked into what little shelter they can find behind rocky headlands, known locally as 'nesses' or 'nabs'. Resembling a giant crocodile's snout, Sandsend Ness is the first of these, and the start of the dark, Jurassic, shale cliffs rising progressively higher the further west you go. **Runswick Bay** is the next haven, hiding behind the heights of High Lingrow, followed by the derelict iron-mining harbour of **Port Mulgrave**. Further west still, at **Staithes** a beck has cut a way through the cliffs to form a spectacular, natural walled harbour. Beyond looms the huge bulk of **Boulby Cliff**, the highest point on the east coast of England, and reputedly the burial place of famed Saxon warrior Beowulf.

Getting there and around

Almost all roads in this region lead to Whitby; plans are afoot for a park-and-ride scheme for the town, and heaven knows it needs it. At busy times (every day in summer, and every weekend of the year) driving to and around the town is a nightmare – so why bother? Why not leave the car elsewhere and take advantage of one of the best integrated public transport systems in the country (0871 200 2233; www.moors.uk.net/moorbus).

Public transport
The Esk valley has its own railway line, linking Middlesbrough and Whitby and

following the river virtually all the way. A magnificently lazy way to see the river as the train crosses it an amazing 26 times within the 1½-hour journey, stopping at or near every village in the dale.

The North Yorkshire Moors Railway (with steam and diesel trains) takes a scenic route along the Murk Esk Valley from Pickering to Grosmont, with some trains continuing into Whitby; another scenic route but much more popular, and pricier, than the Esk Valley line so booking in advance may be a good idea (01751 472508; www.nymr.co.uk; see page 187).

Four main roads link **Whitby** to the outside world, and bus routes use all of them – from Scarborough (93) hourly, from Leeds, via York, Malton, Pickering and Goathland, the Coastliner (840) two-hourly. **Guisborough** is served every hour by the 93 and the coastal villages of **Sandsend**, **Runswick Bay**, **Staithes** and **Loftus** by the 5 hourly.

Within Whitby, seven small 'clippers', an open-top bus tour and a fantastic steam-powered charabanc tour can get you just about wherever you might want to be.

On summer Sundays and Bank Holidays, Moorsbus services (M1, M2, M3, M50, M51) link **Danby** and **Castleton** with the **southern and western moors** (Pickering, Kirkbymoorside and Helmsley) via the spectacular Blakey Ridge.

Boat trips

Whilst there aren't any ferry services within the region, you can still get afloat on a round trip from Whitby, using the following operators:

Cook's Endeavour Cruise Trips Pier Rd ☎ 0845 0450825
🖰 www.endeavourwhitby.com. Half-hour boat trips out to sea on half-size model of Captain Cook's ship. Summer only.
Mary Ann Hepworth Heritage Lifeboat Harbour ☎ 0777 931 8948
🖰 www.oldlifeboatwhitby.co.uk. Half-hour boat trips out to sea on a 1960s lifeboat.
Whitby Coastal Cruises Pier Rd ☎ 01947 601385 🖰 www.whitbycoastalcruises.co.uk.
Half-hour local trips or three-hour jaunts further afield to land for an hour at
Staithes. Whitby's biggest trip boat and the only one with under-cover seating and a
licensed bar.

Boats can also be chartered, usually for angling parties. Details of the 19 boats that operate from Whitby Harbour can be found on www.whitby seaanglers.co.uk/whitby-boat-fishing.php or contact Whitby Tourist Office.

One charter boat operates from Staithes: All My Sons (01947 840278; www.sea-angling-staithes.co.uk).

Cycling

If you can cope with occasional very steep hills, **riding country lanes** in and around Eskdale is great, especially up the quieter side dales. A circuit of Little and Great Fryupdales is my particular favourite, mainly because the slopes are fairly forgiving, but also as the pass between the two dales navigates the delightfully named Fairy Cross Plain.

The picture for the coastal strip is less attractive as few alternatives to the horribly busy A174 exist, except the lane over the top of Boulby Cliff, linking Cowbar and Skinningrove.

Off-road biking is sparse down in the valley bottoms, and tends to be muddy for most of the year anyway, but bridleways and former miners' tracks abound on the moor tops. Danby Beacon and Glaisdale Rigg are two good areas with less challenging routes and are ideal for families. The National Park actively promotes biking in the south and west of the moors but rather neglects this area I think, although their excellent little *Pedal and Puff* guide details routes involving return by train, as both railways in Eskdale allow free bike transport, space permitting.

Horse-riding

Hundreds of acres of moorland, and mile upon mile of bridleway, bode well for potential horse riders, especially if you have your own horse or pony, as opportunities for hiring are limited. Only two trekking stables (below) operate in the region.

Borrowby Equestrian Centre Borrowby TS13 5EH ☎ 01947 840134
🖰 www.borrowbyequestriancentre.co.uk. Rides of ¹/₂ hr, 1hr or more for any ability over four years of age. Children's riding parties can be arranged.
Hollin Equest Hollin Hall, Great Fryupdale YO21 2AS ☎ 01947 897470
🖰 www.hollinequest.co.uk. Number of riders is limited to four on any ride, but with no restriction on age or ability.

Walking

Walkers are very well served here. For long-distance yompers, the Coast to Coast walk and the Cleveland Way both skirt the edge of the area, but the Esk Valley Walk lies wholly within it. Starting at the Lion Inn on Blakey Ridge above Castleton (the highest pub in the North York Moors) and marked by leaping salmon signs, it follows the complete length of the river from its source to the sea at Whitby.

The number of shorter walks, to suit all levels of fitness and enthusiasm, is almost endless. You could for example try a short section of the **Coast to Coast Walk**, like Glaisdale to Grosmont, or vice versa, and take the train back to your start point. As ever, for **information**, the National Park website or visitor centre at Danby are the places to pick up details of waymarked walks or walking guidebooks.

One gem of a walk worth a special mention is the **Rail Trail** from Grosmont to Goathland; rich wildlife, safe river-access for the children to go paddling and wheelchair accessible along most of its three-mile length.

Eskdale

The River Esk flows from west to east, starting at the head of the dale, which the Vikings, not known for their imagination or sense of irony, named Westerdale, and ending gradually by mixing itself with the sea for its last two miles between **Ruswarp** and **Whitby**. In between nestle a string of thoroughly Yorkshire villages; solid but unassuming, chiselled from dark sandstone and growing up the dale-side at each important crossing point. They include rural idylls like **Lealholm** and **Egton Bridge**, the ancient fortified settlements of **Castleton** and **Danby** and two survivors of a brutal industrial past, **Grosmont** and **Glaisdale**.

The mother river is fed by a series of tributary becks along its length, each with its own mini-dale. The largest of these, the Murk Esk, actually qualifies for 'river' status itself, albeit briefly at only 2½ miles long, and navigates even wilder country than the Esk. This is especially so in its upper reaches, through the moorlands and forests near the village of **Goathland**.

① Castleton

Don't come here expecting turreted ruins, as the building that gave this place its name is long gone, with the mound site now occupied by a private manor house. The village is mainly just a service centre for the upper dale, with two pubs, two shops and a petrol station. Visitors do stop here briefly for a café of note and fine art gallery, but Castleton can't really compete in the tourism stakes with neighbouring Danby, which ironically does have a castle.

Most of Castleton village isn't actually in Eskdale bottom, but strung out along a road escaping up the valley side towards Blakey Ridge, arguably the most dramatic moor-top crossing, and a fantastic bus journey to or from Hutton le Hole.

Castleton Tea Rooms Station Rd ☎ 01287 660135. Cyclists always know the best cafés, and my contacts rave about this one, especially the cakes.
Eskdale Inn Station Rd ☎ 01287 660333. Both pubs in Castleton are good but this has the edge. An idyllic river and rail-side position just out of the village.
Montage Gallery Church St ☎ 01287 600456. Rambling and many-roomed building

with locally sourced artwork and home gallery of superb black-and-white photographer, Graham Lowe.

Westerdale Heather Honey The Bungalow, Westerdale YO21 2DE ☎ 01287 660208. Locally produced heather honey.

② Blakey Ridge

A lonely moorland road from Castleton to Hutton-le-Hole heads along the exhilarating Blakey Ridge, which wonderfully encapsulates the wildness of the North York Moors. At the top stand a scattered collection of standing stones, guiding travellers across the moor at the head of three valleys – Westerdale, Danbydale and Rosedale. The tallest stone, named Young Ralph Cross, is the symbol of the National Park, and along with two others, is said to commemorate the survival of three medieval travellers, lost in a deadly fog – Ralph the guide, and Fat Betty and Margery, two nuns from Rosedale.

Not far from the crosses is **Loose Howe**, a Bronze Age burial mound where a 3,000-year-old body was found, prepared for his voyage into the afterlife, armed, clothed and interred in a dug-out boat. In sight of Loose Howe, and surrounded by even older Neolithic burial mounds, the **Lion Inn** makes a most unexpected sight in an astonishingly inhospitable position and 1,325 feet above sea level; like the similarly remote Tan Hill Inn in the Dales it was built to serve miners – those working in coal and iron in this case.

Lion Inn Blakey Ridge ☎ 01751 417320 🖳 www.lionblakey.co.uk. A 16th-century inn in a superb isolated moor-top location. The building, though very large, has low ceilings and open fires which give it a homely feel. Beer is from Theakstons and other guest breweries, and the wholesome meals are very popular.

③ Danby

Five miles from its source, the River Esk is straddled by a pair of Siamese twin villages, joined at a venerable bridge. Both communities sit comfortably in the valley bottom, with old pubs at their centre, the Duke of Wellington on the north bank in Danby, and over the water, the Fox and Hounds in Ainthorpe. The river here is still very young and narrow, and a good running leap could clear it in places, but it carries enough water to power Danby Watermill, whose wheel still turns the internal machinery, but sadly not within public view.

A long history of settlement is evident in the vicinity, with a wealth of Bronze Age earthworks and field systems on adjacent hills (Danby Rigg in particular), a Norman castle, and a medieval packhorse bridge, but despite all this, Danby's most influential building today, the Moors Centre, is predominantly Georgian. **Danby Castle** overlooks the village from nearly a mile away, and has its own access road crossing the river via a structure even older than that in the village. Duck Bridge, built in the 1300s as Castle Bridge, was renamed much later after a local stonemason who renovated it.

The minor road beyond Danby Castle leads into the wonderfully named **Little Fryupdale**, which itself is linked to **Great Fryupdale**. Both valleys, named in honour of the Viking goddess Freya, not a plate of bacon and eggs, offer great potential for foot and pedal exploration. Road cycling is quiet and gentle, a superb off-road route follows the Cut Road around the dale heads, and walking is excellent, especially on the central hill of Heads, which separates the two Fryupdales. It boasts a heathery cap and stunningly beautiful forest in Crag Wood at its northern end. Facing Danby Crag on Heads, across Eskdale, is the prominent **Beacon Hill**, complete with modern commemorative beacon, accessible by tarmac road to the summit. This road continues over to **Scaling Dam reservoir**, the largest lake in the Moors, and a good bird-watching venue – breeding greylag geese and little ringed plovers are specialities, with ospreys as regular passage migrants.

The Moors Centre, Danby

Open every day (weekends only in January and February), this building originated as the palatial shooting lodge for the Dawnay Estate and is now the flagship visitor centre for the North York Moors National Park. You could easily spend a whole day here, especially in fine weather, as there is just as much to do outside as in. Within the grounds short, wheelchair-accessible walks follow the riverside and delve into Crow Wood, an orienteering course and climbing frame can entertain those energetic children, the artistic will enjoy the sculpture trail and if you just want to sit and picnic, there's acres of lawn space. For those happy to wander further afield, five waymarked walks start at the lodge. Recently revamped, the building contains an indoor climbing wall, a gallery with changing exhibitions of arts and crafts inspired by the local landscape, a shop and a tea room.

Danby Castle

In a long and eventful life since it was built in the 12th century, this petite castle has passed through the hand of many aristocratic owners; Catherine Parr, who married into the Neville family, lived here as a young woman long before her recruitment as Henry VIII's sixth wife. As part of the Danby section of the Dawnay Estate, like the Moors Centre, it is owned by Viscount Downe.

After many years of part-ruin, attached to a hillside farm, Danby Castle's latest chapter involves a neat juxtaposition of ancient and modern. Every October the Danby Court Leet, one of the few still in existence, meets in the jury room of the castle, as it has for centuries, to administer the affairs of the local common lands. The same room doubles as a wedding chapel, music venue and corporate meeting room, operated by Danby Castle Events (www.danbycastle.com), a family enterprise comprising Duncan and Carolyn who live in the farmhouse (the southeast tower).

The castle is not officially open to the public, but if you want to nose around the outside of the ruins, just knock on the farmhouse door and ask; it is their garden after all.

Camphill Village Trust Botton Farm YO21 2NJ 01287 661211. Camphill community shop has Botton bread, cakes, milk, yoghurt and cheese.
Duke of Wellington Danby 01287 660351 www.dukeofwellingtondanby.co.uk. A large, rambling but homely village pub on the central crossroads. Cask beer is Tetleys Imperial, Daleside and a guest; there's a selection of pies. River fishing tickets available behind the bar.
Fox and Hounds Brook Lane, Ainthorpe 01287 660218 www.foxandhounds-ainthorpe.com. A big 16th-century coaching inn with quoits pitch nearby. Cask Yorkshire beers and basic pub grub.
Stonehouse Bakery Briar Hill, Danby 01287 660006. Speciality breads, cakes and confectionery to take away or eat in the café.

④ Lealholm

Back in the 1990s I was always baffled as to why Lealholm was not more popular as a place to visit. Granted, the riverbank and quoits pitch would be dotted with picnickers on a sunny weekend, but nothing like the hordes that would descend on Goathland or Grosmont rain or shine. Back then, there was only enough custom to support the pub and one tea shop at the Shepherd's Hall. Now numbers must have perked up, or people are drinking more, because three places supply those wanting to indulge in a cup of tea and a scone, and the pub is busier than ever.

I guess the reason for the influx is that more people are using the Esk Valley line and hopping off at the station here, the growing reputation of the revitalised Board Inn, or the fact that word has got out about the excellent walking and cycling routes from the village.

Two circular jaunts from Lealholm I would recommend are a low-level route and another longer one, partly on the moors above the valley. The beauty of them is that, following bridleways and minor roads, they can be done on foot, bike or horseback for that matter. The shorter of the two starts along the track just below the car park, and following the river eastwards (downstream). At Underpark farm, the route heads under the railway and uphill to Rake Lane. The farmyard can be a bit 'clarty' – the Yorkshire dialect understated way of saying that you may find yourself up to the knees in a mixture of mud and cow muck. A left turn at the quiet dead-ended Rake Lane takes you back to Lealholm via Lealholmside. The longer high-level route climbs up Danby Beacon and back via moorland track and Oakley Walls Road.

Food and drink

Beck View Tea Room Main St ☎ 01947 897310. Attached to the back of the village shop, this snug little café does exactly what it says on the tin, with a fine vista of both Lealholm Beck and the River Esk.

Board Inn Village Green ☎ 01947 897279 ⁂ www.theboardinn.com. An 18th-century alehouse in a glorious riverside position with quoits pitch out front.

Stepping Stones Cottage Bakery Village Green ☎ 01947 897626. Lovely fresh bread and pastries to eat in the sun on the village green opposite.

Shopping

Forge House Gallery Main St ☎ 01947 897901 ⁂ www.forgehousegallery.co.uk. Gallery of contemporary, 19th and 20th-century paintings, and shop with local craft items.

Forge Pottery Main St ☎ 01947 897457. A small pottery workshop opposite the gallery, selling its produce and a few other arts and crafts.

Lealholm Village Store Main St ☎ 01947 897310. This is the only shop in the village so it sells absolutely everything, or seems to. It even incorporates the excellent **Beck**.

Poets Cottage Shrub Nursery Main St ☎ 01947 897424 ⁂ www.poetscottage.co.uk. A serene hideaway just behind the village store, named after the 19th century, Irish-born poet, John Castillo, who lived here.

⑤ Glaisdale

A more rural picture would be difficult to imagine, but the Glaisdale of 150 years ago was an altogether different scene: the river polluted, the air full of black industrial smoke, the clank and rattle of heavy machinery and rail carriages, and its erstwhile pub full of ironstone miners and foundry workers. Glaisdale's industrial revolution was short-lived and the scars have healed, but sharp-eyed industrial archaeologists will still have plenty to find.

The history of this long, straggling village goes way back beyond the Victorian iron boom as the graceful 17th-century packhorse bridge over the river testifies. It was constructed on the instruction of one Thomas Ferris, originally a poor farmer's son, who fell in love with the Squire of Glaisdale's daughter, but was refused her hand in marriage unless he went away and made his fortune. When he succeeded in the task he returned, married his love and built 'Beggar's Bridge' to commemorate his wading of the swollen river to see her during their courtship, and to ensure that later needy suitors kept their feet dry.

At the point where Beggar's Bridge reaches gracefully over the river, a small railway viaduct does the same, though not quite so delicately. Glaisdale Beck joins the Esk through one of its arches, having just flowed down through West Arncliffe Wood. Strangely, this beck has been nowhere near Glaisdale village, which actually resides in Eskdale; the valley of Glaisdale, where the beck originates, is a rarely visited corner nearby. Its one minor road loops up one side of the dale, and back down the other, providing an excellent, gentle, family-cycling circuit.

R H Ford & Son Butchers Main St, Glaisdale village ☎ 01947 897235. Beef and lamb from their own farm; other local farms supply pork for bacon, shop-made sausages and shop-salted hams. The black pudding is legendary and, of the 17 kinds of pie available, Monty Don once declared the pork pie to be the best he had ever tasted. All in all, a pretty good butchers.

Gillbeck Organic Homegrown Low Gill Beck Farm, Glaisdale YO21 2QA ☎ 01947 897363. Seasonal soft fruits for sale.

Padmore's Bank House Farm, Glaisdale YO21 2QA ☎ 01947 897297. Organic beef, lamb and pork straight from the farm.

⑥ Egton and Egton Bridge

The trees that gave 'oak town' its name are gone, but one survivor from the villages past is alive and well. **Egton Show**, on the last Wednesday in August, is the largest of its kind in the North York Moors, and such an event in the country calendar that for many people it is the one and only time they visit during the year. Others may call in to one of the two pubs here, or the village shop whilst passing through, but not much else will hold your attention.

A mile down the road, the ancient river crossing at **Egton Bridge** attracts far more visitors. Like its hilltop neighbour, it has two pubs, one on either side of the river, with a delightful stepping-stone and island-hopping potter between them. A steady stream of admirers always seem to find their way to Egton Bridge, some just happy to gaze at the magnificent 18th-century redwood trees by the river, or to saunter along its banks. Downstream, a flat and just-about wheelchair accessible track leads to Grosmont, whilst the other direction takes you into the spectacular Arncliffe Gorge, and a glorious woodland trail to Glaisdale along the Cleveland Way. Other visitors are Roman Catholic pilgrims visiting St Hedda's church, one that seemed to miss the Reformation and large enough to be dubbed the Cathedral of the Moors. Despite these attractions, the only time it really gets crowded here is at gooseberry show-time.

S⟩ The Postgate Inn Egton Bridge ☎ 01947 895241 ⌂ www.postgateinn.com. Small and cosy pub by the railway station that doubles as the 'Black Dog' in *Heartbeat* but in real life is named after a local Catholic martyr. Exceptionally good food, traditional English, and cask Yorkshire beer.

S⟩ The Wheatsheaf Inn Main St, Egton ☎ 01947 895271 ⌂ www.wheatsheaf egton.com. A comfortable and traditional village pub with an emphasis on good food and fine wines. Best on a winter's evening with a roaring fire in the bar corner range.

Growing giant gooseberries

A world record was broken in Egton Bridge in 2009. It wasn't one that made the national news, but amongst the soft-fruit growing fraternity, the biggest gooseberry ever seen was a major event.

The Egton Bridge Old Gooseberry Society (www.egtongooseberryshow.org.uk) has been holding an annual show on the first Tuesday in August for over 200 years, making it the oldest in the country. Come along in the afternoon for public viewing of the 600 or so entries and prizes for the winners. You will learn about reds, whites, yellows and greens and the relative merits of the Lord Derby, Lord Kitchener and Montrose varieties but you're not likely to see the like of Bryan Nellist's monster 35-dram (two and a bit ounces) Woodpecker, in the foreseeable future.

⑦ Grosmont

In the past two centuries life has almost gone full circle for Grosmont, from rural backwater to industrial centre and back again. Almost but not quite, because, although the ironstone mines and blast furnaces are gone, the railways (two of them) still remain.

The smoke-stained buildings of Grosmont sit at the confluence of two river valleys, the Esk and then the Murk Esk, and are consequently the junction of the two railway lines in those dales. The Esk Valley line is three stations away from Whitby here, and is joined by the North Yorkshire Moors Railway, now a very popular private steam and diesel line crossing the moors from Pickering. Up until recently this was the terminus for steam services, but old locomotives puffing their way through Sleights and Ruswarp to Whitby are now regularly seen in summer.

Such was the impact of the railway when it arrived in Grosmont that its common name changed to 'Tunnel', after the line's short underground journey. It was during the digging of the first small tunnel for a horse-drawn tramway, that ironstone was first discovered and this route has since become a footpath to the **railway engine sheds**. Another footpath, over the top of the tunnels, then follows the rest of the track bed of the old line, planned and built by George Stephenson, the 'railway king'. The Rail Trail crosses the Murk Esk four times on its three-mile journey to Goathland via Beck Hole.

Grosmont Engine Sheds

The public face of the North Yorkshire Moors Railway is the station and level crossing in the village main street: but if you want to see what makes this organisation really tick, then stroll over the footbridge across the river, and through the Stephenson's Tunnel footpath. This will take you to the Grosmont Engine Sheds where the locomotive restoration, maintenance and servicing takes place, and where hard-core enthusiastic volunteers work; there's probably enough oil under their collective fingernails to keep a small car on the road. A public viewing platform lets you watch the work going on and the shed shop sells enthusiasts bric-a-brac.

Grosmont Gallery and Jazz Café Front St ☎ 01947 895007
✆ www.grosmontgallery.com. A wide range of art and craft work displayed; paintings, ceramics, textiles, glass, sculpture, photographs and jewellery. Relax in a café armchair with a cup of tea or coffee whilst you admire the work, and the background jazz music.

⑧ Beck Hole

Almost every approach to this tiny hamlet involves a precipitous hill, to where its dozen or so houses nestle at the bottom of a natural excavation – no surprises where the name came from. Becks' Hole (plural) would be more accurate in fact, as this is the point where Eller Beck, still visibly and audibly excited after its recent fall over Thomason Foss, joins West Beck to create the River Murk Esk. As at Grosmont, ironstone was worked here, and many old buildings served the miners and furnace workers, some as ale-houses.

Only one pub remains, but the **Birch Hall Inn** is the heart and soul of the village; that and the quoits pitch, scene of many sepia-coloured triumphs decorating the walls of the pub. Of all my visits over the years, the most memorable have been on wet winter nights, with a fire blazing in the big bar, a wet dog steaming in front of it and just a handful of locals to share the craic. For me, the Birch Hall is as near perfection as a pub can get, and my favourite anywhere in the country.

On a quiet day, the best sort here, you can hear steam engines pass without stopping on the 'new' line higher up the hill but Beck Hole's station is a 'ghost' on the 1836 route, at the foot of the feature which caused its closure. The incline up to Goathland was way too steep for horses or locomotives to pull carriages up, so ropes and cables did the job, first using an ingenious water-filled counterweight tank coming down, then a big, fixed engine at the top. Rope and cable failure caused mayhem on more than one occasion so, after a crash causing two deaths and thirteen injuries, in 1864 the line was re-routed to bypass the incline.

Scope for walking around Beck Hole is extensive, especially half-day rambles that use part of the old railway track at some stage. For a glorious two-mile woodland and heather circuit, go west to circumnavigate Randy Mere reservoir. Steam enthusiasts will enjoy following the railway to Darnholm and the incline back (another two miles) or of course the full three-mile **Rail Trail** from Goathland to Grosmont is a classic, and you can travel back on the train.

⑧ **Birch Hall Inn** ☎ 01947 896245 ✆ www.beckhole.info/bhi.htm. This little ale-house is a genuine national treasure, made up of two tiny bar-rooms, served by hatches, and a sweet shop sandwiched in between – virtually unchanged for 70 years. Three beers are usually available, Black Sheep, the house brew 'Beckwatter' from the North Yorkshire Brewing Co. and a guest, and food is simple but wholesome; Botham's roll butties and Radford's pies.

⑨ Goathland

I was always a little surprised at the popularity of Goathland even before *Heartbeat* hit our TV screens, as I don't think it has anywhere near the charm and neatness of Lealholm or the character of Grosmont. Now though, its visitor-pulling power is in a different league since it became Aidensfield, and its railway station starred as 'Hogsmeade' in the first *Harry Potter* film. I prefer to pass through, and visit some of the glorious countryside nearby, like **Wheeldale** or the gorges of Eller Beck, towards **Beck Hole**, and West Beck nearer at hand.

A signpost opposite the church indicates the direct route down to the surprisingly verdant netherworld of **West Beck**, with a waterside footpath that takes you past the silky tresses of **Mallyan Spout waterfall**, or under it if you're feeling bold, or hot, or both. If you are up for a challenge, then the mile of public footpath upstream from here is for you, as it follows a deep, narrow and boulder-strewn ravine up to New Wath Bridge on the Egton road. This can be

Quoits

Nothing better reflects the dogged insularity of the Yorkshireman than the game of quoits. It is played virtually nowhere else in the world other than this corner of northeast England, and Eskdale is its heartland.

Norse in origin, as are most things hereabouts, the game involves tossing a metal ring from one end of a pitch to the other, aiming to 'hoopla' a metal pin (a two-point 'ringer'); touch it for one point or at least thunk into the surrounding square of clay nearer than your opponent's quoit.

The tiny hamlet of Beckhole has had more than its fair share of 'world' champions in its time, so I asked Mike Mendelsohn, a multiple winner of that prestigious title, what made a great quoits player.

'A good strong arm's important. That ring weighs five pound, which is a fair weight to be slinging. You don't want to be straining to reach t'pin. It's best to have a bit of distance to spare, which is why me father had us throwing full sized quoits as bairns to build us up. What else do you need? A good eye, a nasty streak and a willingness to go down the pub regularly and practise!'

Almost all the region's quoits pitches are in front of a village pub, and many a visitor has been seen puzzling over the wooden covers and peeping at the mysterious

042

a serious scramble, especially when wet or icy, and West Beck floods the path after heavy rain. Come here on a warm summer afternoon though, and it shows its other face; wood warblers singing in the tops of the oaks, dippers zipping up the rapids and dragonflies snatching a meal from the clouds of gnats that dance over the chattering waters – a glorious place.

⑩ Wheeldale Roman Road and Wheeldale Moor

South of Goathland, a vast tract of land rises as whale-backed hills, pimple-topped with Bronze Age burial mounds and smothered in what is part of England's largest continuous area of **heather moorland**. Two Howes Rigg, Simon Howe and Wheeldale Moor are all Access Areas where you can in general walk where you please: for lovers of peace and tranquillity in the natural world it is a slice of heaven. I have spent many a day up here, striding through the heather or squelching across bogs, with the spicy scent of sweet gale in the air and the bubbling of curlews in my ears, and often not seen another human all day.

Hot summer days are best for wildlife, with the air alive with bees and dragonflies, green tiger beetles scurrying across the sandy soil and an excellent chance of seeing lizards or adders. In August add the bonus of the spectacular flowering of the heather; trillions of tiny blooms combining to form a purple blanket across the hill. Take care from the 12th of the month onwards though, as areas of moor may be closed for shooting.

clay beneath. Turn up on a Saturday and all will be revealed; and what better way to spend a summer evening than discussing the day's walk and sipping a beer to the clink of metal on metal, as local rivalries are settled in an inter-village fixture. You never know, you may even be asked to join in. One of my proudest moments was making up the numbers in a Goldsborough team at home to Fryupdale. I was accosted by my neighbour Alwyn, as I sauntered over to the Fox and Hounds for a swift half one evening. 'Do you fancy a game Mike?' he asked. I laughed and muttered something about leaving it to the experts and having a pint waiting. 'No,' he said, 'I'm serious. Will Lewis is on a coastguard shout and we're down a man.'

So, the upshot was that I was given a quick resume of the rules, watched what the others were doing and attempted to copy them. My practice throws were a bit wayward, a couple of under-thrown bouncing bombs and an over corrected heave that cleared the clay and rebounded into the fence behind. By the time the opposition had arrived and the match got under way I had sort of found my distance and, whilst I never mastered the finer points of throwing 'Frenchman' or laying a 'gater', I didn't let the team down; 'steady away' was the verdict in the bar afterwards. If memory serves me rightly, we came out 21–19 winners.

To find the local quoits summer fixture list, go to www.tradgames.org.uk or to have a go yourself visit one of the many village shows in summer. They often have a come-and-try-it quoits stall.

Wheeldale Moor has a half-mile stretch of the best preserved and excavated **Roman road** in the country. The easiest access is at the Stape Road end where an interpretive board describes the local legend of Wade the giant and his labour of love. Wade lived in Mulgrave Castle near the coast at Sandsend but his wife Bel lived in Pickering castle. To make visiting easier they decided to build a road linking the two, but with only one rock-breaking hammer between them, they had to throw it across the moors to each other. The road is still known locally as Wade's Causeway, but the less romantic reality is that it linked the Roman garrison town of Malton to a chain of coastal signal stations.

⑪ Ruswarp

Twice a day the River Esk does something odd: prompted by the rising tide it flows backwards away from the sea and a mile inland to the village of **Ruswarp**, (pronounced Ruzzup). Its short journey winding under two big viaducts over the estuarine floodplain is a joy, and one that you can follow on foot, by train or, best of all, by boat. Some of the trip boats will venture up the river at high tide and there are possibilities for paddling or rowing your own boat. You're at the richest section of the whole river for wildlife and on the right day it can be a memorable experience: very rare saltmarsh plants like wild celery and hemlock water dropwort grow on the banks alongside vitamin-C-rich scurvy grass, which sailors took as a preventative supplement on voyages. The water teems with tiny opossum shrimps, attracting fish, which in turn bring herons, cormorants, dabchicks and kingfishers. When the sea-trout and salmon are running, seals follow them up the river and otters are here, although dawn and dusk are the only times you are likely to see them, such is their shyness.

Up until the 15th century the Esk was tidal all the way to Sleights along what is still known as The Carrs, meaning flooded woodland, but for 600 years a watermill weir has stopped the tide at Ruswarp. You can get welcome respite from the crowds of Whitby here while still finding things to occupy you; a round of golf on the pitch and putt, a circuit of the miniature steam railway, feeding the ducks on the mill pond or just watching the river go by from the Bridge Inn beer garden.

Sadly, no footpath follows the river for its next languid mile upstream, but half-hourly buses or, better still, the train four or five times a day can take you to **Sleights** where a bridleway picks up the Esk Valley Walk route. The River Esk trickles when it's low or roars at high levels, over another weir at Sleights with a fish ladder at the side. In flood conditions the salmon don't bother with their staircase but jump straight up the main wave, and this is the best place on the whole river to watch them do it. The nearby pub, not surprisingly, is called the Salmon Leap.

Rowing and paddling

Various alternatives exist for you to get afloat at Ruswarp and explore the river using your own muscle power. **Ruswarp Pleasure Boats** (01947 604658; www.ruswarp-pleasure-boats.co.uk) hire out rowing boats or sit-on-top kayaks to explore the non-tidal mile of flat river upstream to Sleights.

If you have access to your own canoes or kayaks you can arrange launching with Ruswarp Pleasure Boats and stay on the flat water or descend the friendly weir and run the tidal section of river to the public slipway at Whitby marina, returning by train. Alternatively, launch at Whitby an hour or two before high tide, drift up with the flood, spend a relaxing hour in Ruswarp, before coming back down river with the ebb-tide.

If all that sounds tempting but the lack of a boat is stopping you then the whole trip can be arranged by East Barnby Outdoor Education Centre (01947 893333; www.outdoored.co.uk). You choose the route and do all the paddling but they provide transport, equipment (including possibilities for wheelchair users) and a guide.

The River Gardens The Carrs, Sleights ☎ 07785573625 ⌂ www.perrysplants.co.uk. Plant nursery and riverside café. Crab sandwiches and local Radford's steak pies particularly good.

⑫ Falling Foss

Just over three miles south of Ruswarp, May Beck's tumble over a 67-foot-tall shale cliff creates Falling Foss, the highest waterfall in the North York Moors, and the centrepiece of a secretive wooded valley. It is possible to drive and park close to the falls but I find it much more satisfying to arrive here on foot along the beck, with the noise of the cascade gradually developing from a distant hiss to a spray-filled roar as I approach. Of the two routes in, the northerly upstream one is probably the more trodden, as the final mile joins up with the Coast to Coast Walk.

It can be started from Sleights railway station and following a tributary of the River Esk which has a confusing habit of changing its name. It is Iburndale Beck for its first mile, then Little Beck as it passes through the rich rainforest-like woods owned by the Yorkshire Wildlife Trust. Just before you arrive at the falls, look out for The Hermitage, a remarkable hollowed-out boulder shelter, complete with seats.

The southerly downstream approach starts at Sneaton Forest car park (grid reference NZ 893024) and follows our stream under its third pseudonym, May Beck, on either bank, along a half-mile nature trail to Midge Hall and its tea rooms on the lip of Falling Foss.

Other very popular Forestry Commission trails head in the opposite direction from May Beck car park, visiting more waterfalls as they enter the vast expanse of Sneaton Forest, a great place to see reptiles and amphibians. Adders and lizards are common in heathery clearings and the plethora of round ponds (World War II bomb craters) boil with frogs, toads and newts in springtime.

Beacon Farm Sneaton YO22 5HS ☎ 01947 605212 🖰 www.beacon-farm.co.uk. A farm that has diversified into Yorkshire dairy ice-cream production with a café attached.
Falling Foss Tea Garden YO22 5JD ☎ 07723477929
🖰 www.fallingfossteagarden.co.uk. The former gamekeeper's cottage of Midge Hall houses an Edwardian tea-garden in a most idyllic woodland site. Recently renovated and restored to sell drinks and snacks. Provides poohsticks for nearby bridge.

⑬ Whitby

'If you want a quiet day in Whitby, try a wet Tuesday in February, with the X Factor final on telly,' was Jim the taxi driver's advice, and his reasoning is plain to see. Whitby is an extremely popular destination, bursting at the seams every weekend, and even midweek if the sun appears. The root of the town's pulling power is its possession of a little bit of something for everyone, seeming to combine in a melting pot all the best that Yorkshire has to offer with a dash of Cornish fishing port and more than a drop of Transylvanian blood. The place is dripping in history, oozing from the pores of every building, like a little York-by-the-sea; Tudor halls, gothic ruins, Saxon churches, smugglers' pubs and fishermen's cottages – they all have their stories to tell. And then, cheek by jowl, you will find the other, more modern Whitby of buckets and spades, amusement arcades and fish-and-chip shops, but even this has a dated and quaintly retro feel to it.

Three figures stand tall in Whitby's past: a woman who famously arrived on a mission, a man who left three times and changed the world, and a character who never even came here, because he didn't really exist. The woman was a Northumbrian princess called **Hild** who came in the year 656 and founded a Saxon monastery on East Cliff, the first Whitby Abbey. The seafarer who repeatedly left in the 18th century, along with shiploads of crewmates, was **Captain James Cook**. He returned twice, but never made it back from his third voyage, having been clubbed to death on a Hawaiian beach – the sort of thing that always upsets your travel plans. Ironically, the most well-known of the three characters is a fictitious literary creation of the Victorian novelist **Bram Stoker**, the infamous Count Dracula. The horrifically evocative Chapter 7 of Stoker's novel *Dracula*, where the Count, in the form of a black dog, leaps off a ship grounded in the harbour, and bounds through the alleyways of the town, should be read on a bench in the churchyard overlooking the scene, for full effect. Dracula's link with Whitby has inspired one of the town's most lively and entertaining annual events, the Goth Festival, which takes place on the weekend nearest to Halloween each year.

Whitby owes its existence to the **River Esk** and the fact that it is a natural sheltered anchorage for ships using the North Sea. This is still what it always was, a working harbour, and going to sea in boats will always be at the heart of the town. In the 18th century fleets of sailing ships left these shores, not just explorers in Cook's *Resolution, Discovery* and *Endeavour* but whalers of world renown like the captains (father and son) Scoresby. In the early 20th century when herring fishing was at its peak, hundreds of boats packed the harbour and it was said you could walk from one side to the other without getting your feet wet. Overfishing and, latterly, European quota setting have been the death knell for the fishing industry and only four deep-sea trawlers operate from Whitby. Their place on the wharf has been taken by a proliferation of pleasure boats; yachts, cruisers, scuba-diving inflatables, and boat trips – tourism is king now.

The river both unites and divides the town, even more so pre-1767 when no bridge linked the two sides. Separation breeds suspicion and the inhabitants of each bank referred to each other as 't'other side o' watter dogs'. Such was the mistrust that when the first bridge was opened, locals celebrated with a pitched battle in the middle. Even today, old-established families say they come from East Whitby or West Whitby, not Whitby. The first bridge lifted to allow boats through but the Victorian replacement that survives today is a swing bridge and is the focal point of the town. Whitby has so much to see that I would recommend splitting it into two trails to visit on foot, both starting here.

Scarborough Borough Council produces two excellent **town trail** books, one for each side of the river and available from the tourist office. The *West Side Trail* visits all the fascinating places you would expect – the *Grand Turk* sailing ship, Baxtergate yards, whalebone arch, Captain Cook's statue and fish quay – but it fails to mention what, to me, should always be a compulsory prime objective, weather and phobias permitting – the pier end. This is as far out to sea as it is possible to get without a boat and an exhilarating experience in rough weather. Whitby harbour faces due north and is one of the few places in the country where watching the sunrise and sunset over the sea is possible on the same day – you are allowed to go for a cup of tea in between. On your way out or back, look out for dinosaur 'fossils' carved into the concrete by local stonemason Darren Yeadon, and take a walk up the spiral staircase in the lighthouse if it's open (01947 601344).

The east side is my favourite; more compact and with fewer new intrusions, this is where I can best let my historical imagination run riot. The *East Side Trail* mentions the jet shops, old inns, lifeboat pier, market square (still operational Tuesdays and Saturdays) and 199 steps up to the church and abbey but stops again at the foot of the pier. Owing to wave damage only half of the east pier is accessible but it's a wild and evocative place, sanctuary for large numbers of sheltering purple sandpipers in winter.

Off the trail, and around the corner under the cliffs, a short mile's wander along the wave-cut platform to Saltwick Bay makes a tremendous diversion, with the return to the abbey via the cliff-top Cleveland Way. Small boats anchored just offshore here may be carrying sub-aqua divers visiting the wreck of the *Rohilla*, a World War I hospital ship which hit Whitby Rock on a stormy night in 1914 with the loss of 85 lives. One survivor, a nurse, had only ever been on a ship once before – the *Titanic*. I don't suppose she ever went to sea again.

Whitby Abbey

If ever a place could be described as having a chequered history, then this is it: founded by Saxons, destroyed by Vikings, rebuilt by Normans, dismantled by Tudors, bombarded by Germans and desecrated by Satanists.

When Princess Hild was sent from Hartlepool in 656 she arrived in the tiny fishing hamlet of Streoneshalh (Whitby was a later Danish name) and became first Abbess of the wooden Columban abbey of St Peter. She later became the patron saint of the town and had many wells and a fossil named after her. *Hildocerous bifrons* is an ammonite common in the cliffs below the abbey and commemorates the legend that St Hilda turned snakes infesting the headland into stone and threw them over the cliff. Medieval monks even carved heads on to them and sold them as 'snake-stones'. During her time a dispute between the Roman and Celtic churches over the date of Easter was settled at the Synod of Whitby and we still use their convoluted formula today, to annual confusion.

After the Vikings razed the original structure, the Normans rebuilt, in local sandstone, the present Benedictine abbey. At the dissolution much of the abbey stone was used to build the Manor next door which now houses the Abbey Visitor Centre.

In one last twist of fate, during World War I, a flotilla of German battleships bombarded the east coast of England. Scarborough and Hartlepool were also targeted but the abbey was particularly badly damaged during Whitby's shelling.

This won't be the final chapter; when the abbey was built it stood half a mile from the sea but in the intervening 900 years that distance has been reduced to 200 yards by the erosional power of the North Sea. In a few more hundred years, the stones of the abbey will be on the beach growing seaweed.

St Mary's Church

I have a soft spot for St Mary's, as it was the church that I was married in, and my daughter was baptised here. That said, I can still safely claim, without being accused of bias, that this is one of the most fascinatingly quirky churches in the country.

Why not St Hilda's you may be thinking, as the church is next door to the abbey of the patron saint. The answer lies in St Mary's antiquity – it was already here, complete with name, when the Princess came calling. The fact is that the heart of this building is older than its neighbour but has been added to piecemeal ever since. The outside is full of interest – Norman arches a-plenty and a strange ship's-deck-style roof – but go inside and you could be in a museum. Rare 17th-century box pews, a three-decker pulpit with ear trumpets for a deaf vicar's wife, a multi-locked treasure chest, and more, all candle-lit and heated from a central pot boiler.

Don't confine yourself to the building but wander around the graveyard surrounding it. Like a mouthful of loose and rotting teeth, this has to be the perfect horror film set. Those gravestones still legible tell of boat sinkings and drownings, master mariners and lifeboat men. One of the eeriest is the Huntrodds memorial, to a husband and wife born on the same day, married on their birthday and dying within hours of each other on... you guessed it, their birthday again.

Whitby Museum

If you enter this building expecting a high-tech, hands-on multisensory modern museum, you will be disappointed. The words hotchpotch and higgledy-piggledy could have been invented for Whitby Museum; it is unashamedly old-fashioned, cramped, politically incorrect, poorly set out, and full of glass cases, but that is what sets it apart and gives it its charm. It is not only a museum of things, but a museum piece of museums.

Themes seem infinitely varied: model ships, stuffed birds, local archaeology, fossils, military clothing, and a brilliant weather-forecasting machine based on leeches, called a tempest prognosticator – a little bit of everything but not much of anything. Don't get the impression that it's all junk in here though. One of the model ships made from food-ration chicken bones by Napoleonic prisoners of war is reportedly worth £250,000 and the carved jet collection is the best in the world, and features two wonderful jet chessboards.

What I like best about this place, though, is the chance to explore and discover things for myself. I read elsewhere of a sea kayak in here, the only one of its design in the world, so I searched and eventually found it, on top of a wall cabinet, unlabelled – that's this place to a tee.

Eating and drinking

Black Horse Inn Church St ☎01947 602906 🖰 www.the-black-horse.com. An unspoiled architectural gem, possibly the oldest pub in town with the original Victorian bar. Traditional in every sense of the word, with up to five cask ales including Whitby Black Dog, Yorkshire cheese or seafood tapas to eat and snuff to sniff.

Elizabeth Botham and Sons ☎01947 602823 🖰 www.botham.co.uk. Long-standing tea rooms; family-run craft bakery since 1865.

Fortunes Smokehouse Henrietta St ☎01947 601659. Traditional kipper-smoking shed with shop attached. Kippers sold in pairs wrapped in newspaper.

Greens Bridge St ☎01947 600284 🖰 www.greensofwhitby.co.uk. Restaurant/bistro specialising in exceptional local seafood.

The Magpie Café Pier Rd ☎01947 602058 🖰 www.magpiecafe.co.uk. World-famous café serving superlative seafood, especially fish and chips. Be prepared to queue.

Royal Fisheries Baxtergate ☎01947 604738 🖰 www.fuscowhitby.com. The locals' favourite takeaway chippy since 1968 when the Fusco family moved here from Pickering. Known as 'Fuscos' in town.

Attractions and shopping

Captain Cook Memorial Museum Grape Lane ☎ 01947 601900
🖰 www.cookmuseumwhitby.co.uk. 17th-century lodgings of James Cook as an apprentice. Unique original exhibits and great view of inner harbour.
Doodlepots Creative Studio Skinner St ☎ 01947 825824 🖰 www.doodlepots.co.uk. Paint your own plain plate/cup/pot/bowl etc, then have it fired to pick up later.
Eagle Turnery Hunter St ☎ 01947 821205. Nick Harty works on his lathe in the shop to produce a wide range of turned wooden objects.
Studio of John Freeman Market Place ☎ 01947 602799
🖰 www.johnfreemanstudios.co.uk. Resident artist working in watercolours.
Sutcliffe Gallery Flowergate ☎ 01947 602239 🖰 www.sutcliffe-gallery.co.uk. Books and black-and-white photographs by the master Victorian photographer.
Wash House Pottery Blackburn Yard ☎ 01947 604995. Customised tiles, planters, house plaques and plates made on site.
Whitby Jet Heritage Centre Church St ☎ 01947 821530 🖰 www.whitbyjet.net. An original Victorian jet works with working craftsmen.
Whitby Lifeboat Museum (RNLI) Pier Rd ☎ 01947 606094. Vintage lifeboat and lots of RNLI memorabilia. Free entry.
Whitby Museum Pannett Park ☎ 0194702908 🖰 www.whitbymuseum.org.uk. Open all year, closed Mon.

The Cleveland coast: Sandsend to Skinningrove

A few years ago from the back of a ferry leaving Newcastle, I saw through binoculars a dark line on the horizon to the southeast. What I was seeing 40 miles away was the great bulge of the northern North York Moors meeting the sea in a line of dark crags. Marauding Vikings approaching from the North Sea over a thousand years ago had the same view, prompting them to name this part of England the Land of Cliffs – Cleveland. This wall of rock stretches, seemingly unbroken, from Saltburn southeast to Whitby and beyond. Prehistoric erosion has breached the wall in a handful of places, allowing the coastal communities of **Sandsend**, **Runswick Bay**, **Staithes** and **Skinningrove** to develop. In the past all have relied for their livelihood on the silver harvest of the sea, and mineral wealth from the cliffs themselves, but now to a greater or lesser degree each depends on tourism.

⑭ Sandsend

This village is certainly aptly named: two miles of golden beach stops abruptly at the foot of The Ness and this cluster of sandstone cottages, hotels and shops huddle in what little shelter it provides. A closer look reveals two hamlets here; one for each of the small streams that flow into the sea 200 yards apart.

East Row, at the beach end, is older but smaller, and hosts the White Hart pub, two cafés, a restaurant, a very tasteful art and craft shop and the main entrance to **Mulgrave Woods**. At the cliff end, most of Sandsend proper hides up the little valley of Sandsend Beck, with a sleepy hobbit village air to it. Even at the height of summer when the beach is crowded, and boy does it get crowded, all stays serene and peaceful up here, with little to disturb the grazing goats.

What the original valley inhabitants were hiding from was the full force of the North Sea. Houses and shops along the seafront are now protected from the worst by a concrete sea-wall, but even this doesn't stop the road being shut at least once a year, when waves from a high spring tide and northeasterly gale combined can send spray over the top of three-storey buildings. The final two buildings at this end of the village are the old railway station and the remains of an alum works, now a café and car park. Beyond lies an industrial archaeologist's wonderland, visited by the **Sandsend Trail**.

The Sandsend Trail

Once you have climbed thirty or so steps up from the car park to join the old railway line, and leant on the station platform to catch your breath, you can relax, because you needn't go uphill again during the rest of this walk.

This cindery track-bed heads along the cliff edge to what locals call 'The Moon', giving grandstand views of wheeling fulmars and surfers on the famed reef-break (known as 'caves' to surfers) below. It weaves its way between vast quarried holes and artificial hills called 'clamps' – remnants of 300 years of the alum industry. Spoil from the works is so disagreeable to plant life that most areas remain completely bare of vegetation, hence the lunar references.

The flat trail ends abruptly at a railway tunnel entrance a mile down the line. You can retrace your steps or continue along the Cleveland Way you have been unwittingly following, and brave the big climb over the tunnel. Roof falls and subsidence have made the underground route unsafe but I did get the chance to traverse its three-quarter-mile length once, whilst searching for a missing person with the auxiliary coastguard. We didn't find anyone, but had a huge scare when torchlight revealed an old wetsuit that some practical joker had stuffed to look like a headless corpse. The air turned blue with relief when we realised our mistake.

Mulgrave Woods

If you can, arrange your visit to Sandsend for a Wednesday, Saturday or Sunday, because these are the days that access is granted to these private woods. Large-scale pheasant rearing has spoilt some parts but this is a big wood and there are still lush, pristine corners; three castles, alum quarries, cement stone mines and a wealth of wildlife – easily a full day's worth of exploration. The woods cloak the two parallel ravines of East Row Beck and Sandsend Beck and the Castle Rigg in between, so a circular walk could take you up one valley and back down the other. Alternatively, a taxi drop-off two miles inland, where the East Barnby road crosses the woods, would allow you a linear walk downhill to the sea.

Espionage, fire water and urine – the alum story

Back in the 16th century, the only known chemical able to fix dyes in cloth was alum, but the complex process for extracting it from rock was known only to chemists in the Vatican. In the first ever documented case of industrial espionage, Henry VIII managed to steal the formula and the English alum industry began. The shale of the Cleveland coast contains 2% alum and to get it, the rock had to be quarried by pick and shovel, piled up and roasted by fire for months, treated with an alkali then dissolved in water and dried, to allow the crystals to form.

Here comes the bit of the process everyone always remembers; the cheapest source of alkali was stale urine, and such volumes were needed that every household in Whitby was required by law to put out all their urine for collection. At the height of the industry demand exceeded supply, so barrels of urine were shipped up from London. Rather than send the barrels back empty they were filled with butter for the rich appetites of the folk in the capital. As the barrels were never rinsed, this is said to account for Southerners' taste for yellow salted butter!

Food and drink

Bridge Cottage Café East Row ✆ 01947 893111. A quaint old building off the track to Mulgrave Woods selling hot drinks, snacks and more substantial meals.

Estbek House East Row ✆ 01947 893424 ⊕ www.estbeckhouse.co.uk. A quietly elegant restaurant next door to the White Hart pub and overlooking East Row Beck, as the name suggests.

Sandside Café East Row ✆ 01947 893916. Fantastic position right on the beach, great surf views while you have your drink or snack.

Shopping

Sandsend Stores Sea Front ✆ 01947 893214. Everything in the village revolves round Dougie and Irene's shop, which doubles as newsagent, post office and delicatessen.

Turnstone Gallery East Row ✆ 01947 893289 ⊕ www.turnstonegallery.net. A tasteful selection of arts and crafts produced by local artisans. Regularly changing exhibitions.

⑮ Runswick Bay

Ice-creams, buckets and spades, multi-coloured wind-breaks and crowds of bank holiday sunbathers; Runswick Bay does all of that, but venture a frisbee-throw away from the car-park and slipways and it shows a much wilder side to its nature.

Halfway round the sandy bay, and just past the yacht club, low shale cliffs begin and the guttural cackles of nesting fulmars compete with the 'swosh' of the waves. This place is known as Hob Holes locally, after the old jet mines at the crag foot. Legend has it that a hobgoblin lived in the darkness with the unexplained ability to cure whooping cough. A chant of 'Hob, Hob, me bairn's got kink cough. Takk it off, takk it off,' was the brief and to-the-point request that was supposed to do the trick.

The Cleveland Way footpath makes its way to the top of the cliff at Hob Holes, so very few people carry on along the shore beyond this point, but the extra effort is well worth it. Just around the corner is the handkerchief-sized beach of Kettleness Sand, a wonderful secluded corner cowering beneath the battleship-grey walls of **Kettleness** itself. Here the only company you can expect are oystercatchers and turnstones ferreting around in the sea-weed, and maybe a nosey seal, head bobbing in the water off-shore.

Take care where you lie and sun-bathe though; too close to the cliff bottom and you are in danger of being landed on by one of the regular small rock falls. Back in the 1990s one family had a very close call when a huge section of cliff buried half of the beach. Fortunately it came down in instalments so they had time to make their escape down to the water's edge. Apparently their tartan rug and Tupperware are still deep under the rocks – an interesting find for the archaeologists of the future!

Cliff falls are maybe not good news for the average visitor to Kettleness Sand, but they certainly are for Mike Marshall, a professional fossil-hunter operating from his workshop at Sandsend (01947 893222; www.yorkshirecoast fossils.co.uk). 'I love going down on the seashore searching,' he said, 'Because you never know what you're going to find. Mostly it's ammonites of course; there are hundreds of different types in the rocks around here and they are my bread-and-butter – what I make my day-to-day living from. They don't take too long to prepare and polish, then I'll sell them to shops in Whitby, or on my website at £10–£30 or so. The really exciting moments are when big, important specimens turn up. I'm still working on an Ichthyosaur (giant fish-like reptile) that I found 15 years ago, which will probably sell for £15,000 when it is finished; that is my pension fund.'

Whilst Mike's sale-quality ammonites and belemnites make great souvenirs, hundreds more lie waiting to be found for free amongst the beach pebbles here. Half the fun is in the searching and children can be occupied for hours; top-tip, take an old dinner knife to split the soft rock and some paper and wax crayons to take rubbings of fossils embedded in big rocks. For more great ideas and free fossil identification sheets visit East Barnby Outdoor Education Centre, two miles from Runswick on the Whitby road. (01947 893333; www.outdoored.co.uk).

On busy days, parking can be a real problem at Runswick Bay, so you might do better to park at East Barnby and walk the four miles to Runswick (all downhill), via Goldsborough Roman signal station and the Cleveland Way cliff-top path. You will be rewarded with magnificent views on the way and a number 5 bus takes you back up the hill to East Barnby at the end.

Fox and Hounds Goldsborough YO21 3RX ☎ 01947 893372
www.foxandhoundsgoldsborough.co.uk. What was a fabulous pub is now an excellent restaurant (shame it couldn't be both). The daily changing menu features local game and Whitby fish. Closed Sun evenings and all day Mon and Tue.

Rock pooling

No trip to the seaside would be complete without a spot of rock pooling, and it was ever thus. How many of us have vivid childhood memories of mornings splashing in the waves, gritty sandwiches for lunch and then, as the tide recedes, ferreting in warm pools with a net and a bucket?

Without doubt, the prime quarry of most rock poolers are **crabs**. My day job involves taking schoolchildren on to the seashore to introduce them to the inter-tidal ecosystem, but sooner or later, even with 'A' level biology groups, proceedings usually degenerate into a 'biggest crab' competition. I have often pondered why we are all fascinated by these creatures, and have come to the conclusion that it is their creepy alien-ness (walking as they do sideways on eight legs) and the thrill of real danger; even a small crab can give a powerful and painful nip.

You will find four common species of crab without much difficulty, and the **shore** or **green crab** is by far the most abundant. Lift up flat rocks amongst the seaweed and they will scuttle away, or dangle a piece of meat-baited string into a deep pool and you could tempt them out into the open. These are the characters that are hauled up on crab lines to fill enthusiasts' buckets in Whitby and Scarborough harbours. **Edible** or **brown crabs** can be found lower down the shore, but only small, young specimens. The adults that end up on the fishmonger's slab live in deeper water. Identification is easy – the only crab with a shell the shape of a Cornish pasty and black mittens. **Hermit crabs** are many people's favourite, living as they do in someone else's shell, usually a periwinkle, top-shell or dog whelk. If you want to get a good view of the creature, place its shell upside down underwater and the crab will slide itself almost all the way out when it thinks the coast is clear and

⑯ Staithes

In many ways Staithes could qualify as a miniature Whitby – a tidal river slicing its way to the sea through steep cliffs, multicoloured fishing cobbles bobbing at their moorings behind the harbour's stone piers, and the same mass of orange pantiled houses, jostling shoulders for space between the cliffs and the water. The two-towns-in-one principle is also at work again, this time officially, with Staithes proper only on the south side of the beck. Not only do the houses on the other bank belong to the separate village of Cowbar, they aren't even in North Yorkshire. The county boundary runs across the middle of the small footbridge over Staithes Beck and Cowbar is in Cleveland. Just to confuse the issue further, the **Staithes lifeboat** is housed here on the Cowbar side.

Staithes' most famous son is undoubtedly James Cook who, after a childhood turn itself right way up. You will know if you have found a **velvet swimming crab** or, more to the point, you will know by the excited squeals if someone else has found one. They are beautiful with velvety backs, electric blue claws and bright red eyes but are without doubt the most aggressive creature on the shore. I have seen one actually jump up off the rocks to attack my approaching hand, and can testify from experience that their pincers are very sharp.

Crabs may be the most extrovert inhabitants of rock pools, but they are by no means the only ones. North Sea rocky shores are incredibly rich habitats, so within an hour or two's searching you could easily find over 30 different species, from deep maroon **sea anemones** and small green **sea urchins** to translucent **prawns** and big knobbly **lumpsucker fish**. Here are some top-tips for the best results:

- Get as far down the shore as you can. A low spring tide is best of all as you can get in amongst the exposed kelp forest.
- Take a deep white tray to put your finds in for examination.
- A small aquarium net is the only way you will catch fast or slippery prawns and fish.
- Take an identification guide. The Field Studies Council (www.field-studies-council.org) produce an excellent waterproof key, the best field guidebook is *The Seashore*, published by Country Life Books, or you can call in at East Barnby Outdoor Education Centre and they will give you a free simple ID sheet.
- The best accessible sites for rock-pools along the North Yorkshire coast are between Staithes and Port Mulgrave, Runswick Bay, Robin Hood's Bay, Scarborough North Bay and Filey Brigg.

One last safety note; take care on wet, slippery rocks and consult tide tables before you stray away from the main beach. Happy searching.

just inland, probably had his first smell of the sea when he worked as a teenage shop assistant in the village. An old harbourside cottage bears a 'Cook Trail plaque' but in reality, the shop he worked in was washed away along with 12 other buildings in the great storm of 1745.

A few yards from Captain Cook's cottage is the labelled entrance into Dog Loup; quite probably the narrowest named thoroughfare in the country, and a good start to a wander around the back alleys, squares and streets. On your exploration look out for the nautical themes in house names, including imaginative ceramic plaques, and the **Heritage Centre** on the High Street. I also recommend crossing the bridge to climb Cowbar Bank for the best bird's-eye view of Staithes to one side, and the mighty **Boulby Cliff** on the other, returning via the allotments footpath and steppingstones.

One of the best short walks in the North York Moors heads off in the opposite direction, but the tide needs to be in your favour to complete it safely (follow the ebb tide out). The route couldn't be simpler; climb the steps at the far end of the harbour, walk along the rocky shore below the cliffs for a mile to

Port Mulgrave and then return along the Cleveland Way. En route you should see oystercatchers on the mussel beds of Penny Steel (and surfers on one of the most testing reef breaks in the country if there are waves), ironstone and jet mines, and alum quarries. You can also experience the best fossil and rock-pool pickings along the whole coast.

If you would prefer expert local guidance in this very wild environment, it doesn't come any better than from Sean Baxter (01947 840278; www.realstaithes.com), local fisherman, member of the lifeboat crew and passionate champion of the town. 'I'm desperate to counter the doom-and-gloom merchants who claim the natural world is dying,' Sean explained, 'It's just not true; there are more fish, whales, dolphins and peregrines around here than ever and I want to show people this rich natural diversity – and tell them about the amazing maritime heritage of my town.' You can accompany him baiting long-lines and emptying lobster pots, ultimately eating your catch as a picnic at Sean's fisherman's hut in Port Mulgrave.

The landlocked city of Leicester wouldn't be many people's prediction of a major lifeboat sponsor but the good people of that city have bought eleven over the years, the most recent being *The Pride of Leicester*. This is the Staithes and Runswick Inshore Lifeboat, to give it its full title, an 'Atlantic 75' class boat which sits on a trailer attached to its amphibious tractor, in a shed in Cowbar. Being the bustling focal point that it is, with crew members often pottering around, the doors are usually open and you are welcome to go in and nose around there and in the RNLI shop which is just a couple of doors down. One certainly shouldn't wish for a lifeboat call-out, but if the maroon does go up (a loud firework to alert the crew) the launch is exciting to watch. You'll have to be quick getting there if you hear it as the Staithes crew pride themselves on being out of the harbour within five minutes of the bang. More predictable is crew training, 6pm on Mondays in summer, and 10am on Sundays in winter.

Food and drink

Captain Cook Inn Staithes Lane ☎ 01947 840200 🖰 www.captaincookinn.co.uk. A very uninviting-looking hostelry at the top of the bank by the old railway (formerly Station Inn) but don't be fooled, the 'Cook' is an oasis. The best selection of real ales within a ten-mile radius, and cheap and cheerful bar food. Regularly hosts a wide range of festivals: folk music, sea shanties and beer, pies and sausages. Regular jazz.

Cod and Lobster High St ☎ 01947 840295. Notable for its position, must be one of the closest pubs to the sea in the country – storm-damaged on more than one occasion. Nostalgic photos line the walls, and three or four cask ales usually on tap. Food available.

Endeavour House High St ☎ 01947 841735 🖰 www.endeavour-restaurant.co.uk. Formerly a seafood restaurant of high renown; Brian and Charlotte now use their kitchen to offer one-or three-day sea-food cookery courses where you go out on a boat, catch your fish, then learn how to prepare and serve it.

Attractions and shopping

Captain Cook and Staithes Heritage Centre High St ☎ 01947 841454
🖰 www.captaincookatstaithes.co.uk. An interesting local museum with an emphasis on the famous seafarer.

Kessen Bowl High St. A gift shop in a quaint little corner building, named after fishermen's glass floats and selling an eclectic mix of products including artists' materials and pharmaceuticals.

Staithes Gallery High St ☎ 01947 841840 🖰 www.staithesgallery.co.uk. A fine display of contemporary artists' work inspired by the old masters from the celebrated Staithes Group. Offers residential weekend courses for artists.

⑰ Boulby Cliff

*'The king was borne, hoary hero,
to Hronesness (Whale Hill).
And firm on the earth a funeral-pile.'*
Beowulf

Viewed from Staithes, the outline of Boulby Cliff is uncannily like the back of a whale, and I would love to share the belief of some, that this was the burial place of that great hero of the Viking age. What is for certain is that his body is no longer there now, after 1,000 years of natural and human erosion. Despite all this cliff reduction, Boulby, at 666 feet above the sea, is still the highest cliff on the east coast of England, albeit in two steps because of the huge alum quarries. Alum is no longer worked here but **Boulby Potash Mine** is a modern mineral extraction operation close by that breaks records in the opposite direction. It is the deepest mine in Europe, and at its bottom, nearly a vertical mile down, tunnels radiate out five miles in every direction, including out beneath the North Sea – a scary thought. The potash, destined to become agricultural fertiliser, is transported to Teeside factories on the only remaining section of the Whitby to Middlesbrough railway.

The four-mile traverse of Boulby Cliff from Staithes makes a magnificent walk, or cycle, and the steep descent at the far end will bring you to a very singular place. The former mining village of **Skinningrove** will never be described as pretty but it has bags of character, and your arrival takes you past some of the structures it has become famous for – pigeon lofts. Skinningrove is one of the racing-pigeon centres of the North East with scores of sheds lining the hillside.

At the bottom of the hill, the beck won't fail to catch your eye either, being as it is luminous orange, a result of pollution from the ironstone mines further up the valley – rust, in essence. The entrance to the old mine at the top of the village is worth a visit as it has been converted into the excellent Cleveland Ironstone Mining Museum (01287 642877; www.ironstonemuseum.co.uk). Not far from the museum, a half-hourly bus can take you back to Staithes, or bring you here if you take my advice and follow the walk in the opposite direction.

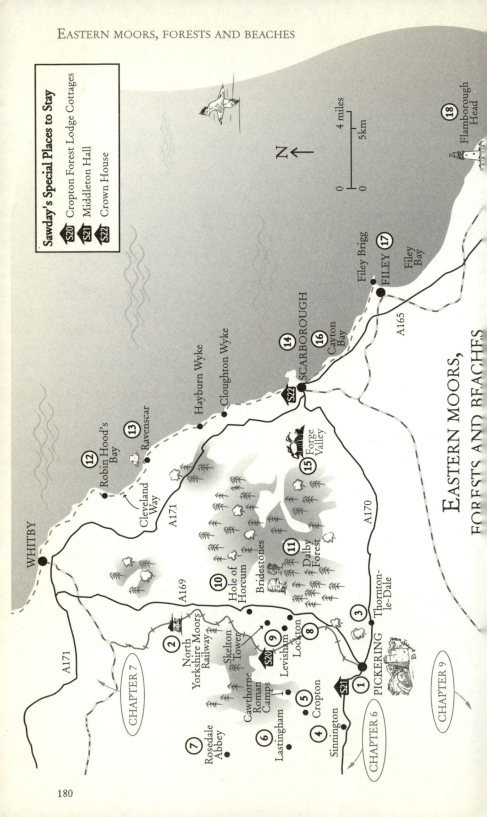

Sawday's Special Places to Stay

S20 Cropton Forest Lodge Cottages
S21 Middleton Hall
S22 Crown House

N ←

4 miles
5km
0
0

Flamborough Head
18

Filey Brigg
FILEY
17
Filey Bay

A165

SCARBOROUGH
14
16
Cayton Bay

Hayburn Wyke
Cloughton Wyke

S22

Robin Hood's Bay
12
Ravenscar
13

Cleveland Way

15 Forge Valley

WHITBY

A171

A170

A169

Dalby Forest
11

Hole of Horcum
10
Bridestones

Thornton-le-Dale
3

North Yorkshire Moors Railway
2

Skelton Tower
S20
9
Levisham
Lockton
8

Cawthorne Roman Camps
5 Cropton

PICKERING
S21
1

CHAPTER 7

A171

Rosedale Abbey
7

Lastingham
6

Sinnington
4

CHAPTER 6

CHAPTER 9

EASTERN MOORS, FORESTS AND BEACHES

8. EASTERN MOORS, FORESTS AND BEACHES

This southeastern corner of the North York Moors is dominated by forest, not the natural English oak woodland that was originally here, but hundreds of square miles of coniferous plantation. The almost-linked forests of Cropton, Dalby and Harwood Dale constitute the Forestry Commission's North Riding Forest Park, at 500 square miles the second largest in England. It stretches from Rosedale in the west to the North Sea coast in the east, across an area of plateaux and deep valleys that some inspired geographer gave the perfect label of Tabular Hills. These uplands don't meet the sea gently, but in a line of precipitous cliffs stretching from **Robin Hood's Bay** in the north to Filey in the south. In the few places where these cliffs relent, there is sand, and where there are beaches there are holiday resorts. **Scarborough**, with two sandy bays, is not only the biggest seaside resort on the Yorkshire coast but claims to be the oldest in the world. Next comes little **Cayton Bay**, literally awash with surfers much of the time, and finally, seven miles south of **Scarborough**, her younger and more modest sister, **Filey**, with the queen of beaches – five miles of glorious Filey sands stretching to the chalk cliffs of **Flamborough Head** and out of North Yorkshire. The only other town in the region is **Pickering**, an old fortified market town sitting just at the point where pancake-flat Ryedale turns hilly: very much a southern gateway to the North York Moors.

Getting there and around

Public transport is actually very good, both for getting here and then for moving around. It is possible to get to virtually anywhere you would want either by train or by bus. If you drive, everywhere is accessible, but it is worth knowing places to avoid at certain times when they become unbearably busy.

The A64 from York and all points west jams up at busy times between Malton and York and also on the outskirts of Scarborough. At most times you may not want to attempt to drive into or through Scarborough – instead you can use the new park-and-rides with 600 places on the A64 and another 600 on Filey Road. Buses run into town every 12 minutes.

Robin Hood's Bay is another traffic bottleneck. I would say park at Whitby and catch the bus there, but Whitby is even worse. My only advice is get here very early to have any chance of parking.

Filey is not quite so bad. It can be very slow getting in but there is lots of parking space at North Cliff Country Park once you are there. Pickering is another place prone to traffic jams as it is at the crossroads of two major routes. If there is a big event on at the showground then divert via Thornton Dale, it will be much quicker.

Trains

Two lines serve Scarborough hourly, the Trans-Pennine express from Manchester via Leeds, York and Malton, and the Hull service which also stops at Filey. The private North Yorkshire Moors Railway runs to Pickering from Grosmont (from where you can carry on to Whitby), with a choice of diesel and steam locos.

Buses

The Coastliner service will deliver you to Scarborough, Pickering, Filey, Thornton-le-Dale or Lockton, all hourly from Leeds or York at half the price of the train. It will be slower though, especially if traffic is heavy. Buses can get you anywhere else; the number 93 every 30 minutes to Robin Hood's Bay from either Whitby or Scarborough, and the Moorsbus services to Dalby Forest (the M6 from Thornton-le-Dale six times a day) and Rosedale Abbey (M50 from Pickering six times a day and M51 from Hutton le Hole three times a day). Look out for good-value deals like the park-and-bus tour from Thornton-le-Dale, where you park your car for free and have unlimited Moorsbus travel for the day from only £4 per person.

Boat trips

At present there are two starting points: Scarborough, and Flamborough. All Scarborough's vessels operate out of the harbour. Numerous boats advertise angling trips, usually with a sandwich board on the harbourside; just turn up and take your pick of the most reputable-looking one. Three enterprises offer pleasure cruises, **Queensferry Coastal Cruises, Scarborough Pleasure Steamers**, and the **Hispaniola**.

One boat, **Emerson's**, operates from Flamborough North Landing, and the RSPB run a trip from Bridlington that tours Flamborough Head.

Cycling

I will stick my neck out and suggest that this is possibly the best area in the country for the cyclist, especially **off-road**. It is absolute two-wheel heaven, and **Dalby Forest** is the focus of it all: it is so good that it was selected for staging the World Mountain Bike Championships in 2010. In the last ten years the Forestry Commission has spent over a million pounds developing biking facilities in the forest culminating in a series of six colour-coded and waymarked trails ranging from the two-mile Ellerburn green trail (easy), a perfect gentle intro for young families, to the black trail (severe), which is a challenge for even expert mountain bikers. The most popular route, and it can get very busy, is the 23-mile red route (difficult) which is possibly the best of its kind in the country. Maps of all the trails are available free in the visitor centre at Low Dalby.

If you want forest track riding to yourself then just go exploring with the 1:25,000 OS Explorer map OL27. There are literally hundreds of miles of deserted tracks in Cropton, Langdale, Broxa and Harwood Dale forests waiting to be ridden, and the Forestry Commission (bless them) are happy for you to do it as long as you take special care near forestry operations. A rewarding gentle ride, for those allergic to hills, starts at Reasty Hill Top car park near Harwood Dale, and covers a flat four-mile triangular route to Barns Cliff End and back; my children had their first exciting forest bike ride here aged five and seven, and still talk about it. It would be too tame for them now of course, but the route can be extended to Broxa, with the uphill return via the delightful, and delightfully named, Whisper Dales.

Another more testing favourite of mine is a meandering exploration of the northern end of **Cropton Forest**, taking in Needle Point and Killing Nab Scar. You can reach the starting point either by car from the hamlet of Stape, or from Newtondale Halt on the North Yorkshire Moors Railway (bikes can be taken on the train).

Still off-road, but not under trees, there are lots of bridleways and green-lane routes on the moors. The moors are not as extensive here as further north and west, but two are crossed by bridleways that make for good biking territory. Levisham Moor is one and is accessible from Levisham village or the Hole of Horcum on the A169 Pickering to Whitby road. The other is Brow Moor behind Robin Hood's Bay, where you could make a circular route by using part of the **disused railway line** at Stoupe Brow. This line is a fantastic, recognised cycle route in its own right and rideable all the way from Scarborough to Whitby, 20 miles of easy cinder track with great sea views.

Good road biking is less easy to find here, but the best of it is a network of quiet minor roads to the west of Scarborough around the village of **Hackness**, which also link up with the tarmac toll road winding its way through Dalby Forest.

Finally, there is a long-distance cycle trail which incorporates lots of what I have already detailed. The **Moor to Sea cycle route** (www.moortoseacycle.net) was developed by local bikers for family cycling and provides four days' worth of the best road, forest, lane and rail riding the area has to offer, linking Scarborough, Pickering and Whitby.

Cycle hire on the Moor to Sea cycle route

Keldy Forest Cabins near Cropton YO18 8HW 'via Cropton' for satnavs ✆ 01751

417510. Bikes, tagalongs, trailer bikes and a tandem for hire. Prices from £16 per day for an adult bike.

Purple Mountain Dalby Forest ☎ 01751 460011 ⌂ www.purplemountain.co.uk. Bikes for hire, and tagalongs, kids' seats, tandems and trailer bikes. Also guided rides, skills courses and weekend breaks. Prices from £25 per day for an adult bike. Café attached.

Trailways The Old Railway Station, Hawsker ☎ 01947 820207 ⌂ www.trailways.info. Bikes, buggies, tandems and trailer bikes for hire. Two hours to multi-day. One-way ride and pick-up by arrangement. Prices from £17 per day for an adult bike.

Horse-riding

The long well-drained tracks here are as good for horses as for bikes, and there are plenty of riding opportunities whether you have your own beast of burden or need to borrow one. The big forests (Dalby and its neighbours) are wonderful venues for riding, and the Forestry Commission welcome you with open arms – free entry into Dalby via the Toll Road for instance. No specific horse-riding routes are designated so you are free to use any of the forest roads or bridleways, but colour-coded bike trails are best avoided as they get so busy.

There are trekking/hacking centres at Staintondale, Robin Hood's Bay and Sinnington. If you are bringing your own horse to the area, the North York Moors National Park produce an indispensable guidebook for horse riders (see page ix).

Farsyde Stud and Riding Centre Robin Hood's Bay ☎ 01947 880249 ⌂ www.farsydefarmcottages.co.uk. Hacking for experienced riders on moors, fields and forests. Trekking on the old railway line for beginners.

Friars Hill Riding Stables ☎ 01751 432758 ⌂ www.friarshillstables.co.uk. Hacking and trekking for those over the age of eight years (not absolute beginners). Also, pony birthday parties and three- or five-day summer camps.

Staintondale Trekking Centre Staintondale YO13 0EL ☎ 01723 871846. Pony trekking for small groups of any ability.

Walking

Four **long-distance footpaths** or unofficial 'ways' have a terminus here. Whether it is the start or the finish is pretty much up to you, except for the Coast-to-Coast walk and Lyke Wake Walk, where the universally accepted direction to travel is west to east, both finishing at Robin Hood's Bay. The other two are the much-frequented, horseshoe-shaped Cleveland Way, which in this area traverses the full length of the coast between Robin Hood's Bay and Filey, and the lesser-known 48-mile Tabular Hills Walk between Helmsley and Scarborough. This route is also sometimes referred to as the Cleveland Way Link as it joins the loose ends of the longer walk to create a circular route of 158 miles.

Shorter day or half-day walks are many and varied, limited only really by your map-reading skills and sense of adventure, because there is a huge network of rights of way and a large area of open access land (see page ix). Avoid busy mountain-bike areas, like some of the bridleways leading into Dalby Forest, and the Moor to Sea cycle route.

Because public transport is so comprehensive here, there are many opportunities for **point-to-point walks with a bus or train shuttle**. I am always more comfortable being driven first and walking back as there is less chance of being marooned and no pressure to make the bus stop or station on time. If you can wangle it so the engine power does more of the uphill than your legs, all the better. A good way to do sections of the Cleveland Way is to use the Scarborough to Whitby bus; Robin Hood's Bay to Cloughton perhaps (ten miles), or Cloughton to Scarborough (five miles). The train can do the same job between Scarborough and Filey (seven miles). Away from the coast, a rover ticket on the North Yorkshire Moors Railway allows you to hop off at one station, walk to the next and hop back on – plenty of scope there.

Tourist information
Filey John St ☎ 01723 383636.
Pickering The Ropery ☎ 01751 473791.
Scarborough Brunswick Shopping Centre ☎ 01723 383636; Harbourside ☎ 01723 383636.

The southern moors and forests

Much of this area is virtually uninhabited, wild territory covered by either trees or heather. Around the sole town, Pickering, are a clutch of rewarding villages: Thornton-le-Dale on the way to Scarborough, Lockton and Levisham towards Whitby and, up the beautiful valley of Rosedale, Cropton, Sinnington, Lastingham and Rosedale Abbey.

① Pickering

Pickering first came to my attention as a case study in a geography lesson at school. It is a textbook example of a ribbon development; a town that grows along an important road instead of spreading sideways. What my geography teacher failed to tell me, though, is that the bits of Pickering away from the busy main road are full of unexpected history and quirky character. By far its biggest visitor attraction is the **North Yorkshire Moors Railway**, of which Pickering is the southern terminus, but the shops and arcades of Market Place and Birdgate come a close second. My favourite part of the town is surprisingly little visited, probably because of the steep walk involved. It is the area where narrow old streets lead up Castle Hill to the town's biggest and oldest building –

Pickering Castle itself. My recommended route would be up Castle Road, from where it begins near the railway station, and back down Castlegate to take in the Quaker meeting house. It is worth detouring along Hatcase Lane, not just to celebrate such a wacky name, but because it will lead you to the fascinating **church of St Peter and St Paul**. This

would be a humdrum building with little interest but for a chance discovery during renovation in 1852. Lime-wash was removed from an interior wall to reveal 15th-century frescoes underneath which Nikolaus Pevsner, the renowned architectural historian, described as, '...one of the most complete series of wall paintings in English churches that give one a vivid idea of what ecclesiastical interiors were really like'. The pictures are multi-coloured affairs mainly depicting the important saints of the time, St George of pest control fame, St John the Baptist, St Thomas of Canterbury and a particularly tall St Christopher, who was reputed to stand 12 cubits high.

On emerging from the front of the church you will be back into the bustle of Birdgate. If another dose of peace and quiet is required try **Beck Isle Museum** at the other end of the market place. You don't even need to go in, although it is well worth the £3 entrance fee, because the beck-side lawn to the front, by the arches of the old bridge, is an ideal place for a tranquil muse or picnic. If you have any interest at all in rural social history, then the 27 rooms of this old agricultural college will keep you well entertained.

Pickering Castle

Pickering's royal connections date back to accounts in a late medieval chronicle of a Briton king called Pereduras living here. A very dubious legend connects him and the origin of the town's name, which involves him losing a valuable ring in the river and it turning up later in the belly of a fish served up on the royal table. The fish was a pike; ring in a pike, pike-ring, Pickering – likely? I don't think so, but there is a pike on the town's coat of arms and a beautifully carved one on a wooden panel in the bar of the White Horse Inn. King Pereduras was around far too long ago to have had anything to do with the present castle but it was a royal residence, having been built at William I's instruction for his personal use when hunting in the Forest of Pickering. Possession of the castle has been passed down the royal line ever since, the present owner being the Duke of Lancaster, better known by her Sunday name – Queen Elizabeth II. English Heritage look after it for her today.

This is a classic Norman motte-and-bailey castle, with the motte, or mound, crowned by the remains of the keep (the King's Tower). I particularly enjoyed the walk on the path around the outside of the walls to detour into the quarries at the back where the limestone for the building was extracted; the North East

Yorkshire Geology Trust have placed information boards explaining how these Jurassic rocks were formed under the sea.

Food and drink

Eleven **cafés** make Pickering a place where it's easy enough to overdose on tea. My top five are **Café Cocoa**, Smiddy Hill (☎ 01751 477755), where the cakes are a work of art; **Café 2 Stop**, Burgate (☎ 01751 471400), with good latte coffee; the very popular **Mulberries**, Bridge St (☎ 01751 472337); **Russell's Café**, Market Place (☎ 01751 472749), the only place to open early for a big breakfast; and the **Tea Shop**, Hungate (☎ 01751 477664), the best place for afternoon tea.

Cedar Barn Farm Shop and Café Thornton Rd ☎ 01751 475614. Own farm Angus beef and free-range eggs plus veg, pies, cheeses and cakes.

Moorland Trout Farm Newbridge YO18 8JJ ☎ 01751 473101. Rainbow trout, whole, fillets or smoked; just north of Pickering. Feed the fish for 50p.

The Organic Farm Shop 6 Eastgate Sq ☎ 01751 473444; web: www.theorganicfarmshop.com. An Aladdin's cave of good things from home-produced beef to ice-cream and groceries.

The White Swan Inn Market Place ☎ 01751 472288 🖰 www.white-swan.co.uk. A coaching inn, not a pub, but the place to come if you want comfort and style. The food is locally sourced in the main, and very highly regarded – one customer wrote a poem about it which is framed on the wall.

Willowdene Watercress and Trout Farm Westgate Carr Rd YO18 8LX ☎ 01751 472769. Traditionally grown watercress and spring-water rainbow trout from the door.

Attractions

Beck Isle Museum Bridge St ☎ 01751 473653 🖰 www.beckislemuseum.co.uk.
Pickering Castle Castle Hill ☎ 01751 474989 🖰 www.english-heritage.org.uk.

② North Yorkshire Moors Railway: Pickering to Grosmont

Very few people aren't moved to a wistful nostalgia at the sight and sound of an old locomotive in full steam, and this is one of the most popular places in the country to enjoy the experience. Some, me included, would argue that it is best to not actually be on the train but watching from outside, but there is no doubt that either way everybody seems to enjoy steam trains immensely. Waving is *de rigueur* of course. I once even saw a group of middle-aged travellers all with a handkerchief to flutter to passers-by.

'It's got to be done,' one of them said, 'The nice man in *The Railway Children* did it so we have to keep up the tradition.' Steam travel is somehow very English. Thank goodness for those few passionate and far-sighted enthusiasts back in

1965 who knew that Dr Beeching had made a big mistake in shutting the line. It is them that we have to thank for the continued existence of the railway here because two years later they started a preservation society. In 1972 they took on one full-time paid worker and now they operate a huge business with 135 paid staff and even more eager volunteers helping out.

The scenic route of this railway also adds to its popularity. Most of the journey follows the spectacular valley of Newtondale, a deep and precipitous ravine with the incongruously small Pickering Beck trickling down the middle. This feeble stream is obviously incapable of excavating such a large valley. That job was done 10,000 years ago at the end of the last ice age, when Lake Eskdale overflowed and emptied into Lake Pickering in a raging torrent.

It is 18 miles from Pickering to the official other end of the line at Grosmont, and your journey will call at four stations, each renovated in a different period style. Pickering recreates the 1930s, Levisham has been decorated as it would have been in 1912 and Goathland boasts a 1922-style tea room. Finally, Grosmont has been left how it was in the 1950s just before closure, and also features the fascinating locomotive sheds (see page 162). If you want to complete the story and visit a modern station then stay on the train because some of them now continue the extra six miles into Whitby courtesy of Northern Rail. Carriages are wheelchair accessible and will carry bikes if there is space (ring to check). Trains run on one of four colour-coded timetables; gold at peak times with nine trains a day on the hour, and red, green or silver, each with six trains a day. Note that some services are diesel-hauled.

Special events trains include Santa specials in December, Pullman Fine Dining runs or extensions to Whitby, and even whole weekends dedicated to the 'Swinging 60s', 'The Railway at War', or 'Vintage Vehicles'.

If just being a passenger is not enough for you and you don't mind getting your hands dirty, then a Footplate Awareness course would be just the ticket. Over the course of one to five days you get the chance to fulfil many a childhood dream, and drive a steam train.

Fares are reasonable and it's only a few extra pounds to Whitby. My advice would be to make a full day of it by catching the first train out in the morning and the last one back, taking full advantage of the hop-on hop-off nature of your rover ticket. That way you can explore around each of the station venues for an hour or so and get the next train that comes along.

North Yorkshire Moors Railway ℡ 01751 472508 🖳 www.nymr.co.uk.

③ Thornton-le-Dale

East of Pickering, Thornton Beck, full of lime from the springs of Dalby Forest, flows between the much-photographed limestone buildings of Thornton-le-Dale. This large village is perennially busy with visitors.

On your first visit to Thornton-le-Dale you may well, like me, have a feeling of *déjà vu* with one building in particular seeming very familiar. Beck Isle cottage is one of the most photographed buildings in the country so the chances are that you have seen it before on a calendar or jigsaw. It isn't the only photogenic view in the village by any means; the combination of village green with cross and stocks, sparkling beck with 15 bridges and 17th-century almshouses has resulted in Thornton being regularly voted the most beautiful village in Yorkshire. This fame attracts visitors of course so if you need any respite from people then take a stroll on the beck-side footpath upstream past Thornton Mill to the sleepy hamlet of Ellerburn. A trout hatchery here takes advantage of the clear, cold, limestone spring water.

A tiny church, part Saxon, has had some unwelcome attention recently due to a wildlife controversy. Rare Natterer's bats live in its roof space, a fact to celebrate you might think, but the bats are not particularly grateful lodgers. Droppings rain down on to the hymn books, sometimes even during the services, and the whiff of bat wee is not really conducive to contemplative worship. The parishioners, understandably, want rid of their guests, but English Nature, also understandably, says no – it's a stalemate at the moment.

If you continue on this route up Thornton beck you will reach **Dalby Forest visitor centre**, a fine walk in itself.

④ Sinnington

Travel four miles west of Pickering and you will reach a crossing of the River Seven, a fraction of the size of its West Country namesake and a different spelling. A detour off the main road here to the village of **Sinnington** is worth the effort just to sit and picnic on the green by the old arched bridge but there are many more active things to do if you wish. The walking and biking along the river upstream are both good and pony trekking can be done from here (see page 184). Keep following the river and you will find yourself in **Rosedale**, a rural idyll now, but a major ironstone mining valley not so long ago.

S⑨ Fox and Hounds Main St ☎ 01751 431577 🖱 www.thefoxandhoundsinn.co.uk. An old coaching inn in a sleepy village. Expect homely panelled bars with open fires and award-winning modern pub food with a European flavour. Cask beers are from West Yorkshire: Copper Dragon and Timothy Taylors. Open every day.
Pearson's Soft Fruits Strawberry Fields YO62 6SL ☎ 01751 433380. Pick your own strawberries, raspberries, gooseberries, redcurrants and blackcurrants or buy homemade jam of all the above. Just west of Sinnington.

⑤ Cropton and ⑥ Lastingham

The main route out of Rosedale passes through the village of **Cropton**, birthplace of the famous Whitby whaling ships' captain, William Scoresby. His local connection is celebrated in the name of a fine beer made in the village, Scoresby Stout. Cropton Brewery is a rarity, a very successful and long-lasting micro-brewery which has been operating from the New Inn for 17 years. It still produces the original 'Two Pints' bitter along with ten other recipes, including my favourite, 'Blackout Porter'.

A gentle two-mile cycle or walk away from Cropton on quiet country lanes is another village of similar size. **Lastingham** is another one of those 'pub and church but not much else' places, but the Blacksmith's Arms deserves all the plaudits it receives in many good pub guides, and **St Mary's Church** is very special. It does not look unusual from the outside but venture in and you will find that it is in effect one church on top of another. Steps lead from the aisle down to a huge vaulted Norman crypt, extraordinarily unchanged since it was built as part of an unfinished abbey in the late 11th century; you won't come across a more atmospheric place too often. It is the only example in this country of a crypt with a nave and side aisles.

The lane east from Cropton towards Newton-on-Rawcliffe passes **Cawthorne Roman Camps**. Here an assortment of humpy earthworks are the remains of a temporary camp and forts for Roman soldiers; the Cawthorn Trail is worth following to bring it all to life.

><><><><

⑤ Blacksmith's Arms Lastingham ☎ 01757 417247
🖥 www.blacksmithslastingham.co.uk. This is almost how you imagine a country pub to be; rambling and dimly lit, very, very old and with legends of a ghost and a secret tunnel to the church crypt opposite. There are always three cask beers on, usually Black Sheep or Theakstons and two other guests, and the food is wholesome and traditional. If there is room then eat in the bar, as it is the most atmospheric part of the building by far. Open every day.

Cropton Brewery Woolcroft, Cropton ☎ 01751 417330 🖥 www.croptonbrewery.com. Brewery tours cost £4.50 per person.

New Inn Woolcroft, Cropton ☎ 01751 417330 🖥 www.newinncropton.co.uk. This is a great beer drinker's village inn with its own brewery (see above) and an annual beer festival in November. Food comes in generous portions and is good value and home cooked. Open every day.

⑦ Rosedale Abbey and Rosedale

Standing on high ground, and casting an appreciative eye over the fields, folds and pastoral corners of Rosedale, you may find it hardly possible to imagine what has gone on here in the past. Today, fewer than 500 people live out a sleepy, rural existence in this valley and it was much the same in 1851. Twenty years later that figure was nearer 5,000 as a Klondike-style rush of miners poured in and turned Rosedale into a loud, smoky, and crime-ridden industrial centre. It wasn't gold they were after but iron: between 1856 and 1926 millions of tons of high-grade ore were extracted and transported to the blast furnaces of County Durham. How they got it there was both dramatic and ingenious: a railway was constructed which stayed almost level, as railways have to do, by contouring right around the head of the valley at about 1,000 feet up. It then crossed Blakey Ridge and into the neighbouring valley of Farndale where it did the same, hugging a high-level line round to a point where descent was possible down a steep incline to join the mainline railway system at Battersby. Fortunately for us, the track bed is still there providing a perfect gentle walk or cycle way which is even wheelchair-accessible in places.

The ironstone boom had a major and lasting effect on the only village in the dale: Rosedale Abbey lost its abbey. The ruins of the Cistercian nunnery were dismantled stone by stone to provide building material for mine buildings and houses. Only one small belfry turret survives, but the village boasts two pubs, a café and a glass-blowing studio.

Rosedale glass – ancient and modern

Not long ago, archaeologists unearthed a furnace last used 400 years ago by exiled French glassmakers who plied their trade using local sand and wood fuel. This ancient local craft is celebrated in a thoroughly modern setting at **Gillies Jones glass-blowing studio** in Rosedale Abbey (01751 417550; www.gilliesjonesglass.co.uk). Steven Gillies and Kate Jones, partners in life and art, work together to produce exquisite works inspired by the Rosedale countryside. Stephen is the glassmaker and Kate the sand-carver and painter. Drop into the studio to see them at work.

Dalby Forest and Levisham Moor

The A169 from Pickering to Whitby has been a route for many centuries, and the name Saltergate, literally 'salt street', refers of course to the journey done in the opposite direction, from Whitby and the coast to Pickering and all points inland, transporting a very important and valuable commodity in times past. Only one part of the A169 still bears that old name, where a hairpin bend takes it past the Saltergate Inn and along the edge of a spectacular crater called the **Hole of Horcum**.

As the road makes its gradual decent from here into Pickering, it bypasses the villages of **Lockton** and **Levisham** to the right, and the wooded ridges and dales of **Dalby Forest** to the left.

A walk on Levisham Moor to the Hole of Horcum

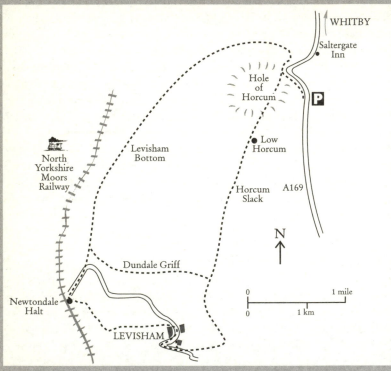

Levisham Moor is all open-access land so you can actually walk wherever you like. However, ploughing through deep heather can be tiring so you may want to follow two of the three public rights of way – one out from your start point and another back to it. For the chance of seeing rare flowers, (green-winged orchids in May and dwarf cornel in August) and great views of steam trains follow the Levisham Bottoms path. For dazzling summer carpets of heather and wide skies go for the moor-top bridleway, and for a close-up view of the enormous natural hollow that is the Hole of Horcum, choose the eastern footpath via Low Horcum and Levisham Brow. The three possible start points for this walk are Hole of Horcum car park, Levisham village or Newtondale Halt on the North Yorkshire Moors Railway. All are accessible by bus or train. Refreshment at the pub in Levisham. Five to seven miles, depending on which route you choose.

⑧ Lockton and ⑨ Levisham

These two neat and tidy moors villages are like a pair of brothers or sisters – close, but separated by a deep valley, always vying with each other over small things, but jumping to each other's defence over matters of importance. In reality the two places are complementary; Lockton has the church and youth hostel, whilst Levisham provides a railway station and pub. There was a small village shop in Lockton and a post office in Levisham until recently, but both have gone the way of many rural businesses, and sadly closed.

One resource neither village is short of is ground water: wells and springs are all over the place, because of the porous Jurassic limestone hillsides hereabouts. Near one of these named water sources, Rowl Spring, you will find the most mysterious building in the vicinity. St Mary's Church, roofless and derelict, is in neither Lockton nor Levisham, but sits

between the two in splendid isolation. Local stories claim that there was a village around the church which was wiped out by the plague in the 14th century, but there is no archaeological evidence for this. Whatever the history, St Mary's Church is an evocative ruin in a memorable setting.

To the north of Lockton and Levisham is a large area of moor and valley, making up the Levisham estate, which was in private hands until 1976 when the national park authority bought it to safeguard its riches. Such is the wealth of archaeological remains there, tumuli, dykes, enclosures and settlements, that Levisham Moor is the largest scheduled ancient monument in England, though you need to poke around carefully with an OS map in hand to spot its ancient features. It is also designated a Site of Special Scientific Interest (SSSI), for its rare breeding birds in particular; this is one of the best places in the country to see golden plover and the dashing little falcon, the merlin.

Skelton Tower

There can be few buildings in the North York Moors with as impressive a position and prospect as Skelton Tower. Perched on the lip of Newtondale, a mile north of Levisham Station, it affords magnificent views up and down the gorge, particularly rewarding when a steam locomotive is grunting up the valley hundreds of feet below.

In reality the tower was a shooting-lodge-style folly built in 1850 by the Rev Robert Skelton, vicar of Levisham. The official line is that he retired there for the peace and quiet required to write his sermons, although unofficial local opinion is that it doubled as his secret drinking den. Such is the sinister aura of the ruins now that they were chosen by local author Ian Johnson as home for the murderous goblin Red Cap in his supernatural novel *The Witcher Keys*.

Food and drink

Fox and Rabbit A169, near Lockton ☎ 01751 460213 🖱 www.foxandrabbit.co.uk. Brothers Charles and Toby Wood have got this pub just about right, very welcoming to travellers to and from the coast, three fine Yorkshire beers (Black Sheep, Theakstons and Taylors) and a wide selection of wines. Their food is simple and traditional.

The Horseshoe Inn Levisham ℂ 01751 460240 ⌂ www.horseshoelevisham.co.uk.
This is a genuine traditional village pub sitting proudly at the top of the Green. Food is
similar to the Fox and Rabbit, well it has the same owners, and the beer is from the
Dales (Black Sheep) and Moors (Cropton).

Shopping
David Stephenson Artist Blacksmith Sunny View, Lockton ℂ 01751 460252
⌂ www.davidstephenson.org.uk. Hand-forged fireside furniture, frames and weather
vanes.

⑩ The Hole of Horcum

Levisham Beck starts its life in a series of tributary, spring-fed valleys. In one of
these deep dales the springs have eaten back into the hillsides evenly over
thousands of years, leaving a dramatic almost circular basin. Our ancestors did
not have the benefit of our geographical knowledge and assumed that there
must be a diabolical explanation for the phenomenon. The Devil, it is said, in
his anger scooped out a vast ball of earth and hurled it over the moors, the
resulting hole being that of Horcum, and the mound where the earth landed,
the nearby hill of Blakey Topping.

Other, more real and sinister goings-on have happened nearby, in the
Saltergate Inn. At the height of the smuggling trade in the 18th century, a lone
excise man chanced upon a meeting of particularly ruthless smugglers in the
pub. He was murdered to keep him quiet and his body hidden under the hearth.
To prevent its discovery (so they say) a fire was kept continuously alight in the
grate for 170 years, and reputedly has never gone out.

Plainly visible to the north of the Hole of Horcum is a much more recent
monument, the pyramid-shaped radar building of **Fylingdales Missile Early
Warning Station**. The 'sandcastle', as it is known locally, is a recent replacement
for the original and famous three 'golf balls' constructed during the Cold War.
Despite regular peace protests here, and with an ironic twist to what we would
normally regard as 'heritage', there was actually a suggestion that the golf balls
should be made listed buildings and preserved; certainly they are said to have
become the subject of the best-selling postcard in the area.

⑪ Dalby Forest

This huge area of woodland has become one of the Forestry Commission's
beacon leisure forests, so much so that it's easy to forget that it still primarily is a
commercial timber production area. The focus of everything here is the purpose-
built forestry village of Low Dalby, which I am covering in this section with slow
transport and economy in mind. You can drive here, but the nearest village by
road is Thornton-le-Dale, and that would involve you paying a £7 toll to drive
through the forest. By foot, horse or bike, Lockton is the closest access point, and
it's free to arrive under your own muscle power. Once you are here you can hire
a bike from **Purple Mountain** (see cycle hire, page 184) if you have walked in,

or treat yourself to a relaxing horse and carriage ride around the forest from **Back in Time**, courtesy of Holly or Maisey (they are the ponies, not the owners).

At Low Dalby the **visitor centre** is designed with all things sustainable and recyclable in mind. It is constructed from wood and glass, has toilet doors made from reconstituted mobile phone cases and is powered by a wind turbine and solar panels. Such a shame then that the architect made it the ugliest box of a building that I've ever laid eyes on. Inside the visitor centre are exhibitions, a shop, an astronomical observatory, a very good café/restaurant and information on the bewildering array of things that you can see and do in the forest itself. Outside are barbecue and picnic areas, two adventure playgrounds, a Go Ape ropes course for adrenaline junkies, and free maps for various waymarked trails. One is a permanent orienteering course, and there are also ten walking trails of varying distance, four of which are accessible to wheelchairs. My favourite of these is the Staindale Lake circuit, which I had the privilege of sharing with a group of students from a special school in Scarborough. One of the children, who was using a wheelchair, said, 'This is brilliant. I've seen places like this on telly with explorers going through the trees and mountains. Now it's me, I'm here and I'm the explorer.'

Staindale is also the best start point for another short expedition of less than a mile, this time to just outside the forest, on the adjacent moor. The **Bride Stones** are a series of wonderfully sculpted sandstone blocks and buttresses, that wouldn't look out of place in a Hollywood western movie, such is their desert-style, wind-eroded profile. Each stone has ended up perched delicately above the heather on an undercut pedestal, and they are in the care of the National Trust, who manage this area as a nature reserve.

Near the new Dalby visitor centre is the building that used to house the old one, now called The Courtyard, and home to various slow or crafty businesses. Purple Mountain bikes and café (see page 184) are here, as is a felt-making workshop and cast glass artist.

Finally, there is a full calendar of events going on throughout the year, from ranger-led nature trails to car rallies and summer rock concerts.

Information

Dalby Forest Visitor Centre ☎ 01751 470702 🖳 www.forestry.gov.uk.

Shopping

Back in Time ☎ 01751 460315 🖳 www.lowdalbywood.co.uk. Horse and carriage rides from 30mins (£5) to 1hr 15mins (£10) along a quiet forest road off the tarmac.

Jenny Pepper-Feltmaker 🖳 www.jennypepper.com. A felt artist's gallery and shop. Workshops available for £35 per day.

Rachel Gretton Glass 🖳 www.rachelgrettonglass.com. An artist working with cast glass using a kiln. Workshops from three hours – weeks offered.

Activities

Go Ape ☎ 0845 6439215 🖰 www.goape.co.uk. High-adrenalin, high-wire forest adventure. £25 adult for 3 hours.

Cycle trails in Dalby Forest

Of everything on offer, off-road biking is Dalby's speciality, and what it is nationally renowned for. Here are the trails available:

- **Ellerburn cycle trail** (green) – a short relaxing and almost flat route perfect for young families that starts and finishes at the visitor centre (two miles).
- **Adderstone cycle trail** (green) – a longer easy circular route starting at the Adderstone field, a five-mile tarmac road ride from the visitor centre (six miles).
- **Dalby blue trail** (blue) – a long intermediate circular route starting at the visitor centre. Still easy terrain but one or two steep hills (eight miles).
- **Dalby red trail** (red) – very long and difficult. One of the best of its kind in the country and justifiably popular. Don't be tempted on here without decent equipment and skills (23 miles).
- **Dalby black trail, Dixons Hollow Skills Park** and **Dalby Downhill** (black) – if you are good enough, then you will already know about these, if not, then don't even think about it!

Robin Hood's Bay to Scarborough

In the twenty or so miles between Whitby and Scarborough, **Robin Hood's Bay** is the only place of any size on the coast. Such is the ruggedness of this coastline there is not even any road access to the shore anywhere else, and the few small villages that exist are perched on top of the cliffs, like **Ravenscar**, or set back inland, like Cloughton and Burniston. Then suddenly there's big, sprawling, friendly **Scarborough**, very much a different world.

⑫ Robin Hood's Bay

Let's get one thing straight from the start. Robin Hood, if he ever existed, never had anything to do with this place. Wild theories abound as to the origin of the name, but not one scrap of evidence that he even came here on holiday. Even the locals in a gesture of embarrassed denial have dropped the Sherwood Forester from the name. 'Bay' or 'Baytown' is what they call their home. Confusing names apart it is certain that there have been outlaws here, in fact in the 17th century it appears that most of the population were actively involved in smuggling. There were tunnels linking cellars, secret passages and hidey holes for both people and contraband. It is said that a bale of silk could pass from the dock at the bottom of the village to the top, without seeing the light of day. If you are feeling adventurous it is still possible to scramble up part of this route by following the beck from the beach up into the tunnel a few hundred yards. All you need is a pair of wellies, a torch and a sense of adventure.

Modern-day Bay is very different from those times when it was considered a more important place than Whitby. Fishing has all but gone, the railway is closed, and no alum or jet is mined here any more. Robin Hood's Bay is now entirely dependent on the tourism industry for its livelihood, but it has embraced it with enthusiasm and does it tastefully in the main, celebrating its own history and heritage well. Of course having the wonderful scenic surroundings and prolific wildlife of a national park on the doorstep helps. The village, or town  as some claim it to be, is tucked into an almost sheltered corner of the coast, behind the Ness (Viking for headland) also called North Cheek. South Cheek sits proudly, three miles across the wide, sweeping bay with the village of Ravenscar on top. In between, when the tide is out, lie the limestone scars of the shore. I hesitate to say 'beach' because sand is in short supply; there is some, but nothing to compare with Scarborough or Filey. The silver lining is that this is the best **rock pooling** territory in the region. This whole section of shore is protected as part of the Yorkshire and Cleveland Heritage Coast.

As for the town and by that I mean the **old village** on the hillside, not the more modern development at the top, my favourite means of exploration is by semi-formal potter. Wandering up and down the many ginnels and alleys on both sides of the main street, seeing which are interconnected and which are dead ends, is the best way to make sure you see everything, and make no mistake, there is lots to see. Amongst the old cottages at Fisherhead, for instance, you will find the town's tiny museum, a whale's jawbone in a garden and ship's portholes as windows. In the maze of alleyways on the other side of Kings Beck, look out for a plaque to mark the spot of John Wesley's sermon, and cottage walls sporting insurance company fire marks, which directed the fire brigade to those houses that had paid to have fires put out, and those unfortunates that hadn't. The abruptly ending King Street is near here, and was the town's main street until its northern end fell into the sea in 1780.

All alleyways and streets lead down to the Dock, now the only access to the shore since the 1975 sea wall was built, and still a focal point. On either side of the slipway sits the Bay Hotel, the eastern terminus of celebrated walks writer Alfred Wainwright's Coast-to-Coast walk (the other end is St Bees Head in Cumbria), and the Old Coastguard Station, now a National Trust visitor centre.

For added spice, do your pottering after dark, from pub to pub maybe, and you will stand a good chance of bumping into some of Bay's other night walkers

– badgers. Apparently the population of the local sett has taken to raiding bins; they are very bold about it and quite easy to see. If you are staying in town, don't leave your front door open late in the evening as one local resident did, to later find a badger wandering around in his upstairs bathroom!

Read all about it!

The residents of Robin Hood's Bay form a close-knit community. There is a real family feel to the place, including 'adoptees', those repeat visitors that come back year after year to the many guesthouses and holiday cottages. Part of the 'glue' that sticks them all together is the monthly town magazine that almost everybody subscribes to. *Bayfair* can tell you virtually everything you need to know about the place, from tide times and local events lists to nature or history articles and details of over 80 places to stay.

'I took it over in 1995 after finishing work at HM Customs and Excise,' said Jim Foster, the editor/designer/printer. 'It was a great move; I was ready to retire but needed something to keep me busy and interested, and *Bayfair* certainly does that. Bay has a real magical quality about it, with its history and all the maritime connections. It draws people in and they stay. I suppose with *Bayfair* we're trying to sprinkle a little bit of that magic about - and inform of course - this is one of the most aware communities on the coast I think. It's time consuming but I try not to do the real hard work; that's the job of the regular contributors who do a great job.' If you are planning to stay in Robin Hood's Bay then *Bayfair* is an invaluable reference and fantastic value at 33p. You can even order it online (www.bayfair.co.uk) before you come.

At the top of the bank you are still in Robin Hood's Bay but a part with a completely different feel to it. It is newer in the main, with many of the Victorian buildings springing up when the railway arrived in 1865. There is not much of interest up here, save one or two good eating houses and the old railway station itself, which is the home of a few slow businesses and organisations.

The Bay

Any Cleveland Wayer worth his or her salt, when heading south from Robin Hood's Bay, would choose to walk on the sea-shore rather than the official cliff-top path, if the tide allows. Not only is it the flat alternative, it is also a delight – part sand, part rock-ledge, but always with the tang, noise and excitement of the sea right by your side.

The first half mile to Boggle Hole could be busy, as this is a popular stroll, and not just with those staying in the youth hostel of that name. This imposing building was originally a big Victorian watermill, built to take advantage of the latent power in the beck that spills on to the beach here. Fewer people make it to the next beach stream, another half mile on at Stoupe Beck, but there is a route on to the cliff-top back to civilisation and even a nearby road.

You are likely to have the remaining three miles of shore-line to yourself – well, you and the oystercatchers, fulmars and turnstones – as there is no escape up the cliffs until Old Peak. I find it incredible that where the looming cliffs are at their steepest, with waterfalls tumbling over the edge, there was once a harbour. A couple of centuries ago, this was where ships loaded up with alum, a chemical extracted from the shale rock that was quarried from Stoupe Brow, hundreds of feet higher up. The remains of the quarries and works are still there to be seen, owned and ably interpreted by the National Trust, both on-site and in their Peakside Centre (see page 201).

Food and drink

Bramblewick Restaurant The Dock ☎ 01947 880960 ⌂ www.bramblewick.org. A good local reputation for breakfasts, afternoon teas and à la carte evening meals.
Dolphin King St ☎ 01947 880337. A rambling old pub on two levels. This fine no-nonsense establishment has a range of real ales and big portions of basic traditional pub food.
Grosvenor Hotel Station Rd ☎ 01947 880320 ⌂ www.thegrosvenor.info. A hotel with a popular lounge bar, pool table and regular live music; Sun is Quiz Night. Bar food includes fish and chips and local lobster.
Laurel Bay Bank ☎ 01947 880400. The smallest pub in town but with bags of olde worlde character. The menu is simple and wholesome and the beers always good. Open every day; quiz night Wed.
The Old Bakery Tea Rooms Chapel St ☎ 01947 880709. The best café in town and in a great position overlooking the beck. Home-baked snacks are particularly good.
Swell Café Bar Chapel St ☎ 01947 880180 ⌂ www.swell.org.uk. A relatively new and innovative venture in an old chapel. Superb views from the café balcony on a good day and surely one of the most unusual cinemas in the country.

Attractions and shopping

Jet Black New Rd ☎ 01947 881206 ⌂ www.jetblackjewellery.co.uk. A range of jewellery made of the prized local Whitby jet.
North East Yorkshire Geology Trust Station Workshops ☎ 01947 881000 ⌂ www.neyorksgeologytrust.com. Provide fossil guides, talks and regular Sun guided walks for £2.
Robin Hood's Bay Museum Fishergate ☎ 01947 881252 ⌂ http://museum.rhbay.co.uk. An enjoyable small, traditional museum run by volunteers and housed in the old mortuary. Free but only open school holidays and weekends.
The Woodcraft Workshop Station Workshops ☎ 01947 881111 ⌂ www.marklaycock.co.uk. Artisan sculptural furniture made from English hardwoods.

Seals

I had heard about the seal colony at Ravenscar, near Robin Hood's Bay, so one clear crisp day in March I went to investigate. It was cold enough to see my breath as I picked my way down the steep cliff path but thankfully there was no wind or I would have needed way more than the thin fleece I was wearing. I heard the seals before I saw them, a slightly forlorn-sounding strangled wail every now and again. At least I knew they were here. I headed towards Peak Steel, the rocky outcrop where the noise seemed to be coming from, and found that I wasn't alone. 'Hello there,' said a man who turned out to be Callum Foster, 'have you come to see the seals as well?'

Callum lives in Robin Hood's Bay where he and his wife run a B&B, but this was his day job and he was accompanied by 12 schoolchildren from York who were staying at nearby East Barnby Outdoor Education Centre. 'We usually take the children on seashore walks nearer the centre but I thought we'd come here today for a change and see the seals,' Callum explained. 'This colony hasn't been here that long. Five years ago, all we'd see were odd individuals out in the bay now and again. But then a few more came from somewhere and started hauling themselves out on the scars here. One winter we noticed some small pups with white furry coats amongst the rocks and realised that they had started breeding. Numbers have increased dramatically, to the point now... how many have we counted today kids?' 'Sixty-five!' piped up the ten-year-old voice of Emma, 'but these are different to the two we saw yesterday. These are grey seals 'cos they've got big noses like Romans, and yesterday's when we

⑬ Ravenscar

There is a major crack in the earth's surface here, well known amongst geologists as the Peak Fault, and it has a lot to answer for. It has indirectly led to Romans and seals taking up residence here and a Victorian property company going out of business. What the fault did was raise the land level to the south 600 feet higher than that to the north, where the bay now is, and it brought different, more resistant rocks to the surface (apologies to geologists, I know it's a lot more complicated than that). The Romans consequently had a convenient high vantage point to build one of their chain of coastal signal stations, where the Raven Hall Hotel is now, and the seals got a protective shelf of hard rock to shelter behind (see above).

As for the property company, this was a group of Yorkshire businessmen who formed the Peak Estate Company in 1885, with the bright idea of creating a seaside resort at Ravenscar to rival Scarborough and Whitby. They spent a small fortune laying out a road system, putting in water mains and digging sewers and then put 1,500 building plots up for sale. Call it naive, but what they hadn't accounted for was that holidaymakers would not want to walk 600 feet down (and more importantly back up) to a beach that was predominantly bedrock and boulders. They sold eight plots and went bankrupt. Details of their ill-fated were canoeing on the river were common seals 'cos they had faces like dogs!'

Emma was right; the Ravenscar colony are grey or Atlantic seals, *Halichoerus gryphus*, which literally means hooked-nosed sea pig, and they probably came as colonists from the big population on the Farne Islands in Northumberland. The adult bulls, at 10 feet long and weighing 300lb, are our biggest wild land animal, if you count lounging on beaches now and again as being terrestrial. They eat 10lb of fish per day which doesn't make them popular with local fishermen – just do the sums, 10 x 65 x 365: that is a lot of fish in a year. Callum is happy to see them here though. 'I think there's a big opportunity here for someone with a boat; "trips across the bay to see the seals" would go down a storm with the trippers. I might even do it myself!'

The common or harbour seals that Emma and her friends had seen the day before in the tidal section of the River Esk are much smaller than grey seals. Their nearest breeding colony is 20 miles north on Seal Sands in the Tees estuary, but adventurous individuals often appear along the Yorkshire coast. They are quite happy to venture up rivers, especially when their favourite food of sea trout and salmon are doing the same. Up to five seals take up residence at times, on a grassy bank of the river, halfway between Ruswarp and Whitby. They are visible from the train, so keep your eyes peeled if you are on it, just after Ruswarp Station, or take a riverside walk up from Whitby. If you want more than a fleeting glimpse from a train, then call in at the Sea Life Centre, Scalby Mills, Scarborough. They operate a seal rescue centre which takes in sick, orphaned or exhausted seals, and pampers them for a bit before releasing them into the wild.

scheme, and much more about this cliff top village, can be found in the National Trust's little visitor centre (01723 870423) near the hotel entrance gate. Retracing the planned road system makes an interesting potter and can be extended down to the old alum works

A coastal walk from wyke to wyke

Between Ravenscar and Scarborough, the walk along the wild section of coast from Hayburn Wyke to Cloughton Wyke and back is a most rewarding one ('wyke' means 'bay' incidentally). It's two miles each way, and you can start at either end; refreshment at the Hayburn Wyke Inn may influence your route plans. Should it be a halfway drink or one at the end – that is the question? There's good rock pooling at Cloughton Wyke and at Hayburn Wyke a stream gushes on to a boulder-strewn cove backed by high cliffs.

Hayburn Wyke Inn Hayburn Wyke YO13 0AU; ☎ 01723 870202
🖰 www.hayburnwykeinn.co.uk. A welcoming pub, that also allows walkers to park their cars there while they go out for the day. Extensive, traditional menu with a Sunday carvery. Open every day.

The Station House Tea Rooms Station Lane, Cloughton YO13 0AD ✆ 01723 870896 🖰 www.cloughtonstation.co.uk. Set in the old railway station with half an acre of garden. Open fires, tempting cakes, low prices and good service – what more could you ask for?

⑭ Scarborough

Scarborough has an old provenance; a Roman signal station, a Viking name, a Norman castle and the tourist industry that started in the 17th century. It is also a modern seaside resort, and a 'fast' one at that, with many visitors coming for the nightclubs, amusement arcades, lager and speed-boat trips. The words 'go slow' and South Bay seafront fit together as comfortably as, well, a square peg and a round hole. It is all relative though; in the loud-brash-tacky stakes it is not in the same league as Blackpool or Margate and you can still savour its genteel Georgian class in some hidden, serene corners.

A good place to start is the starting point of the resort itself, the Spa at the foot of South Cliff, where the original therapeutic spring was discovered in 1626. Behind the elegant **Spa complex**, with its concert hall and café, **South Cliff Gardens** cling to the steep hillside. You could easily spend half a day exploring the three miles of zigzagging path on foot, wheelchair or bike (there are no no-cycling signs) and enjoying stunning views over the sea. In summer you can walk down and take the **Spa Cliff Tramway** back up. Even on busy days the gardens are remarkably quiet, especially at the non-town end. For the more intrepid a walk in this direction does not need to stop at the end of the gardens but could continue along the shore, on to Black Rocks and around White Nab, tide permitting. South of town, the cliff-top is accessible again at **Osgodby Point** and your two-mile return follows the Cleveland Way path. This route crosses debris from the famous 1993 landslip, when a huge section of cliff suffered a 'rotational slip' taking the Holbeck Hall hotel with it. You can find out all the details of this event and much more about local geology in the **Rotunda Museum** near the Spa.

If you can brave crossing the seafront (on the beach itself is the most pleasant route) the other end of **South Bay** has Scarborough Castle on the headland. From the top of this promontory you can see down on to Scarborough's other beach in **North Bay**, where you can enjoy more sand and less people. Halfway round North Bay, where the road ends, is Peasholm Park, once a huge tourist attraction but now dilapidated and scheduled for redevelopment. Two welcome exceptions here are the Peasholm Glen Tree Trail (map from Tourist Information) described in the National Tree Register as 'one of the richest and most diverse tree collections of any English town', and the North Bay Railway.

Scarborough itself is not in the North York Moors National Park but the boundary comes close to the town in the north near Cloughton, and especially the west, where Raincliffe Woods and **Forge Valley** are very accessible.

The Rotunda Museum

Historically and architecturally this is one of the most important small museums in the country, but the Rotunda is a real riches-to-rags-to-riches-again story. It was built in 1829 to the specific design of the geologist William Smith, one of the most significant men of the 19th century. He almost single-handedly produced a geological map of England and Wales, the first of its kind in the world. Near the end of his career he wished to celebrate his discoveries, and the rich fossil beds of northeast Yorkshire, by displaying his huge collection in the same vertical layers that they occurred in nature, the youngest on the top floor and the oldest in the basement. This graceful 50-foot-high Doric-style building with a viewing spiral staircase was the consequence, and a roaring success in Victorian society. Simon Winchester lamented in his 2001 biography of Smith, *The Map that Changed the World*, that in recent years the building had become a shadow of its former self and had lost its fossils. To their eternal credit, Scarborough Museums Trust have since done a fantastic job of returning the Rotunda to its former glory, and in 2008 it reopened as the William Smith Museum of Geology.

Scarborough Castle

On the lofty headland between North Bay and South Bay, this is such a textbook defendable site it's no surprise there has been a fort here since Iron Age times. The Romans also had a signal station here and finally the Normans built the present building. Actually, to call it a building is stretching a point a bit, because little is left except the barbican, curtain walls, and the tottering remains of the keep. Parliamentarians did most of the damage in the Civil War, and that was added to last century by the Germans – not as you may suspect, World War II aerial bombing, but an artillery attack from a battleship in 1914. What is left is a big castle site but not an awful lot to see. It is a great place for a family picnic though, with plenty of grassy space for the little ones to run around in, and English Heritage produces free activity sheets for them to do while you sit and have a cup of tea in the café.

Just outside the castle entrance is another building worth a visit, especially for those with a literary bent. **St Mary's Church** is old, but not remarkable, save for a much visited grave outside. It is a memorial to part of the tragic family history of the Brontës, being the resting place of Anne. She moved to Scarborough in May 1849 to take the restorative sea air and try to avoid the fate of her brother Branwell and her sister Emily who had already died from tuberculosis, or consumption as it was known then. It didn't work; she died of the same disease within the month and was buried in St Mary's graveyard. To add insult to injury, there were five errors on her original gravestone which her surviving sister Charlotte replaced with the present one, but even that has a mistake – she was 29 at her death not 28 as the stonemason's engraving claims.

A seafront tour

The best of what Scarborough has to offer is by the sea, between the Spa and Scalby Mills, but these two are almost three miles apart. That's a little too far to walk there and back, and probably the last thing you would want to do is even attempt to drive through town. Here is a suggested multi-transport tour of the seafront, starting at either of Scarborough's park-and-rides, although it could just as easily start at the Scalby Mills car park.

Pack your bags for the day, and take the **park-and-ride bus** into town, getting off at Aquarium Top. Just around the corner is the Spa where you can catch the **Shoreline Suncruiser bus** (every 15 minutes between March and October) and enjoy the open-top views, weather permitting. This will take you around South Bay, the harbour, the kittiwake colony on the castle headland and North Bay to **Peasholm Park**. Just across the road from the park, in Northstead Manor Gardens is the southern terminus of the **North Bay Railway**, a narrow gauge line dating from 1931, where you can take a short ride to Scalby Mills. If you have to wait for your train, then there are always the pedal boats nearby, or a cup of tea in the fantastic Glass House Café. At Scalby Mills you may be tempted into **Sea Life Scarborough** (£3 off on production of your train ticket), but it was a little too much like a zoo for me, so I had a pint in the excellent Scalby Mills Hotel instead, and a stroll along the cliff-top path to watch the seabirds.

Cafés

Scarborough probably has more than a hundred cafés, so to find out which were the best, I approached Sarah Dowey and Victoria Addis-Brown, two locals who review cafés for the local paper in their spare time. Here are the best three in the experts' opinion:

Bonnets Huntress Row ☎ 01723 361033. In the heart of town, adjacent to its own famous chocolate shop, Bonnets is definitely the cream of Scarborough cafés. It offers a tantalising choice of homemade cakes and light meals and with its chocolatier heritage, deserves a visit for the hot chocolate alone.

The Glass House North Bay ☎ 01723 368791. Tucked away opposite Scarborough's miniature railway, the Glass House is a hidden gem. With its selection of freshly made meals and speciality theme nights this bistro is definitely worth making a stop for.

The Stained Glass Centre Tea Rooms Killerby Lane, Cayton ☎ 01723 585146. Nestled at the bottom of a rambling country lane, the Stained Glass Centre Tearooms have a relaxed country atmosphere; idyllic views offer the perfect retreat to enjoy the unobtrusive service and generous homemade fare.

Pubs

Valley Valley Rd ☎ 01723 372593 ⏚ www.valleybar.co.uk. For a Yorkshire pub to be voted the best in the whole country for cider and perry, something special has to be going on. This is first and foremost a drinkers' pub, with eight ciders, six draught beers and 100 Belgian bottled on offer. Food is home made and very good value, especially the locally caught fresh fish. No food Sun evening.

Boat trips

Three boats make sightseeing trips:

Hispaniola West Pier slipway ✆ 01723 355480. Short cruise around South Bay. Easter–end of Oct, every day weather permitting. £2.50 adult, £2 child.

Queensferry Coastal Cruises West Pier slipway ✆ 01723 379126 / 07834 410309. A 37ft open launch offering 1hr 45mins trips to seal colonies. Easter–Sept, every day from 11am. £6 adult, £4 child.

Scarborough Pleasure Steamers Lighthouse Pier ✆ 01723 363605 / 07855 381139. A big boat with covered bar, food and entertainment. A 1hr trip up or down the coast dependent on weather. Opening seasonal. £3.50 adult, £1.75 child.

Places to visit and activities

North Bay Railway ✆ 01723 368791 🖰 www.nbr.org.uk.

Rotunda Museum ✆ 01723 353665 🖰 www.rotundamuseum.co.uk.

Scarborough Castle ✆ 01723 372451 🖰 www.english-heritage.org.uk.

Scarborough Surf School Cayton Bay ✆ 01723 585585 🖰 www.scarboroughsurfschool.co.uk.

Shoreline Suncruiser Buses Falsgrave Rd ✆ 01723 360969 🖰 www.shorelinesuncruisers.co.uk.

The Stained Glass Centre Killerby Lane, Cayton ✆ 01723 581236 🖰 www.stainedglasscentre.co.uk.

⑮ Forge Valley

The River Derwent follows one of the weirdest routes of any river in the country. It rises on Fylingdales Moor near Robin Hood's Bay, a mere two miles from the sea, but then decides to wander inland and south for another 50 miles, finally joining the River Ouse to empty into the Humber. Before the last ice age it was a normal and much shorter river, finding a fairly direct route to the sea at Scalby Mills. All changed when this exit was blocked by the massive North Sea ice sheet and the river was dammed to form a lake in the Hackness valley. Water always finds a way out and the lake eventually overflowed south cutting a new channel through the Tabular Hills – the gorge we now know as Forge Valley.

What we are left with is a steep-sided wooded ravine with a flora and fauna rich enough to warrant its designation as a National Nature Reserve, and a crystal-clear trout stream babbling along its centre. Forge Valley really is a delightful place, the only intrusion into its wildness the traffic noise from the road that follows its whole length. Natural England have provided excellent boardwalk paths for walkers and wheelchairs (but not bikes) and riverside picnic areas with feeding stations that attract masses of woodland birds.

Special flowers to look out for are broadleaved helleborine, and birds' nest orchids; exciting birds you may see include woodwarblers, redstarts and woodpeckers. The wooded section of Forge Valley is only a mile long but if you are walking here it is worth extending your route a little to include the remains of Ayton Castle (small but picturesque) and Raincliffe Woods (extensive and quieter than the main valley).

Three pubs in surrounding villages stand out:

SP The Anvil Sawdon YO13 9DY 01723 859896 www.theanvilinnsawdon.co.uk. This welcoming little hostelry is housed in a 200-year-old forge in the back of beyond, with the bar where the blacksmith's workshop was. The food is inventive and locally sourced, and the beer all from Yorkshire too (Daleside and Copper Dragon). A place worth seeking out, off the A170. Open every day, not Mon lunch.

SP The Coachman Inn Snainton YO13 9PL 01723 859231 www.coachmaninn.co.uk. The York–Scarborough mail coach stopped here in Georgian times and it's still old fashioned, but in a 1930s Arts-and-Crafts style now. The food is excellent and decidedly modern, leaning towards local game and fresh fish. Cask beers are from the local Wold Top brewery. Closed all day Mon and Tues lunch.

The Moorcock Inn Langdale End YO13 0BN 01723 882268. An absolute rural gem and local institution. Langdale End is a tiny, isolated hamlet, between Forge Valley and Dalby Forest. Food is traditional bar meals with the steak pies especially popular. Yorkshire micro-brewery ales served though hatches to both bars. Can be busy in summer but winter opening hours are sketchy so ring first.

⑯ Cayton Bay

This small beach resort has changed dramatically within the past 20 years. Back in the days when Butlins and Pontins were fashionable, Wallis's Holiday Camp at Cayton Bay was very popular and the beach here almost an east-coast Blackpool. There is still a large caravan park but a big new road separates it from the beach which is consequently much quieter. The beach is a classic in the holiday-postcard tradition, a small, almost perfect semi-circle of soft sand, but with a rocky reef in the centre of the bay that makes this one of the best surf spots on the Yorkshire coast.

Not having any of your own gear is no excuse for not having a go in the waves, as Scarborough Surf School have a base here. You can hire a wetsuit and board for £20 and just go and play for half a day, or you can sign up for a lesson at any level, complete beginner to competition coaching, for £25. As this price includes your gear hire, you effectively get 2 ½ hours coaching, a shower and a hot drink for £5 – fantastic value.

If the idea of squeezing yourself into a rubber suit and venturing into the cold North Sea fills you with horror, then head to the quiet north end of the beach. You can bask in the sun or rummage amongst the pebbles for gemstones.

Cornelian – a Yorkshire gem

Cornelian, or carnelian, is a semi-precious stone with a deep orange colour, often found on the beaches of North Yorkshire. One beach, between Scarborough and Cayton Bay, is a particularly good hunting ground and has earned itself the name Cornelian Bay. Geologists class cornelian as iron-oxide-stained chalcedony – rusty quartz in other words – but that doesn't stop it polishing up into beautiful jewellery. The cornelian pebbles have had a long and eventful journey to these beaches because they do not originate from the local Jurassic cliffs. They have actually been washed out of the cliff-top boulder clay which was left here by the last North Sea ice sheet 10,000 years ago. The ice must have brought the pebbles from the nearest source of cornelian – Scotland!

Just inland from Cayton Bay lies the village of Cayton, nice enough but unremarkable – except that is for a small craft business tucked away down the back lane to Killerby. The Stained Glass Centre is run by Valerie Green, keeping her family tradition going, as her grandfather was a master glass stainer in 19th-century Bradford. Valerie and her team produce stained glass and leaded lights for businesses all over the country, but also sell items in the centre shop and run very popular courses for you to learn how to do it for yourself. The tea shop is excellent.

South from Scarborough: Filey Bay

Filey Bay is huge, stretching ten miles from **Filey Brigg** in the north to **Flamborough Head** in the south and straddling not just two counties but two geological time zones. The brigg marks the end of the Jurassic series of rocks, whilst Flamborough, in East Yorkshire, is the start of the Cretaceous chalk that makes up the foundations of the Yorkshire Wolds. **Filey** itself is the only settlement on the bay at all, and it is tucked away at the northern end. The wide sweep of the rest of the bay is backed by fast-eroding clay cliffs and is not fit for any permanent buildings, so consequently it is capped by a rash of caravan parks and holiday villages – decidedly non-slow.

⑰ Filey

As part of the Yorkshire Riviera, along with Scarborough and Whitby, Filey has been a holiday venue for many years. It was the planned destination of my mother and her friend Ena on a hare-brained tandem trip in the 1940s. They never got there as it turned out (brake failure before even leaving Lancashire, and recuperation in Blackburn Royal Infirmary) but, had they managed it, their first impressions would have been pretty much the same as today. Filey seems to exist in a time warp of sorts and its very old-fashionedness is what many of its visitors like.

'I hope your book won't go bringing more people here,' commented Bella, the elderly lady I shared a park bench with, 'We don't want anything changing. It's just right as it is thank you very much.'

Parts of the resort are crowded, like the short seafront, but on nothing like the scale of Scarborough or Whitby, and there is always some deserted tranquillity a few yards around the corner. Between the buildings of Beach Road and the rest of the town are a line of public gardens which make a pleasant walk between two wooded valleys at either end of the town. Martin's Ravine is at the southern end and The Ravine to the north. The latter was the pre-1974 boundary between the old North and East Ridings with most of the houses on one side and the church and graveyard on the other. This led to the cryptic traditional saying, 'Yon'll straightly be off t' North Riding,' meaning so-and-so's not in good health and could soon find themselves in the graveyard. The old fishermen's cottage community of Queens Street is nearby, two of which have been converted into **Filey Museum**, a fine local collection (01723 515013; www.fileymuseum.co.uk). Don't be put off by the motto over the door; 'The fear of God be in you' was a reminder to 17th-century fishermen, not a dire warning to us.

Naturalists may well wish to visit **Filey Dams** (open all year round, free entrance; www.ywt.org.uk), a freshwater marsh nature reserve on the inland edge of town. It is managed by the Yorkshire Wildlife Trust, mainly to protect its rare newts, dragonflies and plants, but it is also a magnet for migrating birds, and a long list of unusual visitors has been seen from the hides.

Good pubs are in short supply in Filey, but this one definitely meets the standard:

Bonhommes Bar Royal Crescent Court ☎ 01723 514054.
Named after the ship of the American rebel, John Paul Jones, the *Bonhomme Richard*, which sank in Filey Bay. This hidden-away gem is worth searching out. It is a friendly and lively local with music, quizzes and a rotating range of guest cask beers, including brews from Filey's own East Coast Brewery Company. No food. Open every day.

The café picture is very different: there are loads to choose from; these are my best five:

Brontë Vinery Café Belle Vue St ☎ 01723 514805. Good all round and fair value.
The Clock Café Station Ave ☎ 07786 634480. A cosy café, particularly recommended for breakfasts but the cakes are nice too.
Country Park Café Northcliff ☎ 01723 514881. Serves free-range and fair-trade products. The sandwiches and vegetarian food are particularly tasty.
Frothies Coffee Shop Union St ☎ 01723 514114. Wide range of teas and coffees and good-value snacks sold.
The Lighthouse Belle Vue St ☎ 01723 512191. Homemade cakes and scones, and proper fresh ground coffee in a traditional tearoom.

Filey Brigg

Filey owes its existence as a fishing settlement to this narrow promontory of hard Jurassic limestone, as it keeps the worst of the North Sea's waves from reaching the town's boat landing areas and essentially converts Filey Bay into a huge harbour. It forms part of North Cliff Country Park where a caravan park with shop and café sits cheek by jowl with a large car park. There is a big green space here for children to be let loose in, but for me the place to head for (with care) is the cliff edge. Unofficial descent points here are used by anglers and youths in wet suits engaged in the dangerous sport of 'tombstoning' – leaping off the cliff into the sea.

You can easily spend hours watching people pursuing their contrasting leisure activities, ships and seabirds passing or just waves thundering into the rock wall below. Or you could amble along this end section of the Cleveland Way but, unfortunately, not down to the wave-wasted rocks of the brigg-end itself. Erosion has caused the steep end path to collapse so access has to be across the beach from the other end of the country park, via the yacht club. It is worth the effort though; it's an exhilarating place to be, especially in heavy seas, and the rock pooling here is excellent. There are some huge tame prawns in the upper shore pools who will investigate a wiggling finger or even take food from your hand. Strong currents off the end of the brigg attract seals and porpoises so take your binoculars down with you if you have them.

⑱ Flamborough Head

Flamborough Head is not really part of this region politically or geologically but since you can hardly help seeing it in the distance along the coast from Filey, I feel it deserves an expedition to what is an extremely special place. Pedantically speaking, only the relatively low cliff at the very end of the headland qualifies for the name but when most people talk of Flamborough Head they are referring to the whole area of land between Bridlington and the sands of Filey Bay. This enormous chunk of chalk, an extension of the Wolds, sticks out a good six miles into the North Sea, with its highest cliffs an awesome, vertical 400 feet at Bempton on its northern side. These cliffs face Filey but such is their size they don't look anywhere near their actual distance of seven miles away.

Flamborough has always been a very separate place, indeed the Bronze Age people here cut themselves off from the rest of the country completely by constructing a massive earth wall and ditch now mistakenly known as 'Danes' Dyke'. There is a strong Scandinavian connection here though, with many colloquial terms, stories and traditions dating from Viking times. The annual sword dance that is still performed, even if only by local village schoolchildren now, is probably the most famous of these old traditions.

Flamborough Head's exposed position has always been a hazard to shipping; over 50 shipwrecks are recorded close by, so it's no surprise to find a lighthouse here. What is unusual is that there are two, the present working one built in 1806 and its predecessor, a wonderful octagonal chalk edifice whose beacon was a basket of burning coal. Dating from 1674, this is the oldest standing lighthouse in the country.

Other attractions apart, what draws most people to Flamborough Head is its birds. Two nature reserves are dedicated to the protection of the huge seabird colonies here, Bempton Cliffs Nature Reserve (RSPB) and Flamborough Head Nature Reserve (Yorkshire Wildlife Trust). If you want to have an extended walk along the coast, the village of Flamborough inland makes a handy starting point, with easy links by footpath to the coast north, south and east. The most satisfying way of doing it is to walk along the southern part of the peninsula to Flamborough Head, then along the much more spectacular, indented cliffs on the north side before heading back into Flamborough village.

Seabird cities

This is almost a sensory overload experience I am going through. There is deafening cackling all around and the constant pattering of feet on water, so many individuals are coming and going carrying fish that I cannot keep up, and an overpowering fishy smell pervades everything. Where am I? A busy Scarborough chip shop on a Friday night perhaps? No, I am bobbing on the swell in a small boat at the foot of Flamborough Head cliffs, taking in one of the most spectacular wildlife experiences that Britain, never mind Yorkshire, has to offer. Most of the pattering fish-carriers are members of the auk family; puffins mainly, but also guillemots and razorbills that have surfaced with a beak full of sand eels to feed their young. They manage to get themselves airborne with a whirring of their small wings and a frantic leg-sprint over the sea surface before banking over to their cliff-top nest. As they leave, the next shift arrives and plops beneath the surface. I lean over the side and watch enthralled as one puffin flaps its way under our boat (they swim by flying underwater), its progress through the clear water visible because of a silver layer of air clinging to its waterproof feathers.

What sound like two sharp gun-shots pull my attention to the other side of the boat, just in time to see the cause of the noise as a gannet folds its wings back at the end of its 30ft dive and 'thunks' into the water at breakneck speed. Two others surface, both with a wriggling mackerel that they wolf down headfirst – what gannets! There is so much going on it is tiring; a seal's head in the water to port, was that a porpoise fin on the starboard side? Yes, there it is again – two of them! After a while though, childish excitement slackens enough to observe and see order in the apparent chaos. Seven or eight species of bird breed on the chalk cliffs of Flamborough and Bempton, 200,000 in total, most feeding on small fish, sand eels

Food and drink

Ship Inn Post Office St ☏ 01262 850454 ⏀ www.theshipinnflamborough.co.uk.
The name is apt, as you will feel as if you have walked into the Captain's cabin when you enter the varnished, wood-panelled bar. This is a traditional local, with darts, pool, dominoes and cards available to play, and John Smith's and other guest cask ales to drink. The grub cooked here is wholesome and very good value, especially the seafood.

Information and boat trips

Bempton Cliffs Nature Reserve Bempton ☏ 01262 851179 ⏀ www.rspb.org.uk.
Open every day, all year, entry £3.50 per car but free if you walk or bike there.
Emerson's North Landing slipway ☏ 01262 850575 / 850704. Boat trips to see the birds and caves of Flamborough Head. Summer season only.
Flamborough Head Nature Reserve ⏀ www.ywt.org.uk. Reserve open every day, all year, free entry.

and sprats. Kittiwakes and guillemots are the most numerous and nest on ledges high on the most vertical sections of cliff with gannets and razorbills preferring the lower sloping sections. The puffins here are unusual – elsewhere in the country, such as the Farne Islands in Northumberland, they raise their young in soil burrows at the cliff-top. At Flamborough, natural cavities in the rock face do the job and puffins have the unusual experience of tenement living with fulmars as neighbours.

In the past, the vast numbers of birds here were seen as a harvestable resource by locals. Gangs of 'climmers' would make a hair-raising descent by rope from the top of the cliffs to collect both eggs and young birds for food. This sustainable harvesting worked fine until Victorian times when things got out of hand. Shooting birds from boats as holiday sport caught on and many more eggs were collected to supply private collections, but the activity that caused a change in the law was kittiwake collecting. Thousands were massacred to provide feathers for fashion hat accessories and to stuff mattresses. So to prevent their complete wipe-out, the first Bird Protection Act of 1869 was introduced to the statute book and today the birds are very well protected.

As my boat chugs back to North Landing at Flamborough I marvel at what a special place of superlatives this is. It is the most northerly outcrop of chalk in the country, England's biggest seabird colony, and the only mainland gannet colony in Britain. Most of all, it provides one of the most exhilarating wildlife experiences to be found anywhere.

If you fancy a boat trip to see, hear and smell the birds of Flamborough Head, there are a few options (see page 182) but being afloat is not the only way to experience the birds of course. You can see them with a good pair of binoculars from the beaches at North Landing and South Landing or from the cliff-top path looking down. The RSPB have some excellent viewing points at the top of Bempton cliff.

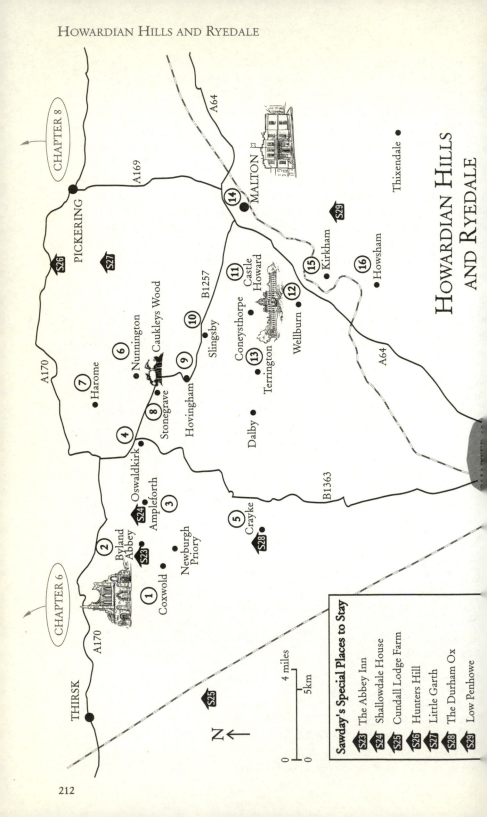

CHAPTER 8

A64

CHAPTER 6

THIRSK

A170

CHAPTER 6

N

4 miles

5km

0
0

Howardian Hills and Ryedale

A169

MALTON

Thixendale

(14)

S29

(15) Kirkham

(16) Howsham

A64

(11) Castle Howard

Coneysthorpe

(12) Wellburn

(13) Terrington

Dalby

B1363

B1257

Slingsby

(10)

(9) Hovingham

(6) Nunnington Caukleys Wood

(7) Harome

(8) Stonegrave

(4) Oswaldkirk

S24 Ampleforth

(3)

(2) Byland Abbey

S23

(1) Coxwold

Newburgh Priory

(5) Crayke

S28

PICKERING

S26

S27

A170

S25

Sawday's Special Places to Stay		
S23	The Abbey Inn	
S24	Shallowdale House	
S25	Cundall Lodge Farm	
S26	Hunters Hill	
S27	Little Garth	
S28	The Durham Ox	
S29	Low Penhowe	

9. Howardian Hills and Ryedale

I f Yorkshire is England in miniature, then this is its Cotswolds. The Howardian Hills are gentle, rolling and agricultural, with more than their fair share of trees; no big forests but some sizeable woods and lots of clumps and copses, dark pillows lying on a rumpled patchwork quilt of a landscape. This arable pastoral embroidery hides a scattering of honey-coloured hamlets and villages, one of which is my home. It is no coincidence that the look and feel of the place is so similar to the Cotswolds as it is the same Jurassic limestone that underlies both, prompts a similar land-use, and forms the warm, yellow stone walls of the old buildings.

This is archetypal well-off countryside: sleepy, self-contained and quintessentially English, with each village seeming to have its old manor house, very old church and huge vicarage. I can easily imagine Miss Marple taking tea with the Colonel in Bulmer or cycling past the green in Hovingham. The Edwardian landed gentry feel to this place is no illusion. Feudal old England is alive and well here, with a fair proportion of the Howardian Hills still owned and run by three families as their country estates. The Wombwells rule the roost in the west at Newburgh Priory near Coxwold, the Worsleys' family home is Hovingham Hall but pride of place for pomp, opulence and grandeur must go to the Howards. Not only do they have a castle named after the family, but a range of hills named after their castle; now that is true arrogance – oops, sorry, I mean influence.

Nunnington sits alongside the River Rye just as it leaves the Howardian Hills Area of Outstanding Natural Beauty (AONB) and slides lazily out into the floodplain of its own making, Yorkshire's fenland. Scenically, lower Ryedale is nothing to write home about. Most people would go as far as to say it was boring, unless they had a thing about crop rotation, yields per acre or the relative merits of David Brown tractors over Massey Fergusons, because this is prime arable farming country. It does have attractions though; its rivers, the Rye and its tributaries, are wonderful linear reserves of nature and tranquillity.

The River Rye empties into the bigger River Derwent. Three miles below this confluence sits the town of Malton, on the north bank, with its twin Norton facing it from the other side of the river. This has always been an important river crossing even back to Roman times and Malton is still very much the social hub of this region. When people from **Terrington**, **Hovingham** or **Welburn** say that they are going into town, this is where they mean; likewise, local farmers taking their beasts to market will also head this way. **Malton** is a market town, but a real one that still does what it says on the tin.

Downstream from Malton the River Derwent winds its way south, through Kirkham gorge and away down the western edge of the Wolds, finally joining the sea at the Humber estuary.

Getting there and around

Quiet, affluent areas don't tend to have good public transport, so it's no surprise that in the Howardian Hills it's average at best and terrible in places.

Trains

Getting to Malton is fine and dandy, with the trans-Pennine Manchester to Scarborough train service calling every hour via Leeds and York. This is the only rail link here, although Thirsk station, on the East Coast Main Line, is only a bus ride away from the western side of the region.

Buses

The Coastliner bus service is another excellent means of getting here, running half-hourly from Leeds and York to Malton where the service splits to go to either Pickering and Whitby hourly or Scarborough and Filey hourly.

Getting from Malton to anywhere else is the tricky bit. The villages on the fringes of the area do not fare too badly, with an hourly service to Hovingham (194) via all the Street villages, and connecting three times a day with the 195 and 196 to Helmsley, via Nunnington and Harome, or Gilling East and Oswaldkirk. The service is frustratingly Monday to Saturday, daytime only and none-too reliable; more than once I have stood and waited for a non-existent or very late bus.

Castle Howard can be reached by services 183, 194 and 842, which together provide a roughly hourly service. The 183 also visits Welburn, Terrington and Scackleton four times a day.

The villages of lower Ryedale have the sparsest service, just one bus today on four days a week. The 175 and 176 links Malton with Pickering or Kirkbymoorside via Great Habton, Great Barugh, Brawby, Salton, Normanby and Marton. Kirby Misperton is very well served by buses to deliver the thousands of daily visitors to the Flamingo Land theme park which, as one of the fastest destinations in the country, is very definitely outside the remit of this book.

Over in the west, Coxwold, Byland Abbey and Ampleforth are served by four buses a day from Thirsk to Helmsley (59, M7, M71) with more on Mon and Fri, and two a day from York to Helmsley (31X, M15).

Cycling

It is mixed news on the two-wheeled front. The good news is that **road biking** in places is superb, mainly because the minor roads around here are so quiet. I once cycled from home in Barton le Street, in the middle of the day on a circular route, through Butterwick, Brawby and Salton. The sun was out, skylarks and yellowhammers were singing throughout the whole nine miles over minor tarmac roads, and I did not see a single motorised vehicle; come to think of it, I did not see another person at all. Ryedale has the added advantage of being flat as a pancake mostly, so is very forgiving for the less athletic biker.

The Howardian Hills half of the region is not quite so gentle; the clue is in the 'hills' bit of the name. There are still some lovely quiet road circuits like Hovingham to Stonegrave to Gilling East to Coulton and back to Hovingham, or west from Terrington along Bonnie Gates Lane and back via Steersby and Skewsby, but some of the hills on the way are killers. Dalby Bank, up from the beck to the hamlet, is my nemesis, but what the heck, there is no shame in getting off and pushing every now and again.

Off-road biking is less promising. The areas of the OS map devoid of bridleways suspiciously correspond to the biggest estate lands. Gilling Castle and Newburgh Priory estates seem to have been particularly good at keeping peasants off their land in the past, which is reflected in the lack of rights of way today. A decent network exists elsewhere, with Castle Howard lands being surprisingly rich. One of my particular favourites is a circuit linking Hovingham and Coneysthorpe, with much of the northern leg following the Centenary Way, and the parallel southern return on the Ebor Way. This is a lovely nine-mile ridge route predominantly under trees and with lots of alternative options to shorten or lengthen the ride. Wildlife encounters are likely, with hares lolloping away from you across every field you pass and buzzards soaring on the up-draught at any point on the ridges. If you are early or late in the day you have an excellent chance of seeing badgers bumbling along the track side, roe deer melting into the trees or barn owls drifting along hedgerows. Other recommended off-road hill routes are Caulkleys ridge from Nunnington (six miles) and a circumnavigation of Welburn, (five miles ; see page 236).

Down on the flats of Ryedale, off-road biking is not recommended unless you can see from the OS map that the bridleway follows a farm track. The chances are that those marked in bold green across the fields, or along river banks, do not in reality exist on the ground, or are complete quagmires. I have had some nightmare walks-with-a-bike in swampy fields between Butterwick and South Holme and, worse still, had my bike gears completely destroyed by wheat stalks that had been planted over a bridleway, jamming in the mechanism.

Cycle hire

Golden Square Campsite Oswaldkirk ☎ 01439 788269. Off-road bikes and baby seats from £9 per day.

R Yates and Sons Railway St, Malton ☎ 01653 693215 🖰 www.yatescycles.co.uk. Road, off-road and tandems available from £20 per day.

Horse-riding

Sadly, and surprisingly for such a horsey area, there is a dearth of facilities for riders here. **White Rose Riding School** at Park House Farm near Coxwold (01347 869001/07764 575249) is the only one offering horses, hacking and lessons, although there are four not so far away in bordering regions. These are at Sinnington and Rosedale (see page 184) and Hawnby and Helmsley (page 130). It is good riding country though, so if you can bring your own horse you will have a field day. Grazing, feed and a secure tack room are available at Manor Farm, Old Byland (01439 798247) and other horse accommodation can be found in neighbouring areas at Boltby, Gillamoor, Hawnby, Helmsley, Pockley and Sproxton (see chapter 6) and Appleton le Moors, Cropton, Ebberston and Sinnington (chapter 8).

Sloe motion

Hedgerows in the Howardian Hills are often full of dazzling white flowers in April, and tiny wild plums in autumn. These are sloes, the fruit of the blackthorn bush, and although they are far too sour to eat as they are, they make a delicious natural flavouring for other foods and drinks.

Jonathan Curtoys and his colleagues have made a business out of the sloe taste. Their company, 'Sloe Motion' (0844 800 1911; www.sloemotion.com), based at Green Farm, Barton le Willows (south of Howsham, see page 244), collect sloes using an army of local pickers, and produce a range of rich and fruity products. Traditional sloe gin is their biggest seller, but have you ever tried sloe vodka, sloe brandy, sloe whisky, sloe chutney or sloe truffles? No, I hadn't either and I didn't know what I was missing – they are delicious. Buy on-line or from farmers' markets, shows and good specialist food stores.

Backpacking and walking

Although the options for walks are more limited here than in the neighbouring North York Moors, the quality is high. Because the Howardian Hills are so compact and small-scale, one walk can visit a variety of landscapes in a short distance. The brief section of the Centenary Way north of Welburn is a good case in point. Within two miles it crosses arable farmland, follows a small beck through ancient deciduous woodland containing a fen nature reserve, visits classically managed parkland, cattle and sheep pasture and finally dark conifer plantations. The drawback is that this is the whole list of what the area has to offer; you won't find proper hilltops or fast flowing rivers; and the only open-access land is a small area of woodland near Yearsley voluntarily opened by the Forestry Commission.

Three **long-distance footpaths** visit the area in passing, the Ebor Way en route from Helmsley to Ilkley, the Centenary Way from York to Filey and the Foss Walk briefly, through Crayke.

As for shorter and more practically achievable ventures, the Howardian Hills AONB authority has produced two excellent leaflets with suggested representative circular walks. The start points are Hovingham (see page 230) and Welburn (page 236), with the walks ranging from three to nine miles. North

Yorkshire County Council has produced a similar leaflet for Terrington.

Point-to-point walks using public transport are possible, but require a bit of forward planning, because buses are so few and far between. The simplest strategy is to catch a bus from Malton to Welburn, Castle Howard, Terrington or Hovingham and walk back. It is best done this way round with unreliable buses, to avoid being marooned in the sticks. For shorter walks, the 'Street' bus can be caught for a few stops, and the return made along the Centenary Way ridge, Hovingham to Barton (five miles) for instance, or Slingsby to Appleton (four miles).

The Rye, with its tributaries, is a lovely river, so it is worth trying to search out the few footpaths that follow them. Pickering Beck south towards Kirbymisperton is a delightful stroll, as is the mile along the River Seven from Marton to Normanby, or vice versa, but the longest and best stretch is the Rye itself from Helmsley to Nunnington via Harome. This convoluted five miles can be extended by one more to West Ness, or two more to Salton.

Information
Malton Tourist Information Centre Malton Museum, Market Place ☎ 01653 600048.

An abbey road – Ampleforth, Byland and Coxwold

Where the northern edge of the Howardian Hills butts against the southern slopes of the Hambleton Hills the village of Gilling East sits astride a narrow gap often called the Gilling gap. Its centuries-old use as a transport route is not surprising: as well as having a road and disused railway line, it is a known Roman route. What is not quite so clear is why it was such an ecclesiastical magnet, as within six short miles, from **Oswaldkirk** to **Coxwold**, are two abbeys, (**Ampleforth** and **Byland**), two very old churches, (Oswaldkirk and Coxwold), and a priory at **Newburgh**. This little corner's pulling power does seem to have waned though, as it never seems anywhere near as busy as nearby Helmsley, Sutton Bank or Nunnington. For us lovers of undisturbed walks or traffic-free cycling this is no bad thing of course.

To the south of Coxwold lies the quietest corner of the Howardian Hills, with the hill-top village of **Crayke** perched at its edge.

① Coxwold

'I am as happy as a prince in Coxwold, and I wish you could see in how princely a manner I live. Tis a land of plenty.' So wrote Laurence Sterne, vicar of Coxwold in the 1760s, and this small village is still a very desirable place to live. In 2008 it was rated in the top ten best villages nationally, on Five TV's Property List.

I would also rate it highly in a list of desirable places to visit, but the two are very different things. At first sight it seems like just another Cotswoldy village typical of this corner of the Howardian Hills but beneath the surface lies a rich vein of quirky eccentricity. **Shandy Hall** at the top of the village is the best example; a singular building that was lived in by a very singular man, Laurence Sterne himself. As vicar of the village he spent a good deal of time, though not as much as he should have spent apparently, in **St Michael's Church**, the next large building down the main street. He almost certainly spent too much time in a building opposite the church, the Fauconberg Arms, although it was not called that then. The pub name has followed the family name of the residents of nearby **Newburgh Priory**, being the Bellasis Arms in Sterne's time although it has not so far changed to the Wombwell Arms in honour of the present family name. Two lines of honey-coloured stone buildings lead down the broad main street with an ancient crossroads at the bottom. Wakendale Beck crosses the road by the old schoolhouse, changes its name to Green Beck and passes the old mill it used to power. Both buildings are worth calling in on; the former is now the Schoolhouse Tearooms and the latter a craft courtyard housing two artisans, Coxwold Cabinet Makers and Coxwold Pottery.

Shandy Hall

Shandy Hall is the oldest building in Coxwold and it looks it. It is a wonderfully rickety maze of a place that would merit preservation in its own right, but the

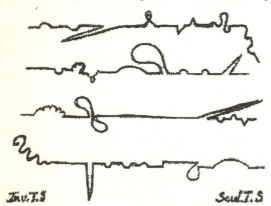

reason it is a museum is not for what it is but for who lived here. In 1670 this was the Parsonage, and the new parson, Laurence Sterne, was part-way through writing what would become his most famous novel, *Tristram Shandy*. He finished it in this house along with *Sentimental Journey*, both books written in a surreal comedic style way ahead of their time and a touch ribald for a country vicar. Sterne enjoyed eight years of fame, and a little controversy, before succumbing to ill health and dying in 1678. After Sterne's death the re-named Shandy Hall became a place of literary pilgrimage and in the 1960s was bought by the newly formed Laurence Sterne Trust, which has looked after the house and gardens ever since. The present curator Patrick Wildgust lives in the house with his wife Chris. 'My job is to celebrate the life of this great writer and introduce other people to his work, but there are things here to appeal to all sorts. Sterne was never a dedicated gardener, as he said himself he would sometimes "weed, hack up old roots or wheel away rubbish", but the gardens he has left us are lovely. Much like the man really, a complex contradiction; two acres of old-fashioned roses, formal walled garden, and semi-wild old quarry. If you want an apt Sterne quote for your book, my suggestion would be these four squiggles.'

Shown on page 218, these are the plot lines for *Tristram Shandy* showing how it didn't just take the shortest, fastest route from A to B but deliberately digressed off on interesting tangents. And, as for *A Sentimental Journey*, it's a spoof of a travelogue of France and Italy.

Shandy Hall is open from the beginning of May to the end of September, on Wednesday and Sunday afternoons only.

St Michael's Church

The Pope wrote to the King of Northumbria in 757 instructing him to repair Coxwold Minster so we know this is a very old church site — in fact there was probably a pagan temple here before then. The present building is not that old (1430) but some really unusual features inside and out justify an exploration. As you would expect, there are lots of connections with the Bellasis/ Fauconberg/Wombwell family — monuments, memorials, tombs and the like — but Laurence Sterne has also left his mark. He installed a three-decker pulpit (now reduced to two) and box pews, and his gravestone sits just by the porch outside. In a bizarre chain of events typical of Sterne, he was buried three times: firstly in Westminster Abbey, then again after his body was stolen for medical research but reclaimed, and finally in 1960 when the London graveyard he lay in was built on. The Laurence Sterne Trust obtained permission to bring his head up to Coxwold and its final resting place near his beloved Shandy Hall.

Newburgh Priory

Just south of Coxwold, this house (01347 868372; www.newburghpriory.co.uk) is one of those places whose brilliance lies in its differentness. For a start, it is not a priory but a stately home, and a refreshingly un-heritage one at that. The building is a  hotchpotch of styles with some of it derelict and roofless, and the grounds are very randomly set out with no apparent plan, but the whole place has a serene, informal air about it.

It is a special place for me because I so much savoured a sense of discovery, chancing upon it with no pre-knowledge of its existence, and just turning in off the road on spec. I was lucky as opening times are very singular; just the month of June and then only during the afternoon on Wednesdays and Sundays. It was late afternoon on a Sunday when I was greeted at the entrance shed by a dapper, elderly gentleman dressed in slacks, shirt and straw trilby. He listed the attractions, each with a vague directional point. 'There's the lake of course, but you can see that. The walled garden is splendid at the moment (it was). The basin pond and water garden are over there (vague point), and should you feel like you can tackle the hill behind the house, you will find a view over to the Hambleton Hills (cursory wave) absolutely marvellous.'

'Is there a map or guidebook at all?' I asked.

'Oh no – it's very much a go and find it for yourself experience here,' was the reply.

So I went and searched, and in the walled garden I found leeks growing in tubes, new potatoes part-harvested, a pink climbing rose with an overpowering perfume, a lily pond with dancing blue damselflies and newt tadpoles just below the surface. At the side of the house, a series of 'Royal Trees' were planted by visiting monarchs, and a small fenced-off area near the water garden contains the graves of family dogs.

Inside the house is just as quirky and interesting. The compulsory tea-shop visit at the end was, as expected, very non-National Trust. The handwritten sign 'Tea Shop' directed us through the old servants' quarters and into the dining room with its faint smell of lavender and mothballs. Old paintings lined the walls; each small table had a single rose in a small vase and the clock on the wall tick-tocked slowly. Such was the peaceful atmosphere in the room, the two people already there were actually whispering.

The rest of the house has the usual lines of family portraits, wood panels and Chippendalesque furniture, but then suddenly you come face-to-face with the death mask of Oliver Cromwell on an attic vault door, with his headless corpse inside by some accounts. Visiting the house in June is by guided tour only, but on odd days throughout the year the house is open for informal wandering. If that is when you happen to be here, give yourself a least an hour to search out all the little things.

Food and drink

Fauconberg Arms ✆ 01347 868214 ⌂ www.fauconbergarms.com. An ancient inn that was rescued from closure in 2006, and had new life breathed into it by the present owners, the extended Rheinberg family. They have done a great job. I was informed independently by three family members that, 'This is a pub first and foremost, but we do very good food', and they are right on both counts. Top-quality Yorkshire cuisine and (bravely, I feel) Thwaites Lancashire beer.

School House Tea Rooms ✆ 01347 868077 ⌂ www.coxwoldtearooms.co.uk. Basic, cosy café handily placed at the bottom of the village near the craft workshops.

Shopping

Coxwold Cabinet Makers ✆ 01347 868530 ⌂ www.coxwoldcabinetmakers.co.uk. Makers of bespoke hardwood furniture. Some real works of art, all with the Wombwell unicorn motif.

Coxwold Pottery ✆ 01347 868344. Peter and Jill Dick carry on the local tradition of earthenware production (archaeologists have found large quantities of medieval pottery around the village). Closed Mon and winter weekends.

② Byland

Two things catch your attention on first sighting the ruins of Byland Abbey. The first, from a distance, is the amazing rose window (the first of its kind to appear in England), or rather half rose window, and the question of what is keeping it up, it looks so precarious. The second, with a closer view, is likely to be the size of the place; the site is huge with the abbey church alone as big as some cathedrals. Other features to look for are the 13th-century ceramic mosaic floor tiles, still in their original position and made on site, and said to be of world heritage significance as far as ceramics go; and a medieval doodle of the rose window scratched into the wall beneath the window itself, on the left as you come in (not at all easy to spot without some expert guidance).

Not all monks are nice

Byland Abbey has boasted many colourful characters over the years, too many to mention, but one story in particular deserves to be told. The 'most audacious acts and merited misfortunes' of Wimund the Blind Monk were recorded by William of Newburgh.

Although of humble origins, Wimund learnt to write and became a monk at Furness Abbey. His 'ardent temper, retentive memory and competent eloquence' resulted in quick promotion (sounds like a few politicians I can think of). After a meteoric rise he became bishop of the Isle of Man but still yearned for greater acclaim and more power (definitely a politician, then). He announced that he was the rightful heir to the earldom of Mowbray and that the King of Scotland was depriving him of his inheritance. Gathering an army of followers he invaded Scotland, 'wasting all before him with rapine and slaughter'. Sensing military defeat, the king of the Scots decided on a more subtle strategy that would use Wimund's own arrogance against him. He granted large areas of land, including Furness, to the rebel knowing that Wimund would not be accepted by those who once knew him as a low-born monk. Sure enough, as he was parading his army around the area, a trap was set and he was captured. His punishment was to be blinded, castrated and sent to Byland Abbey as a lowly monk once more (politicians take note). He remained there, humiliated but unrepentant until his death, moaning to all who would listen of his woes. 'Had I the eye of the sparrow, my enemies should have little occasion to rejoice at what they have done to me.'

The fact that the abbey was built here at all is down to a strange series of 12th-century events and a long journey by 13 Savignac monks. Amazingly, we know all their names; they were: Gerold the Abbott, Robert, Tocka, John, Theodore, Hormi, Roger, Alan, Wido, William, Peter, Ulfus and Bertram (an interesting study in which names survive nearly 1,000 years and which don't – I certainly don't know any Widos or Hormis). The 13 were sent out from Furness Abbey in Lancashire to found a new abbey, and tried four sites before ending up here. Their penultimate choice was five miles due north of the present abbey at a place still called Old Byland. The apocryphal reason for them leaving there after only four years was that they were too close to Rievaulx Abbey and their church bells clashed with those of the established Cistercian community. The monks finally settled near the village of Wass, converted to Cistercianism and, in 1170, started to build their magnificent monument. During the next 370 years Byland prospered and became a very rich and powerful organisation/landowner until the catastrophic Dissolution in 1538.

S☉ Abbey Inn Byland Abbey ☎ 01347 868204 ✍ www.bylandabbeyinn.com. Over the road from the Abbey and with the same owner, English Heritage, which has restored it with an eccentric, tweedy elegance. Food is British-based and interesting but quite pricey. Closed Sun evenings and all day Mon and Tue.

③ Ampleforth

Ampleforth is an unusual and not overly attractive place, or should I say, two places. There is a village, but mention the name of 'Ampleforth' and most people will think of the abbey and associated private college. These two are tenuously attached to the village but very definitely culturally separate. The whole lot is strung out along two miles of busy and often congested road. Surprisingly, the village is much older than the abbey and college, it being mentioned in the Domesday Book whilst the latter was only founded in the 19th century.

Ampleforth Abbey is one of the few living and active Benedictine monasteries in the country, and certainly the largest. Until recently, the monastic community kept its slow and peaceful lifestyle pretty much to itself and the students of the college. But, times have changed, and an outreach venture that has really taken off in the last year or two has been the sale of abbey produce. At the heart of this has been Father Rainer and his cider-making, which made the columns of the national press back in 2008.

Ampleforth Abbey Tea Room ☎ 01439 766000. A pleasant modern room decked out with Mousey Thompson wooden tables and serving home-produced scones and cakes. Fruit from the abbey orchard features prominently. Open Tue–Sat and Sun mornings.

Ampleforth Cider

Ampleforth Abbey has a historic five-acre organic orchard with 49 varieties of apple trees, which until recently was largely unloved and untended; most of the apples went to feed autumn wasps and blackbirds. Father Rainer Verborg had other ideas, first producing apple juice to sell to local farmers' markets, and then moving on to cider-making.

The production plant, in old abbey farm buildings, now makes over 3,000 litres a year, but could sell twice that amount, such is the popularity of the distinctive pale, dry brew.

Father Rainer's cider is available in the abbey shop and various delis locally such as Castle Howard farm shop and Hunters of Helmsley. Look out also for the Ampleforth cider brandy – it's delicious.

④ Oswaldkirk

This tiny village clings precariously on to the hillside known, not too flatteringly, as Oswaldkirk Hag. Most of the village buildings sit on the slightly less steep south side of the road and fall within the jurisdiction of the Howardian Hills AONB, whereas those on the other side lie within the North York Moors National Park.

Oswaldkirk has two buildings of note and these are, as is so often the case, the church and the pub. I suppose for decency's sake I ought to deal with the church first, especially as the village was named after it. It is a lovely, peaceful little building, especially the side away from the road where the sloping grave-yard allows panoramic views across the Vale. There was probably a wooden Saxon church here originally but the present building is a humble mixture of Norman and more modern stonework.

There are no prizes for working out that the church is dedicated to St Oswald but the story of the man himself is much more obscure. He was a Saxon King of Northumbria in the 7th century, and one of the original 'Christian soldiers'. It was he who invited St Aidan to establish the original monastery at Lindisfarne. In the year 642 King Oswald was killed in battle against the heathen King Penda and he was sainted soon afterwards. A cult surrounding him developed, resulting in many St Oswald's churches in the Saxon areas of eastern England. His head, as a prized relic, was taken to Lindisfarne and, when the Viking raids threatened, was put into St Cuthbert's coffin for safekeeping. It is still in the coffin now, buried in the foundations of Durham Cathedral.

I like old churches, but I love good pubs and the **Malt Shovel** is one of my favourites, with a real two-buildings-in-one feel to it. The side by the road has two dark, low-ceilinged rooms, one a cosy bar and the other a flag-floored pool room and, during many visits to the Sunday quiz, this is all I saw. It was only when my neighbour, on a sunny day, suggested a pint from the back bar to be drunk in the beer garden, that I saw the original front of the building – and it is magnificent. From here its origins as a manor house are obvious, a storey higher than the back because it is lower down the hill, and with stunning views over the terraced gardens and patchwork of fields and woods in the vale.

The Malt Shovel looks as if it should be haunted, and apparently is. The official ghost is of a five-year-old boy, Thomas Bamber, who died in the house in the 1890s and whose mother, unable to accept the death, kept his body for weeks. He is still said to be there, in his bedroom – now the ladies' toilets. 'I've never seen Tom,' said the landlady as we chatted in the lounge bar, 'but I have seen a bloke in here. No idea who he was but he drifted across the room and through the wall there. It doesn't bother me – they can't hurt you can they? That only happens in films.'

Malt Shovel Oswaldkirk ☎ 01439 788461. A gem of a place (see above) and the cheapest beer in Yorkshire courtesy of Sam Smith's Brewery. Not renowned for its food but that's not why you would come here.

Barn Owls

A white owl bounces over the hedge top
As if on puppeteer's strings
So bright and alive it illuminates the dusk
So buoyant, it seems its wings are stretched
To keep the Earth from losing it
What heart this bird must have
To fill so slight a body with such energy...

Barn owls have inspired poets and artists since ink and paint existed. They provoke conflicting feelings of love and fear, being the nation's official favourite farmland bird but also a traditional omen of death. In living memory they were skinned and nailed to doors to ward off lightning storms. These eclectic birds are in trouble though. Nationally, their numbers have dropped by 75% since the 1930s, and yet I have seen more barn owls in the last two years in Ryedale than in the whole of the rest of my forty-odd years of bird-watching elsewhere in the country. What is it about this part of northeast Yorkshire that suits *Tyto alba*? The obvious person to ask was Robert Fuller. Robert is one of Britain's leading wildlife artists, but also a passionate conservationist with a special interest in barn owls. He directs operations from his home and studio at Thixendale on the Wolds side of the Derwent Valley.

⑤ Crayke

The charming village of Crayke sits on top of an little eminence with staggering views across the Vale of York. This isolated Howardian Hill, cast adrift from the rest, is thought to be the one that the Grand Old Duke of York famously marched his 10,000 men up and down.

Crayke has very strong ties with County Durham; in fact until 1844 it was still officially a remote enclave of the county. St Cuthbert founded a monastery here, giving his name to the church, and the Prince Bishops built the original castle which is now a private house. It is said that the saint's body was hidden from marauding Vikings here before its final burial in Durham Cathedral.

S⁀ Durham Ox Westway, Crayke ☎ 01347 821506 ⁀ www.thedurhamox.com. This is an unashamedly high-quality food and wine establishment and it does it brilliantly, seafood and local game being specialities. Open every day.

Lower Ryedale

Lower Ryedale is part of what is now called the Vale of Pickering, but a few thousand years ago it was Lake Pickering which stretched some twenty miles

'I set up the Wolds Barn Owls Group with friends a couple of years ago. It's a real hands-on project where we make and put up barn owl boxes on farms on the Yorkshire Wolds. We're a really enthusiastic team and have had great support from the local community. Barn owls have had problems from all angles. A lot of their habitats have changed because there are bigger fields these days and different farming methods. And the old traditional brick farm buildings they liked to nest in are no longer used... a lot of them have been converted, knocked down or fallen down, so it is important to provide them with an alternative nesting site. Dutch Elm disease has been a big problem as well. The elm trees were often important as they had good hollows for owls to nest in, but now all those trees have fallen down and rotted away.

I've designed my own nest box for the project. Normally the male barn owl has to find a new home once the chicks are born and people tend to put out two boxes. But my boxes have two compartments – there is a little penthouse area for the male to live after the chicks arrive. We've now put up nearly two hundred boxes across our area and about half are occupied – that's a healthy population of owls. It is good to know that, despite their other pressures of habitat loss and harsh weather limiting hunting, at least the barn owls around here won't be short of a place to nest. I've always had a particular affinity for barn owls and they often feature in my paintings – it's nice now to give something back.'

from Ampleforth in the west to Scarborough in the east, making it probably the biggest lake in Britain at the time. Lake sediments make fabulously rich farming soils and agriculture here is productive and very lucrative. Stand atop one of Lake Pickering's old islands, now small hillocks, like Great Edstone or Normanby Hill, and turn through 360°; all you will see is a flat carpet with a repeating pattern of wheat, barley, spuds, hay, wheat, beans and barley – thank heaven for a break in this monotony. The saving grace is the River Rye itself, and its tributaries the Dove, Seven and Costa Beck. They are ribbons of oasis in the desert, willow-fringed and hidden away behind flood banks. Wherever footpaths and bridleways meet them it is a joy, especially so to float down in a kayak or canoe in the few places not policed by landowners or fishermen. In summer they're bejewelled by iridescent blue and green damselflies, and in winter, when they burst their banks to temporarily re-form Lake Pickering, they're alive with cackling and honking flocks of ducks and geese.

⑥ Nunnington

All most visitors see of Nunnington is its stately home. Granted, Nunnington Hall is well worth a visit, but there is more to explore here. The hillside village is bigger than it seems: you could spend a pleasant hour pottering up and down its two lanes. The church of All Saints and St James at the top of the village is unremarkable except for two stories recorded in the porch; one of a local St George-style dragon slaying and the other a framed piece of writing that I found particularly moving. It was a 'thank you' note to the villagers, and his guardians in particular, from a war-time evacuee (or 'vaccy', as they were known), with an accompanying drawing of the church he did himself as a child in the 1940s.

Not far down from the church is the Royal Oak. Some pubs just belong exactly where they are, and this one, slotted into a row of other hunched, yellow, limestone buildings, does just that.

The River Rye winds its way lazily around the bottom of Nunnington. I have seen it cold, brown and uninviting after winter rain, but in summer it is delightful. Leaning over one of the village's three bridges and gazing into the gin-clear water, with its long slowly waving tresses of water crowfoot and hanging trout shadows, can be an hypnotic experience.

By now, halfway round your potter about here, you may like to head for Low Farm which backs on to the river. The farmyard buildings have been converted into **Nunnington Studios**, a series of craft outlets, one of which houses Honey Pot tea rooms. For the grown-ups there is Victoria Interior design and furniture (01439 748212; www.nunningtonstudios.co.uk) and Clang Jewellery. If you have children with you, they will love The Pottery (01439 748510; www.nunnington-pottery.co.uk) and the chance to have a go on a potter's wheel or make and paint a pot. While I was there one group of excited girls taking part in a pottery birthday party seemed equally engrossed in the painting and the cute farm dogs. The studios are open Wednesday to Sunday and on bank holidays.

Nunnington Hall

By the standard of its near neighbours, this is not an exceptional stately home. Hovingham Hall is bigger, Castle Howard is more spectacular and Newburgh Priory is older. What Nunnington Hall has though, is a just-rightness and great charm, with everything that a stately home should have – stone-flagged floors, oak panelling, old paintings and tapestries, a giant, creaky staircase and a haunted bedroom. The restored walled garden, with a local-variety apple orchard and flower beds, is a balanced mix of practical and ornamental and the Hall's location, tucked into a bend of the River Rye, is serene.

So it is not surprising that the National Trust accepted the Hall and gardens from the Fife family in 1952, or that it is one of their most popular properties with visitors. Many come here specifically for what is in the attic, the old servants' quarters, which houses a permanent exhibition of miniature rooms and buildings (the Carlisle Collection), which has nothing to do with Nunnington; it is just a convenient place for the National Trust to store it. Other attic rooms house constantly changing exhibitions from rock musicians' photographs to Victorian cartoons.

In summer Nunnington Hall is open every day except Monday, but it's weekends only in November and December and closed all January and February. Entry to the tea shop and tea gardens is free and if you're not visiting the hall there's a reduced fee for the garden.

It can get very busy here, especially early afternoon with folk calling en route from Castle Howard to Helmsley, or vice versa. Being such a small place, crowds can spoil the experience here so my advice would be to go midweek if you can, or if not, be first at the door when it opens in the morning.

Honey Pot tea rooms Low Lane ☎ 01439 748517. No-nonsense, good-value tea, coffee and homemade snacks with seating inside and out in the crafty yard.
Nunnington Hall tea room ☎ 01439 748283 ⏚ www.nationaltrust.org.uk. The tea room, originally a dining room, has been restored with the original dark decor which makes it a bit dingy, and service is quite formal. In good weather, the tea garden by the river is much the better choice. Usual National Trust good quality and value, locally sourced produce.
Royal Oak Church St ☎ 01439 748271. Warmed by log fires and with an assortment of jugs, flagons and old keys hanging from the beams, this is a little too much restaurant and not enough pub for me but has very good food and well-kept local beers.

Nunnington's water bats

The Hall is closed, the car park is empty and the crowds have gone: this is the best time to enjoy the River Rye, a balmy summer evening with the last yellowing of the sky reflected in the water under the old bridge arches. Wait a few minutes longer, if you can bear the attention of the dusk midges and mosquitoes, because these insects will soon tempt out some of Nunnington's special residents. In crevices and crannies in the stonework of the bridge lives a healthy population of bats, and not any old flitter-mice either; these are Daubenton's bats, a species that loves to live near, and hunt over, water. When they appear they are unmistakable, whizzing around in circles and figures of eight, inches above the river, sometimes setting off ripples as they grab a hapless insect from the water's surface. You will get about half an hour's watching in before the light goes; the bats will carry on hunting of course, but you can retreat to the pub to enjoy a glass of wine or beer and scratch your new midge bites.

⑦ Harome

This must be one of the most mispronounced place names in the country. I have heard 'Ha-rowm', 'Ha-rom' and 'Har-rowm', to name but three, but the correct one apparently is 'Hair-um'.

One of the village's claims to fame is its seven thatched cottages, the most of any place in Yorkshire, giving it more of a West rather than North country feel. What brings most people to Harome though is not its chocolate-box look but the gastronomic delights available in the Star Inn, Pheasant Hotel and shop, all run by the Pern family.

Pheasant Hotel ☎ 01439 771241 🖰 www.thepheasanthotel.com. A country hotel in buildings that were once barns and a blacksmith's workshop. This is part of the Pern family stable and head chef Peter Neville came from the Star Inn, so high-quality service and food are both guaranteed; they're also open for morning coffee and afternoon tea.

S? Star Inn ☎ 01439 770397 🖰 www.thestaratharome.co.uk. Possibly the best food anywhere in Yorkshire, in a low, rambling building with a nicely old-fashioned bar as well as a sleek dining room and plenty of space to sit outside; decent beer too. Gastronomic Michelin-starred heaven, but meal prices reflect the quality so save it for a special occasion, like a birthday, anniversary or holiday.

The Star Inn

For a little backwater village, Harome is becoming very well known, even beyond the bounds of Yorkshire. This fame is almost solely down to one man, Andrew Pern and his wife Jacquie. Put simply, Jacquie is the landlady of the village pub, the Star Inn, and Andrew is the chef. In reality the two of them are at the helm of a burgeoning business that is fast becoming an empire.

It all started in 1996 when the pub came up the sale and the newly wedded Perns, working for another nearby pub, had their offer accepted. It was a brave move, as Andrew remembers. 'It was knee-high in weeds and ridden with mice. We left the Milburn Arms on June 10, 1996, and were faced with opening our new venture just ten days later. There was just me in the kitchen, Jacquie out front and her Mum behind the bar. We were serving off plates that were our wedding presents, and washing them at once to serve the next customer. On the first day we ran out of food, beer and change as an avalanche of people fell into the place. The encouraging thing was that the avalanche never stopped. We worked 18-hour days for 20 months virtually without a break, until our first child, Daisy, was born.'

Their hard work paid off in 2001 when the Star Inn was awarded a coveted Michelin star with more to come in 2006 when it was rated the best Gastropub in the country by Egon Ronay.

The success of Andrew and Jacquie's business has allowed them to expand to the point where now it seems like they are taking over the village. They now have catered accommodation at Cross House Lodge, Black Eagle Cottage and The Farmhouse and have opened The Corner Shop opposite the pub and selling specialty foods and local produce. Their most recent acquisition is the village hotel, The Pheasant.

Andrew is very aware of the importance of his local roots, and values not just the quality but the 'localness' of his supplies.

'Taste and smell are potent in their ability to evoke faces and places, times and events. Looking back to my childhood on a farm, I can instantly recall the waft of bacon frying, the aroma of roasting beef, the gamey scent of partridge in the oven, and the tang of blackberries as I plucked them, purple-fingered, from the hedgerows. The North York Moors was an idyllic place to live and learn about nature's larder; seafood from the North Sea, lamb, beef and pork reared by people with pride in their produce, game from the rough shoots alongside the Esk Valley and especially grouse from the purple-cloaked moors of Egton, Rosedale and Danbydale. The food you were eating was teaching you about the seasons.

The 'Street' villages

The Romans were famously good road builders. Contrary to popular belief though, their roads did not always follow the straightest route, but they did invariably choose the easiest course. Consequently, when they decided to link the garrison town of Malton (Derventium) with Aldborough (Isurium) near Boroughbridge, they avoided the direct line across the steep ups and downs of the Howardian Hills. Instead they followed the flat land to the north, through Lower Ryedale and the Gilling Gap, but just uphill enough to avoid the swamps. This is the course of the present B1257, known locally as the 'Street' in recognition of its antiquity. A string of old villages punctuates this road, from Broughton in the east to Hovingham in the west, with two of them, Appleton and Barton, even having 'le Street' tacked on to their name to distinguish them from nearby Appleton le Moors and Barton le Willows.

⑧ Stonegrave

I have a rule: any place that I pass through on a busy road thinking 'Ooh, this looks nice', by definition isn't, and what spoils it is the very busy-ness of that road. Stonegrave suffers from this phenomenon unfortunately as the whole hamlet is strung out along the well-used Malton–Helmsley road, the B1257. There are three consolations though: a lovely short circular walk nearby, a truly ancient church, and the rarest native tree in England.

The walk is a tour of **Caukleys Wood** east of the hamlet; go clockwise if you prefer your uphill bit first, along the top of the wood, with panoramic views of the moors to the north, then down Caukleys Bank to return under the trees at the bottom of the wood. Do it in reverse if you need a warm-up before any ascent.

Any church with Minster as part of its name is usually very old or has been very important at one time; **Stonegrave Minster** is both. Sadly, the building has suffered many 'modernisations' over the years so only part of the tower is original Saxon, but you can see fragments of intricately carved 9th-century crosses on display just inside the porch.

⑨ Hovingham

This is arguably the prettiest village in the Howardian Hills, and certainly one of the most popular with visitors. Hovingham is a sunny-Sunday sort of place, somewhere to lounge and stroll, because to be honest there is not an awful lot else here to do. It has more than enough to be a living, working village – a hotel, a pub, two shops, two cafes and a bakery – but for me its biggest attractions are the buildings themselves. It does 'grand', notably Hovingham Hall itself which dominates the village green, and All Saints' Church with its impressive Saxon tower, but it is the little buildings which make Hovingham special for me, especially some of the tiny cottages hidden away behind the church and the strangely gothic primary school. Historically, the hall and church were the epicentres of the community, but now on most days, and especially weekends, the focus is the Spa Tea Room and adjacent beck. Everybody seems to gravitate there, grown-ups to sit with a cup of tea outside if it's warm, inside if it's not, and children to paddle and fish for bullheads in the limey waters of the brook.

The Black Poplar

I will be honest; I was not overawed when I first saw the Howardian Hills' only surviving black poplar tree. It is a handful of feeble regrowing shoots sprouting from an old dead stump of the original tree that blew over in 1996. But, such is its value as a sole survivor that cuttings were taken and pampered lovingly in local nurseries, and are now being replanted in hedgerows around the region. Black poplars need this helping hand because they have lost the ability to germinate from seed and are very fussy about the soil they grow in – it has to be silt over gravel. So if you are walking in the Yearsley, Brandsby or Hovingham areas and see a ditch-side sapling with a protective mesh guard, then the chances are it's one of the VIP baby poplars. The parent tree is in a hedgerow just south of Stonegrave village on the Cawton road, with an AONB information board telling you all about it.

Hovingham Hall

Most stately homes are extravagant status symbols, built to be viewed as much as to view from. To this end almost all of them sit in splendid isolation, with a definite front on display to the world.

Hovingham Hall is an exception. It is right in the middle of the village, presenting a not very imposing façade to the main road, but neither is the other side particularly impressive. The odd reason for this is that Hovingham Hall was never built as a house at all, but comprises huge, ornate riding school and stables with the living quarters tacked on as an afterthought. The man responsible, back in the 1750s, was Thomas Worsley, known as Thomas the Builder to differentiate him from the other five Thomases. The Worsley family, incidentally, are an amateur genealogist's nightmare, specialising as they do in duplicate names. Since 1563 there have been six Thomases, six Williams, six Roberts and we are now on a run of Marcuses in the present day.

Thomas the Builder is regarded as an eccentric today, but when he was alive he was considered completely disreputable by his fellow aristocrats, for two reasons. Firstly, he married a servant, his half-sister's governess, but more seriously, his riding school did not teach proper riding for hunting, but strange prancing about that Thomas had seen on his travels in Europe – dressage to you and me.

Two generations after Thomas, in the 1800s, one of the Williams changed the layout of the building to make it more habitable for humans, but its equine origins are still very obvious.

The next obsession to shape the house and grounds was cricket. Sir William number five was a cricketer of note, captaining the Yorkshire county team himself in 1928 and 1929. He had the field behind the house made into a cricket pitch and converted one of the rear stables into an outdoor pavilion. An indication of Sir William's priorities can be seen in his proclamation that, if a batsman broke a window in the house with a strike for six, then five pounds was payable, not by the player as a fine to cover the damage, but *to* him as a reward for such a good shot. This area in the hall's history is commemorated by one of the village pubs. In the Worsley Arms, facing the hall on the main street, the Cricketers' Bar has old photos of famous visiting teams, signed bats and other memorabilia.

Like Newburgh Priory, Hovingham Hall has a pleasant family-home feel to it, basically because it still is. On my last visit, the guided tour had reached one of the staircases just on the hour, and we were listening to an antique grandfather clock playing an intricate baroque tune which echoed around the domed stairwell. As we stood there we were joined by the baronet Sir Marcus himself, just passing through. He offered a prize for anyone who could recognise the tune, and breezed off again.

All Saints' Church

'There is a church and a priest here' said the Domesday Book of Hovingham in 1080, and there still is, although the priest is now a vicar shared with the other three street parishes. Most of All Saints' Church is a Victorian rebuild, but a very sensitive one that has incorporated many of the original medieval features and, thankfully, left the fantastic Saxon tower completely untouched. With a bit of searching inside and out you should find other even older relics which show that the Saxon church was itself a replacement of a still more ancient church. Here is your tick list: an Anglican cross above the west doorway, a Danish wheel cross over the South Belfry opening, and a Viking carved cross on the altar.

The Worsley family obviously had a strong influence on All Saints' from the 1500s onwards, paying for the Victorian rebuild for instance, so it is no surprise to see memorials aplenty, of various baronets and ladies, and the family mausoleum in the churchyard.

McConnell Thomas Ltd Park St ℃ 01653 628080 ⌨ www.mcconnellthomas.co.uk. A wonderfully hippyish, organic and ethical local produce store, deli, and internet café. Open seven days a week.

Quarton Country Meats Farm Shop Moorhouse Farm YO62 4LR ℃ 01653 628249 ⌨ www.quartonscountrymeats.com. Pork, bacon, sausages, lamb, beef, chicken and eggs, all produced on the farm.

Spa Tea Room High St ℃ 01653 628898. A very welcoming and popular café with bakery attached. Everything is well done but the bread and pastries are particularly good, as you would expect.

Worsley Arms Hotel High St ☎ 01653 628234 🖰 www.worsleyarms.co.uk. There is a restaurant but I much prefer the atmosphere in the Cricketers' Bar for eating and drinking. Food is very good, beer is well-kept local Hambleton Ales and the owners are justifiably proud of their well-stocked wine cellar.

⑩ Slingsby

This is the largest village in the Howardian Hills but also one of the least well known. Even temporary residents on its two caravan sites tend to use the place as a base from which to go and visit more entertaining places, but its castle and its maypole make it worth a look.

Slingsby has a tradition of impressive **maypoles** which probably goes back over a thousand years, but the first documented one was in 1799. The tallest, at 91 feet high, was erected in 1895 but the villagers are just as proud of the current 41-footer, which stands on the village green right in front of the primary school entrance. If you want to see the pole in action, then go on May Day bank holiday Monday. You will see Slingsby completely out of character, in a frenzy of fertility-rite excitement, with the maypole the central attraction of a bustling village fete. With a summer fair in early July the only other exception, Slingsby soon settles down after May Day to its normal, quiet existence with life just ticking along.

I find **Slingsby Castle** fascinating because it is a ruin; not just in the sense of having no roof and not being lived in, but in its state of utter dilapidation. There are no mown lawns or interpretive signs here, but a series of completely overgrown and dangerously teetering walls and tall towers. Underlying these is a series of interconnecting, vaulted, basement chambers and the whole lot is surrounded by an intact but dry moat. At twilight, with owls hooting in the trees and bats emerging from the cellars, it is like a scene from a Gothic novel – a hugely memorable place.

The castle is owned by the Castle Howard estate, and unfortunately has no public access, but public footpaths pass close enough for you to get a distant glimpse.

Castle Howard and around

⑪ Castle Howard

Castle Howard (01653 648333; www.castlehoward.co.uk) still does what it was always designed to do – dominate and impress. What is in effect one building is the focal point of the whole area, having for instance more attached shops than the nearby villages of Terrington, Welburn, Bulmer, Crambe, Whitwell and Coneysthorpe, put together.

As for its origin, well I like to imagine the scene.

It is 1699 and Charles Howard, the third Earl of Carlisle, is in London and sitting in the Trumpet Tavern with other members of the Kit Kat club. Drinking brandy with him is a chancer, ex-soldier and playwright John Vanbrugh, and they are discussing the Earl's intention to build a house on his Yorkshire estate.

Vanbrugh: So Charles, who is going to design this big house of yours?
Charles: I don't know. None of the chaps I have so far have come up with anything I like.
Vanbrugh: Really... now that is interesting. Charles, I'll do it for you.
Charles: Would you? Splendid! How many similar projects have you done before John?
Vanbrugh: Erm... not many, but what say, how difficult can it be?
Charles: John, exactly how many buildings have you ever designed?
Vanbrugh: Well, none – but I am a quick learner...

It reads like a *Blackadder* script, with Rowan Atkinson as Vanbrugh, Hugh Laurie as the Earl, and Mrs Miggins hovering nearby with pies, but astonishingly it is more or less true. Quite how Vanbrugh managed to convince Charles Howard he was the right man for the job is anyone's guess but he did, and over the next ten years their joint dream became a magnificent reality, probably with more than a little help from a lowly clerk of works who happened to be Nicholas Hawksmoor, one of Christopher Wren's apprentices. Oddly, the iconic great dome, such a signature feature of Castle Howard today, was not part of the original design, but added almost as an afterthought well after the building work had begun, and was reconstructed after World War II. Vanbrugh died in 1726 and the third Earl followed in 1738, but their work was continued by two subsequent earls and various architects and landscape gardeners, during the rest of the 18th century. Castle Howard in its entirety, that is the mansion, park, lakes, temples, mausoleum, road and monuments, was complete by the start of the 19th century.

All that has happened since then has been tinkering really, and a massive repair project after a fire in the main building in 1940. World War II nearly saw the end of Castle Howard. First the disastrous fire reduced the mansion house itself to a burnt-out shell and the dome was destroyed, then the heirs to the title began to drop like flies in the war in Europe. Mark, the eldest son, died on the Normandy beaches and the next in line, Christopher, was killed flying with the Dam-busters. Things were looking so bad for the estate that the trustees began to sell off the mansion's contents, assuming that it would never be lived in again. Enter a hero; George, the third son, returned wounded from the war and turned everything around. He moved into the house and set about the mammoth task of repairing the damage and restoring the building to its former glory, dome and all. The house and gardens were opened to the public in 1952 and the estate has not looked back since. The palatial grandeur of the house, inside and out, is instantly familiar to anyone who has seen the filmed version of Evelyn Waugh's novel *Brideshead Revisited*, either the wonderful 1981 TV 11-hour adaptation, or the 2008 movie.

Today, Castle Howard is a multi-million-pound business run by a private company, of which two of George Howard's sons, Nicholas and Simon, are the directors – and business it very definitely is. At the stable courtyard, your first port of call if you arrive by car or bus, are five castle shops selling books, gifts, local farm produce, plants and chocolate. There is also a café, and a glass-blowing studio run by one of the only female glass blowers in the country (01653 648555; www.jorvikglass.co.uk). Tours and talks, constantly changing exhibitions, events and outdoor concerts are on offer throughout the year; in fact no end of expensive things to do with lots of other people. But, if it is peace and quiet you prefer, then the gardens and grounds are for you. They are big enough to escape the crowds and get lost in: public rights of way thread through the wider estate, allowing you to get some choice glimpses for free of the house, the majestic 20-column Mausoleum and Palladian splendour of Temple of the Four Winds from a distance. The hamlet of Coneysthorpe, built for estate workers around an oblong green, makes a handy starting point for walks, with scope for getting close up to the house and lake to the south and a fine section of the Ebor Way to the north, which gets choice views of the Vale of Pickering.

There is wildlife here as well if you care to look, especially around the lakes where there are breeding flocks of greylag and Canada geese all the year. The Great Lake is even more of a magnet for birdwatchers in winter when large numbers of migrant waterfowl arrive; pochards, wigeon, goosander and goldeneye brightening up the chilly season. For those interested in furry, as well as feathery, flyers, some of Castle Howard's ancient hollow oak trees are important roost sites for noctule bats.

Castle Howard has a high season (March–October and December) when the house is open, while in other months just the gardens are available. There is no getting around it, entrance fees are very high (£11 for an adult in summer) so consequently many people don't get past the free café and shop area, making do with distant views of the house. Fortunately those wanting more affordable parkland walking can find it in the nearby Arboretum at half the price.

The Arboretum

This delightful rural escape is always a lot less crowded than the big house next door, but it is rapidly being discovered by more and more people. Although it is sited on the Castle Howard estate and was set up by the Royal Botanic Gardens at Kew, the Arboretum trust (01653 648598; www.kewatch.co.uk) is independent of both. It exists to manage the huge collection of trees planted here in 1975, and to entertain and educate visitors in all things woody. There is lots to do here, especially for families, with the most obvious being a walk to see the trees, either on the one mile short trail or on the long trail of two and a half miles into the wild corners for the more energetic. For keeping children entertained, the treasure hunt, leaf bingo and orienteering course work really well. I overheard one lad, running past me with a map, say to his mate in a broad Leeds accent, 'This is mint, innit? Much better than that castle place wi t'fountains over t'road.'

The trust have worked hard to make everyone welcome – those with an artistic bent can enjoy a community sculpture trail, visitors with limited mobility can hire a motorised buggy, and dogs and their walkers are actively encouraged. The Arboretum is open from March to November.

Arboretum Café ☎ 01653 648767 🖰 www.kewatch.co.uk. Very welcoming and cheaper than the nearby Castle Howard Stables Courtyard Café. More importantly it is much quieter, with seating inside and out and wide, green views over the arboretum park. Open daily from March to November.

⑫ Welburn

What a difference a pub and a shop make. Bulmer has neither and Welburn has both and consequently the latter is very much the livelier and busier of these two neighbouring villages. There was a time though when the balance of power was reversed, when the church was the focus of village life and Bulmer's old St Martin's served both villages as a joint parish. Welburn got its own church in 1865 thanks to monies from the then Earl of Carlisle: its recent resurgence is almost solely due to its proximity to Castle Howard. Two routes to the 'big house' passed through Welburn, the present public road being originally for aristocracy only, as it took them from the private Castle Howard railway station at Crambeck. This now sadly defunct station was built for one visit of Queen Victoria to the castle in 1850. The proletariat's route by road from the main York road, now the A64, to Welburn was from Whitwell village along what is now a green lane and a very pleasant cycle or walkway. As it broaches the ridge-top above Welburn you get your first view of Castle Howard. Such was the impact of this first sight that a gateway was built for extra emphasis and the posts of the 'Exclamation Gate' are still there for you to lean on and frame your photos of the castle.

Welburn is the base for another one of those excellent AONB 'History and Habitats' walks leaflets, although their selection of three by no means exhausts the wide choice of others nearby. A particularly nice two-miler circles the village keeping your walk's-end refreshment venue in sight most of the way round, whether at the café or in the Crown and Cushion.

Crown and Cushion Main St ℂ 01653 618304 ✆ www.crownandcushionwelburn.co.uk. This is a pub with a nice balance. Well-kept guest real ales. A fine basic bar, but also a comfortable lounge/dining area with good food. Game a speciality. Open daily.

Pattacakes Tea Room and Shop Main St ℂ 01653 618352 ✆ www.pattacakes.co.uk. Good-value hot and cold drinks, soups and snacks, plus sandwiches to take out on a local walk.

⑬ Terrington

On the face of it Terrington seems much like other nearby villages of a similar size, with neat limestone houses set back on the wide main street, a relatively modern looking church on an old site, a big Victorian rectory building and one central pub.

What is different here is the modern bustle about a place that has had a very slow and uneventful past. As one local historian put it, ' History has its place in Terrington, but nothing big ever happened here.' It has never had a castle or an abbey and the Victorian railways were always too far away to have any influence. Other villages have had, and lost, these exciting things and feel as if they are having a well-earned rest; Terrington gives the impression of waking up after a big sleep.

Much of this new life is centred on the shop, Terrington Village General Stores, the only proper shop for five miles in any direction and consequently one of those admirable sell-a-bit–of-everything sort of places. It also has an internet café attached and a little art gallery around the back with the no-nonsense name Back o' the Shop Art Gallery. Terrington's exceptionally good summer arts festival is masterminded from the shop.

The road west out of Terrington runs along one of the Howardian Hills ridges, giving spectacular views to Sheriff Hutton and the Vale of York beyond. The best place to enjoy this vista is just on the edge of the village at the **Yorkshire Lavender Farm**, or you can carry on for a couple of miles to the hamlet of **Dalby** and the Church of St Peter. This has to be one of the most serene little buildings anywhere; plain, unassuming and so quiet you will feel obliged to whisper. The view from the porch, through the trees and down the hillside, could grace any calendar.

If you travel east on Terrington's only road you will first pass the enormous rectory that later became Terrington Hall, and since 1920 has been a private preparatory school. A mile down the road is the hamlet of Ganthorpe, birthplace of Richard Spruce, an apt name for an eminent Victorian botanist, who is buried in All Saints' churchyard.

My preferred choice for exploring around Terrington, though, is on foot rather than by car, and North Yorkshire County Council have obliged by producing two **walks** leaflets, *Walking in the Howardian Hills from Terrington* (No 19) and *Two more walks from Terrington* (No 20), detailing five walks in total. They are good, if a little dated, but are due for revision by the AONB in 2010.

Terrington's Storyteller Brewery

Country pubs are going out of business at the staggering rate of over 30 a week, and micro-breweries are such difficult businesses to get established that there seems to be a constant stream of new ones starting up and others folding. So, for Rob Franklin to simultaneously take on the running of his first ever pub, the Bay Horse in Terrington, and start his own micro-brewery without any training would seem like a business act of suicidal naivety. That may be so, but against all the odds, the Storyteller Brewery is booming, mainly because of Rob's determination and talent as a beer maker.

'None of this was planned really', said Rob. 'It all started with bees. I was driving up and down the M1 as a door salesman, not door-to-door but a salesman selling doors, and I wanted something a bit more interesting and exciting to do so I decided to keep bees. I bought one hive off a bloke in York and after two years they had expanded to four hives, and I had more honey than I knew what to do with – we couldn't sell it fast enough and there's only so much honey ice cream you can eat. So, in the end I decided to try to make honey beer, which I did first by just adding honey to homebrew beer kit syrup. It was rubbish of course so I went on the internet to find out how you made real beer from the base ingredients of grain, hops and yeast and tried again. This time it worked – well my mates in the curry club enjoyed it – so I joined the Craft Brewers Association and made some different beers for us all to try. It's not rocket science, it's just following a recipe really – like making curries – and I love doing both, experimenting with flavours and suchlike. The Craft Brewers competition was a big step; there was a regional round in a bowls club in Manchester and I just turned up with four bottles and said, "I'm Rob from York. Where do I put me beer?" They said, "Put it down there, and stick some labels on it." One happy afternoon tasting later my beer came second to the president's and a big fella from Bradford picked me up and said, "This bloke will be a champion brewer one day." That qualified me for the national finals in Derby and I took four beers that time; "Wycary" (a beer flavoured with cardamom and coriander to be drunk, you guessed it, with curry), "1402" (named that because the recipe was written on Valentine's Day) and "Fireside Stout" (called such because that's the best place to drink it). When the results came through I couldn't believe it, Wickery came second in its class and Fireside was voted best stout. One of the judges said that I should either go and work for Guinness or set up my own brewery – so here I am.

As for the name well that's down to my Dad. When he was a lad at school, he had to read Chaucer's *Canterbury Tales* in old English and he hated it. He passed his exams, but when he shut the book for the last time he vowed he would never read another book again, and he hasn't. He told me this story when I was a nipper, and the fact that one of the characters in the book was called Franklin, who had to tell a story to win a meal in a pub, led me to the brewery name.'

Yorkshire Lavender Farm

What started off as a plant nursery specialising in herbs, the Yorkshire Lavender Farm (Terrington YO60 7PB; 01653 648008; www.yorkshirelavender.com; open daily) has evolved over the years into an award-winning celebration of all things lavender. Everything in the café and shop is either coloured or flavoured lavender, the walls, the chairs, the cake, the tea and the custard! I found it all a bit death-by-mauve but loved the outside, wandering around the gardens, watching the children feed the deer and admiring the 'Spirit of Yorkshire' cricket game sculptures – all with the heady scent of fresh lavender in the warm summer air. Very relaxing, and free.

Bay Horse Inn ☎ 01653 648546 🖰 www.thestorytellerbrewery.co.uk. A lively village pub with lots going on. On-site brewery supplies award-winning beers (see box opposite) and food very popular, especially Sunday lunch.

EJ's Tearoom Yorkshire Lavender Farm YO60 6PB ☎ 01653 648008 🖰 www.yorkshirelavender.com. You could just have a coffee and a biscuit, but where else is it possible to have lavender cake, lavender and blueberry cheesecake and a lavender scone washed down with lavender tea? It wouldn't be quite right not to try at least one.

The City of Troy

Eight ancient turf mazes survive in England, and this one, the smallest in Europe, sits by the roadside near the hamlet of Dalby. It is a seven-ringed puzzle based on the classical labyrinth of Crete, and named after the walls of the Trojan city. Why it is here, when it was made and by whom, is a mystery.

Malton and the Derwent Valley

When asked where I live, my reply of, 'Near Malton', usually prompts the response, 'Isn't that the place that flooded? Where exactly is it?' Malton is not a well-known place outside of northeast Yorkshire, even though tens of thousands of holiday visitors pass close by every weekend on the A64 or railway on their way to Whitby, Scarborough and Filey. This is not a place geared to mass tourism and that, I think, is where its attraction lies. Malton is very much a small work-a-day, rural market town serving the people of Ryedale and the Wolds, and they know it very well.

⑭ Malton

Getting to know the town takes time though, because of its very strange and confusing layout; it took me months to get my bearings when I first moved here.

What most people describe as Malton town is actually three separate places welded together, Old Malton, Malton and Norton. Even Malton proper is confusing as it has no one obvious centre but a scattering of focal points that reflect areas of shifting importance through history. The Derwent bridge and adjacent fort was the Roman town centre, but emphasis shifted in medieval times to Castlegate where the Lodge Hotel now stands on the old motte and the roads from York, Beverley and Helmsley all meet at the old crossroads. The market place was the hub in days past, and still is on Saturdays, but the cattle market is now a shadow of its glory days. Like most towns of its size Malton has its fair share of necessary but not very welcome 'new', like 1950s housing estates, high-street chain shops and the Ryedale Borough Council offices, but it is slow and sleepy enough to have retained some genuinely old-fashioned traditional shops and businesses.

Malton also has a regular **Saturday market** and a big **farmers' market** (01653 692151) on the last Saturday of every month except August and December. May 2009 saw the first Malton Food Festival which was a roaring success and likely to be a regular feature in future years.

Four **town trails** are detailed in an excellent leaflet produced by the tourist information centre, three on the Malton side of the river and a fourth around Norton. To be honest, I got the impression that the Norton Trail was a token one included so as not to offend the good people south of the river, as most of the interest is on the north bank. The shortest trail, barely half a mile long, stays within the town centre and can be done easily in an hour. It visits both of Malton's old parish **churches** and five historic **pubs**, including one with a medieval hospice crypt (the Cross Keys) and one with an excellent micro-brewery (the Crown hotel or 'Suddabys'). It will also lead you up two alleyways; Chancery Lane, downhill from the marketplace, has Charles Dickens connections. Also here is the fabulous small, traditional, **Palace Cinema**, a very informal, family-run establishment where you can relax with a glass of wine or cup of tea while watching your film – very civilised.

Uphill from the market is the **Shambles**, like its more famous namesake in York, an historic site of butchers' shops. There are none there today, but just around the corner is the acclaimed Derek Fox's, as traditional a butchers as you will see anywhere, and supplier of the extraordinary Yorkshire Pot. This is a local delicacy produced at Christmas and by order only, comprising four boned birds, one inside the other in order of size, and ready for roasting. For one recent Christmas I shelled out £60 for a partridge in a pheasant in a duck in a turkey; it was delicious and it lasted for weeks.

The intermediate town trail extends the short one by a further hour and will take you along a short section of the **River Derwent** and over both the town's bridges. It also allows you to explore the sites of Malton's old **fortifications**, first the Roman legionary camp of Derventio followed by Malton Castle. Don't get too excited – there are no buildings left to see at either place, just mounds, banks and ditches. Having said that, Orchard Fields, where the Roman fort was, and Castle Gardens are very pleasant and peaceful green areas and the nearest Malton has to a park. Information boards are on hand to describe the sites, explaining the strategic importance, and huge size (22 acres), of the Roman fort and turbulent history of the castle.

The long town trail is a further loop tacked on to the previous two taking you through the lovely riverside trees of **Lady Spring Wood** to Old Malton. Boardwalks keep your feet dry as you visit the limestone springs and marshes and a mosaic trail marks the route. Take care in wet weather; the water meadows here become lakes when the river gets very full and even the boardwalks won't stop your feet getting wet.

Two artists in wood

One small shop on The Shambles in Malton is, quite literally, the shop window for the art of **Mark Bennett**, working under the name of Woodlark (01653 691124; www.thewoodlark.com). Mark is a genius at producing, he would say 'finding', the beauty in wood. In his nearby workshop he works in many different timbers, sometimes in-laying metals and gemstones, and combining different woods. Whatever the finished product, whether it be a functional ash and yew jewellery box with gold inlay, a bog-oak toilet seat or just a hand-carved ornamental spiral, they are all beautiful.

In complete contrast, **Nick Nixon** (01653 695525; www.nixoncricket.co.uk), in his workshop 50 yards away from Mark's shop, works with two sorts of wood only, willow and cane, and makes just one finished product – cricket bats. These aren't just any bats though, they are handcrafted, bespoke items, shaped by an ex-player who loves the game and knows his stuff. Nick makes over 600 bats a year, and though they are only used for whacking a lump of leather around, each one is a work of art. As Nick says, 'There are only two ways of making a bat worthy of the great game, the wrong way and the right way'.

Malton Museum

Don't be put off by the austere-looking entrance to this ex-town-hall building in the Market Place (web: www.maltonmuseum.co.uk), because this is anything but a boring museum. 'Oh yes, we may be very small as museums go,' the lady at the desk said, as she fixed me with an enthusiastic eye, 'but we are *very* good,' and after a few minutes of wandering around the downstairs mainly Roman display, I had to agree. Some of the artefacts were very impressive (the best example of a Roman central-heating chimney in the country gets amateur archaeologist visitors most excited) and information boards were pitched just right for me, neither frivolous and trendy nor dull and dusty. And there's no doubt about the appeal of the children's favourite room – the hands-on-and-do annex has a dressing up box complete with chain-mail and helmet, mosaic tile jigsaws and a chance to grind grain to flour with a Roman hand mill.

Old Malton

A confusing name this, because it is in fact younger than 'new' Malton's Roman settlement, but presumably this was the bigger of the two places in Saxon times when the new non-Latin names was given. It was certainly a very important place in the 1150s when the large priory of St Mary was built here on the site of an earlier church. What was unusual was the monks that occupied it; they were Gilbertines, an exclusively English order that had 26 priories or churches across the country. All are now complete ruins except St Mary's; it is considerably reduced in size from its original but it is the only Gilbertine church in the world still in use, and incidentally the only church that I know of with a medieval barn-owl nest box built into the tower wall (see box, page 224). Such was its importance in its heyday that it spawned two chapels of ease in 'new' Malton, that later became the joint parish churches of St Michael's and St Leonard's. In 1971 the Church of England had a rush of ecumenicalism and donated, or should that be returned, St Leonard's to the Roman Catholic church. The rest of Old Malton village consists of the main road into Malton (from the A64) with two pubs almost next door to each other, and some attractive, old stone buildings, two of which are thatched.

Just outside the village though, and on the other side of the A64 dual carriageway, squats a very singular museum. I say 'squats' because the buildings of **Eden Camp** (01653 697777; www.edencamp.co.uk) are all low, single-storey Nissen huts, which would be very inconspicuous were it not for the banking spitfire suspended above the entrance. This excellent museum of World War II is housed in an old prisoner-of-war camp from that very conflict. It is open daily.

Pubs in Malton

Malton's pub story is a sad but familiar one. Ten or fifteen years ago the town was regarded as a haven for the traditional inn lover, with a string of town pubs to rival York. Most of these have now gone night clubby, downhill or out of business, save for a few oases in the desert, notably:

Crown Hotel: Suddaby's Wheelgate ℂ 01653 692038 🍺 www.suddabys.co.uk. A grade 2 listed coaching inn which has been run by the Suddaby family for 138 years. The brewery was, until recently, in the old stables behind the pub, but has now outgrown the building. One of the house beers, Double Chance, takes its name from a Grand National winner once stabled here. Don't come here for decor and comfort; Suddaby's is a basic boozer, but the beer quality is second to none, whether it is brewed on the premises or not. Three beer festivals a year (Easter, summer and winter). An attached shop stocks over 200 bottled beers and some wine. No food.

Spotted Cow Cattle Market ℂ 01653 692100. As befits a pub in the middle of the cattle market, this has a country farmer's inn feel to it. Excellent beer, and bustling on market days. Limited food.

Royal Oak Town St, Old Malton ℂ 01653 699334. This is a very welcoming village pub, with a comfortable ambience, especially in the front snug or back beer garden. A well-kept range of Yorkshire beers are served and food is also sourced locally. Meals are served at weekends and on an extremely popular 'pies only' evening on Thu. Closed Mon.

Other food and drink

Ambiente Tapas Restaurant Market Place ☎ 01653 691992 ◌ www.ambiente-tapas.co.uk. A very friendly and welcoming place with delicious Spanish food.

S⒫ Grapes Inn Great Habton YO17 6TU ☎ 01653 669166 ◌ www.thegrapes-inn.co.uk. Northwest of Malton, this is not the most inviting of buildings or villages, but there's always a warm welcome and excellent food. Very good value as well, lots of thoughtful extras for the price. Closed all day Mon and Tue lunch.

Leoni the Coffee House Wheelgate ☎ 01653 691321. A fabulous place. Voted best coffee shop in Britain in 2006 and still run by award-winning barista Simon Robertson. 'I want good coffee to be seen in the same light as good food', said Simon, 'Just like food, the difference between good coffee and bad coffee is passion. Like a chef I am passionate about creating something beautiful'. Leoni also does food with an Italian slant, snacks and lunches made from listed local sources.

Malton Relish Market Place ☎ 0845 116 1378 ◌ www.maltonrelish.co.uk. This delicatessen opened in 2007 selling specialist foods from Yorkshire and beyond. Now you don't have to wait until you get home to sample the wares, just sit at one of the small tables in the corner with whatever takes your fancy from the shop and wash it down with a brew from behind the counter.

Old Lodge Hotel Old Maltongate ☎ 01653 690570 ◌ www.theoldlodgemalton.com. Afternoon tea and coffee isn't cheap, but it's worth it for the sumptuous surroundings and view of the croquet lawn. The herb teas are rather special, supplied by 'Mighty Leaf' – you get to smell leaf samples before choosing your flavour and the 'bag' is a woven silk pouch. Fortunately they taste good too and come with a piece of shortbread. Food quality is kept high by the three house chefs indulging in a most-sales competition with their signature dishes.

Thai House, Cross Keys Wheelgate ☎ 01653 696117 ◌ www.crosskeysthai.co.uk. Stuart, the landlord, moved his successful Thai food operation from the Bay Horse in Terrington over to here in 2008, and has been turning away customers ever since. The all-you-can-eat buffet on a Mon evening is particularly good value, but book early. This is still also a proper pub with a traditional food menu and real ale. Closed Tue.

The Derwent Valley: ⑮ Kirkham and ⑯ Howsham

Not long after leaving Malton the River Derwent enters Kirkham Gorge and reverts to its wild state after the last twenty or so miles of agricultural straightening and urban encroachment. This is the start of the river as a linear nature reserve of national importance, because the wildlife here is so rich. The Derwent was one of the few rivers where otters never died out in the 1970s and they are now thriving, sustained by more than twenty species of fish that swim in these clean waters – including salmon, which are making a comeback (see page 262). Although this is an historical navigation route all the way up to Malton from the sea, no boats use the river now as it has been designated a site of special scientific interest (SSSI) and the right of navigation removed.

The only way to see the delights of this waterway is on foot or by train; the Malton–York line accompanies the river through the gorge. Walking, it's almost possible to hug the riverbank all the way from Malton to Howsham by following the Centenary Way five miles to Kirkham on the left bank, then swapping to the right bank for the remaining three miles. No buses run to either of these places and sadly, the train no longer stops anywhere between Malton and York, so a point-to-point walk is awkward.

Kirkham is best known for its Augustinian Priory (01653 618768; www.english-heritage.org.uk), its riverside situation as glorious the building itself. It is open in summer except Tuesday and Wednesday, but open every day in August. The OS map does not indicate much of interest to **Howsham** but that is misleading. The small village is quiet and pretty and the old hall was a private school until recently, but the real interest is down by the river. Canoeists and kayakers have long known about the weir here as a play spot, but since 2004 it has been the mill it serves next-door that has hit the headlines (see below). Once the river water has done its job at Howsham Mill it slides downstream towards the fantastic floodplains of the Lower Derwent, but out of our area.

Howsham Mill

Howsham Mill was built in 1755 in the Gothic revival style and was operational until 1947 when it was abandoned. In 2004 it was taken over by the Renewable Heritage Trust. 'This is a wonderful Grade 2 listed building that desperately needed rescuing back then,' explained Dave Lister, one of the volunteer restorers. 'Our plan was not just to restore it but to put it back to work harnessing energy from the river. This time it would generate "green" electricity via the water wheel, plus two modern Archimedean Screw turbines, enough for the whole thing to be completely self-sustaining. The building could then be given over to use by the community – a residential environmental centre. We got enough support for the idea to actually win the Northern England round of the BBC's *Restoration Village* programme in 2006 – that was a massive boost. Since then it's just been a lot of hard graft by a few dedicated volunteers. We've had ups and downs (mostly vandalism) but we're getting there. The Archimedes screw is in and working, funding everything now – the electricity it generates we sell to the National Grid, £15,000 a year would you believe? Things are looking good.'

To visit the mill, cross to the east side of the Derwent bridge at Howsham, follow the path under the bridge and then upstream along the boardwalk. After a few hundred yards of pleasant river-side walking, you will cross a small footbridge to the mill on its own little island.

Ryedale Vineyards

England is now firmly on the map when it comes to producing wines of internationally recognised quality but most of the commercially viable vineyards tend to hug the southernmost regions of the country. Ryedale Vineyards have crossed that north–south divide by becoming the most northerly commercial vineyards in Britain.

Close to the village of Westow, the vineyards are owned and run by Stuart and Elizabeth Smith, an established name in the commercial world of grape growing, as the Smiths have been running a vine-supply business for over twenty years.

The vineyards began in 2006 when seven acres of a gently sloping hillside were planted to vines. Said Elizabeth, 'Before we bought the land, we made regular trips over the course of twelve months to see the plot in all different weathers – to see if it sat in a frost pocket in early morning for example, which could be extremely damaging to the vines. But the vineyard is on a south-facing slope, the ideal orientation.' With such a lovely rural spot, the Smiths are keen to enhance the wildlife and are working with the RSPB to ensure that bird species such as tree sparrows and barn owls are protected by their activities.

A selection of modern, disease-resistant red and white grape varieties are grown at the vineyard in addition to some small test plantings of the more familiar French Pinot Noir and Chardonnay grapes, in the hope of producing some delicious sparkling wine in the future. 'Because we are so far north, our vines have been selected specially to ripen early, before the harsh frosts arrive, although we try to put off harvesting for as long as possible to raise the sugar levels in the grapes, which makes a better-quality wine. The Pinot Noir and Chardonnay grapes tend to ripen later in the season so they are being trialled to see what happens.'

Their first commercial vintage was produced in 2008, most of which sold out instantly. 'We were really thrilled to win several awards with our first vintage,' said Elizabeth. 'Our rosé, "Yorkshire Sunset" won a national award and our aromatic white, "Wolds View", won a trophy as the best dry white wine in a regional competition.'

The public are invited to help out with the harvest – a very sociable occasion with a privileged opportunity to witness a lesser-known aspect of North Yorkshire. For those who prefer to sit back and hold a glass of wine, there are vineyard tours (see the website below). Wine tastings are also available to bed-and-breakfast guests staying in the adjacent farmhouse that Elizabeth runs. Wine can be bought from the vineyard by prior arrangement.

There is also the opportunity to rent a vine, which includes a name plaque on a row of vines, a bottle of wine from the following harvest and an invitation to a special preview tasting when the wines are released.

Ryedale Vineyards Farfield Farm, Westow YO60 7LS ☎ 01653 658507
🖱 www.ryedalevineyards.co.uk.

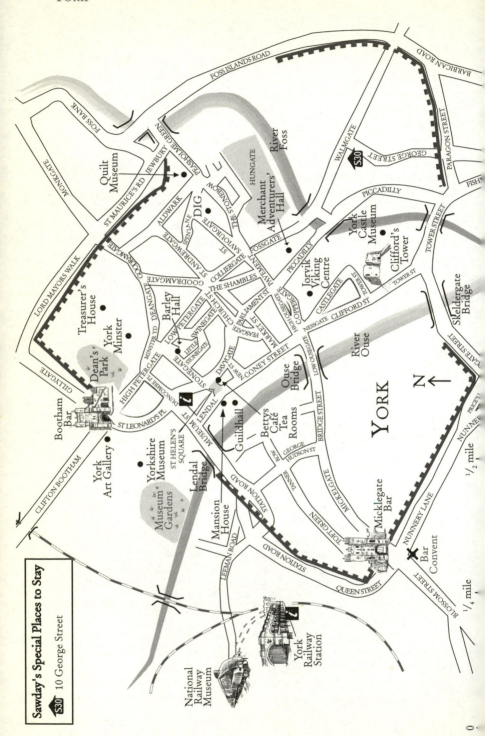

Quilt Museum

Merchant Adventurers' Hall

River Foss

WALMGATE

S30

GEORGE STREET

PARAGON STREET

BARBICAN ROAD

FOSS ISLANDS ROAD

FOSS BANK

MONKGATE

ST MAURICE'S RD

JEWBURY

PICCADILLY

FISH

DIG

ALDWARK

ST ANDREWGATE

ST SAVIOURGATE

SPEN LANE

STONEBOW

HUNGATE

FOSSGATE

York Castle Museum

Clifford's Tower

TOWER STREET

TOWER ST

Jorvik Viking Centre

Skeldergate Bridge

LORD MAYOR'S WALK

GOODRAMGATE

DEANGATE

MINSTER YD

THE SHAMBLES

COLLIERGATE

CHURCH ST

TAVERN ST

PARLIAMENT ST

PAVEMENT

CASTLEGATE

COPPERGATE

KING'S SQUARE

PICCADILLY

GEORGE ST

SKELDERGATE

Treasurer's House

York Minster

Barley Hall

LOW PETERGATE

SWINEGATE

LITTLE STONEGATE

FEASEGATE

MARKET ST

CLIFFORD ST

NESSGATE

LOW OUSEGATE

River Ouse

BRIDGE STREET

YORK

N

Dean's Park

GILLYGATE

Bootham Bar

HIGH PETERGATE

DUNCOMBE PL

STONEGATE

MUSEUM ST

LENDAL

DAVYGATE

NEW ST

CONEY STREET

Ouse Bridge

Guildhall

Bettys Café Tea Rooms

GEORGE HUDSON ST

MICKLEGATE

½ mile

PRICEY ST

NUNNERY

CLIFTON BOOTHAM

York Art Gallery

Yorkshire Museum

ST HELEN'S SQUARE

ST LEONARDS PL

Lendal Bridge

Mansion House

STATION ROAD

TANNER ROW

TOFT GREEN

Micklegate Bar

NUNNERY LANE

Bar Convent

BLOSSOM STREET

¼ mile

Museum Gardens

LEEMAN ROAD

STATION ROAD

QUEEN STREET

National Railway Museum

York Railway Station

Sawday's Special Places to Stay

S30 10 George Street

0

10. YORK

Caroline Mills

'It isn't possible to love and to part. You will wish that it was. You can transmute love, ignore it, muddle it, but you can never pull it out of you.'
E.M. Forster, A Room With a View

And so it is with the city of York. It's not possible to visit York without wishing to return; you will never be able to 'pull it out of you'. At least that's how it seems with anyone who has visited or lived there. Its character has a bewitching quality that will implore you to return again and again.

York has a history that is hard to match. While other British towns and cities have a history that's recorded in books, York still has, more than perhaps anywhere of its past visible to the eye. And yet, with the help of vibrant industries aside from tourism, it has managed to avoid becoming a stereotypical tourist city with little else to offer the wider community.

My first historical encounter with York, long before I lived there, involved eating ice cream – a fine history lesson for a youngster. The delightful block of frozen loveliness, wedged between two rather soggy wafers, was made by the Ebor Ice-Cream Co Ltd (sadly no longer in existence). I was told that Ebor was short for Eboracum, the Roman name for York.

The city and Legionnaire's fortress, built some two thousand years before the ice-cream-eating incident (though I swear the wafers may have been artefacts from the era), was one of the most important places on the map of Roman Britannia. The remnants are still evident – a column from the Roman headquarters, the remains of the fortress in the basement of the Minster, the Multangular Tower – a part of the old Roman bastion – in the Museum Gardens, stone coffins by the city walls and the ghostly figures of a marching army trampling through the basement of the Treasurer's House, heading who knows where along an old Roman road.

However York is perhaps more famous for its Viking history, with archaeological digging uncovering all manner of important finds. While I lived in York, I really took all this Viking talk for granted. It was not until I visited Trondheim in Norway that everything fell into place about York's Viking history. There were distinct similarities – the streets were named gates, the town gateways were *bars* and St Olave, a name that crops up repeatedly around York, stood on a column in Trondheim's centre, the patron saint of Norway. Indeed, the penny dropped – the Vikings made their mark in York.

They too are ever-present, be it at the **Jorvik Viking Centre**, one of the city's major tourist attractions following archaeological excavations more than a quarter of a century ago, or in the most recent findings buried under years of medieval rubbish at **Hungate**.

Yet these invasions are only the start of York's story, with medieval merchants profiteering from get-rich-quick schemes, infighting royals, men loyal to the royals, guys not so loyal to the royals, highwaymen, railway men, chocolate makers and Quakers all making an impact on the way the city looks today. You don't need an in-depth history of York to enjoy the city's pleasures – like partaking of a hot-buttered teacake in a tea-room, aiding the profits of the independent retailers that line the streets or relaxing on a grassy knoll in the Museum Gardens – but a brief understanding does help to explain a few things.

Whenever I return to the city, I usually head straight for a walk 'around the block': down **Stonegate** (arguably York's most atmospheric pedestrianised street); along **Low Petergate** for a look back at one of the most iconic views of the Minster; to **King's Square**, often frequented by buskers; down the minuscule 'Shambles' towards **Parliament Street** where street markets prevail; and along **Davygate** returning to **St Helen's Square** to visit the civilised world of **Bettys Café Tea Rooms**, where tea drinkers look out through the great glass window on to the world of York. From there a trip to the **Minster** is a must for me, to marvel at the size and scale of the creamy exterior walls and the hundreds of years of craftsmanship that have gone into creating and preserving them. Finally a wander around the **Museum Gardens** would top off a visit, especially on a day filled with sunshine.

Dividing the centre of York into segments is somewhat arbitrary for there are really just two main parts to York – inside or outside the city walls. For the sake of honouring York's chocolate heritage, I've broken the city centre into three bite-size chunks that are more easily digestible by a visitor on foot – Around the Minster, Traders' and Debtors' York, and South of the River Ouse.

The York Pass

If you plan to visit lots of fee-paying attractions, and you're in town for more than a day, it's worthwhile purchasing a **York Pass** (www.yorkpass.com). The pass allows entry into more than fifty places of interest, including several outside York mentioned elsewhere in this book such as the North Yorkshire Moors Railway (see page 187) and the RHS gardens at Harlow Carr in Harrogate (see page 115). Passes can be purchased for one, two, three or six days, with greater savings for the longest stays, in advance by post or from the tourist information centres below.

Food and drink

As York's a cosmopolitan city, you can grab a sandwich or a pasty for pavement food, dine in any number of international restaurants or sink a pint of regional brew in one of the many town-centre pubs and bars. But this is Yorkshire, and the city has not forgotten its roots, with a plethora of cafés and tea rooms serving a traditional afternoon tea. With such a compact centre you could eat all day moving from breakfast to brunch, lunch to tea and evening drinks to dinner without leaving a street.

The area around Newgate and Parliament Street is the place to pick up goodies in the open air. Newgate hosts a daily **market** while Parliament Street is the scene for **York Farmers' Market** (first Friday of every month) and several **continental markets** held throughout the year, including a large one around Christmas.

Cafés and restaurants

The Bar Convent 17 Blossom St ☎ 01904 643238 ✆ www.bar-convent.org.uk. Quiet café, serving delicious homemade food throughout the day in relaxed surroundings.

Bettys Café Tea Rooms 6–8 St Helen's Sq ☎ 01904 659142; and **Little Bettys** 46 Stonegate ☎ 01904 622865 ✆ www.bettys.co.uk. The epitome of Yorkshire (see page 116), Bettys overlooks St Helen's Square with a huge curved plate glass window from which to survey the world while listening to some classic coffee-shop tunes from the in-house pianist. Little Bettys is much more intimate and cosy, looking like an old shop from a Dickens novel. Both serve excellent food and drinks, and their fantastic bakery products, teas and coffees can be bought to take away from the premises too.

The Blake Head Bookshop & Vegetarian Café 104 Micklegate ☎ 01904 623767 ✆ www.theblakehead.co.uk. Lots of discounted books and a quiet café with good home-cooked vegetarian food.

The Blue Bicycle 34 Fossgate ☎ 01904 673990 ✆ www.thebluebicycle.com. Well-talked-about restaurant specialising in seafood. By no means the cheapest in town but good quality, fresh ingredients used and plenty of ambience.

Café Concerto 21 High Petergate ☎ 01904 610478 ✆ www.cafeconcerto.biz. A bistro that has gained quite a reputation for good food and ambience; in a prime location overlooking York Minster.

Earl Grey Tea Rooms The Shambles ☎ 01904 654353. Cosy tearooms on York's most famous street with a hidden courtyard where you can enjoy a quiet cup of tea and cake or light bite.

Grays Court Chapter House St ☎ 01904 612613 ✆ www.grayscourtyork.com. Next door to the Treasurer's House, this is a really extra special place to eat for either a relaxing mid-morning coffee, lunch or afternoon tea. The entrance to this magnificent 11th-century historic building is through a peaceful cobbled courtyard. You can relax on sofas or private window seats in the oak-panelled Jacobean long gallery, or find a table overlooking the garden, itself overlooked by the city walls that line the Lord Mayor's Walk. My pick of daytime eateries throughout the whole of York.

The Langhe Peasholme Green ☎ 01904 622584 ✆ www.lelanghe.co.uk. Good Italian deli-like café in the grounds of the York Conservation Trust garden, right next door to the Quilt Museum and Gallery.

Plunkets 9 High Petergate ☎ 01904 637722 🖱 www.plunkets.co.uk. Not terribly Yorkshire in taste but quite an institution in York, having been in business for over 30 years. Mexican and Deep South menu; the gourmet burgers are legendary.

Treasurer's House Chapter House St ☎ 01904 624247. A National Trust tea-room, open to all (not just those visiting the house).

York Minster Tea Rooms College St ☎ 01904 634830 🖱 www.yorkminster.org. Good for people-watching over a coffee, this sits in the zebra-like timber-framed building of St William's College. With a few tables on the pavement outside, it overlooks the east front of the Minster. There's also a nice courtyard away from the crowds.

Pubs

🆂 **Blue Bell** 53 Fossgate ☎ 01904 654904. Unpretentious, small front-room pub that's full of character and knick-knacks.

Guy Fawkes Tavern (Youngs Hotel) 25 High Petergate ☎ 01904 671001. One of the reputed birthplaces of Guy Fawkes, with a tiny bar.

Golden Slipper 20 Goodramgate ☎ 01904 651235. A traditional English village pub in the heart of the city. Look out for the giant golden slipper shoe hanging outside.

Ye Olde Starre Inn off Stonegate ☎ 01904 623063. Prepare for some ghostly sights while mulling over a pint. The pub sign spans the street – one of the few in Britain to do so.

Snickleway Inn 47 Goodramgate ☎ 01904 656138. Another of the pubs claiming to be the most haunted in York.

Yorkshire Terrier 10 Stonegate ☎ 01904 676722 🖱 www.york-brewery.co.uk. Pub owned by York Brewery serving their own ales and a few guest beers. In a beautiful old building, the pub sits behind and above the brewery's shop.

Tourist Information

Visit York Information Centre 1 Museum St, York YO1 7DT ☎ 01904 550099 🖱 www.visityork.org.

York Railway Visitor Information Centre Station Rd ☎ as above 🖱 as above. Wheelchair accessible.

Getting around

Much of the beating heart of York is pedestrianised so the very best way – indeed the only way – to see the main proportion of the city within the walls is on foot, or at least by pedal cycle. Public transport only helps when crossing the city or getting from the outskirts to the centre.

By bus

Buses from the suburbs to the city centre are run by **First Bus** (0845 604 5460;

www.firstgroup.com/ukbus/yorkhumber/york). These are colour-coded routes for ease of use, with the main terminus at Station Road outside the railway station and Rougier Street, a five-minute walk from the railway station. These buses won't particularly help you to see the sights of York but they will help visitors staying in accommodation away from the city centre.

However, one way to reach some of the attractions of York is by taking the **York City Sightseeing Tour** (01904 655585; www.yorktourbuses.co.uk). It's a hop-on, hop-off ride stopping at 22 points of interest. With tickets valid for 24 hours, the tour skirts the city walls and is useful for gathering your bearings, or for those with mobility problems (the buses are wheelchair and pushchair 'friendly'), but it cannot replace foot-stomping through the streets. **York Pullman** (01904 622992; www.yorkpullmanbus.co.uk) provides a similar open-top tour, with tickets that can last up to 48 hours. Tickets can be bought for both tours from the driver at any of the hop-on, hop-off locations.

By taxi

Taxis are readily available directly outside the railway station but there are also licensed taxi ranks in various locations around the city centre including St Saviourgate and St Leonard's Place (useful for evening performances at the Theatre Royal).

By car

Frankly, this is not a good idea. By far the easiest and most cost-effective thing to do with your car if visiting for the day is to use the convenient park-and-ride scheme (city-centre car parks are expensive). With free parking in five locations, all well-signposted around the city ring road, the bus, with a reasonable fare, transports you right into the city centre, stopping at several points around the city.

Cycling

To get to York, the **National Cycle Network** Route 65 (The White Rose Cycle Route) has much off-road cycling from Selby to York, connecting with Hull and Middlesbrough, plus several new routes in the offing, including a trans-Pennine route from Manchester to York.

York is officially the safest place in the UK in which to cycle, based upon recent research by the Cyclist Touring Club, and has been granted 'Cycling City' status from Cycling England. There are many traffic-free cycleways to keep you off the busy streets, with bike parking facilities in the city centre. **Bike hire** is available from **Europcar** (01904 656181) at the railway station and from **Bob Trotter Cycles** (01904 622868; www.bobtrottercycles.com) in Lord Mayor's Walk.

As for **maps**, pick up a free copy of York's *Cycle Route Map & Guide* from Visitor Information Centres and local libraries or download it from www.york.gov.uk/cycling. This details all cycle routes throughout the city as well as off-road tracks for safer cycling.

Walking

The very heart of York, enclosed by the **city walls**, is compact and easily manageable on foot. With your head down, you could cross the centre from wall to wall in approximately 20 minutes, though in reality you'll take far longer because there is so much to see. It is by far the best way to see York, and many of the main streets are pedestrianised. Rather than cross the heart of the city, you can circle it with a walk along the city walls providing one of the best vantage points from which to view the centre, particularly as an introduction before tackling the core. Originally built by the Romans and beefed-up with stone in the 13th century to keep out the Scots, the castellated walls include an inner parapet-like walkway that is approximately three miles long. They are a significant feature of the York landscape and can make a good short cut in places. My favourite section is to start at **Micklegate Bar**, considered to be the royal entrance to York as the gate through which all members of the royal family have passed on state visits to the city, and walk towards **St Leonard's Place**. Besides the superb golden glow of trumpeting daffodils hugging the banks in springtime, there are fabulous views, when walking this part of the walls, of the curving Victorian arches at the railway station, the beautiful Dutch-looking former headquarters of the North Eastern Railway Company and one of the most magnificent views of the Minster. It's the West Front of the Minster that you see from this particular section of the walls and on sunny afternoons, the stone from the façade glows with such vigour as to bring it to life.

York has built a tourist industry around walking and for visitors who prefer to be guided by a knowledgeable local, there are any number of themed walks provided by various organisations. One of the most notable is **Yorkwalk** (01904 622303; www.yorkwalk.co.uk) which begins its tours from the main gates of the Museum Gardens on Museum Street. Regular walks include useful themes for first-time visitors such as Essential York and Secret York. Other tours are more specific – the Bloody Execution Tour, Roman York, Women in York History and the infamous Historic Toilet Tour, a unique approach to uncovering aspects of social history within the city.

For self-guided trips, **Visit York** has created a series of 'Exploring York' themed walking trails. Leaflets detailing each walk with a pocket history can be picked up from the Visitor Information Centres. Walks include exploring the history of Guy Fawkes (see page 258), the Mystery Plays (see page 260), Medieval Churches and Roman York. They have also produced two walking trails especially for young children: *Little Feet* explores the city centre, pointing out places of interest that might appeal to little ones, all the while searching for 'clues' that appear on buildings and along streets; the *Retrace York Rubbing Trail* encourages children to walk the city walls, searching for rubbing panels along the way that collectively create a map of York. A complete pack, including paper and a rubbing crayon, is available from the Visitor Information Centre.

York Snickelways

Snickelway seems such a lovely word, one that you will not find in any dictionary – yet. Mark Jones created the word by taking certain syllables from three other words – snicket, ginnel and alleyway. A long-time York resident, Mark is very specific about what a snickelway should be but, in essence, they are described as narrow medieval passageways.

There are dozens of snickelways within York – tiny routes that squeeze between buildings, darting about across the city, linking more well-known, grander streets and squares; it's not difficult to imagine the hustle and bustle of a noisy medieval life while wandering these routes, even though they remain peaceful in modern times. Mark has devised a fantastic walk using many of the snickelways in what could be described as a very enjoyable game – totally disorientating even for those who know the city well. If you follow the route exactly, it uncovers all kinds of hidden gems that cannot be found simply by strolling along the main streets. Time is essential to really appreciate the walk and to accept a fair amount of distractions in the form of nosing into yards, window-shopping and stopping off en-route for a coffee or a leisurely pint in a pleasant looking pub. I'd recommend that you get to know York a little via its main streets before attempting the Snickelways to appreciate them.

The Snickelways walk is disorientating because, despite being $3^1/_2$ miles long, it is confined to an area within a quarter of a mile from **The Shambles**, one of York's most famous streets (and deemed a snickelway), so the route of the walk twists and turns every few paces. The game, however, is that you do not re-cross the path from whence you came or retrace your steps, although you do occasionally need to walk on the opposite side of the street to avoid this. Like The Shambles, there are some fascinating street names that crop up as you pass through, each with a historical narrative all of their own such as Hornpot Lane, Lady Peckett's Yard, Mad Alice Lane and Whip-ma-Whop-ma-gate (yes, really!), a name that would sound more at home in a recently-penned rap song than a medieval tongue twister.

Yorkwalk (see above) cover this walk within their selection of themed tours. However if you would prefer to amble along at your own pace, Mark Jones has produced a fascinating guide entitled *A Walk around the Snickelways of York*, available in the Visitor Information Centre and various bookshops. Try the walk with children, searching for the names of the various snickelways and sticking to the rules of the game.

Around the Minster

York Minster

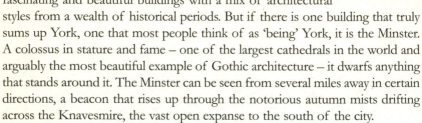

The character and ambience of York is owed to a multitude of fascinating and beautiful buildings with a mix of architectural styles from a wealth of historical periods. But if there is one building that truly sums up York, one that most people think of as 'being' York, it is the Minster. A colossus in stature and fame – one of the largest cathedrals in the world and arguably the most beautiful example of Gothic architecture – it dwarfs anything that stands around it. The Minster can be seen from several miles away in certain directions, a beacon that rises up through the notorious autumn mists drifting across the Knavesmire, the vast open expanse to the south of the city.

This is one of the few positions from which to survey the whole of the Minster. As you move closer to the structure, fragments disappear behind other buildings; even when you are standing right by it, when its sheer size is overwhelming, you cannot possibly see all of it. As you gaze skywards, you'll feel a pain in the neck creep in, unaware just how long it has been that you have studied the delicately carved decorations, mighty flying buttresses and magnificent **stained-glass windows**. From inside, these windows glint and gleam with every passing sunlit flicker, as if taking on a life of their own. The rose window in the south transept is one of the most famous in the world, not least for the painstaking restoration that was required following the lightning-bolt fire in 1984 that destroyed this work of art. The window joins the red and white roses of Lancaster and York, a symbol marking the end of The Wars of the Roses, a horrific and bloody period of history during which the Plantagenet families of Lancaster and York spent many a year bickering. When King Henry VII married Elizabeth of York, daughter of King Henry IV, in January 1486 in York Minster, the two 'roses' were conjoined to create the Tudor Rose.

Other windows are equally beautiful, their colours dancing across the gigantic walls and pillars within the Minster, such as the Great West Window, known as 'The Heart of Yorkshire' owing to the shape of the stone carved into it, and the unique Five Sisters Window in the north transept, with five elegant columns of glass. You can take a tour of the Glass Conservation Studio, to view the medieval stained glass at close quarters and see the restoration methods used. Tours of the studio, which is housed in the Bedern Chapel close by, take place on Wednesday and Friday afternoons, leaving from the Group Desk in the Minster.

Another way of seeing parts of the Minster that are otherwise inaccessible when walking around the cathedral, is to take one of three **Hidden Minster Tours**. The Early Minster Tour looks at the walls of previous cathedrals built on the same site – the walls that you see from the exterior are not the originals – such as the remains of columns in the western crypt from the church built in the 11th century or the extensions to the church that were added in 1160. It's believed that the extension used pieces of highly polished and carved stone from the Roman fortress (the foundations of which can be seen in the Minster's

Undercroft). The tour also takes you on a walkway above the beautiful Five Sisters Window, at 55 feet the tallest lancet window in the world.

A second tour takes you to the west end of the Minster and the towers that house the 32 bells; as York's highest point, it gives some spectacular views across the city. But my favourite of the three tours is to the Chapterhouse Roof and Mason's Loft. Above the vestibule of the church, the mason's loft incorporates a giant drawing floor, the markings created by draughtsmen and masons from centuries ago while working on new pieces of stone architecture for the cathedral. There are some fascinating stories told on the tour, such as why a stone toilet should have been incorporated into the room – possibly for private contemplation by King Edward III on a royal visit!

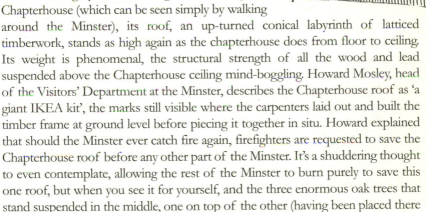

But by far the greatest architectural gem of the Minster is the oldest part, the **Chapterhouse roof.** Above the highly ornate ceiling of the octagonal Chapterhouse (which can be seen simply by walking around the Minster), its roof, an up-turned conical labyrinth of latticed timberwork, stands as high again as the chapterhouse does from floor to ceiling. Its weight is phenomenal, the structural strength of all the wood and lead suspended above the Chapterhouse ceiling mind-boggling. Howard Mosley, head of the Visitors' Department at the Minster, describes the Chapterhouse roof as 'a giant IKEA kit', the marks still visible where the carpenters laid out and built the timber frame at ground level before piecing it together in situ. Howard explained that should the Minster ever catch fire again, firefighters are requested to save the Chapterhouse roof before any other part of the Minster. It's a shuddering thought to even contemplate, allowing the rest of the Minster to burn purely to save this one roof, but when you see it for yourself, and the three enormous oak trees that stand suspended in the middle, one on top of the other (having been placed there goodness knows how in 1260 without the aid of modern lifting equipment!), you begin to understand the sentiment and the reasoning.

The Minster grounds

To best appreciate the acoustic qualities of York Minster, listen to one of the concerts held occasionally or listen to the attractive peal of the bells on a Sunday morning, slowly dragging persistent slumberous souls into the awoken world. To concentrate on this musical campanology, head for the **Dean's Park**; it's a quiet (but for the bells!) and restful green space overshadowed by the north face of the Minster.

The Treasurer's House

Behind the Minster is the 17th-century **Treasurer's House**, so called because it stands on the same site of the medieval mansion used by the Treasurer of York Minster. Owned by The National Trust, it was used by a bachelor, Frank Green, to house his collection of antique furniture in period settings. His portrait that

Restoring York Minster

The walls of York Minster might have been built almost a thousand years ago, but this most celebrated of buildings could be likened to Trigger's broom, the prop that made an important appearance in the sitcom Only Fools and Horses. The unlikeliest of analogies, I know, but in a famous scene Trigger describes how his original road-sweeping broom has lasted for 20 years adding that the broom has had 17 new heads and 14 new handles.

York Minster is a little bit like that. So soft is the limestone used to build and decorate the Minster that every stone only lasts for approximately 150 years. Hence it's difficult to find much genuinely original stonework.

The stone restoration is a mammoth task so the Minster has its own stoneyard, housed on Deangate. Peer through the gates and you're likely to hear the sounds of giant circular blades slicing through stone like soft butter and when the whirring stops (remembering that the original masons didn't have such a useful tool to summon into action), there's the gentle tapping of the stone-carver's chisel and mallet, creating some masterpiece to adorn the face of the Minster for future generations. Beautiful these creations are not, though the work is first-class, for it's often grotesques that these stone-carvers are creating – ornate figures that do nothing but punctuate the Minster's walls by sticking out a tongue at an unsuspecting passer-by.

The Stoneyard is open to the public occasionally. If you're not in town when a tour is planned, accept that you'll get neck ache and take the time to admire the stonework on the Minster. Generations of stone-carvers have plied their trade and thousands of man-hours have gone into making the Minster look the way it does.

I chatted to Geoff Butler, Head Stone-Carver at the Minster Stoneyard, as he carved one tiny section that will sit on the East Front, the area of the Minster currently being restored. The piece of stone Geoff was working on was approximately 16 inches high and 8 inches wide, indicating just how laborious the restoration task is. Geoff was about to carve a crocket, a leaf-shaped decoration that's particular to gothic architecture, on to a small, decorative pinnacle that had been marked out. He described the process: 'We receive large, sawn-cut blocks from the quarry. The masons put a template on the block and saw away some of the stone and then it comes into me to carve. From the ground the crockets appear like knobs on pinnacles but when you get close to them (an opportunity afforded to those visitors who climb

hangs in the hall shows quite a friendly looking chap although his frequent notices to staff left around the house suggest a rather pedantic figure – his request for workmen to wear slippers in the house would not pass a health and safety assessment now! There's another chance for a view of the Minster from the drawing room but the Great Hall is really the attraction here, with a hidden minstrel's gallery complete with a small leaded-light window from which to glance at passing visitors below.

the steps to the Minster roof), they're quite intricate. We have to put the design back as it was because we're trying to maintain the original medieval pattern.'

It's when designing the decorative grotesques that the carvers can let their imagination run. Each one is entirely unique and doesn't always follow the designs of their stone-carving forefathers. Geoff explained, 'On the latest restoration area, the old grotesques are either missing or too eroded to tell what the designs were. I decided that we would make them into figures from the time of the medieval carvers that originally worked on the cathedral and then base them upon illnesses of the time. So we have figures that are suffering from the plague, toothache or backache.'

Geoff pointed to a magnificent decorative figure hanging over the workbench being sick, the figure's smoothly carved, hunched back appearing to be desperate for some tender hand to relieve his suffering. Geoff continued, 'That one is the Black Prince, a character from the period when this section currently being restored was built. He represents dysentery as that is what he factually died from and we like to make the detail historically accurate on whatever we are carving.' Accurate indeed, the Black Prince's coat of arms was intricately carved on to his shield, the poor wretch clutching at his stomach with terrible cramps.

Geoff pointed to another figure serenely waiting on a bench; work in progress by Lee, a stone-carver who had recently finished his apprenticeship. 'That one is the result of a visit by the Duke of York. He suggested representing the soldiers in Afghanistan and Iraq. Lee, who carved the figure, chose to base it on the angels carved into the stonework on the east end and depicted in the stained glass of the east window too. Lee decided that this angel was "the keeper of souls" and the regimental badge that the angel is holding is that of the Yorkshire Regiment.'

I asked how long each figure takes to carve and when the stone-carver knows his work is finished. 'Well,' Geoff said, you always see something that you've missed but at some point you have to say "that's it".'

Geoff has worked as a stone-carver at the Minster's stoneyard for over forty years and was awarded a British Empire Medal by the Crown for his services helping to mend the south transept of the Minster that was so badly ravaged by fire in 1984. More than 2,500 stones need to be replaced by the stonemasons and carvers on the East Front of the Minster. Even if you can't visit the stoneyard in person, you can sponsor a stone, with sponsors' names recorded in a book held in the Minster.

A city of gates

The word gate comes from the Scandinavian word *gata*, which actually means road, and many of York's roads are named this way, often describing the occupation of the original residents that would congregate in the same place – **Swinegate** was the old pig market, **Stonegate** was the thoroughfare to bring the stone from the River Ouse to the building site of the Minster, **Coppergate** residents made cups. Many of these gates are, perhaps rather obviously, in the very heart of York where the Viking residents lived. It's these most ancient of streets that provide the character of the city around the Minster, each one similar and yet dissimilar to others, the plethora of independent retailers, restaurants and bars a refreshing change from the cloned High Streets found in many towns today. From **Bootham Bar**, the city's northwest entrance, the narrow **High Petergate** runs up past the Minster's west front, crossing Stonegate to meet with **Low Petergate**.

Opposite the Minster, on the edge of High Petergate, sits a far smaller church named **St Michael-le-Belfrey**. Though in the shadow of the mighty Minster, it is significant to York history – indeed British history – by being *the* church where a baby was baptised as Guy Fawkes. He was born yards away (a couple of buildings in High Petergate and Stonegate lay claim to being the birthplace) as a Protestant son of York; his father and grandparents are buried in the Minster.

Guy Fawkes in York

Ironically, King James VI of Scotland passed through York in 1603 on his way south to become King James I of England. He stayed at **The King's Manor**, in St Leonard's Place, yards from his potential murderer's place of birth and baptism. As he had a Catholic wife, it was hoped that James I would provide greater security and tolerance for Catholics than they had known since King Henry VIII's abolition of Catholicism in England. It was not to be. Guy Fawkes had become a Catholic some years earlier while at St Peter's School, quarter of a mile from Bootham Bar, and was aware of the antagonistic feeling occurring among Catholics within the city before taking part in one of British history's most notorious events. And while many enjoy burning a Guy on top of a roaring fire each November to commemorate the event, it is a practice that, to this day, St Peter's School does not partake in, it being considered unsporting to burn the effigy of a former pupil!

Of all the streets in York, **Stonegate** is what I feel to be at the very heart of the city. With the River Ouse, the medieval **Guildhall** and the **Mansion House**, home to the Lord Mayor, behind you, Stonegate runs from **St Helen's Square** towards the Minster. It was originally the Via Praetoria that went to the main gates of the Roman fortress long before the Vikings renamed it. There are glimpses of the Minster from time to time, drawing you ever closer towards this giant beast of a building. But ponder a while along Stonegate; its charm lies within the York paving beneath your feet and the fact that no two buildings are the same. The rooflines, the building materials, the paint colours of the window frames and the decorative iron signs advertising small boutiques, tea shops and ancient inns are all different and all add something to the character of the street. It can get busy around Christmas but there's room for all, including the odd busker or two, their independent tunes turning into a cacophony of sound or a melodic harmony depending on their proximity to one another.

Mid-way along Stonegate, an unusual pub sign runs across the full width of the street, directing you to **Ye Olde Starre Inn**, hidden down a tiny alleyway. It's the oldest pub in York and reputedly has a posse of ghosts to alarm punters. **The Punchbowl**, also in Stonegate, claims to have a good bunch of ghostly goings-on too, but then, given the number of ghost tours and bump-in-the-night walks, hauntings are big business in York so it makes good financial sense to have a ghost or two running about to scare customers.

For a more serene experience, take a peak into Coffee Yard, a tiny 'snickelway' off Stonegate, where the medieval **Barley Hall** stands. It was re-discovered in the 1980s, hidden behind the façade of a derelict office block being demolished, and has now been restored to the beautiful timber-framed home of a 14th-century Lord Mayor. Community involvement is an element of the building's restoration: there's an oral history project still going on to involve anyone who has ever lived or worked in or around Stonegate.

York Art Gallery

Within a stone's throw of **York Theatre Royal** (01904 623568; www.york theatreroyal.co.uk), a good provincial performing arts house, is **York Art Gallery** (01904 687687; www.yorkartgallery.org.uk) in St Leonard's Place, free and accessible to all. It has a vast collection of paintings – over a thousand in number – but not the space to exhibit them all at the same time. Consequently there is always a variety of changing exhibitions as well as some fine permanent displays grouped into themes in large, light rooms. On the ground floor, in the South Gallery is a collection of 17th-century Dutch works, a strong collection of early religious paintings and some rather harrowing scenes grouped together under the title of 'Sacrifice', some so gruelling you feel it inappropriate to look for too long. Though one that I couldn't take my eyes off was a painting by Bernardino Fungai entitled *The Martyrdom of St Clement*. It's cartoon-like in character, a giant Noah-style boat dominating the picture over a startling turquoise blue sea; it's only later that you see the thin line of the anchor noose wrapped around the neck of St Clement as he's tossed overboard, while many of the crew appear totally nonchalant about the action, busying themselves with their own tasks.

The painting could easily have fitted into any one of the three other permanent themed displays upstairs in The Burton Gallery under the headings 'People', 'Places' and 'Stories', where each picture in the collection contains a narrative. As a travel writer, I felt naturally drawn to the Places collection, not least because many of the paintings are by artists with Yorkshire connections or are of Yorkshire scenes. The gallery has a couple of York-based paintings by the matchstick-men master, L S Lowry, including one of **Clifford's Tower**. It's a painting that was commissioned by the art gallery in 1953 and is so typically 'Lowry', it seems quite surreal to see such a well-known York landmark painted in a style that is more akin to industrial factory scenes. There's also an enchanting seascape entitled *Coastal Scene with Shrimpers* by York-born artist Henry Moore (not to be confused with the Yorkshire-born sculptor of the same name) who studied at the Royal Academy. Its glowing sunset, reflected in the calm waters, is a very restful picture, unlike its neighbour in the gallery, *La Vague* (*The Wave*) by Roderic O'Conor, an Irishman who went to school at Ampleforth (see page 222) in the North York Moors. His oil painting of a thundering sea comes out of the frame as if it will fill the room with water.

The art gallery puts on regular events for visitors to learn more about either particular paintings or styles of painting with curators' talks and opportunities to take part in practical art activities such as painting or felt-making workshops.

The York Mystery Plays

I had a crush on God – or the performer who played him, at least, in York's famous Mystery Plays, when I got involved with a production some twenty years ago. Earlier, these plays launched the professional career of a young Dame Judi Dench. A daughter of York her first theatrical outings, both facing the stage and on it, were in the city. She performed as the Virgin Mary in the 1957 production of the York Mystery Plays, one of the first revivals since the original pageants were banned in 1568 courtesy of religious in-fighting under Elizabeth I.

Originating in the 14th century, the York Mystery Cycle was a collection of community plays put on by the various Guilds in the town, each one responsible for a particular Christian story, from the Creation to the Last Judgement. Held around the festival of Corpus Christi (late-May to mid-June), they were a way of educating the largely illiterate townsfolk while providing eagerly anticipated entertainment. Each play was performed on pageant wagons that processed around the city streets, a spectacle that lasted from sunrise to well beyond the midsummer sunset.

The mobile pageantry disappeared for the 1950s revival; the plays were performed instead on a fixed stage in the Museum Gardens until the 1990s. Though not conforming to the original idea of mobile performances, it was a spectacular setting and one that I remember well, having become involved with a production like so many other residents before and after, performing alongside university students and schoolchildren.

The York Mystery Plays continue to be performed every four years (2010, 2014 and so on). But the plays have been returned to their rightful place – on the city streets. The community is still involved: the modern Guilds of York are once again in charge of the productions and pageant wagons as they were in medieval times.

With such a long gap between cycles, the best way to appreciate the atmosphere in between times is to follow the York Mystery Plays Trail, a walking route that takes in the route and wagon stations where the original plays were performed in the 14th century. It's an interesting way to see the city centre, looking out for some of the old medieval buildings that were important at the time, and where some of the plays are performed today. You can download details of the trail from www.visityork.org/explore or purchase a trail guide from the York Visitor Information Centre.

The Museum Gardens and the Yorkshire Museum

Shrouded with daffodils in spring and multi-coloured blooms in summer, the **Museum Gardens** just north of the River Ouse are still my favourite place to relax in York, finding a sun-strewn piece of Benedictine wall to prop oneself up against, the empty arches of the delicately carved windows towering above. The distant traffic crossing **Lendal Bridge** disappears as the birdsong whistling from the window ledges takes over, the occasional clanging of the Minster's bells ringing out the passing time.

The creamy wall – for there is only one full wall left standing – of St Mary's Abbey, blackened by centuries of decay, belonged once to the largest Benedictine monastery in the north of England. Founded in 1055, it became one of the casualties of Henry VIII's Dissolution. Other parts of the Abbey remain scattered around the gardens like discarded rubble, the stumpy foundation stones of once-magnificent pillars appearing to grow from the grass; they are now the back-scratchers for idle bookworms and lunchtime gatherers escaping the bustle of the city streets and offices.

Behind the abbey, just outside a redundant part of the city walls, is **St Olave's Church** in Marygate. Built in 1055, the parish church is the oldest monument dedicated to the patron saint of Norway, King Olaf, who had died in combat 30 years earlier. The church became the foundation for the Benedictine community that built St Mary's Abbey. In a quiet back street, bordered by the Museum Gardens and close to the river, it is a very peaceful and a quite beautiful sanctuary, well away from the hubbub. The six bells are rung every Sunday morning at service in full view of the congregation and visitors are welcome to witness the bell-ringing practice, held every Wednesday from 7pm to 9pm.

Elsewhere in the Gardens, the **Yorkshire Museum**, being refurbished at the time of writing, has an extensive collection of antiquities from the city and around, including the famous Middleham Jewel. It is due to re-open in August 2010: the new displays focused on the city's Roman heritage promise to add another layer to the city's extraordinary range of archaeological attractions.

The River Ouse

Below the Museum Gardens is the **River Ouse**. Its usually mild-mannered waters entertain visitors on river cruises or dawn-breaking university rowers most days. Sometimes, when the weather has been cruel in the distant Dales forcing the water ever higher, the river forgets its manners, turning into a savage torrent that bullies its way into the front rooms of neighbouring houses and upturning bar stools in the ever-patient **Kings Arms**. Every time it happens, the landlord marks the flood's height on the wall.

When it's not deep under water, the Kings Arms is a great place from which to view aspects of the **Jorvik Viking Festival** (www.yorkfestivals.com), an event every February where longboats sail down the river in homage to the time when the Viking raiders used to head out to the North Sea to trade around the world. Other events take place elsewhere around the city including battle re-enactments and saga-telling.

A river cruise provides yet another perspective on York. It is one of the best ways from which to view the medieval Guildhall that backs on to the Ouse close to Lendal Bridge. **YorkBoat** (01904 628324; www.yorkboat.co.uk) plies the river in a variety of red-and-white cruisers, departing either from Lendal Bridge, close to the Museum Gardens, or Kings Staith, just outside the Kings Arms. The York City Cruise, with on-board commentary, gives a good introduction to York from the river. An alternative one-hour cruise downstream to Bishopthorpe Palace, the home of the Archbishop of York, gets you out of the city centre for a while. YorkBoat run lunch and dinner cruises too if you wish to combine a meal with a river cruise but one of the most atmospheric of trips is to take the Floodlit Evening Cruise to Bishopthorpe Palace, when the lights of York play games on the water and buildings such as the Guildhall take on another dimension.

The Salmon of York

Mike Bagshaw

If asked to name an English salmon river, very few people would suggest the River Ouse, which slides its way through York. But it's not a typically polluted city river, fed as it is by the clear Dales rivers of Swale, Ure and Nidd.

Bob Drake was a lad in the 1940s, struggling to live on wartime rations in York. 'We'd look forward to late autumn nights, just after a high tide, because that's when the salmon would run. A net across the river, hidden under the railway bridge at Poppleton for a few hours, would always land a few fish, five or ten – enough for our family and a few friends. I know it was poaching, but the river was teeming in those days, and they were desperate times.'

What makes this abundance all the more remarkable is that these are the fish that got past the commercial netters way downstream below York, at Naburn and Cawood, the limit of the tide, and they took nine tons of salmon every year – that's a lot of fish.

Fast forward to the 1970s. The Dales rivers that feed the Ouse were still as clear and clean as ever, pike, perch, roach and bream still swam under the city's bridges, and trout in its tributaries, but the King of Fish was gone, not one salmon to be seen. What went wrong? The answer lay in the fatal combination of the fish's incredible life-cycle, and what was going on in 1950s West and South Yorkshire.

Atlantic Salmon (*Salmo salar*) are famously born in fresh water, migrate to the sea to feast and put on weight, returning a few years later to their home river to mate, spawn and produce the next generation of fish. What complicates the situation in

Mercantile York: trade, debt and industry

Not surprisingly much of the historical trading area of York grew up between the two rivers of York, the River Foss flowing into the River Ouse a little southeast of Skeldergate Bridge. Viking traders brought goods in and out of the city via the River Ouse, which flows into the North Sea. Many of the Viking artefacts associated with trading have been found in the **Coppergate** area just east of the riverbank while medieval merchants, with a rapidly increasing wealth, chose to position their headquarters, the **Merchant Adventurers' Hall**, in a prominent position next to the River Foss, with water-level storage rooms for goods to be brought in and out.

By contrast to these wealthy merchants' quarters, **York Castle**, built by William the Conqueror as a defence post, became the debtors' prison in the 1800s followed by the felons' prison in the 1900s. The whole area was, and still is, synonymous with law and justice – the Crown Court is still found opposite **York Castle Museum**, where the various prisons were until their closure in 1934. One of York's most infamous 'traders', if he can be called that for his 'trade' was somewhat one-sided, was Dick Turpin, or John Palmer as he liked to call himself in Yorkshire to escape his crimes further south.

Yorkshire, and which almost resulted in the salmon's extinction here, is the dominance of the Humber estuary. All of Yorkshire's major rivers join forces as the Ouse, and flow into the sea together in the Humber. The salmon could not survive the level of pollution in the water in the Rivers Don and Aire which entered here from industrial Sheffield and Leeds, and either died as young fish on their way out to sea, or as adults on their way back.

If the salmon's story had ended their it would have been a tragedy, but in the past ten years or so rumours of a possible comeback have been confirmed; some are now making it back up the Humber and returning to their old haunts. 'This is a completely natural recolonisation,' explained John Shannon of the Environment Agency, 'We've not done any stocking of the Dales rivers at all. What we have worked hard at is habitat restoration, and in particular water quality lower down, and the fish have done the rest themselves.'

The future looks good for Yorkshire salmon, and consequently all the other living parts of the river ecosystem, especially the fish-eaters. Not many people see them, because they're very shy and nocturnal, but otters are back in York as well – possibly because gourmet fish are back on the menu.

If you want to stand a good chance of seeing a Dales salmon, you need to be in the right place at the right time. They tend to run upstream in late autumn, November is the peak time, and when the rivers are full and fast. Weirs and small falls, where the salmon have to leap out of the water, are the best places. Try watching from the weir and fish-pass at Naburn near York or Westwick weir at Ripon.

York Castle Museum and Clifford's Tower

York Castle Museum (01904 687687; www.yorkcastlemuseum.org.uk) was one of my favourite places to visit as a child, the old sweet shop selling sugar mice

along the cobbled Victorian street being a truly memorable experience. It's brought the social history up to date since then, with room scenes depicting many different eras to the present day but Kirkgate, the Victorian street, is still the best in my opinion. Next door are the very cells that locked up Dick Turpin and other notorious criminals as well as those who got into severe financial debt, a lockable offence in the 1800s.

Originating from the castle built by William the Conqueror in 1070, **Clifford's Tower** remains a symbol of the Normans' triumphant defeat over the Vikings. The tower sits in a perfect defensive position, snugly between the rivers Ouse and Foss. Despite the magnificent display of daffodils in spring helping you to forget your calf-pulling ascent, the mound is no easier to climb now than it was in 1070, with the exception of a moat to cross and the arrow slits in the circular tower thankfully remaining redundant for anything other than a pigeon's resting place. There are some great views of the city from the top, but that's about all there is now, the tower open to the elements following an unfortunate incident that blew the roof off in the 17th century when gunpowder was stored there.

Fairfax House

To the north of Clifford's Tower is **Castlegate**, a road that runs from the castle into the centre of town. The street is home to **Fairfax House** (01904 65554; www.fairfaxhouse.co.uk), considered to be one of the finest examples of an 18th-century townhouse in Britain. Its façade is imposing in a very classical, ordered way, the symmetry just so, the Georgian windows perfectly aligned. You can imagine how this would have been the talk of the town among society, the windows filled with light and chatter during social evenings and carriages arriving to chauffeur away young ladies and gents. Inside, the rooms have been restored perfectly to the fashion of the day with brightly painted walls and elegant furnishings, including the Noel Terry collection of 17th- and 18th-century clocks, and cabinets full of secret compartments that, in their day, must have held the hidden secrets and affairs of many a society scandal.

Friargate and Coppergate

On the corner of Castlegate and tiny Friargate is the Friends' Meeting House, the main place of worship in York for the Society of Friends, otherwise known as Quakers. It's a very plain, simple building and deliberately so, owing to the beliefs of the practising Friends. There are no amazing stained glass windows, no elaborate choir screens or decorative stonework but the result is a very restful building where the sun bounces off the cream coloured walls and fills the building with light.

Quakers and chocolate

The Quakers have a long tradition in York that goes back way before the Rowntree family, but it is the Rowntrees who put Quakerism, or Quaker values, on the map in York. Although perhaps more renowned for Kit Kat and Smarties, they played a vital philanthropic role within the city that included creating a garden village for their factory workers in New Earswick and providing land for the two Quaker schools in the city – the Mount School for girls and Bootham School (where Joseph Rowntree, the founder of the chocolate factory, went to school). They also created **Rowntree Park** on the south bank of the River Ouse in memory of those who lost their lives during World War I. A Rowntree Walk through the city has been created, highlighting places relating to the Rowntree family, including the building where the cocoa business began before it moved to the current Haxby Road site (now owned by Nestlé) and the Friends' Meeting House in Friargate. It provides a break from the Roman and Viking history that abounds in the city and gives you the chance to look at a completely different side to York from the more recent past. A trail leaflet is available from the York Visitor Information Centre in Museum Street or you can download a copy from the Rowntree Society website: www.rowntreesociety.org.uk.

Between 1979 and 1981, the **Coppergate** area of town was scoured for clues in one of the largest archaeological digs ever in Britain, revealing a complex of 10th-century Viking buildings and some 40,000 finds. The result was the creation of the **Jorvik Viking Centre** (01904 615505; www.jorvik-viking-centre.co.uk), one of York's most visited attractions, beneath the 1980s shopping centre erected on the site. Not always obvious to the thousands of queuing visitors about to descend to this phenomenally successful display (pre-book to avoid the wait) is that they are going to see the genuine Viking archaeology of York in its original position, The site includes timbers preserved in the wet ground, which are only now underground because over them lie the deep deposits created by medieval and later rebuildings of the city. Reconstructions, sound tracks and even authentic aromas from fish markets and cesspits, all highly innovative when the Jorvik first opened in 1984, bring the scenes to life: if you are resistant to the idea of the ride which you have to take to see it, bear in mind that this is proper archaeology, meticulously researched and far from just a theme park: the electric 'cars' were the only feasible way to move large numbers of visitors safely around such a compact and fragile site. Jorvik continues to bring in funds to support the work of the York Archaeological Trust, such as the activities at **DIG** (01904 615505; www.digyork.com), housed in St Saviour's Church, Saviourgate, where archaeologists explain what they do and children especially enjoy digging in specially prepared pits of clean 'earth' (actually recycled rubber crumbs) for genuine York artefacts, and the current archaeological project nearby in

Hungate: 969 and all that

One thing that can epitomise slow travel is visiting an archaeological dig, or even more so, taking part in one. To some extent time moves quickly on an archaeological dig – two thousand years of history stripped back in a few years – but in a visit to York, a trip to Hungate Dig shows time moving rather slowly, before your very eyes.

The Hungate Dig is a six-year project in an area of York that is due for redevelopment in 2012. Until then a team of professional archaeologists, together with anyone from the general public who wishes to get involved, will unearth history with trowels, fingertips and sieves.

Peter Connelly, the Project Director for the Hungate Dig, showed me the accessible-to-all archaeological site. Describing a Viking timber building, found beneath the surface, as 'treasure', Peter explained 'We know that the building is built in the early 970s but, by analysing the growth rings of the wood used for the building, we've also established that at least two of the posts were split from a tree that was cut down in the summer of 969' said Peter. And there were many more astonishing facts like that too.

Peter enthused, 'Archaeologists look for patterns in the soil. So in that soil face you actually have the bands of time: there's a big band of grey soil – that's Roman – and then on top of it, the orange band is laid during the Viking age and dug into it is our Viking-age house; then as you build your way up' Peter continued, gesticulating eagerly, 'we've got a stone lime pit which is actually a 17th-century cess pit. Cut into that is a late 18th or early 19th-century well. Behind that you've got the drainpipe for a house that was built here in the late Georgian period. So within a single space you've got evidence of occupation from the Romans right up to the present day.' Seeing it laid out, I could understand why Peter gets so enthusiastic.

Hungate, where visitors can take part in a major excavation, to my mind the most exciting of the three archaeology attractions.

Shambolic merchants: The Shambles and the Merchant Adventurers' Hall

I've always loved the sound of the street named **The Shambles**, York's finest medieval street. Despite the name referring to the butchers' shops that once lined the street, it so aptly depicts the topsy-turvy nature of the top-heavy houses that lean precariously towards one another on either side of the narrow lane. Each house seems close enough that you could quite easily shake hands with neighbours on the opposite side of the street by merely opening a top floor window.

The Shambles is almost too quaint to mention but the charm in its lack of architectural uniformity, a mixture of brick, timber and rendered buildings, is

'You've got this continuity of time that people can come and see when they visit here,' Peter said. 'They can see the plots, where the house stood and where the toilets were!' Pointing to a couple of archaeologists with mucky boots, shovels and a wheelbarrow, he was understandably keen to stress that the project is not about trained professionals hidden away but about getting people – anyone – involved. 'We run site tours several times a day, which give people the opportunity to ask questions as we work. Then every summer York Archaeological Trust runs "Archaeology Live", which is open to the public – no experience necessary. You can do a one- or two-day taster course during which you'll do some digging, find out how we do our archaeological photography and how we record things, and you wash any artefacts that you find.

There are week-long courses too and we also run events throughout the year such as the Introduction to Fieldwork weekend.

To ensure that no artefact of importance is missed, all visitors are supervised by our fully trained archaeologists. We'll accept anyone above the age of 16 and if they are under 16, we ask that they come with a parent. Our lower age limit tends to be 12, as the work can be quite intensive.'

Peter finished, 'We have people who come on Archaeology Live digs and make it their holiday. If you join the Friends of York Archaeological Trust (www.yorkarchaeology.co.uk), you get a discount on the digs and a discount into the other attractions run by the Trust.'

DIG Hungate The Stonebow ℓ 01904 615505 (tours) 07908 210026 (Archaeology Live training days) ✆ www.dighungate.com. It is advisable to pre-book scheduled guided tours, which begin from DIG at St Saviour's Church (St Saviourgate), a short walk from DIG Hungate. Archaeological dig courses are based at the DIG Hungate site.

unavoidable. Today the butchers have gone, the bow-fronted windows of the tiny shops taken up with a succession of tourist paraphernalia that you could probably do without, but will buy anyway as a souvenir of the street. However, of a more sobering thought that might curtail the spending is the shrine to Margaret Clitherow, half way along the street. She was the wife of a butcher who harboured catholic priests at a time when it was not the done thing to do. She was found out and her punishment was to be crushed to death.

It's the ability to lure passing trade, as shown in The Shambles today, that turned York citizens into wealthy merchants 650 years or so ago. These medieval traders built their communal building, the **Merchant Adventurers' Hall** (01904 654818; www.theyorkcompany.co.uk), in Fossgate to be able to meet socially and transact their business affairs. It's a fantastic building with timbers the size of tree trunks and a totally uneven floor that slides into the centre of the room. From the outside, the hall sits restfully in its own peaceful garden by the River Foss, though this has caused flooding problems in the past as can be seen from the watermarks in the Undercroft, the flood heights steadily rising since they were first recorded in 1831. The coats of arms of 22 of the medieval guilds hang in the Undercroft too and the accompanying exhibition puts into perspective just how powerful and important the Guilds were. The building, including the guild chapel, is still used for regular events both by the current members of the guild and by outside organisations, which helps to ensure that it remains a living and breathing part of York rather than a dusty museum.

The Quilt Museum and Gallery

Sandwiched between St Saviourgate and Hungate is **The Stonebow** leading to **Peasholme Green**, where one of York's newest museums, the **Quilt Museum and Gallery** (01904 613242; www.quiltmuseum.org.uk), is housed in St Anthony's Hall, on the corner with **Aldwark**. This half-stone, half-brick building, built in the 15th century, was once a medieval guildhall too so it is apt that it is now home to The Quilters' Guild of the British Isles. The structure is worth visiting to see the Great Hall alone, its timber roof juxtaposed nicely against the giant quilts and textiles that hang from the walls. But, like the Merchant Adventurers' Hall, this too is a living building and visitors can take part in events organised by the Quilters' Guild, with craft workshops, gallery demonstrations, talks and activities on the programme. The hall also houses the guild library with a collection of 3,000 quilting books and a shop selling quilting and craft equipment too. Outside, the recently created York Conservation Trust garden, partly surrounded by the city walls, is open to the public and provides a lovely area to sit.

Across the Ouse

From the **Quilt Museum and Gallery** in Peasholme Green, a short stroll up Aldwark takes you towards the Minster and the very heart of York. However, wander along **The Stonebow** past the hideous concrete monstrosity known as The Stonebow building, and you come to the market square bordered by Pavement and Parliament Street. It's where all the major banks congregate if you're short on ready cash, but it's also where regular food markets take place and any other festivities that can happen in a temporary marquee; it's the home for many of the events during the annual York Food Festival (www.yorkfoodfestival.com).

Continue along High Ousegate and you'll cross over Ouse Bridge, the oldest of the bridges in York, to Micklegate.

Micklegate

I find **Micklegate** one of the nicest – and longest – streets in York. The first few hundred yards, closest to the bridge, are a bit messy, with shops that seem to frequently change hands and the Park Inn Hotel, another of York's buildings that might not be classed as the city planning department's finest hour. But as you begin to climb the steady slope past this small area in desperate need of a facelift and crossing George Hudson Street, Micklegate becomes a quiet gem. There are no distinguishing tourist attractions along the street, making it appear blissfully uncrowded, but it has some striking Georgian townhouses, built by the wealthy merchants who found the street to be a good trading route when it was the main road into the city centre. Among a clutch of good independent shops is **Ken Spelman** (70 Micklegate; www.kenspelman.com), a secondhand bookshop that has been there since eternity. It doesn't matter what books are placed in the window display, there is always something that will catch your eye. A little further up the hill towards Micklegate Bar is the **Blake Head Bookshop**. By comparison with the all-conquering book chains, this is a minnow but a very pleasant one and with a vegetarian café behind that has gained a good reputation in the twenty-odd years it has been running.

On the opposite side of the street to the shops is **Holy Trinity Church**, a conventionally built stone church, set back from the street line, in its own peaceful grassy graveyard. It's all that remains from a once powerful Benedictine monastery destroyed by Henry VIII. However, the monastery would have been there when previous members of the royal family found their heads being strewn along the top of **Micklegate Bar**, following the Battle of Wakefield during the Wars of the Roses. Micklegate Bar was *the* place for several centuries upon which to find the head of a losing army, traitor or dignitary, royal or not.

The Bar Convent

In a Georgian building on the busy corner of Blossom Street and Nunnery Lane, just beyond Micklegate Bar, the Bar Convent (01904 643238; www.bar-convent.org.uk) is the oldest living convent in England. It was founded in 1686 at a time when persecution of Catholics was rife and has been a major part of the York community ever since. Originally set up as a school for girls, the convent and the founding order has a fascinating history with links to Guy Fawkes and the gunpowder plot.

The convent still has a sense here and there of school-ness inside with long corridors covered in aging linoleum, but the architectural secret is a covered chapel, designed by a York architect in the mid 18th century to be completely hidden from view. And indeed it is – you would never know it was there from the street. The chapel, which is open to visitors and still in regular use, has a beautiful gilt-decorated dome that is completely concealed by a pitched roof from the outside. The chapel also has eight exits and a priest hole – necessary security measures at the time it was built.

The convent is a great place to visit to get away from the bustle of the city centre. The plant-filled Winter Garden, the entrance hall to the convent, has a striking glass roof and mosaic-tiled floor. It's a quiet place for a cup of tea, as is the peaceful back garden that's tended by the few remaining sisters. For here you can sit with your lunch and not notice a sound coming from the busy roads that surround the building. Jo Dodds, who works at the Bar Convent, commented on how restful a place it is. 'You don't have to be religious to come here and get something out of the place,' she says, 'It's a place to sit quietly and be able to relax; it has a very soothing environment.'

The National Railway Museum and York station

York has one of the most famous railway stations in the world – with a walkway through to the free-to-view **National Railway Museum** (08448 153139; www.nrm.org.uk), complete with one of the world's most iconic trains, the Flying Scotsman. Even if you are not particularly a train enthusiast, something here will make you catch your breath, whether it's the sheer scale of the great steam engines, appearing all the larger if you see them from the ground rather than from platform height, or the charmingly changing period detail of the Royal Carriages from different eras. The Warehouse, an open store for some three-quarters of a million smaller railway objects such as sign boards, benches, buckets and china, is big enough to lose yourself in – it's like being surrounded with props from *Brief Encounter*.

With its Victorian arched, glass and iron canopy, the **main railway station** is also evocative of tearful goodbyes on a black-and-white film set, and is worth a visit even if you are not arriving or departing by train. Short of being underneath the glass roof, the best place to view the station is from the city walls opposite.

On the opposite side of the city walls from the railway station, underneath the arch through which Station Road disappears, is the **former headquarters of the North Eastern Railway Company**. Built in 1906 as a grand status symbol to signify the company's importance, it simply bristles with chimneys and fancy gable ends. The building now has a new use as York's first five-star hotel and spa, due to open in 2010.

Glamorous camping in York

I've been lucky enough to stay in a wonderful place before now when visiting York that allows you to see all the sites and then retreat to the countryside a short way northeast of the city (midway between York and Malton) – a 15-minute drive from the centre. At **Jollydays Luxury Camping**, it's like staying in a hotel in the woods except that your walls are made of canvas and you can hear the hoot of an owl rather than the honk of a car horn at night. Carolyn, who runs Jollydays, describes it as 'glamping' – glamorous camping – and indeed it is.

My safari tent was huge, set upon a large timber base with two bedrooms including a very comfortable four-poster bed (with all the bedding provided), an en-suite shower with hot running water and loo, and a kitchen. The log-burning stove turned the living and dining area into a more than cosy and relaxing space, with a sofa bed together with shabby-chic furniture and furnishings. Outside on the terrace, complete with barbecue, I could sit quietly and listen to the nothingness-sounds coming from the 200-acre woodland that surrounded the tent or make a visit to the communal log fire for a chat with others on site. My tent very comfortably slept six but within the woodland there are some smaller bell-tents, still luxurious by comparison with standard camping, but without the en-suite facilities; instead visiting the immaculately kept showers.

Carolyn is so welcoming and the reception tent, adorned with fabric bunting and a chandelier, sells the most fantastic homemade cakes and hot drinks upon arrival.

To really get into the communal spirit and have the opportunity to be involved in the woodland campsite, Carolyn and Christian offer a barter scheme whereby a tent for up to four people is supplied free of charge in exchange for 20 hours of work in a week, the remaining time available to visit York and the surrounding area. Jobs include managing the woodland, collecting wood for the stoves, planting tree seedlings and helping on changeover days. A rustic feast is provided on one evening in the week too.

Jollydays Luxury Camping Village Farm, Scrayingham, York YO41 1JD ☎ 01759 371776 🖰 www.jollydaysluxurycamping.co.uk.

Photography holidays in York

Capturing York through the eye of a lens can put a whole new perspective on this incredibly photogenic city. John Potter (01904 797222; www.jpotter-landscape-photographer.com) is a professional landscape photographer and teacher based in York; he runs landscape photography holidays and courses with personal tuition for up to four people at a time. The 'Viewfinder' one and two-day workshops are tailor-made and involve photographing York and potentially visiting either the Yorkshire Dales or the North York Moors to take pictures too, followed by tuition to turn the prints into professional-looking images. It's the ideal opportunity to glean some useful tips from an exhibition-quality photographer and take a look at York in a completely different way.

Index

Page numbers in **bold** refer to main entries